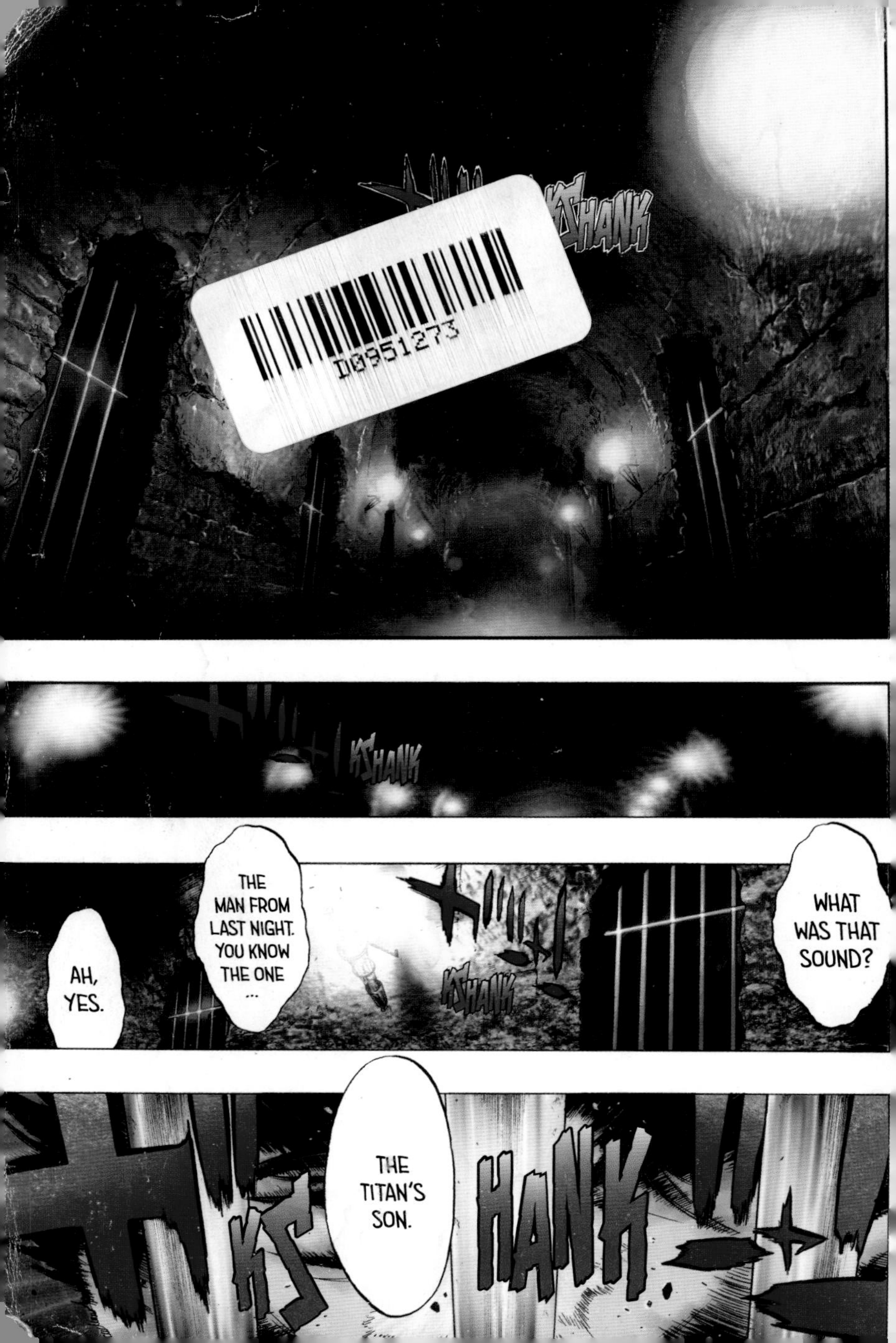
KSHANK
KSHANK
WHAT WAS THAT SOUND?
THE MAN FROM LAST NIGHT. YOU KNOW THE ONE ...
KSHANK
AH, YES.
THE TITAN'S SON.
KS HANK

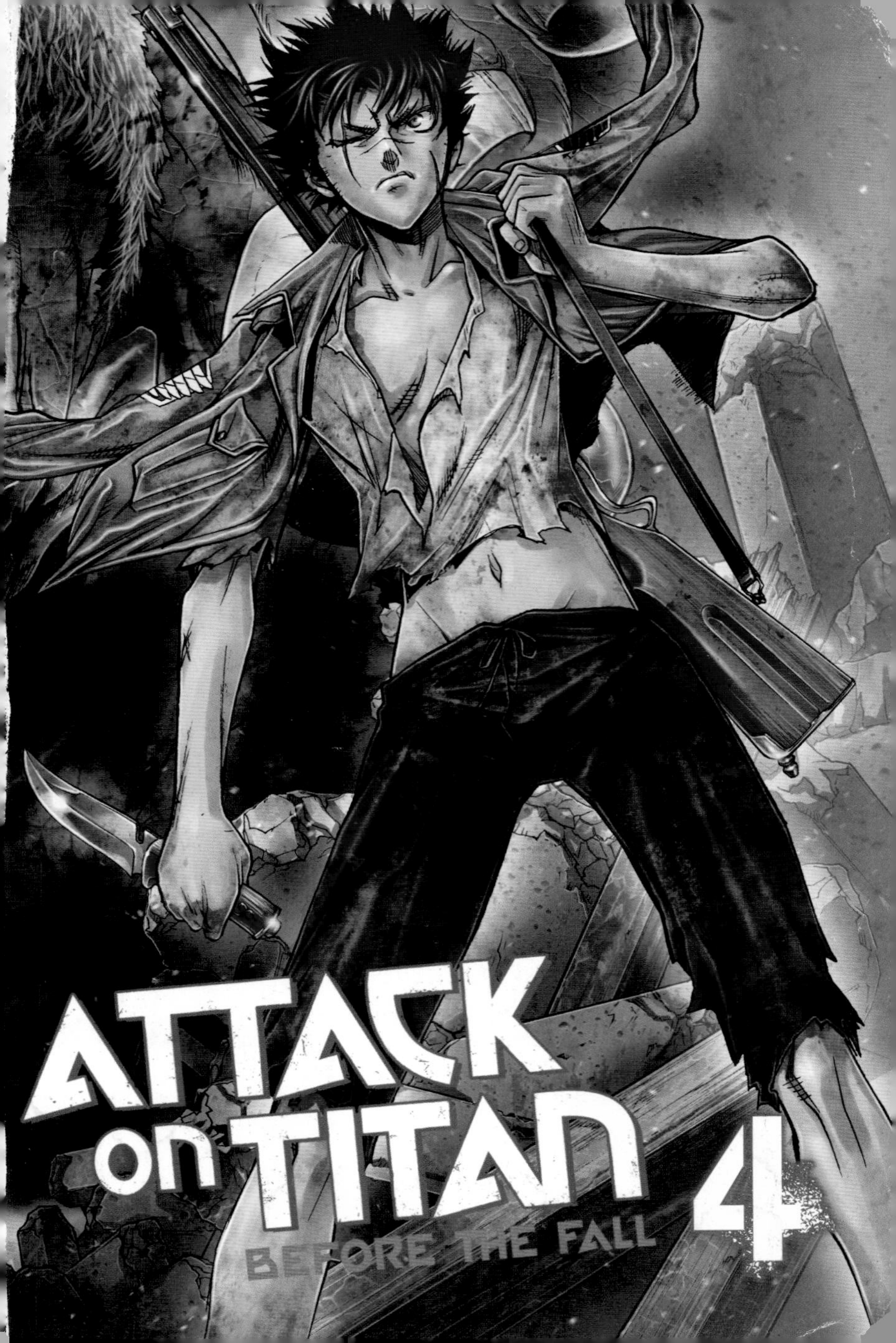
ATTACK on TITAN 4
BEFORE THE FALL

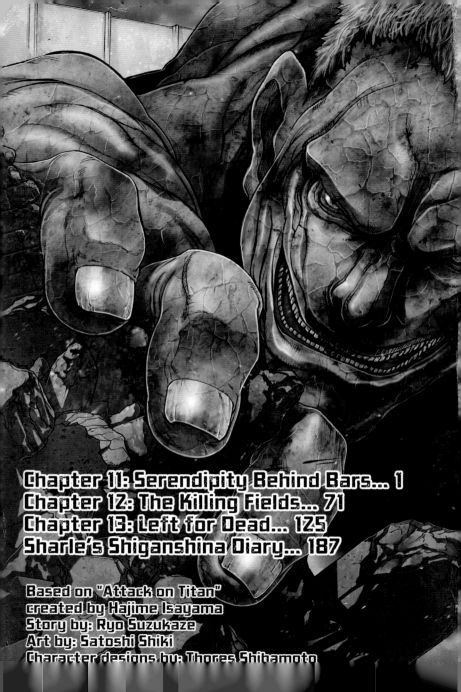

Based on "Attack on Titan"
created by Hajime Isayama
Story by: Ryo Suzukaze
Art by: Satoshi Shiki
Character designs by: Thores Shinamoto

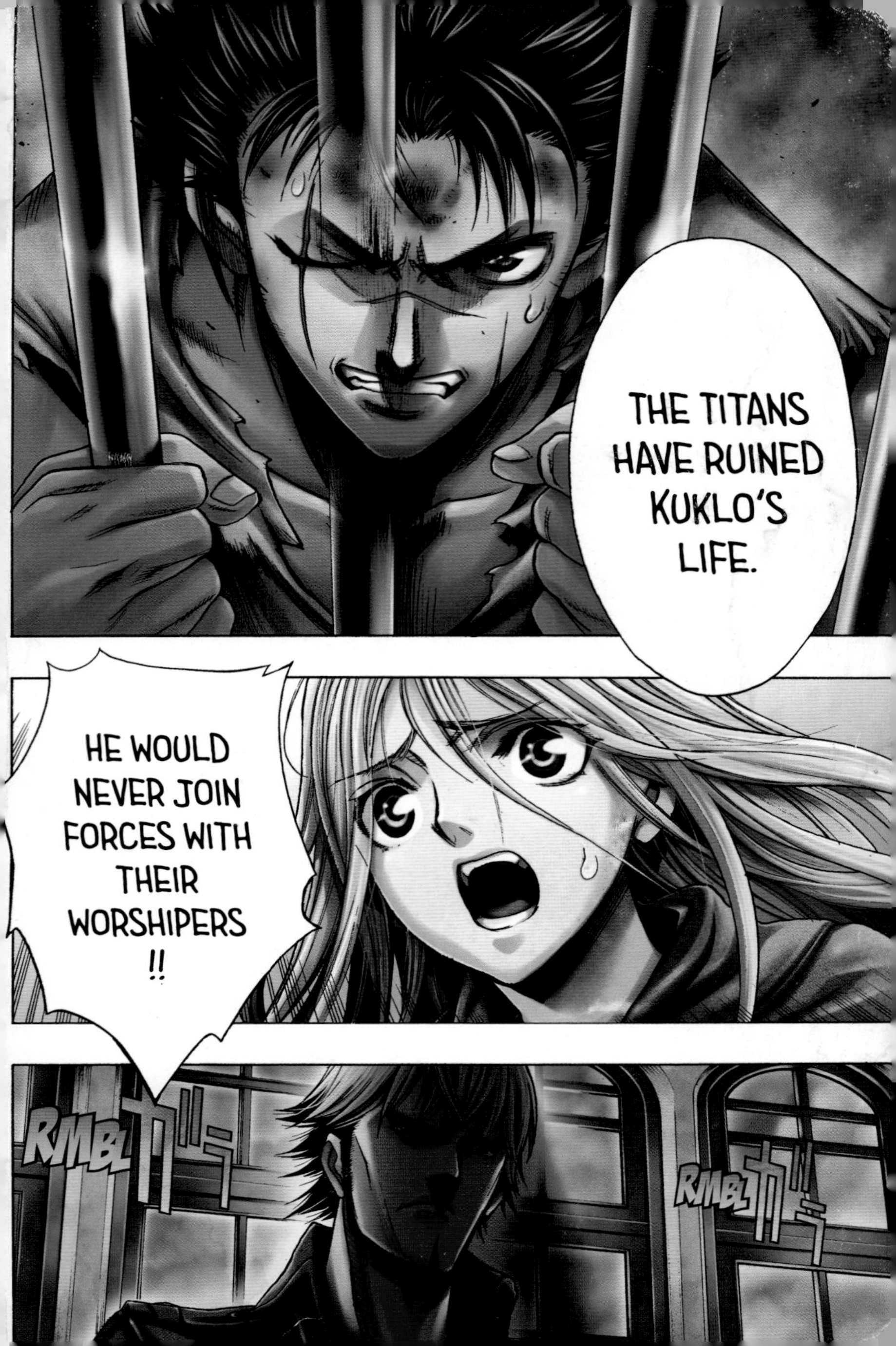
THE TITANS HAVE RUINED KUKLO'S LIFE.
HE WOULD NEVER JOIN FORCES WITH THEIR WORSHIPERS !!
RMBL
RMBL

Character Profiles

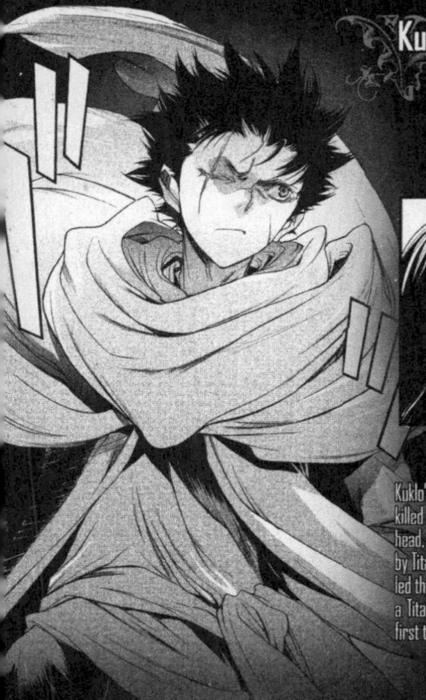

Kuklo

A boy born from a dead body packed into the vomit of a Titan, which earned him the moniker, "Titan's son." The wealthy Inocencio family bought him from a sideshow hut. His father was Heath Mansel, squad leader in the Survey Corps, and his mother was Elena, who helped bring a Titan inside the Wall. He escaped the Inocencio mansion when it was attacked by Titan-worshipers. Currently 15 years old.

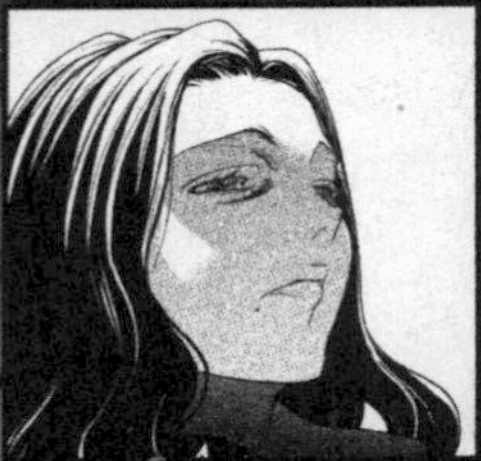

Elena

Kuklo's mother. Her husband Heath was killed by a Titan. When she saw his severed head, she went mad; and was manipulated by Titan-worshipers. Heavy with child, she led the cultists who opened the gate. When a Titan made its way inside, she was the first to be eaten.

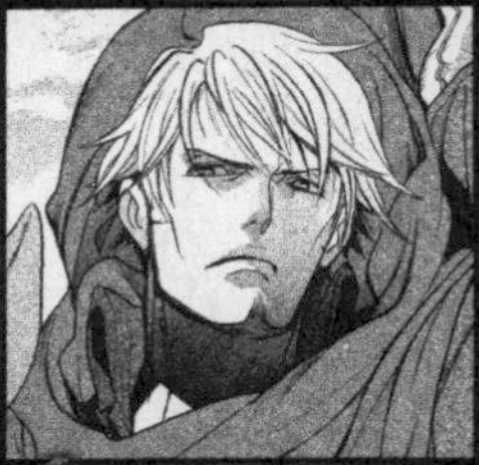

Carlo Pikale

A Survey Corps captain. He joined the same time as Heath, Kuklo's father. As a simple soldier at age 18, he discovered Elena's remains in the Titan's vomit, and witnessed Kuklo's birth. Now the captain of the newly-reformed Survey Corps, he is 33 years old.

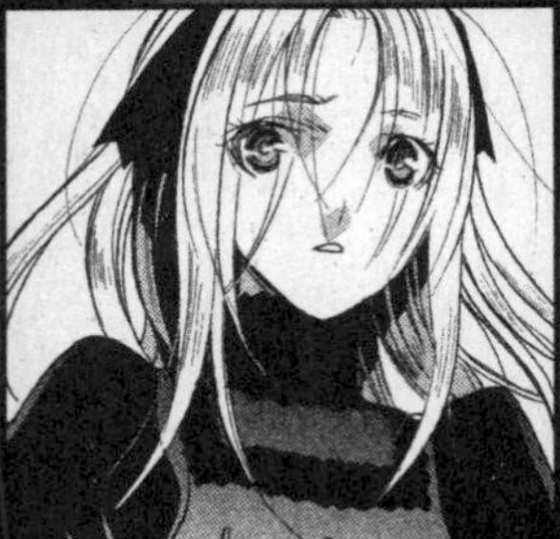

Sharle Inocencio

First daughter of the Inocencio family. She attempted to kill Kuklo after he was brought to the mansion, but became his only friend and taught him language when she realized that he was human, not a monster. When Titan-worshipers invaded her home, she left with Kuklo and had a falling out with her brother Xavi. Currently 15 years old.

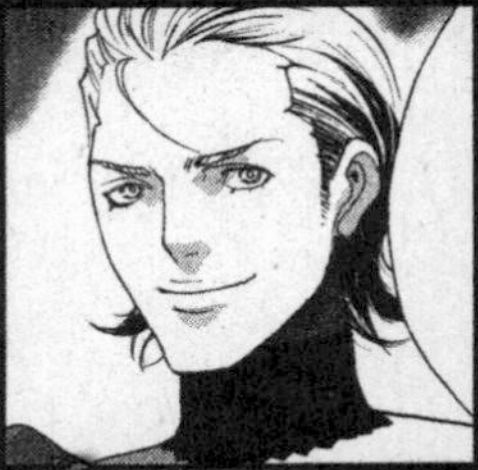

Xavi Inocencio

Sharle's brother, firstborn of the Inocencio children. His father Dario raised him to lead the military. He beat Kuklo nearly every day for two years, claiming to have "conquered the son of a Titan." This gave him an arrogant leader's air. He believes that Kuklo brought the Titan-worshipers into his home.

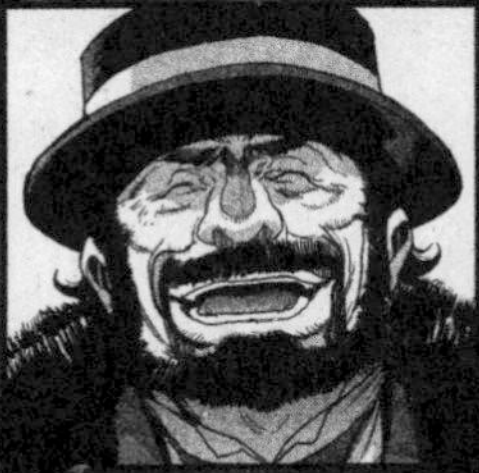

Dario Inocencio

One of the top merchants behind Wall Sheena, innermost of the walls. He had close ties to politicians, and hoped to arrange a marriage between Sharle and the son of Bruno Baumeister, a prominent conservative leader. He was slain by Titan-worshipers who intended to free Kuklo.

The Story So Far

When a Titan terrorized Shiganshina District and left behind a pile of vomit, a baby boy was miraculously born of a pregnant corpse. This boy was named Kuklo, the "Titan's son," and treated as a sideshow freak. Eventually the wealthy merchant Dario Inocencio bought Kuklo to serve as a punching bag for his son Xavi. But Xavi's sister Sharle decided to teach him the language and knowledge of humanity instead.

Kuklo put together an escape plan over two long years, but on the day of the escape, tragedy struck the Inocencio mansion. A group of Titan-worshipers invaded, seeking to take back the Titan's son. They murdered Dario and many of the servants. Kuklo narrowly managed to save Sharle and Xavi from harm, but Xavi accused him of being in league with the attackers, and cut out his right eye. Kuklo took Sharle and escaped from Wall Sheena into Shiganshina.

In Shiganshina District, the Survey Corps was back in action, preparing for its first expedition outside of the wall in fifteen years. Kuklo wanted to see a Titan to assure himself that he was indeed a human being. He left Sharle behind and snuck into the expedition's cargo wagon. As he hoped, the Survey Corps ran across a Titan, but it was far worse of a monster than he expected. The group suffered grievous losses, but thanks to Captain Carlo and Kuklo's ingenuity, they managed to retreat to Wall Maria.

Kuklo helped the Survey Corps survive, but inside the walls he was greeted by the Military Police, who wanted the "Titan's son" on charges of murdering Dario. As Sharle watched from the crowd, Carlo had no choice but to turn Kuklo over. Sharle rushed to Carlo's office to plead Kuklo's case, but learned that the accuser was Xavi, her own brother.

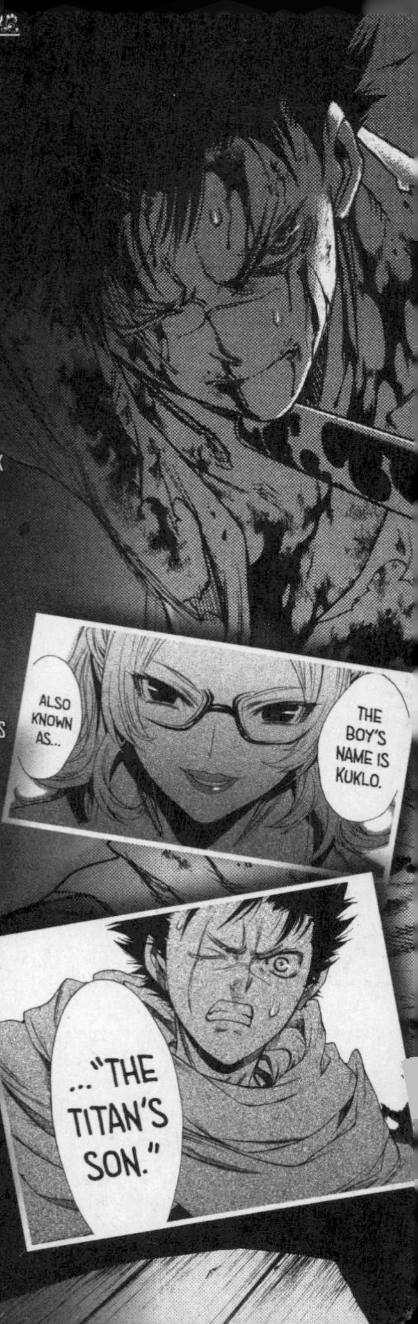
THE BOY'S NAME IS KUKLO.
ALSO KNOWN AS...
..."THE TITAN'S SON."

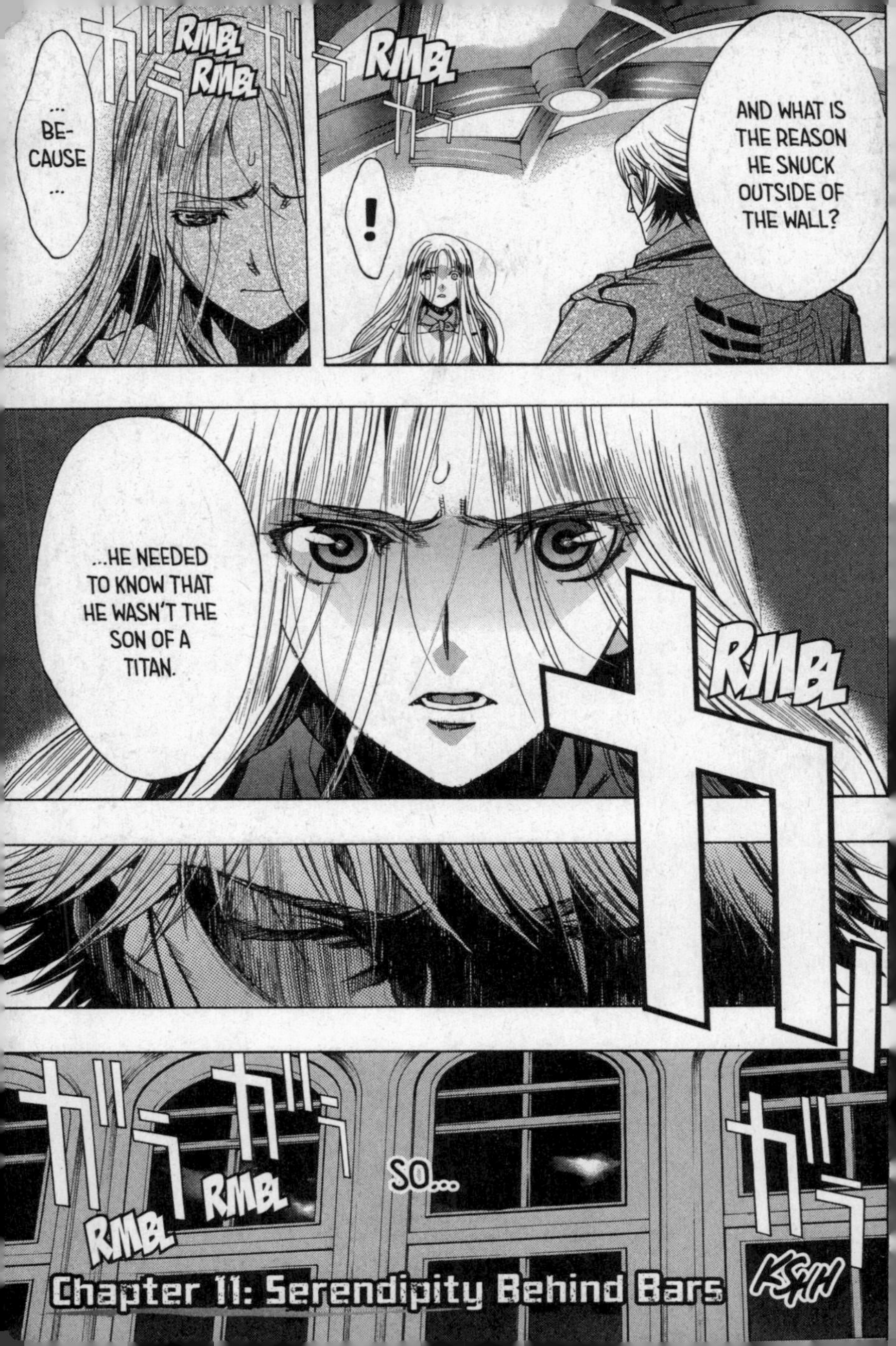
AND WHAT IS THE REASON HE SNUCK OUTSIDE OF THE WALL?
!
RMBL
RMBL
RMBL
... BE-CAUSE ...
...HE NEEDED TO KNOW THAT HE WASN'T THE SON OF A TITAN.
RMBL
KSHH
SO...
RMBL
RMBL
Chapter 11: Serendipity Behind Bars

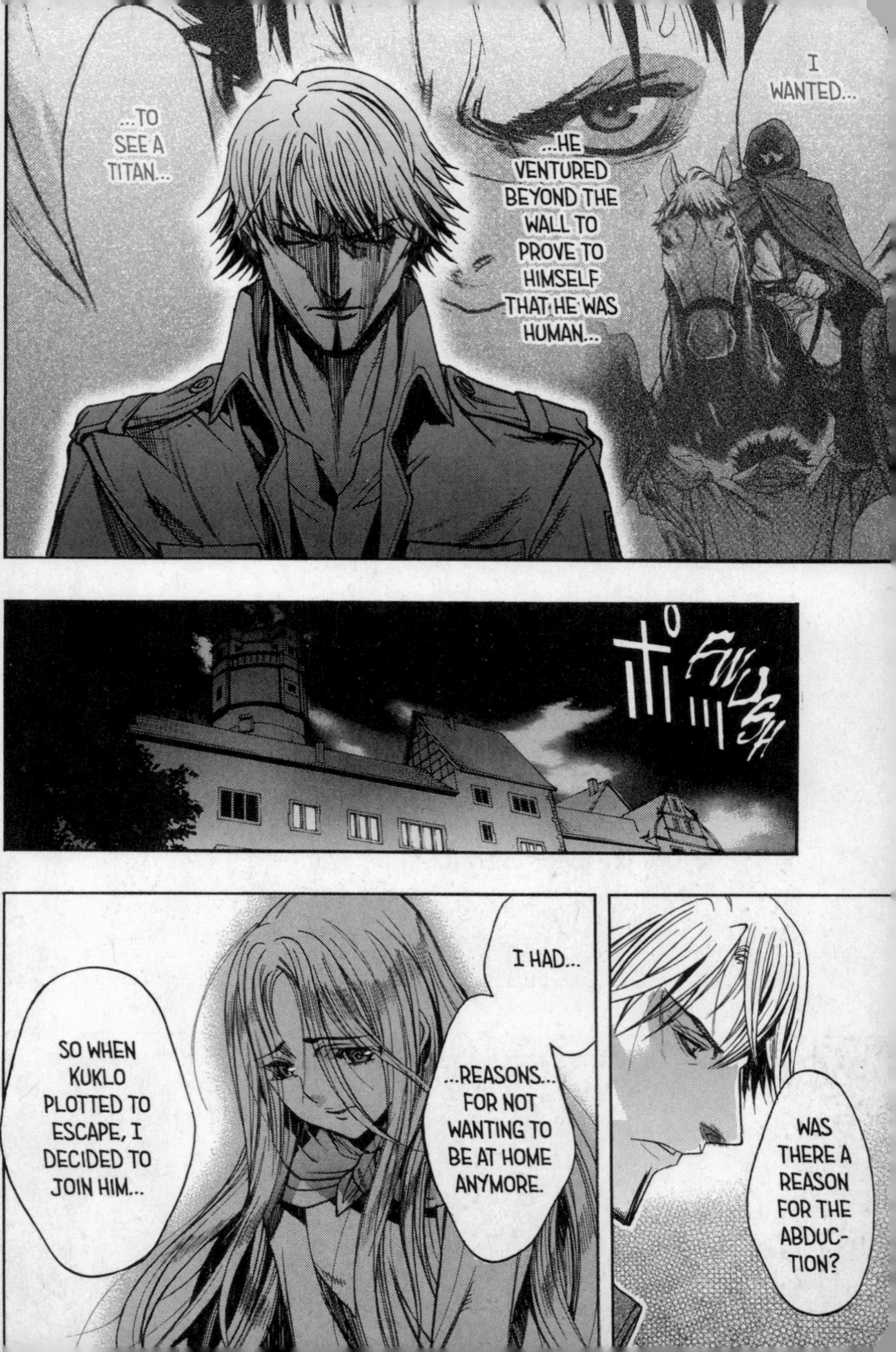
I WANTED...
...TO SEE A TITAN...
...HE VENTURED BEYOND THE WALL TO PROVE TO HIMSELF THAT HE WAS HUMAN...
FWUSH
WAS THERE A REASON FOR THE ABDUCTION?
I HAD...
...REASONS... FOR NOT WANTING TO BE AT HOME ANYMORE.
SO WHEN KUKLO PLOTTED TO ESCAPE, I DECIDED TO JOIN HIM...

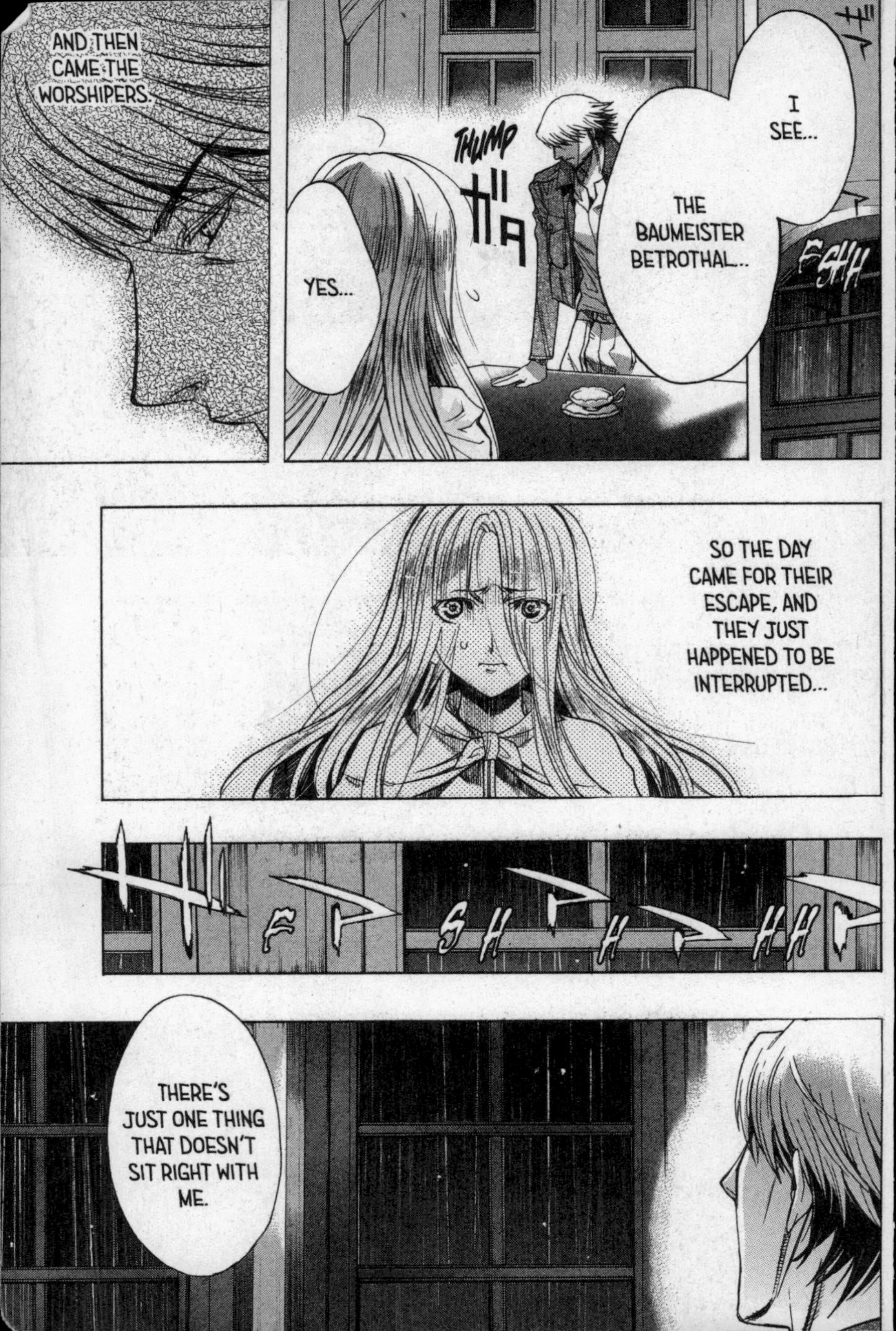
FSHH
I SEE...
THE BAUMEISTER BETROTHAL...
THUMP
YES...
AND THEN CAME THE WORSHIPERS.
SO THE DAY CAME FOR THEIR ESCAPE, AND THEY JUST HAPPENED TO BE INTERRUPTED...
F SH H HH
THERE'S JUST ONE THING THAT DOESN'T SIT RIGHT WITH ME.

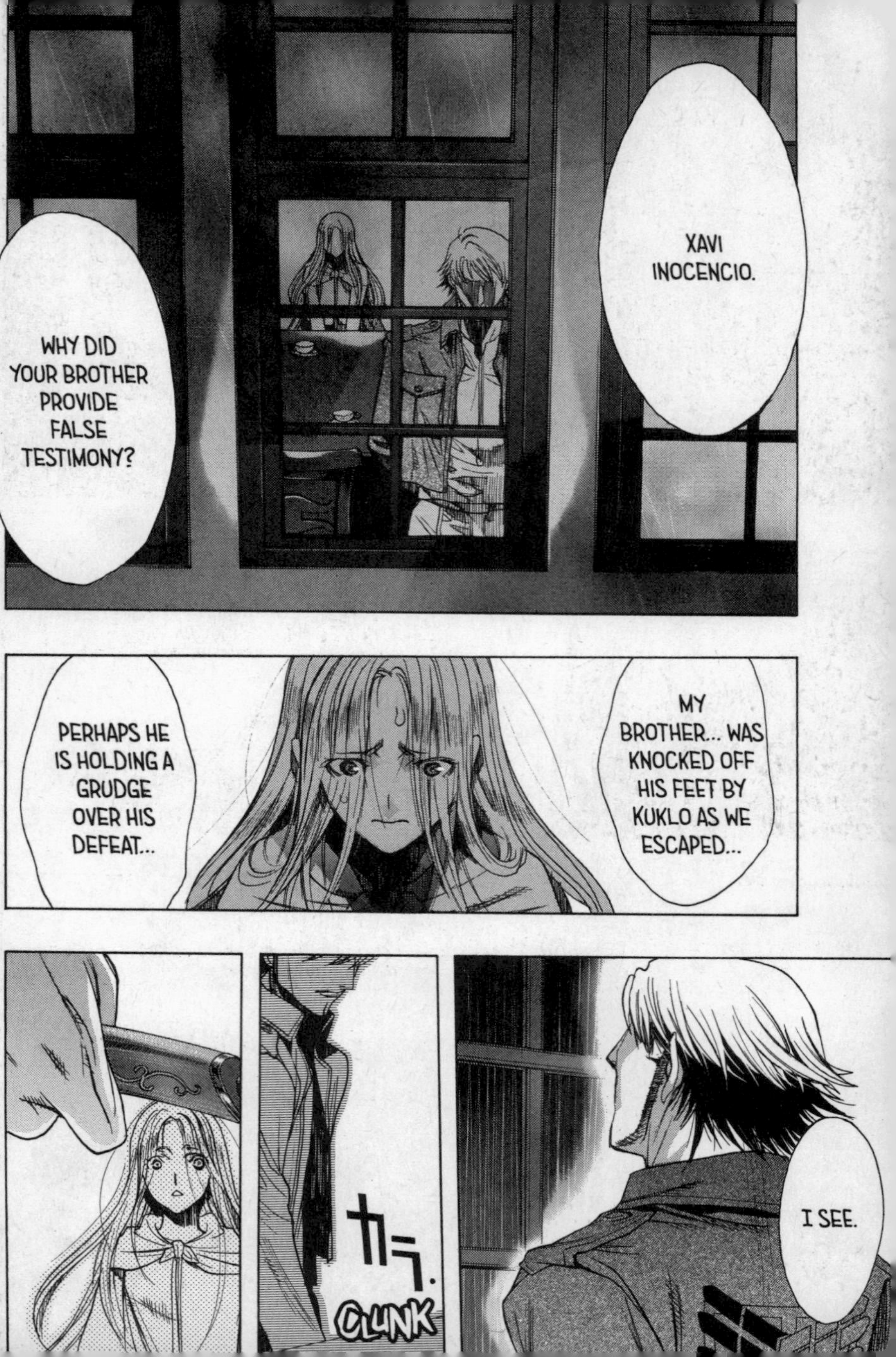
XAVI INOCENCIO.
WHY DID YOUR BROTHER PROVIDE FALSE TESTIMONY?
MY BROTHER... WAS KNOCKED OFF HIS FEET BY KUKLO AS WE ESCAPED...
PERHAPS HE IS HOLDING A GRUDGE OVER HIS DEFEAT...
I SEE.
カラ.
CLUNK

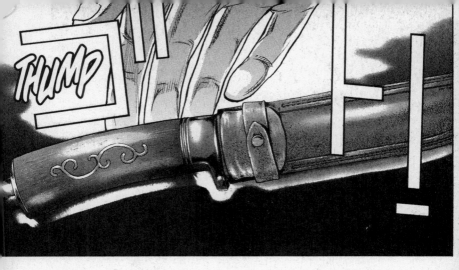

THUMP

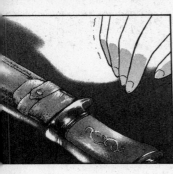

THE KNIFE...

....!

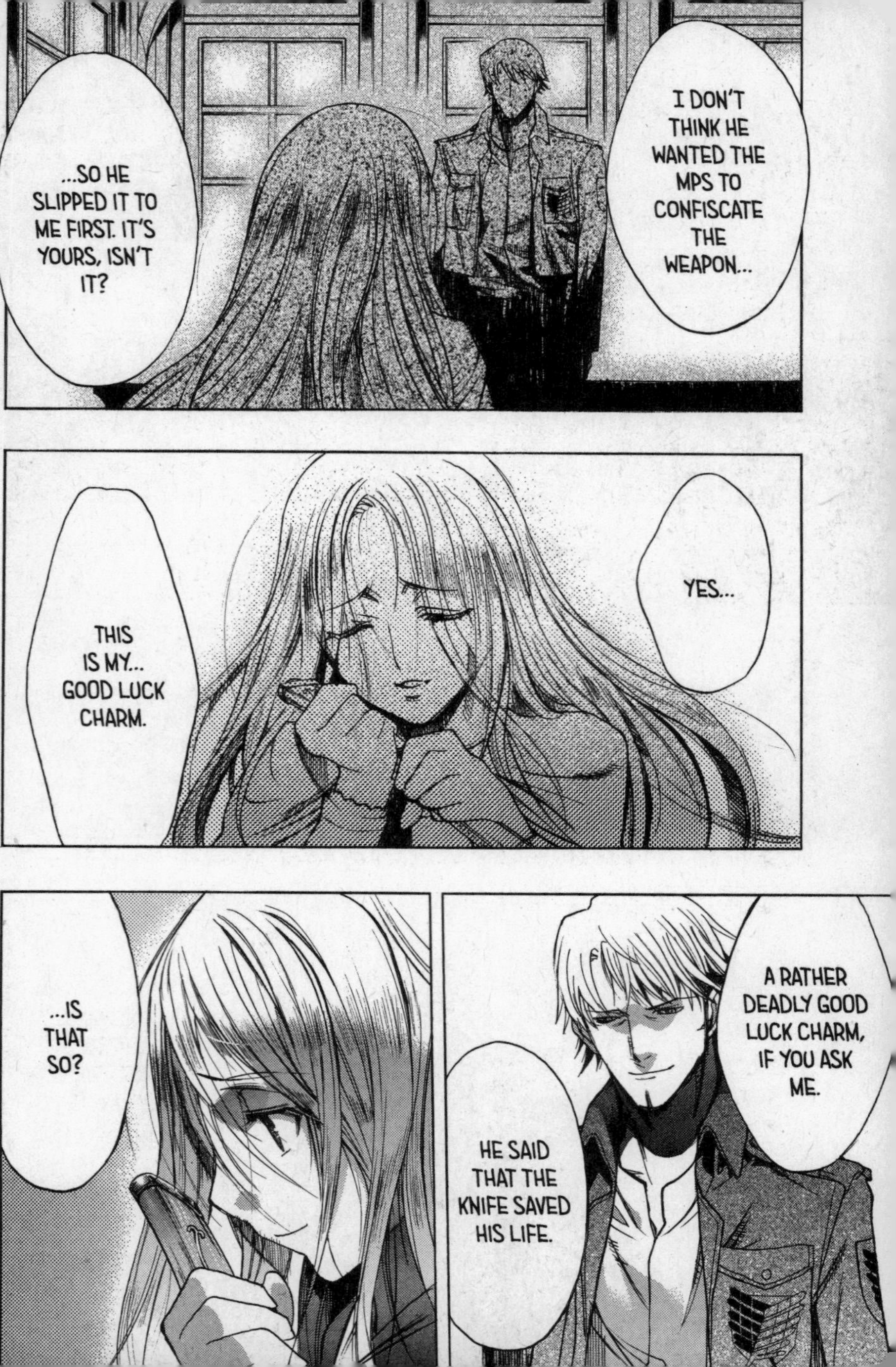
I DON'T THINK HE WANTED THE MPS TO CONFISCATE THE WEAPON...
...SO HE SLIPPED IT TO ME FIRST. IT'S YOURS, ISN'T IT?
YES...
THIS IS MY... GOOD LUCK CHARM.
A RATHER DEADLY GOOD LUCK CHARM, IF YOU ASK ME.
HE SAID THAT THE KNIFE SAVED HIS LIFE.
...IS THAT SO?

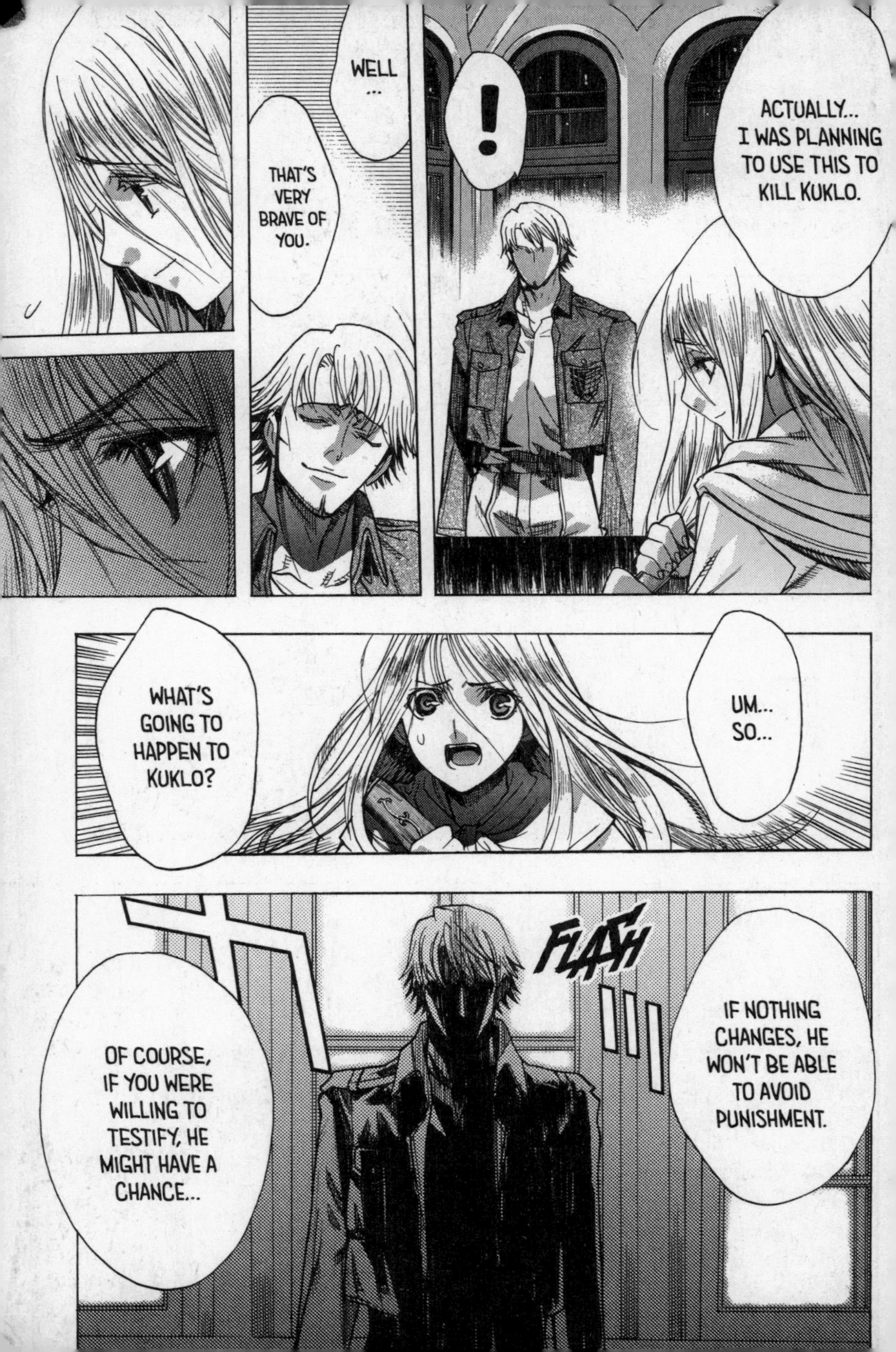
ACTUALLY... I WAS PLANNING TO USE THIS TO KILL KUKLO.
!
WELL ...
THAT'S VERY BRAVE OF YOU.
UM... SO...
WHAT'S GOING TO HAPPEN TO KUKLO?
FLASH
IF NOTHING CHANGES, HE WON'T BE ABLE TO AVOID PUNISHMENT.
OF COURSE, IF YOU WERE WILLING TO TESTIFY, HE MIGHT HAVE A CHANCE...

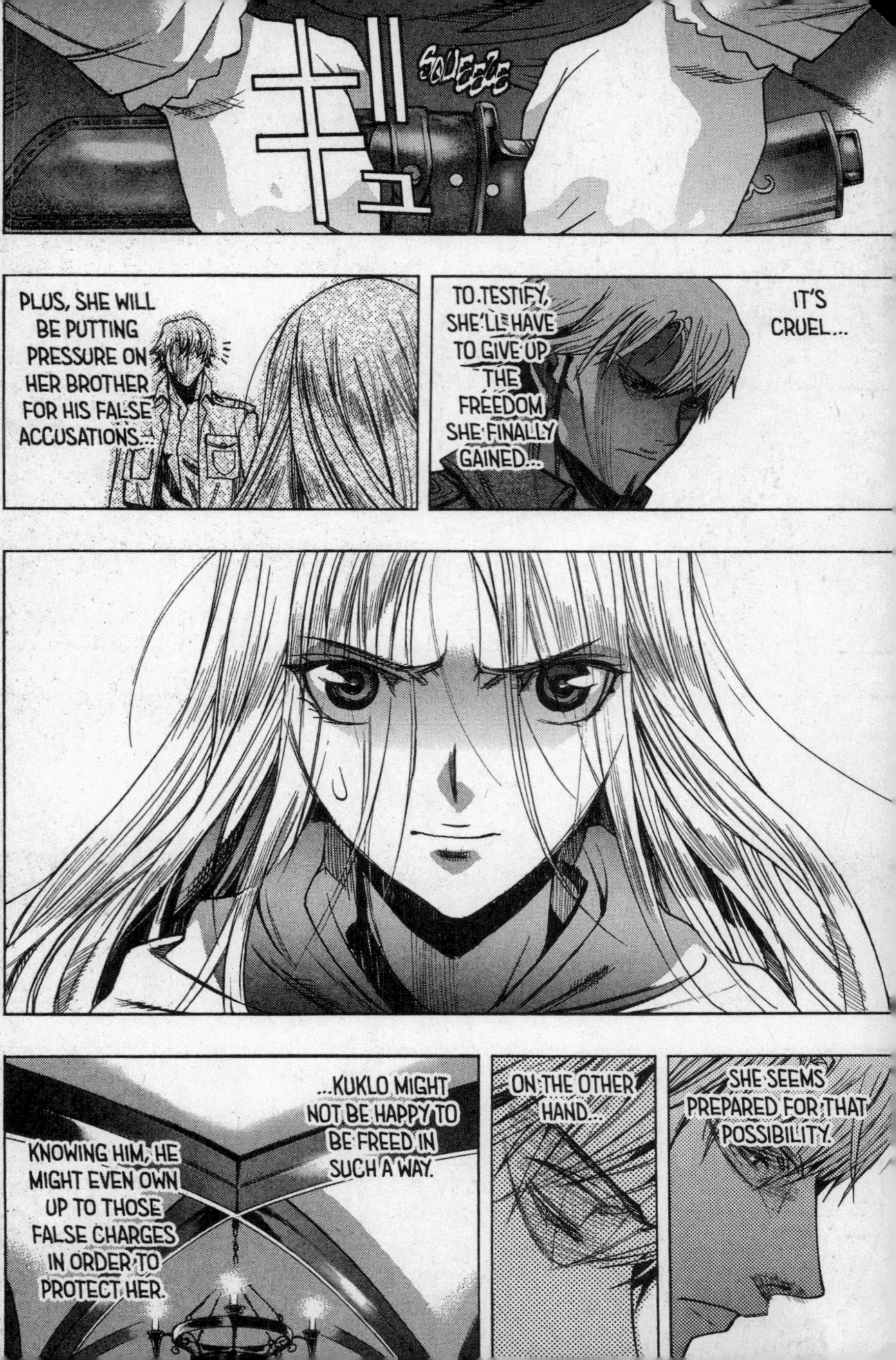
SQUEEZE
IT'S CRUEL...
TO TESTIFY, SHE'LL HAVE TO GIVE UP THE FREEDOM SHE FINALLY GAINED...
PLUS, SHE WILL BE PUTTING PRESSURE ON HER BROTHER FOR HIS FALSE ACCUSATIONS...
SHE SEEMS PREPARED FOR THAT POSSIBILITY.
ON THE OTHER HAND...
...KUKLO MIGHT NOT BE HAPPY TO BE FREED IN SUCH A WAY.
KNOWING HIM, HE MIGHT EVEN OWN UP TO THOSE FALSE CHARGES IN ORDER TO PROTECT HER.

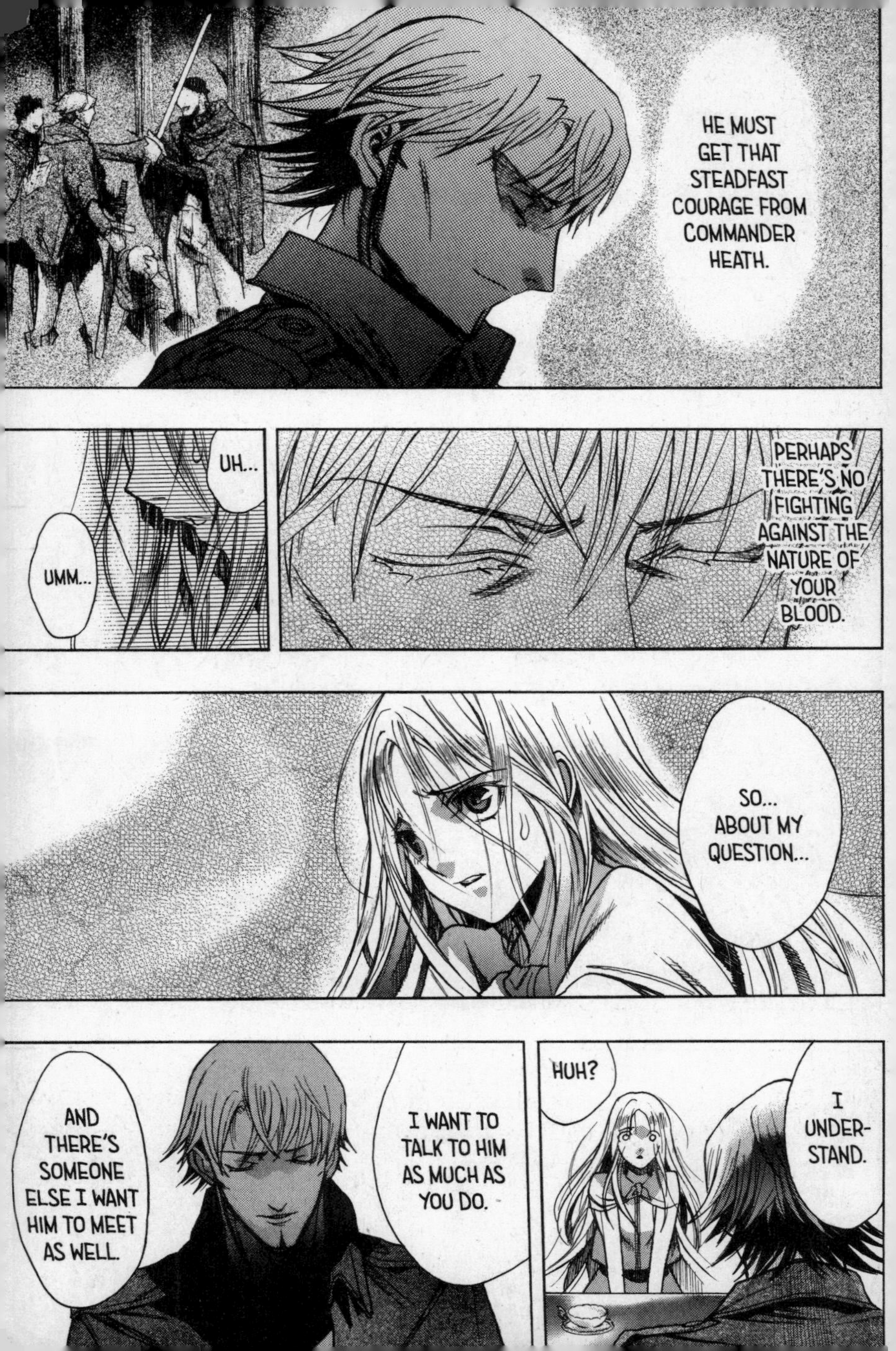
HE MUST GET THAT STEADFAST COURAGE FROM COMMANDER HEATH.
PERHAPS THERE'S NO FIGHTING AGAINST THE NATURE OF YOUR BLOOD.
UH...
UMM...
SO... ABOUT MY QUESTION...
I UNDER-STAND.
HUH?
I WANT TO TALK TO HIM AS MUCH AS YOU DO.
AND THERE'S SOMEONE ELSE I WANT HIM TO MEET AS WELL.

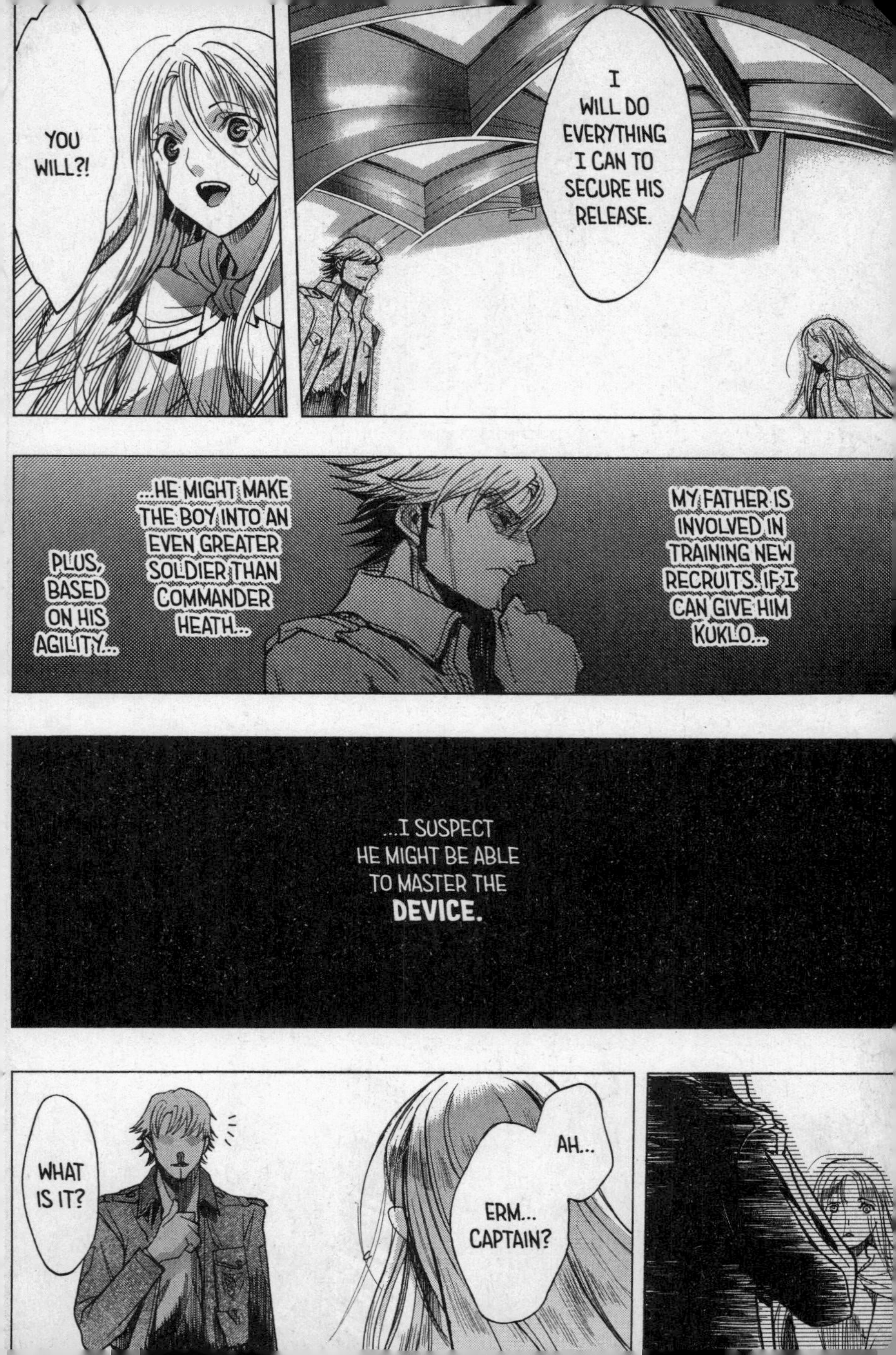
I WILL DO EVERYTHING I CAN TO SECURE HIS RELEASE.
YOU WILL?!
MY FATHER IS INVOLVED IN TRAINING NEW RECRUITS. IF I CAN GIVE HIM KUKLO...
...HE MIGHT MAKE THE BOY INTO AN EVEN GREATER SOLDIER THAN COMMANDER HEATH...
PLUS, BASED ON HIS AGILITY...
...I SUSPECT HE MIGHT BE ABLE TO MASTER THE DEVICE.
AH...
ERM... CAPTAIN?
WHAT IS IT?

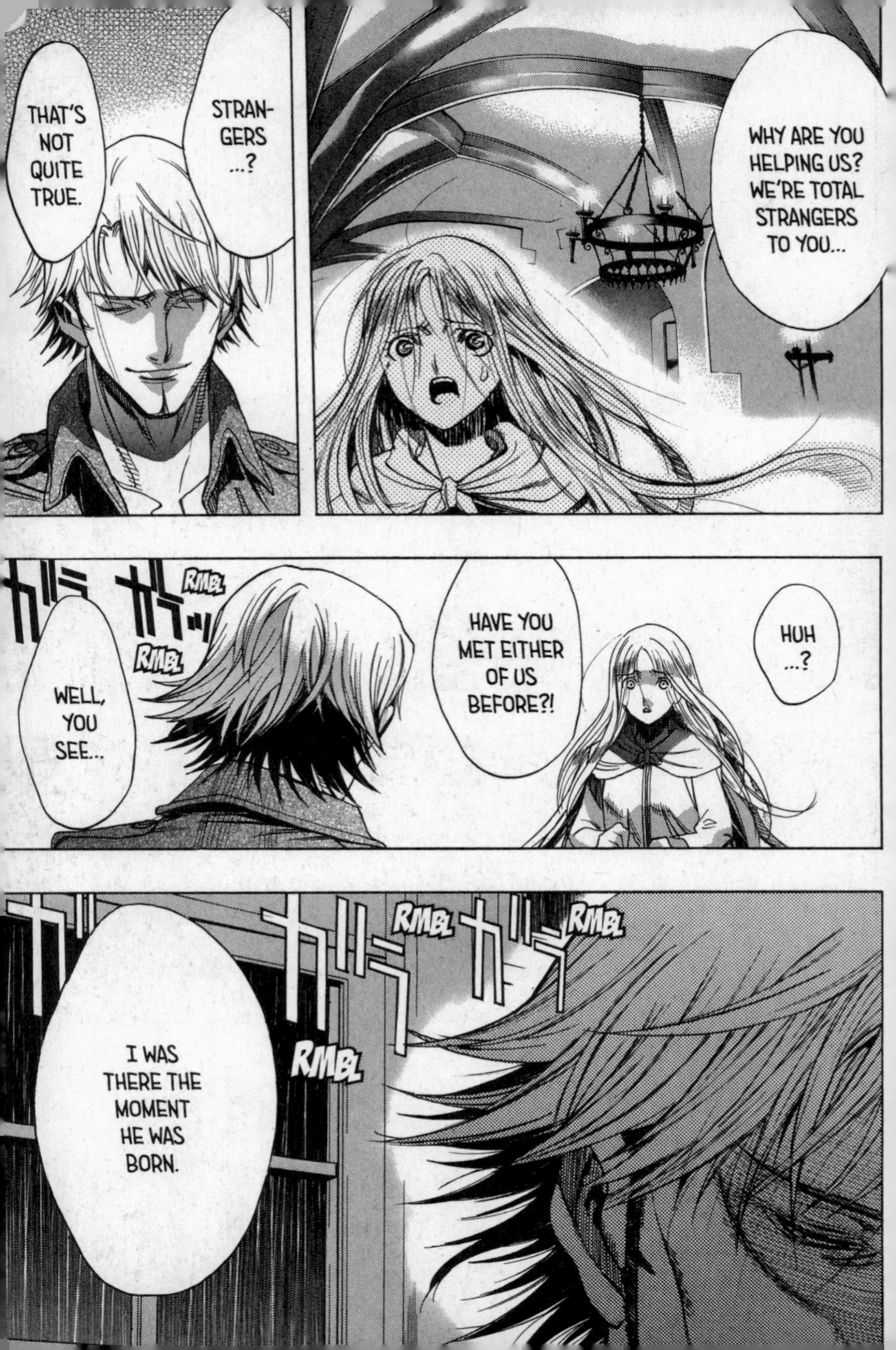
WHY ARE YOU HELPING US? WE'RE TOTAL STRANGERS TO YOU...
STRAN-GERS ...?
THAT'S NOT QUITE TRUE.
HUH ...?
HAVE YOU MET EITHER OF US BEFORE?!
RMBL
RMBL
WELL, YOU SEE...
RMBL
RMBL
RMBL
I WAS THERE THE MOMENT HE WAS BORN.

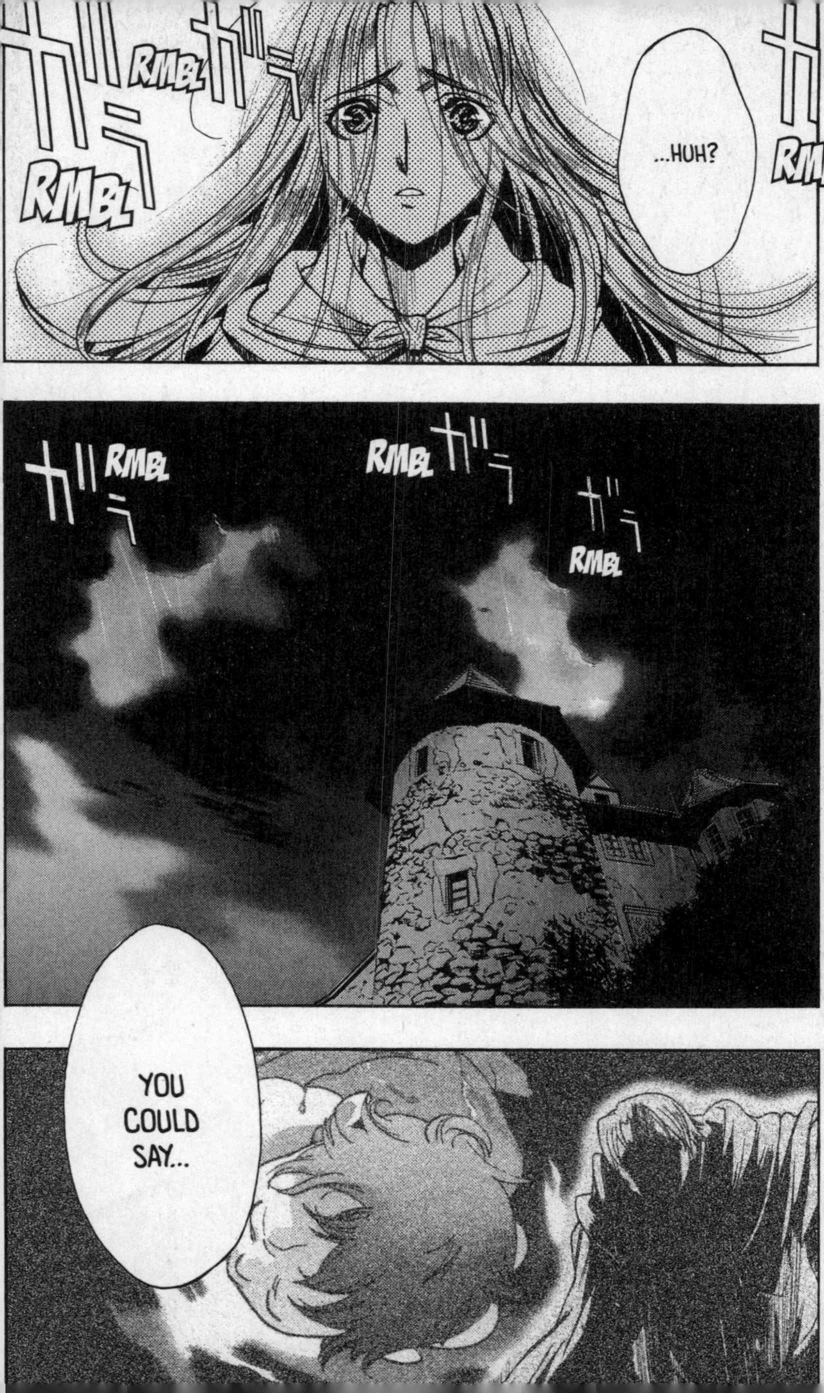
RMBL
...HUH?
RMBL
RMBL
RMBL
RMBL
RMBL
YOU COULD SAY...

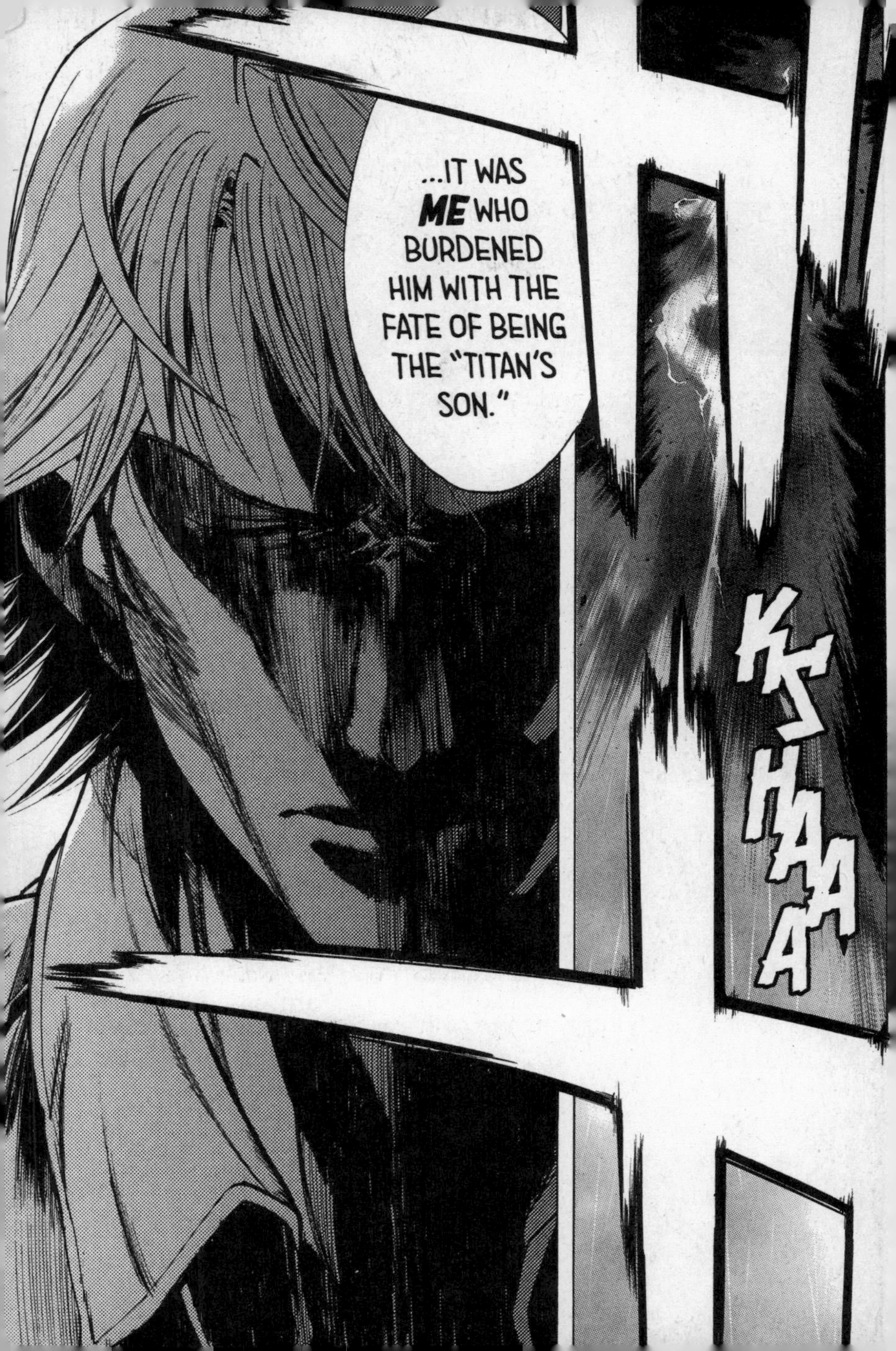
...IT WAS **ME** WHO BURDENED HIM WITH THE FATE OF BEING THE "TITAN'S SON."
KSHAAAA

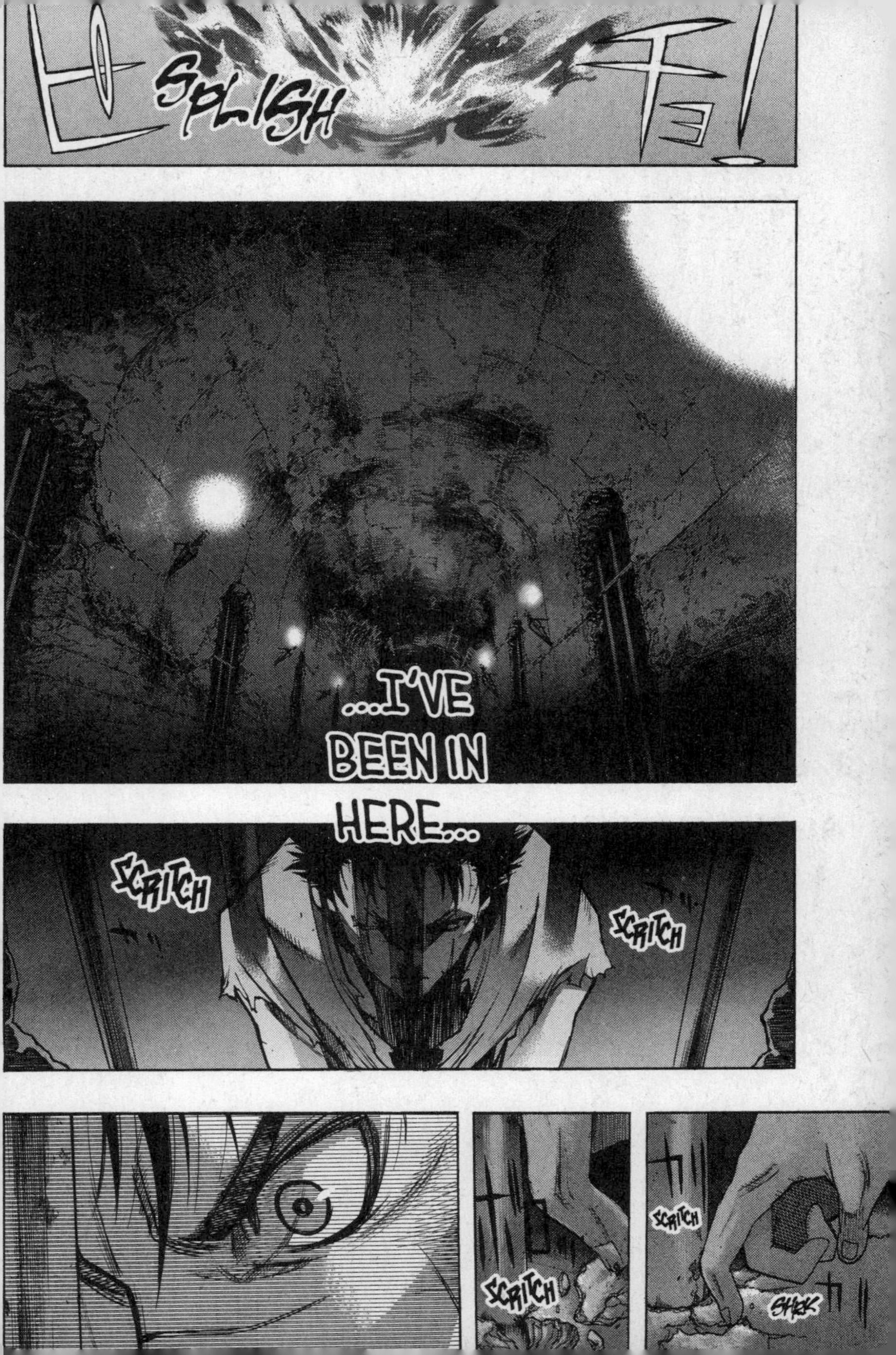
SPLISH
...I'VE BEEN IN HERE...
SCRITCH
SCRITCH
SCRITCH
SHAK
SCRITCH

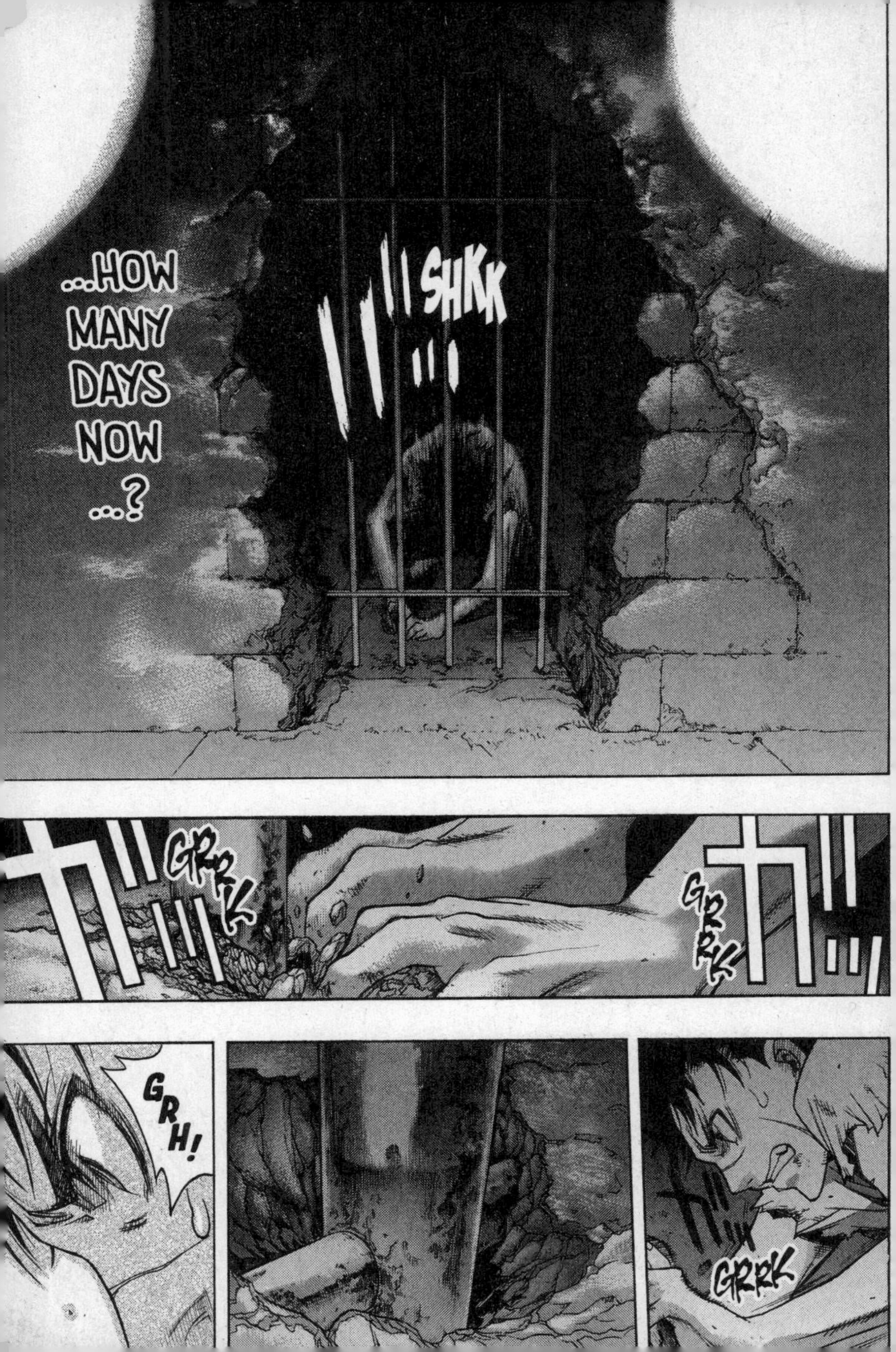
SHKK
...HOW MANY DAYS NOW ...?
GRRK
GRRK
GRRK
GRH!

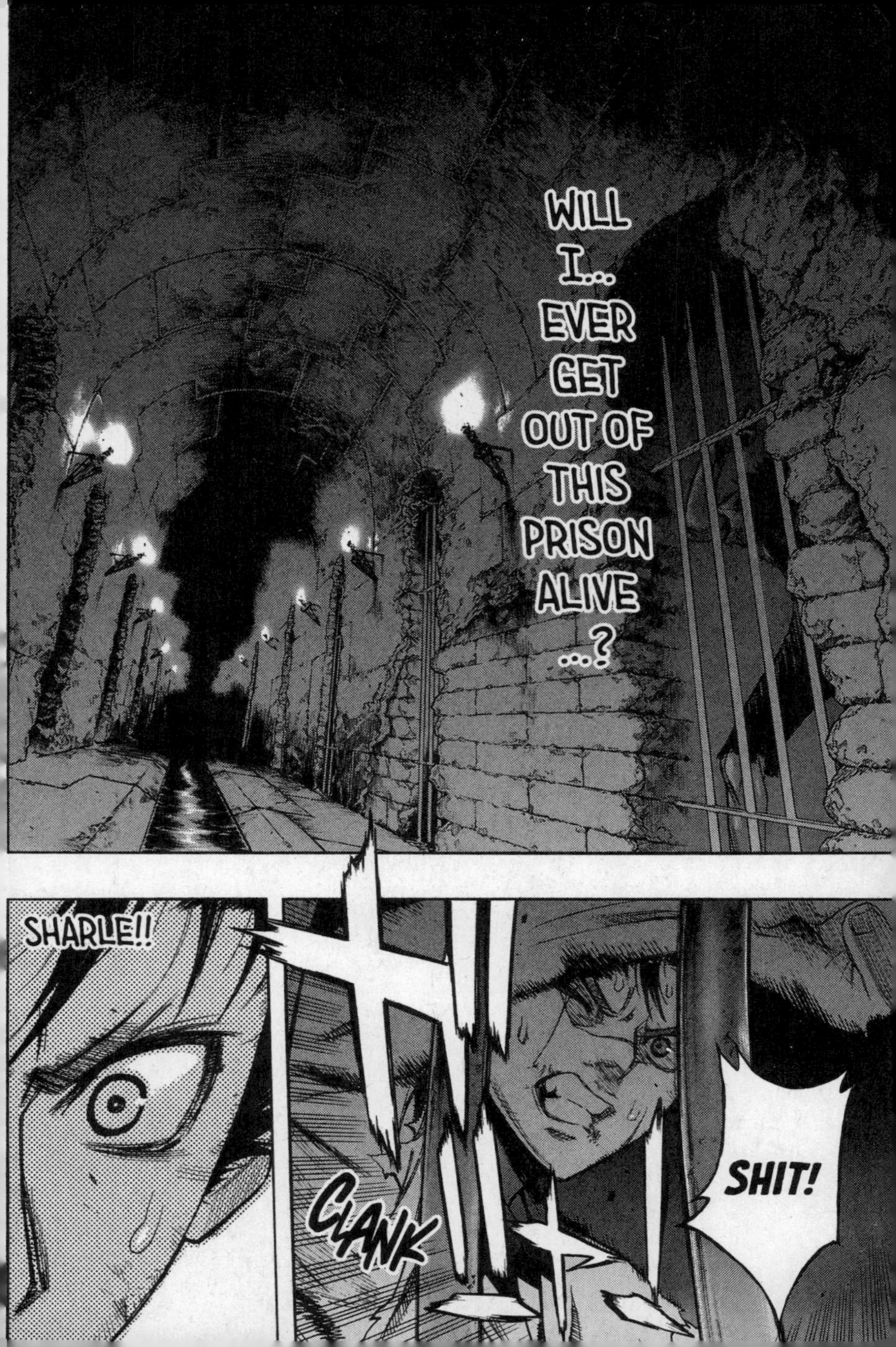
WILL I... EVER GET OUT OF THIS PRISON ALIVE ...?
SHIT!
CLANK
SHARLE!!

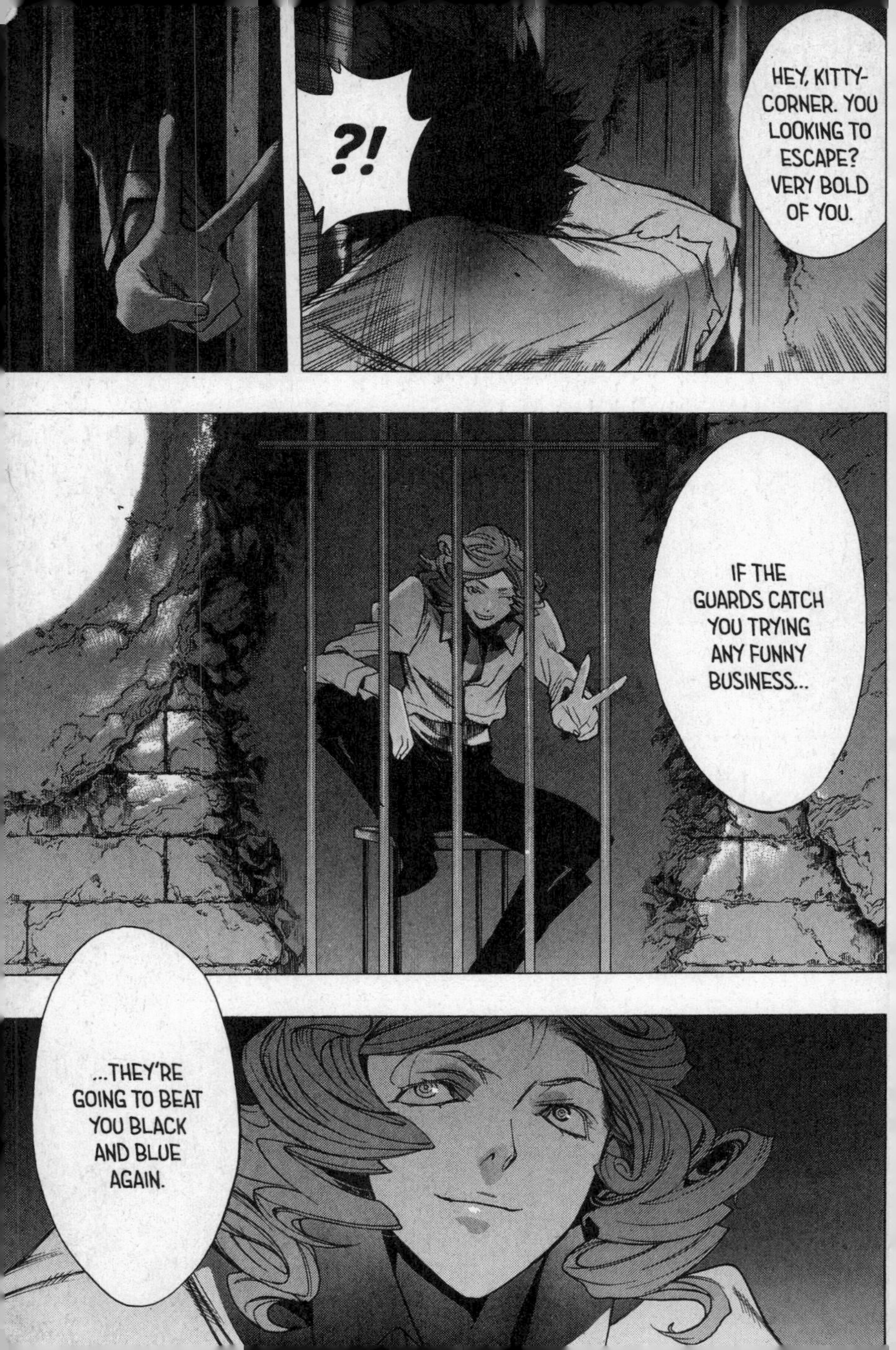
HEY, KITTY-CORNER. YOU LOOKING TO ESCAPE? VERY BOLD OF YOU.
?!
IF THE GUARDS CATCH YOU TRYING ANY FUNNY BUSINESS...
...THEY'RE GOING TO BEAT YOU BLACK AND BLUE AGAIN.

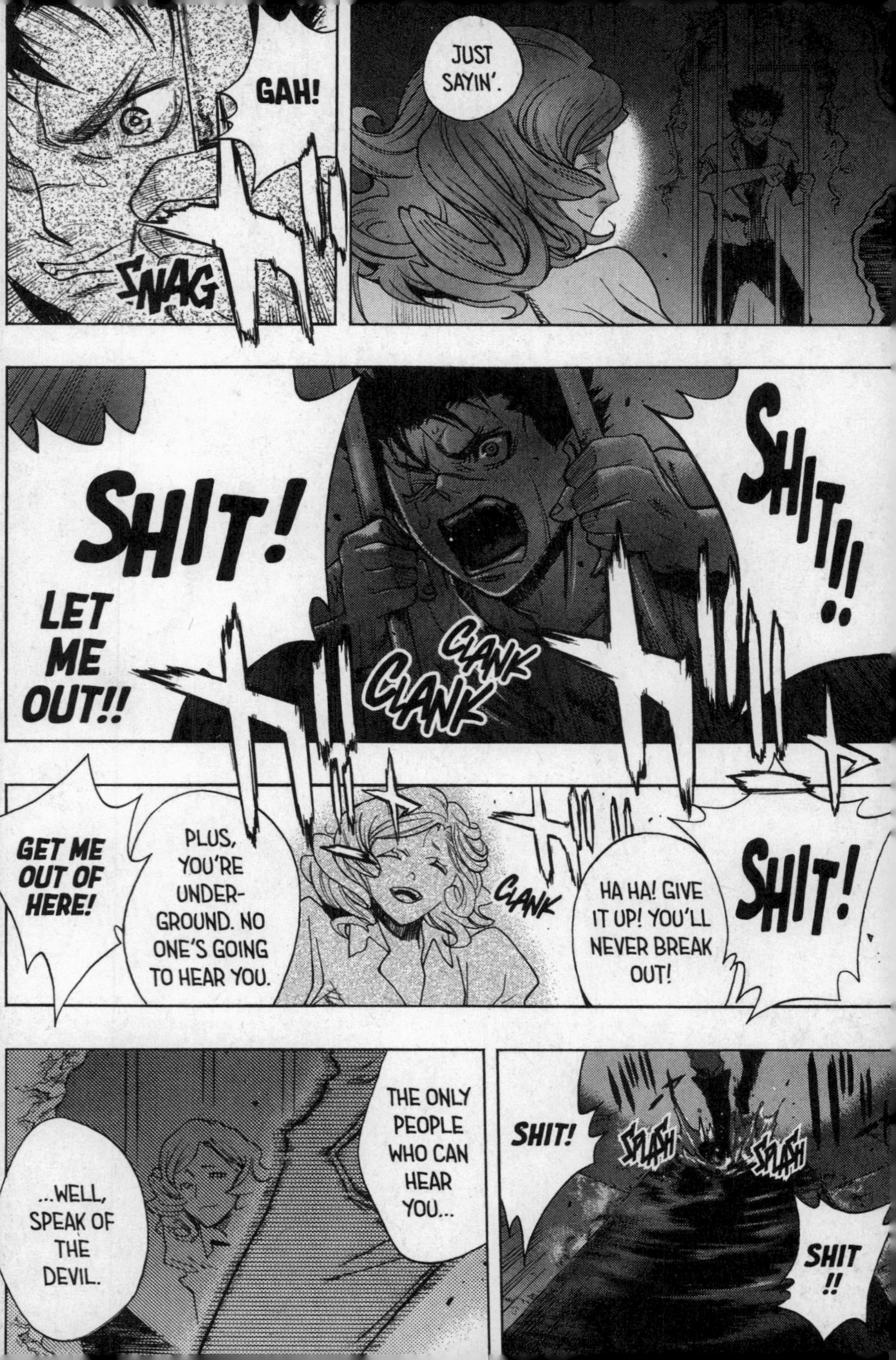

JUST SAYIN'.
GAH!
SNAG
SHIT!!
CLANK
CLANK
SHIT!
LET ME OUT!!
SHIT!
HA HA! GIVE IT UP! YOU'LL NEVER BREAK OUT!
CLANK
PLUS, YOU'RE UNDER-GROUND. NO ONE'S GOING TO HEAR YOU.
GET ME OUT OF HERE!
SPLASH
SPLASH
SHIT!
SHIT!!
THE ONLY PEOPLE WHO CAN HEAR YOU...
...WELL, SPEAK OF THE DEVIL.

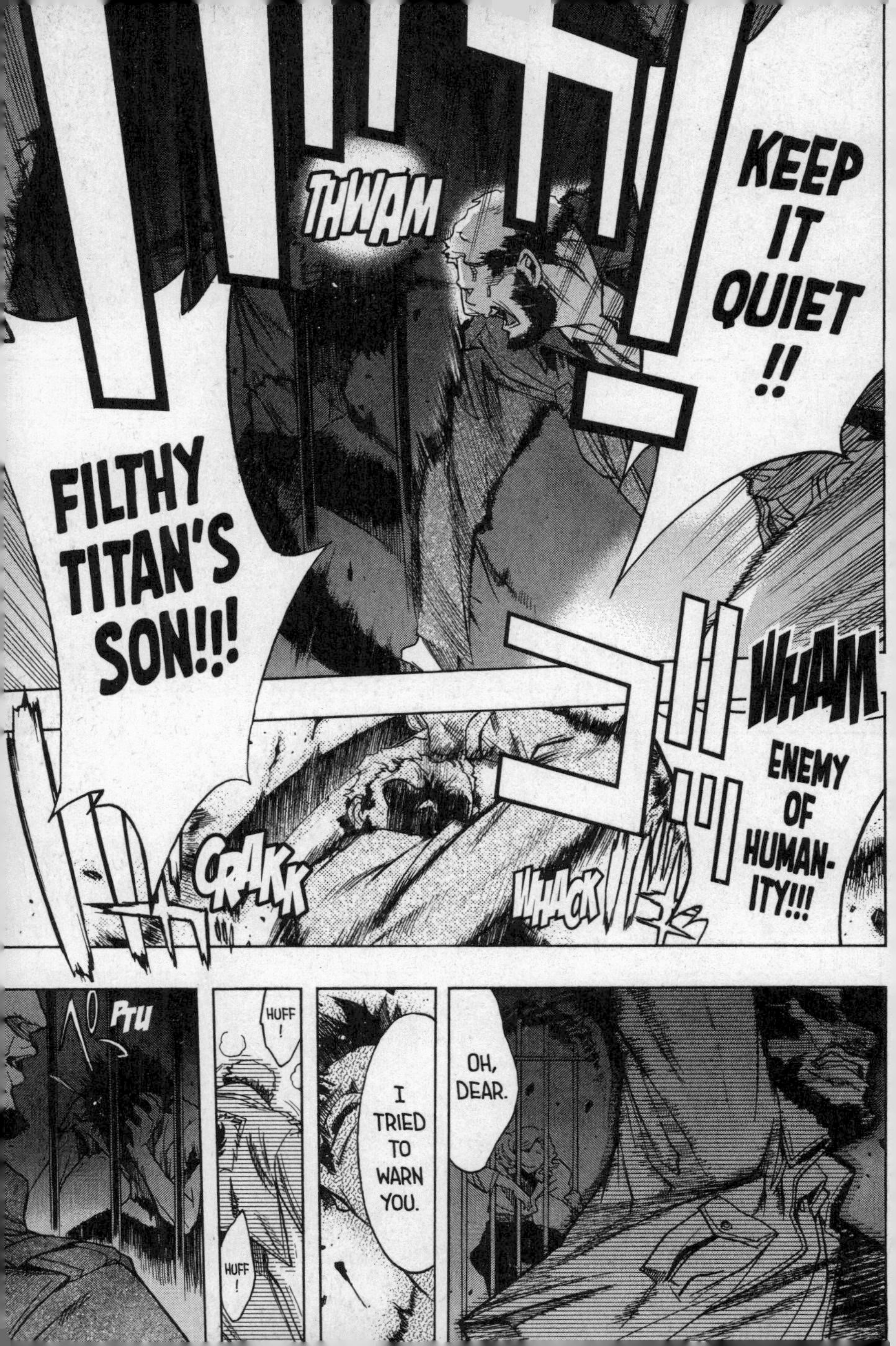
KEEP IT QUIET!!
THWAM
FILTHY TITAN'S SON!!!
WHAM
ENEMY OF HUMAN-ITY!!!
WHACK
CRAKK
OH, DEAR.
I TRIED TO WARN YOU.
HUFF!
HUFF!
PTU

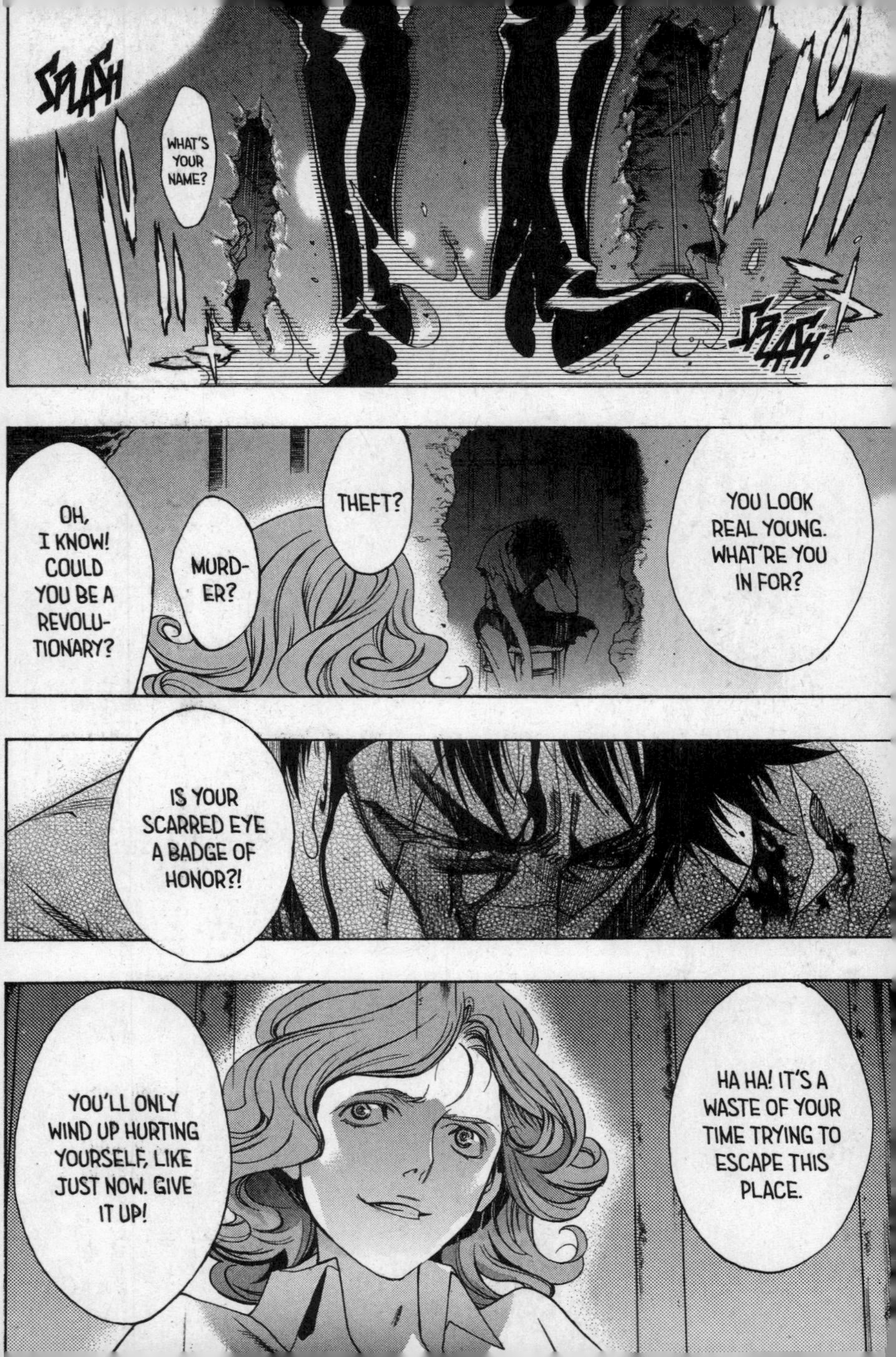
SPLASH
WHAT'S YOUR NAME?
SPLASH
YOU LOOK REAL YOUNG. WHAT'RE YOU IN FOR?
THEFT?
MURDER?
OH, I KNOW! COULD YOU BE A REVOLUTIONARY?
IS YOUR SCARRED EYE A BADGE OF HONOR?!
HA HA! IT'S A WASTE OF YOUR TIME TRYING TO ESCAPE THIS PLACE.
YOU'LL ONLY WIND UP HURTING YOURSELF, LIKE JUST NOW. GIVE IT UP!

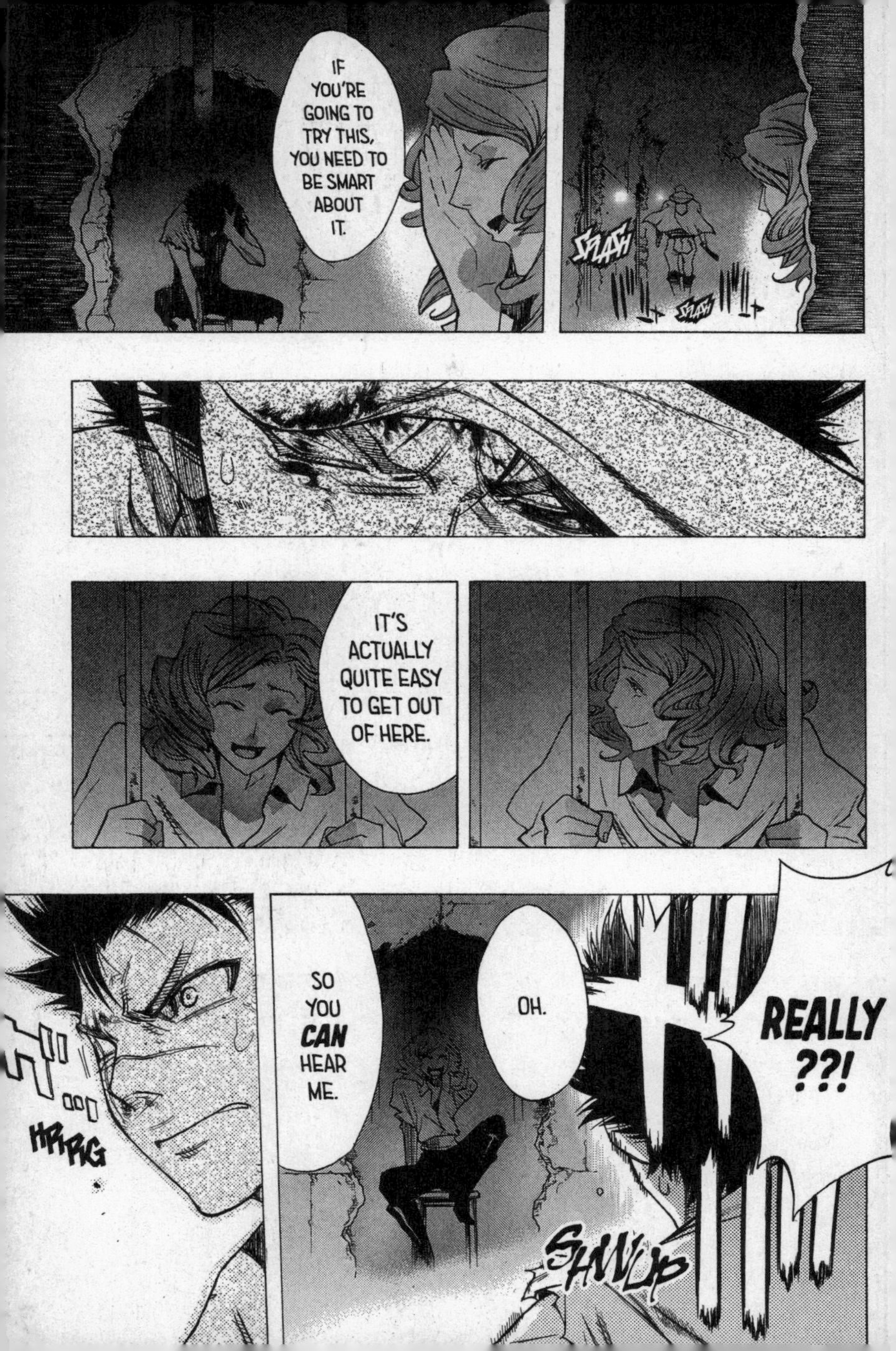
SPLASH
SPLASH
IF YOU'RE GOING TO TRY THIS, YOU NEED TO BE SMART ABOUT IT.
IT'S ACTUALLY QUITE EASY TO GET OUT OF HERE.
REALLY ??!
SHWUP
OH.
SO YOU **CAN** HEAR ME.

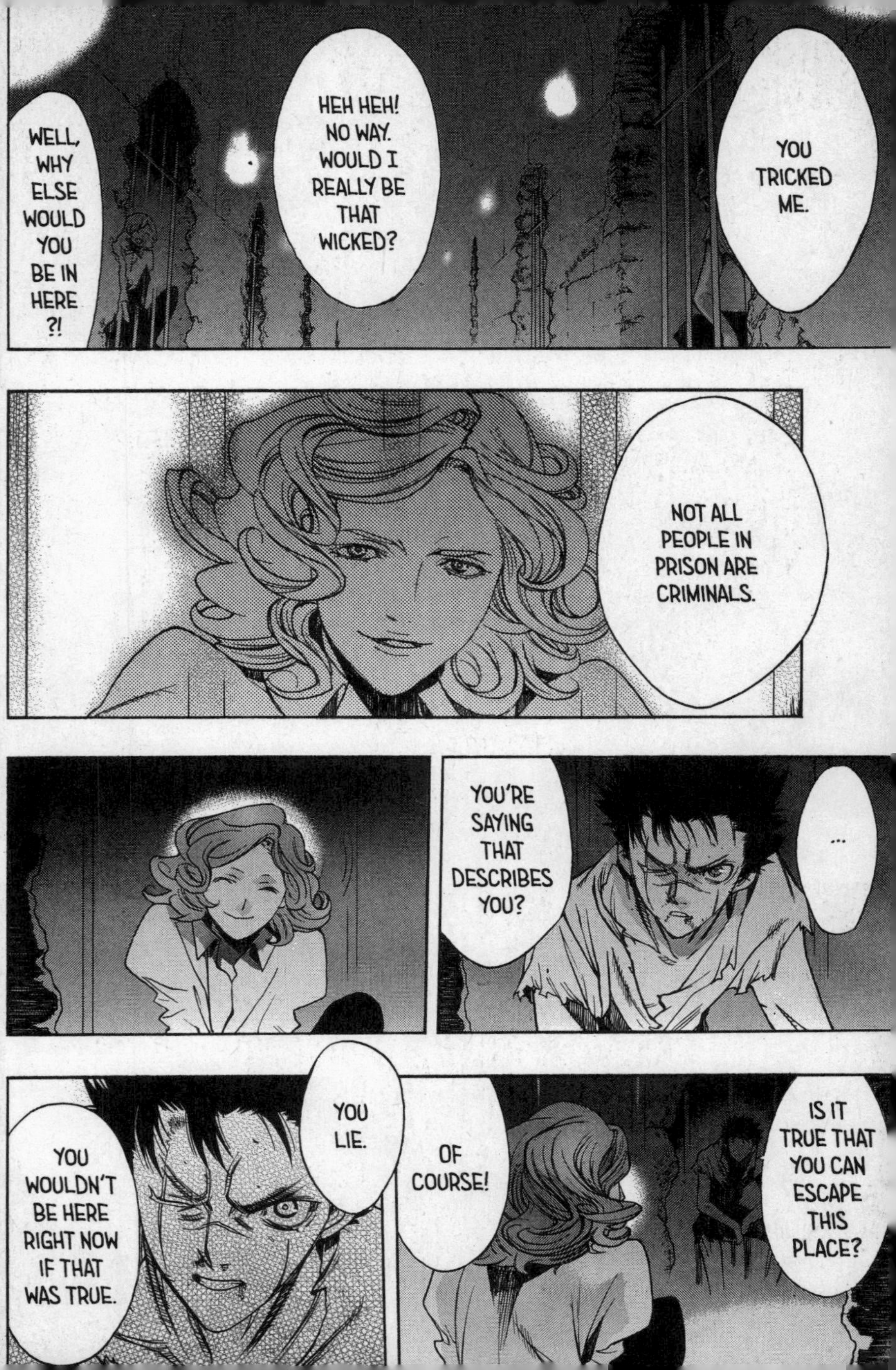
YOU TRICKED ME.
HEH HEH! NO WAY. WOULD I REALLY BE THAT WICKED?
WELL, WHY ELSE WOULD YOU BE IN HERE?!
NOT ALL PEOPLE IN PRISON ARE CRIMINALS.
...
YOU'RE SAYING THAT DESCRIBES YOU?
IS IT TRUE THAT YOU CAN ESCAPE THIS PLACE?
OF COURSE!
YOU LIE.
YOU WOULDN'T BE HERE RIGHT NOW IF THAT WAS TRUE.

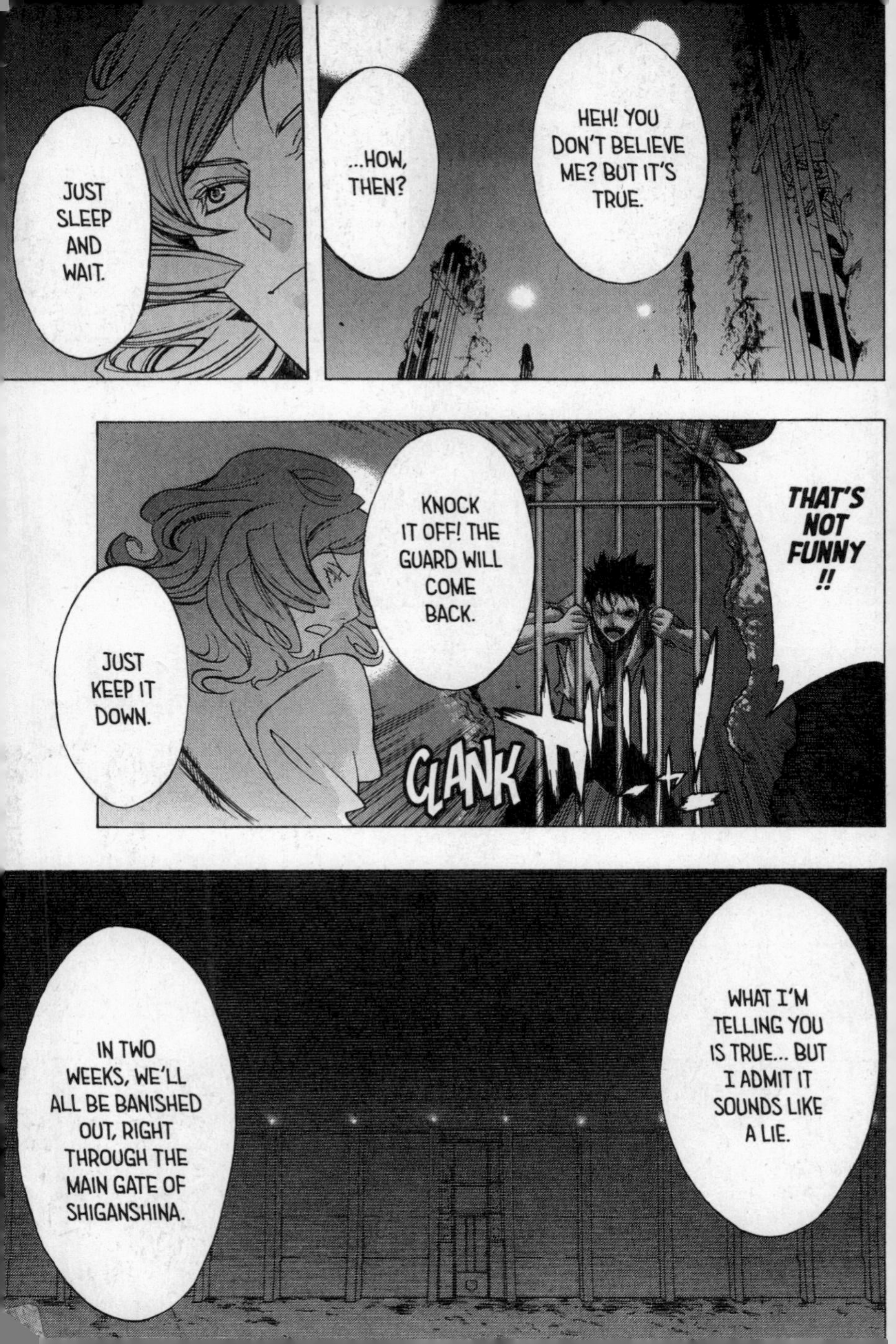
HEH! YOU DON'T BELIEVE ME? BUT IT'S TRUE.
...HOW, THEN?
JUST SLEEP AND WAIT.
THAT'S NOT FUNNY!!
CLANK
KNOCK IT OFF! THE GUARD WILL COME BACK.
JUST KEEP IT DOWN.
WHAT I'M TELLING YOU IS TRUE... BUT I ADMIT IT SOUNDS LIKE A LIE.
IN TWO WEEKS, WE'LL ALL BE BANISHED OUT, RIGHT THROUGH THE MAIN GATE OF SHIGANSHINA.

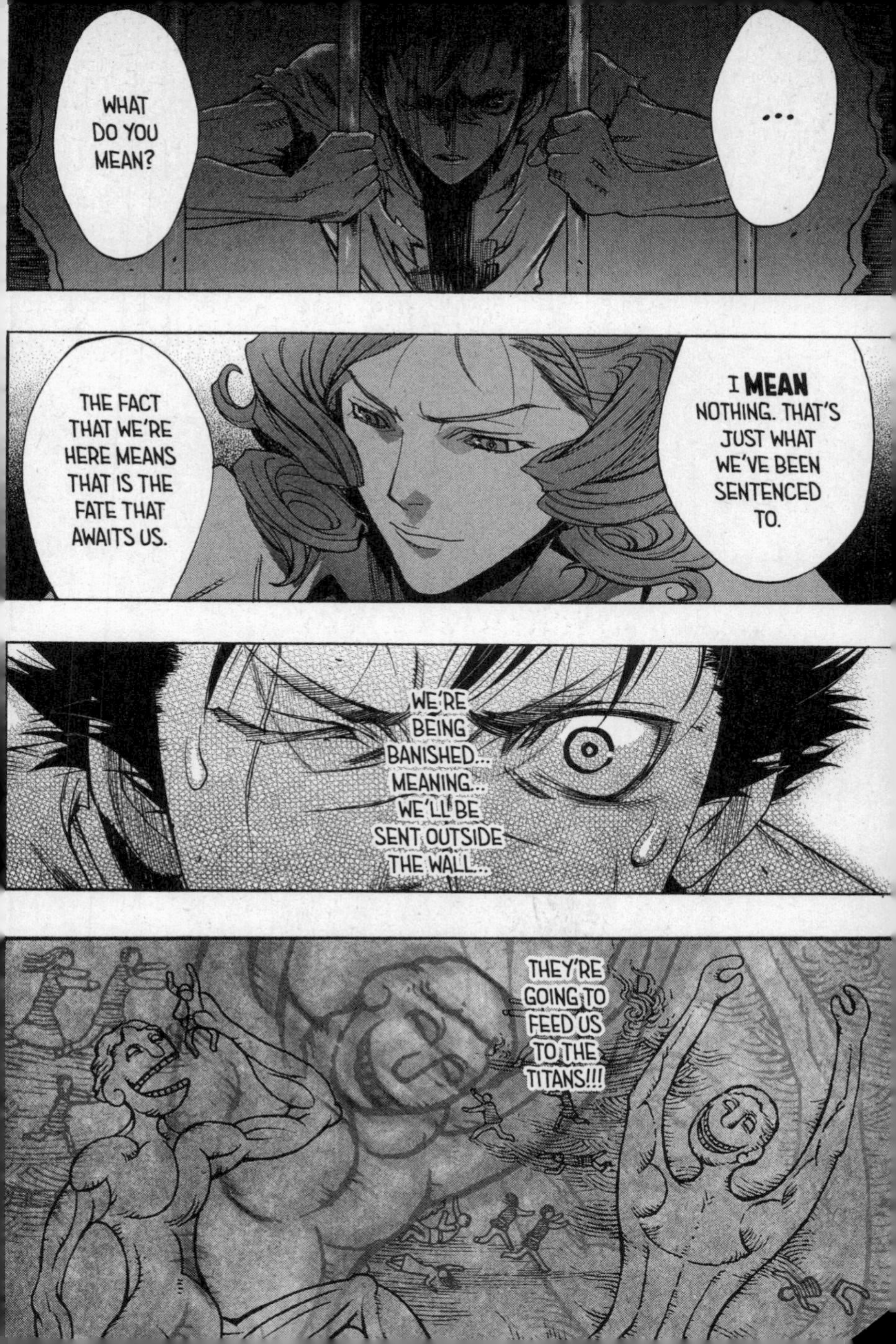
...
WHAT DO YOU MEAN?
I **MEAN** NOTHING. THAT'S JUST WHAT WE'VE BEEN SENTENCED TO.
THE FACT THAT WE'RE HERE MEANS THAT IS THE FATE THAT AWAITS US.
WE'RE BEING BANISHED... MEANING... WE'LL BE SENT OUTSIDE THE WALL...
THEY'RE GOING TO FEED US TO THE TITANS!!!

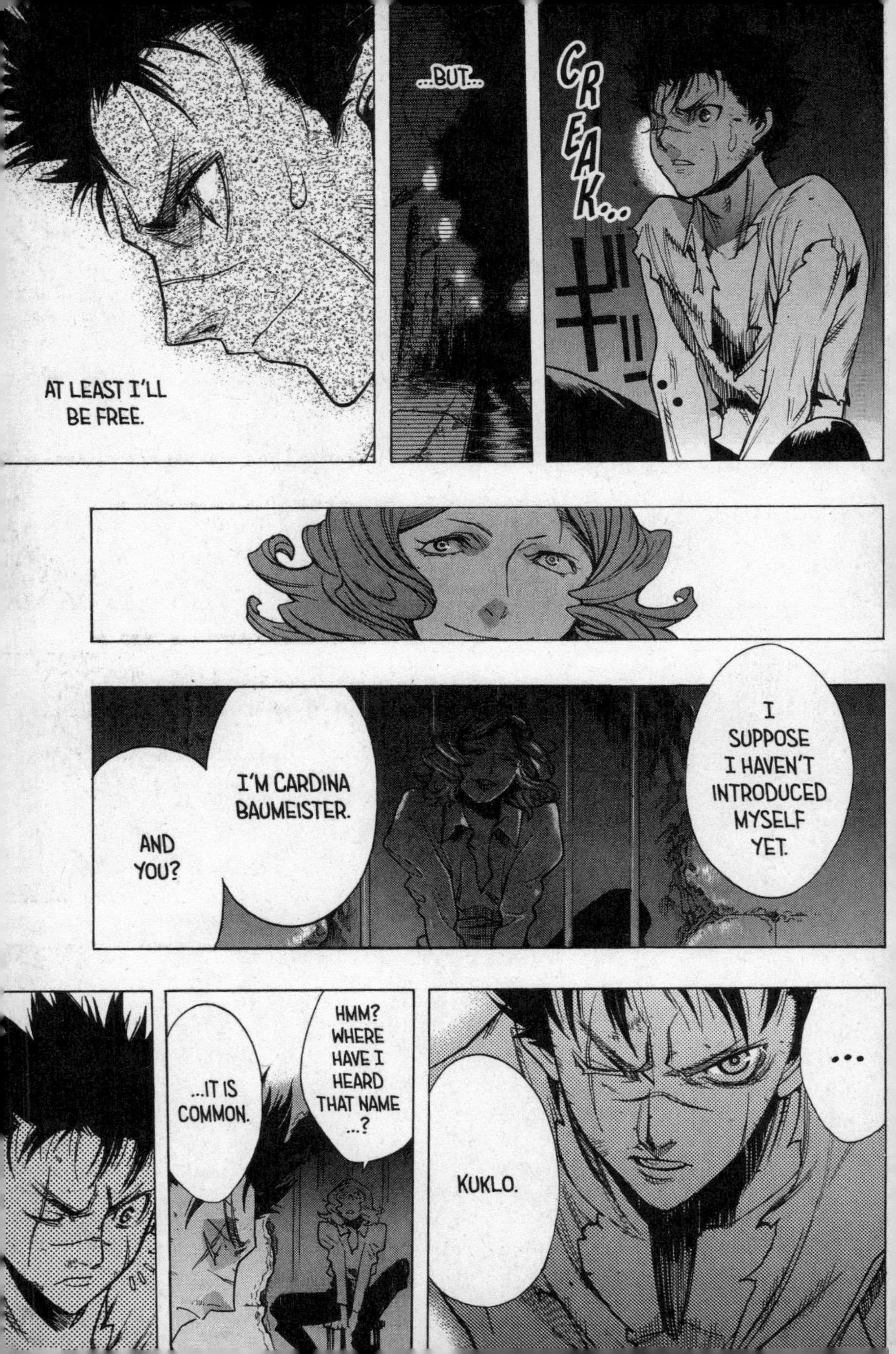
CREAK...
...BUT...
AT LEAST I'LL BE FREE.
I SUPPOSE I HAVEN'T INTRODUCED MYSELF YET.
I'M CARDINA BAUMEISTER.
AND YOU?
...
KUKLO.
HMM? WHERE HAVE I HEARD THAT NAME ...?
...IT IS COMMON.

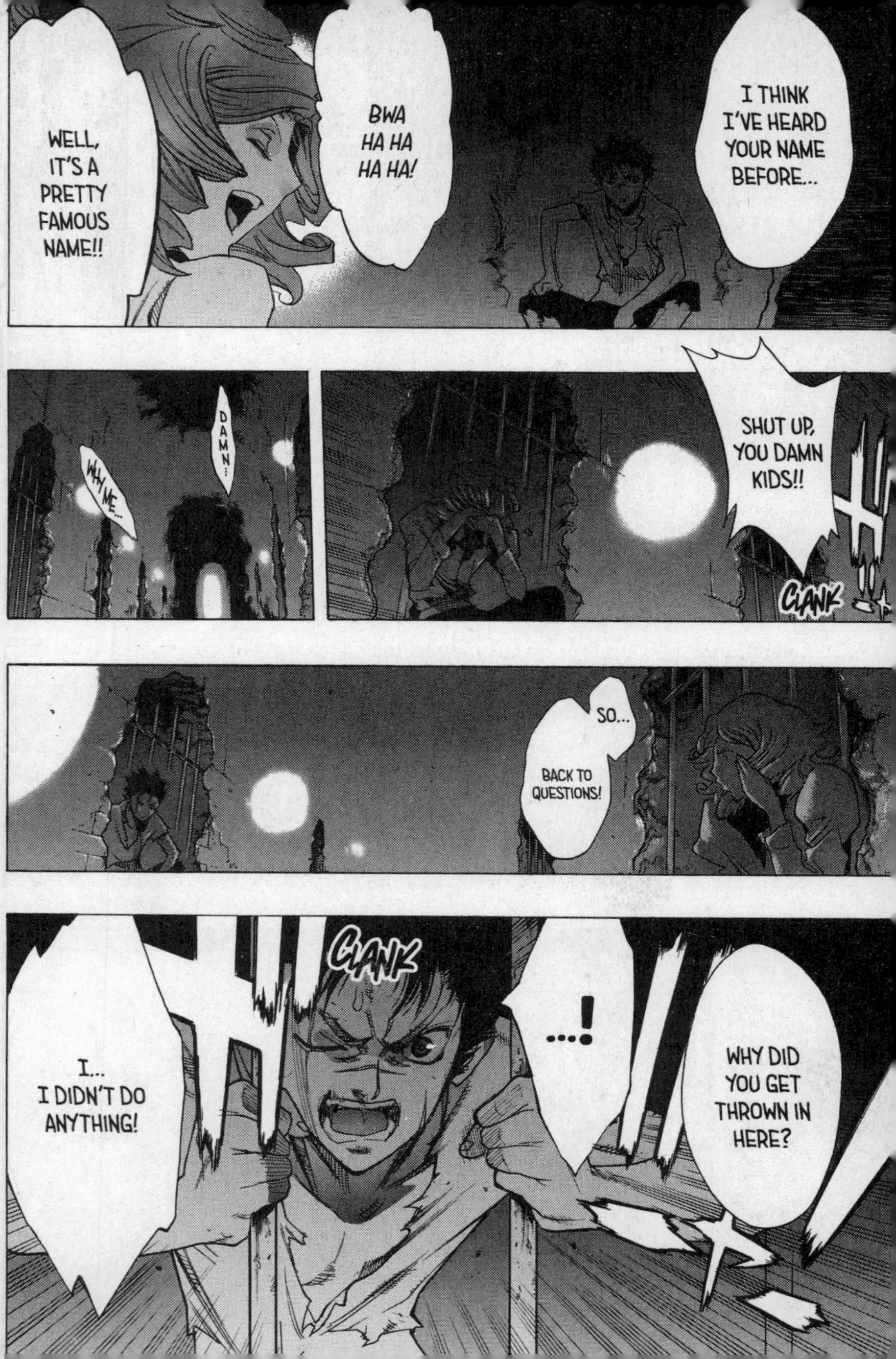
I THINK I'VE HEARD YOUR NAME BEFORE...
BWA HA HA HA HA!
WELL, IT'S A PRETTY FAMOUS NAME!!
SHUT UP, YOU DAMN KIDS!!
CLANK
DAMN...
WHY ME...
SO...
BACK TO QUESTIONS!
WHY DID YOU GET THROWN IN HERE?
...!
CLANK
I... I DIDN'T DO ANYTHING!

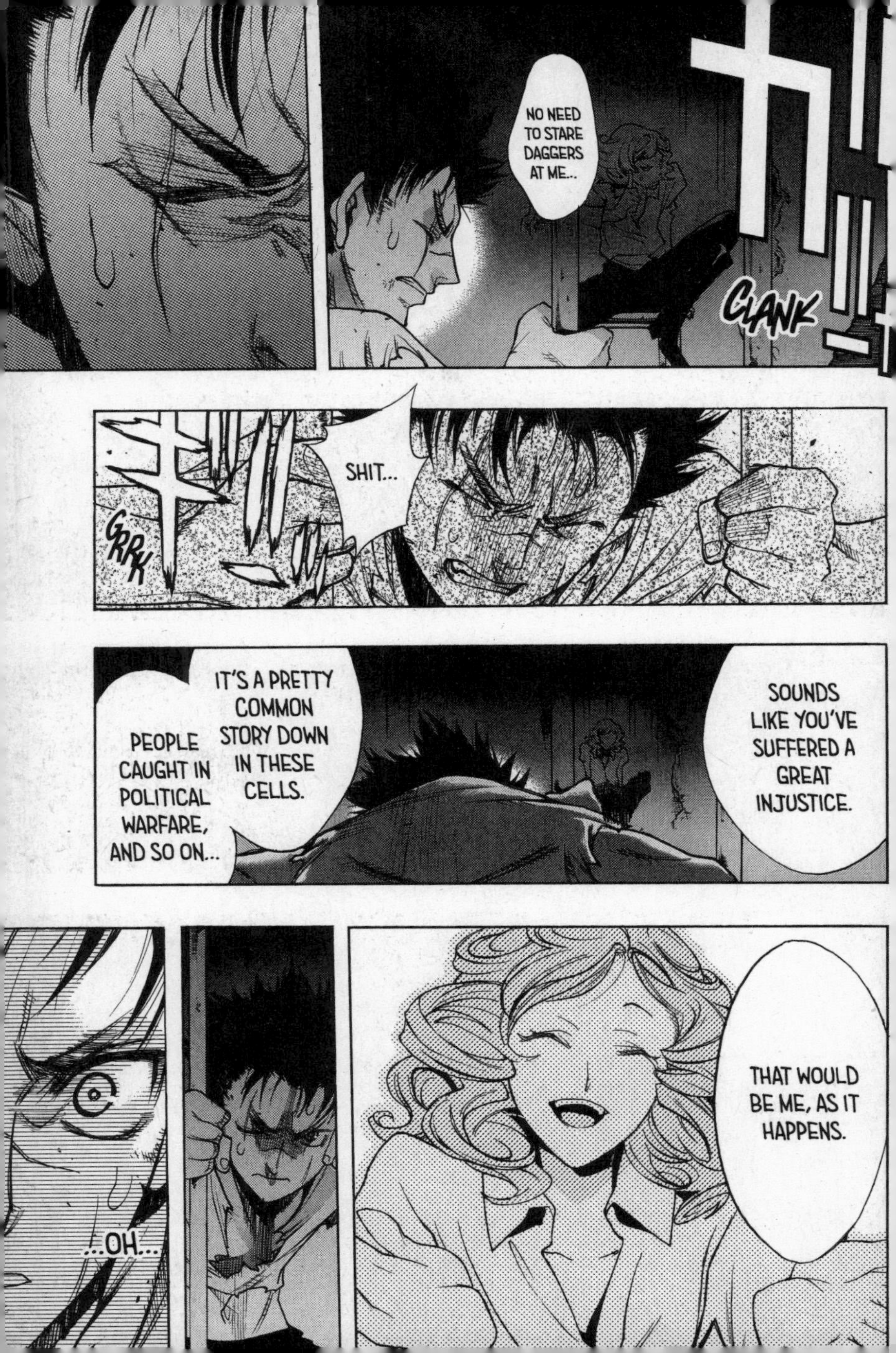
NO NEED TO STARE DAGGERS AT ME...
CLANK
SHIT...
GRRK
SOUNDS LIKE YOU'VE SUFFERED A GREAT INJUSTICE.
IT'S A PRETTY COMMON STORY DOWN IN THESE CELLS.
PEOPLE CAUGHT IN POLITICAL WARFARE, AND SO ON...
THAT WOULD BE ME, AS IT HAPPENS.
...OH...

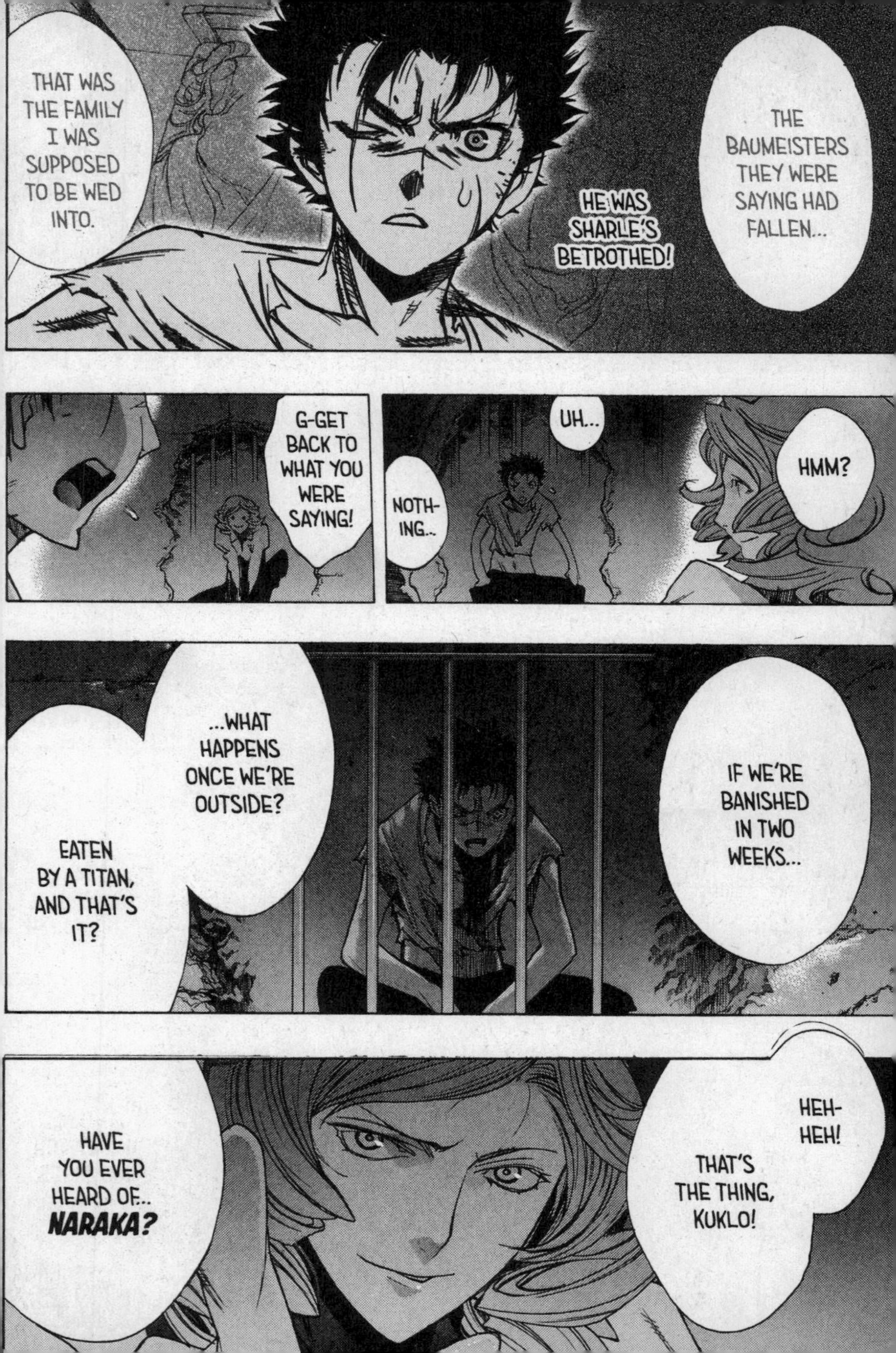
THE BAUMEISTERS THEY WERE SAYING HAD FALLEN...
HE WAS SHARLE'S BETROTHED!
THAT WAS THE FAMILY I WAS SUPPOSED TO BE WED INTO.
HMM?
UH...
NOTH-ING...
G-GET BACK TO WHAT YOU WERE SAYING!
IF WE'RE BANISHED IN TWO WEEKS...
...WHAT HAPPENS ONCE WE'RE OUTSIDE?
EATEN BY A TITAN, AND THAT'S IT?
HEH-HEH!
THAT'S THE THING, KUKLO!
HAVE YOU EVER HEARD OF... **NARAKA?**

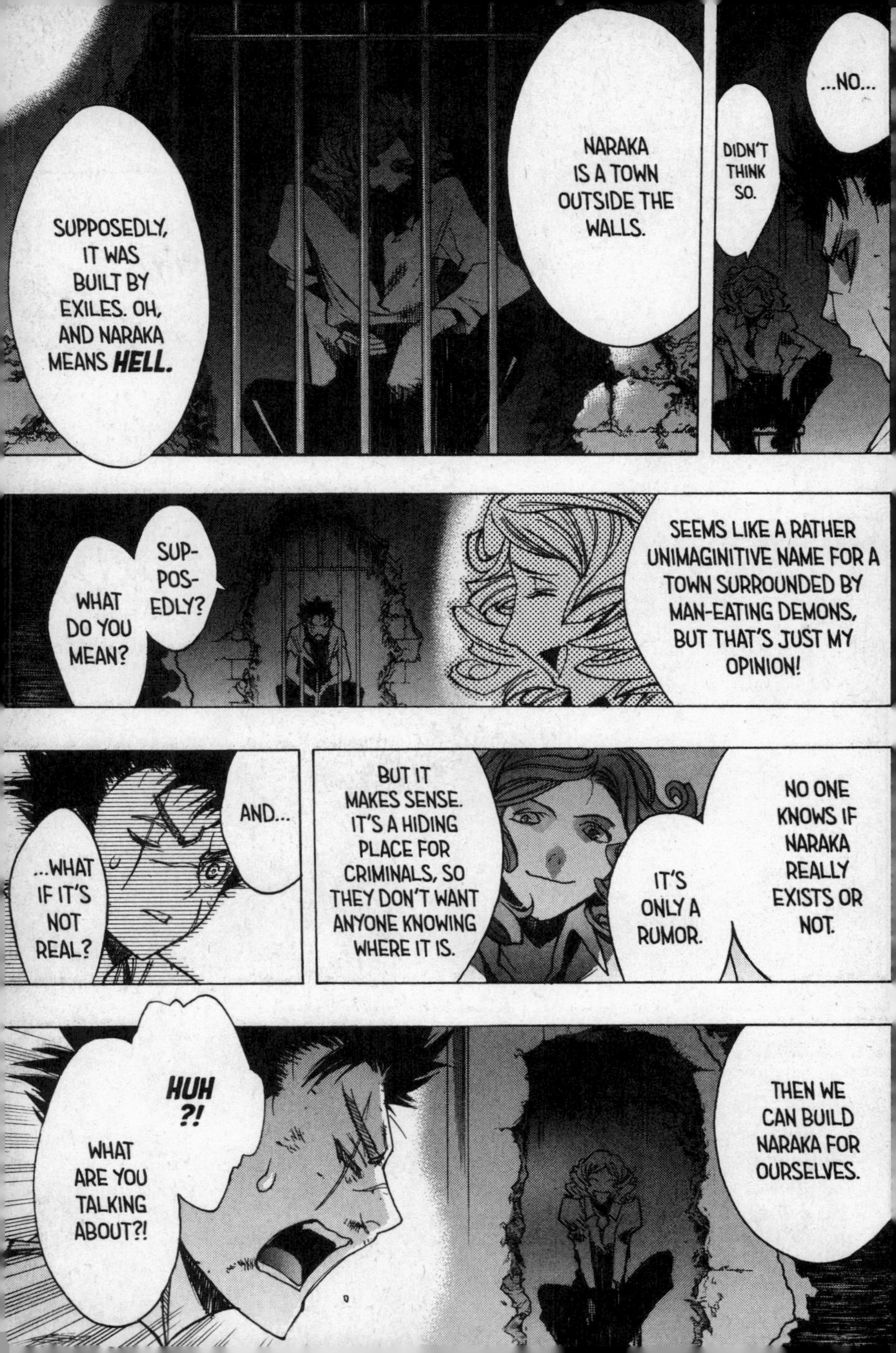
...NO...
DIDN'T THINK SO.
NARAKA IS A TOWN OUTSIDE THE WALLS.
SUPPOSEDLY, IT WAS BUILT BY EXILES. OH, AND NARAKA MEANS **HELL.**
SEEMS LIKE A RATHER UNIMAGINITIVE NAME FOR A TOWN SURROUNDED BY MAN-EATING DEMONS, BUT THAT'S JUST MY OPINION!
SUP-POS-EDLY?
WHAT DO YOU MEAN?
NO ONE KNOWS IF NARAKA REALLY EXISTS OR NOT.
IT'S ONLY A RUMOR.
BUT IT MAKES SENSE. IT'S A HIDING PLACE FOR CRIMINALS, SO THEY DON'T WANT ANYONE KNOWING WHERE IT IS.
AND...
...WHAT IF IT'S NOT REAL?
THEN WE CAN BUILD NARAKA FOR OURSELVES.
HUH?!
WHAT ARE YOU TALKING ABOUT?!

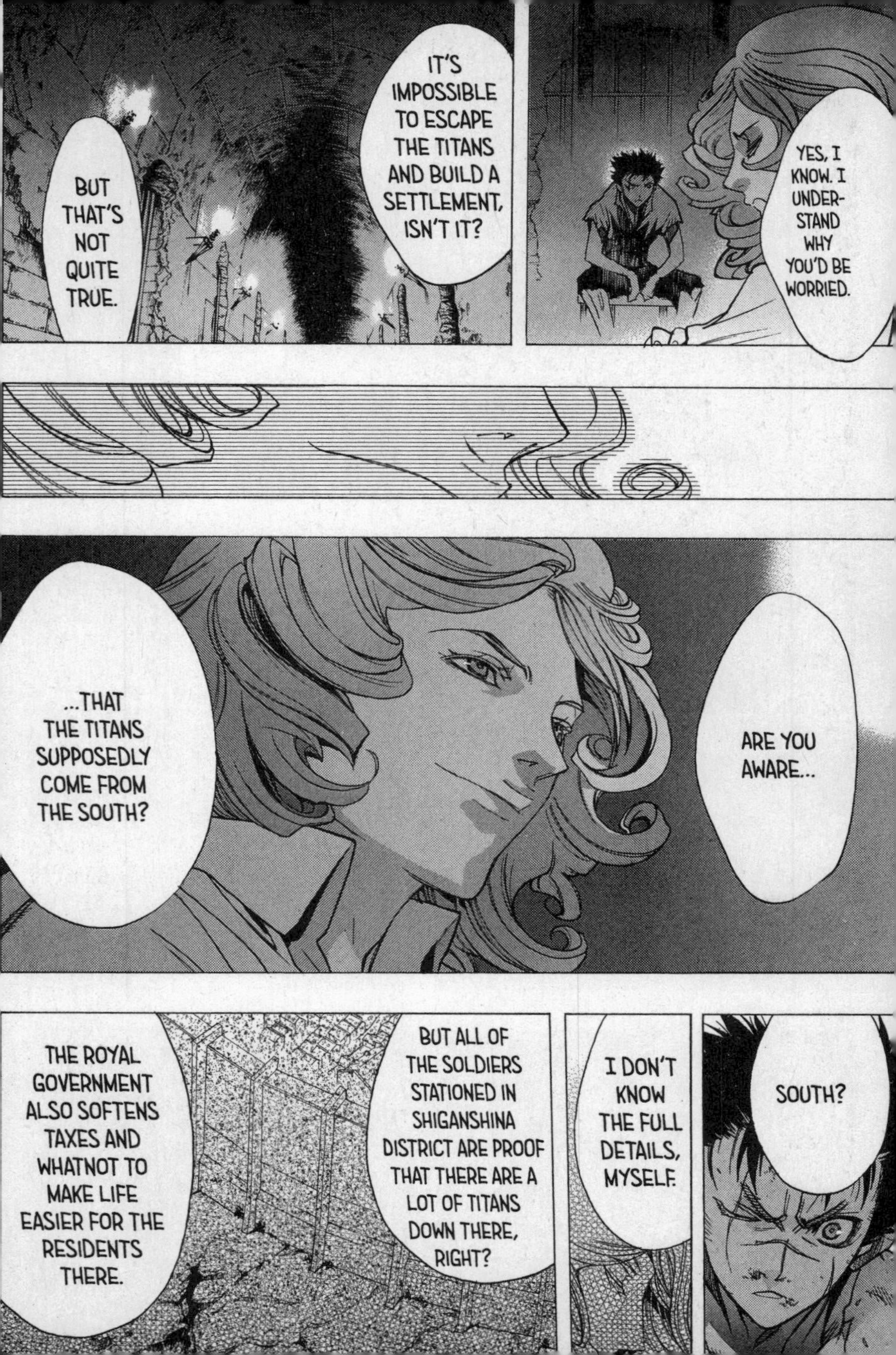
YES, I KNOW. I UNDERSTAND WHY YOU'D BE WORRIED.
IT'S IMPOSSIBLE TO ESCAPE THE TITANS AND BUILD A SETTLEMENT, ISN'T IT?
BUT THAT'S NOT QUITE TRUE.
ARE YOU AWARE...
...THAT THE TITANS SUPPOSEDLY COME FROM THE SOUTH?
SOUTH?
I DON'T KNOW THE FULL DETAILS, MYSELF.
BUT ALL OF THE SOLDIERS STATIONED IN SHIGANSHINA DISTRICT ARE PROOF THAT THERE ARE A LOT OF TITANS DOWN THERE, RIGHT?
THE ROYAL GOVERNMENT ALSO SOFTENS TAXES AND WHATNOT TO MAKE LIFE EASIER FOR THE RESIDENTS THERE.

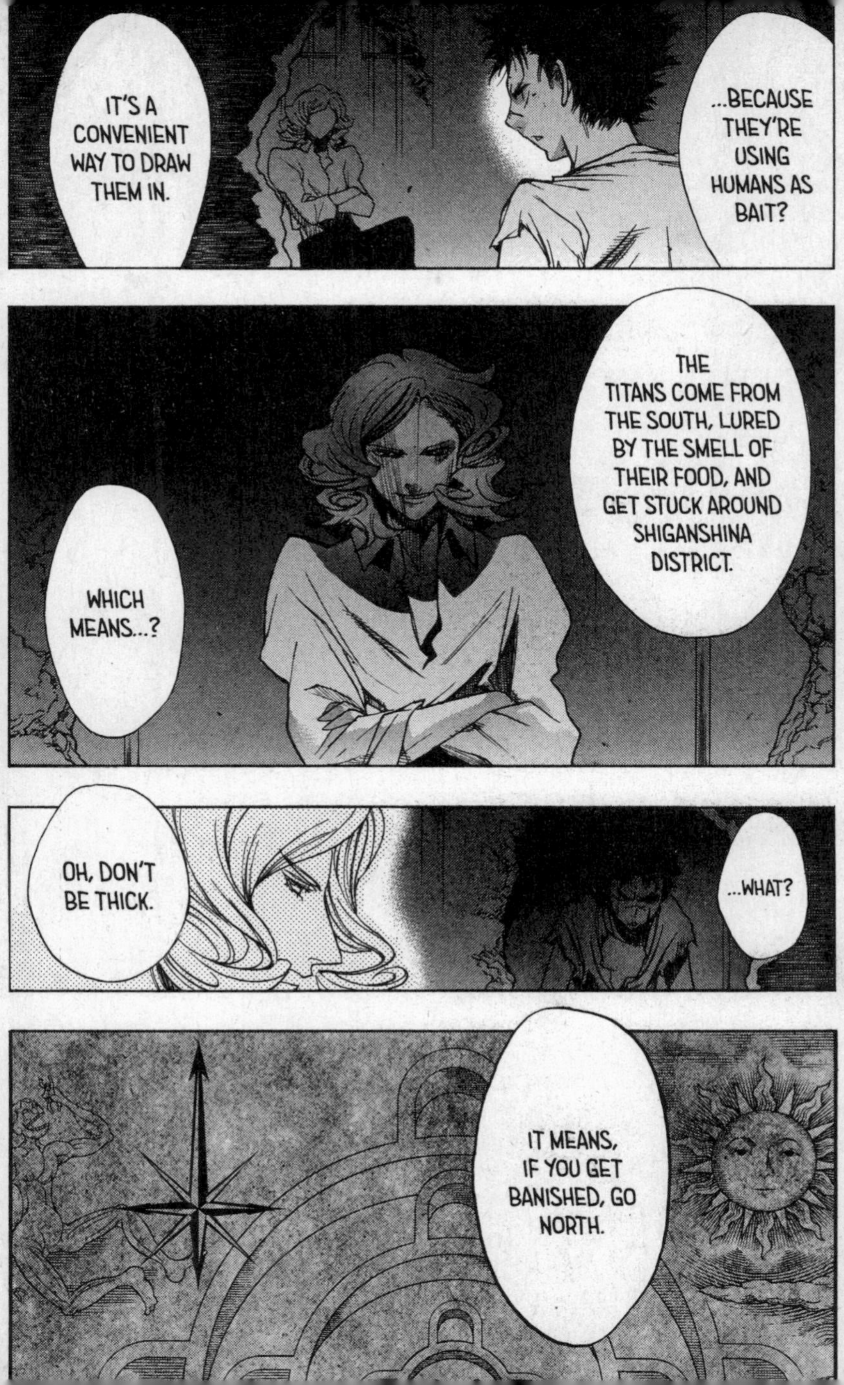
...BECAUSE THEY'RE USING HUMANS AS BAIT?
IT'S A CONVENIENT WAY TO DRAW THEM IN.
THE TITANS COME FROM THE SOUTH, LURED BY THE SMELL OF THEIR FOOD, AND GET STUCK AROUND SHIGANSHINA DISTRICT.
WHICH MEANS...?
...WHAT?
OH, DON'T BE THICK.
IT MEANS, IF YOU GET BANISHED, GO NORTH.

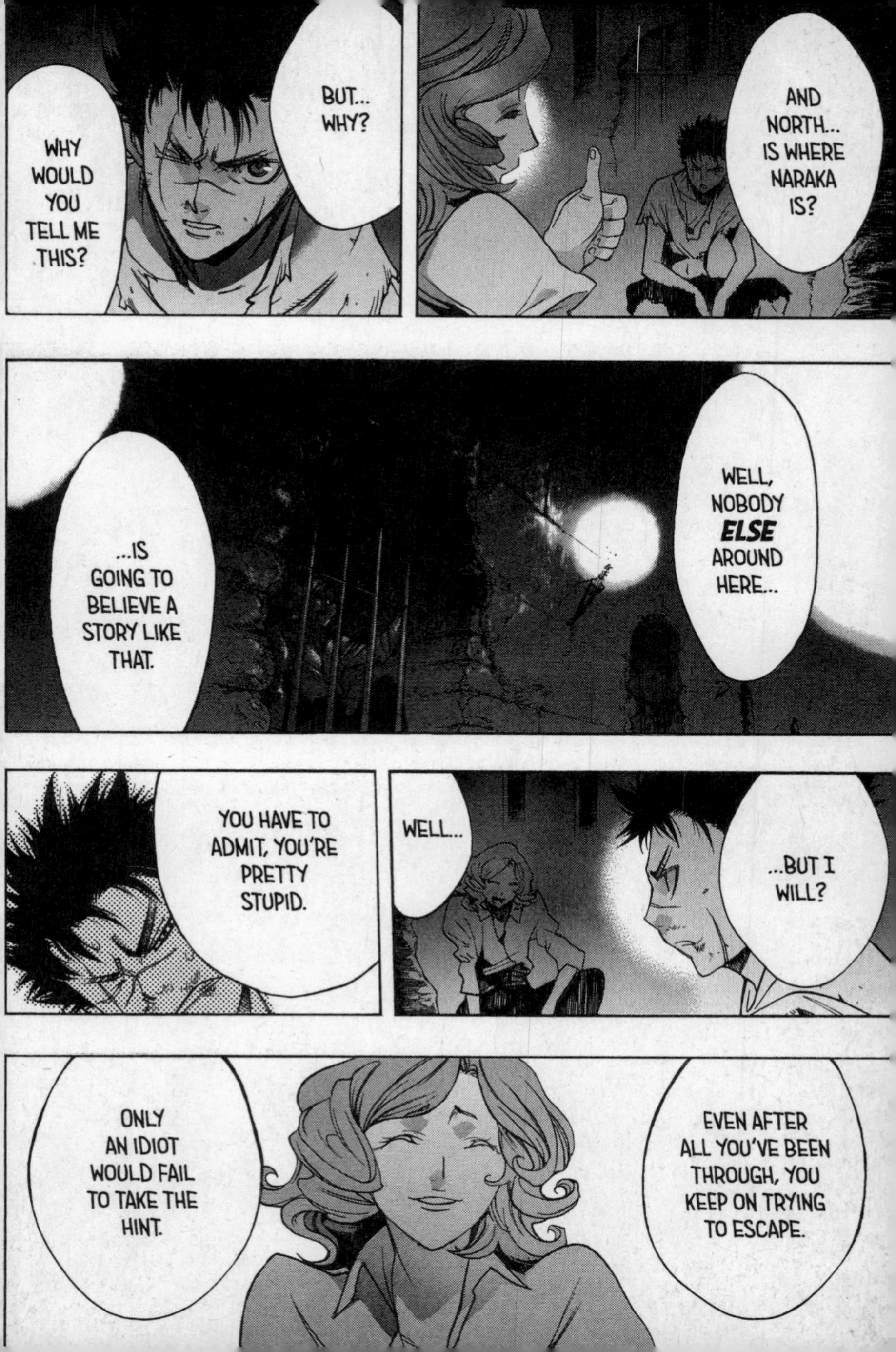
AND NORTH... IS WHERE NARAKA IS?
BUT... WHY?
WHY WOULD YOU TELL ME THIS?
WELL, NOBODY ***ELSE*** AROUND HERE...
...IS GOING TO BELIEVE A STORY LIKE THAT.
...BUT I WILL?
WELL...
YOU HAVE TO ADMIT, YOU'RE PRETTY STUPID.
EVEN AFTER ALL YOU'VE BEEN THROUGH, YOU KEEP ON TRYING TO ESCAPE.
ONLY AN IDIOT WOULD FAIL TO TAKE THE HINT.

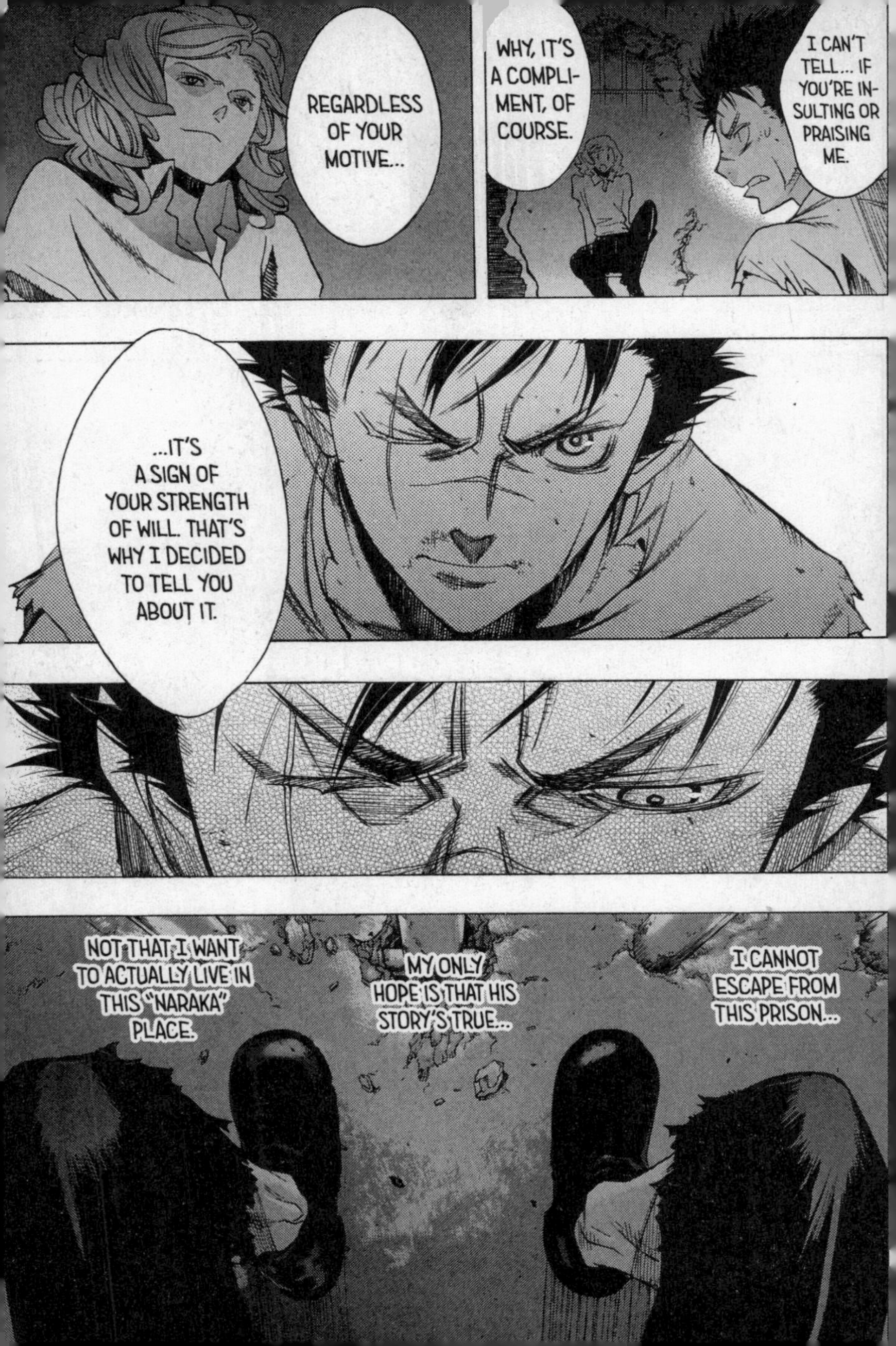
I CAN'T TELL... IF YOU'RE INSULTING OR PRAISING ME.
WHY, IT'S A COMPLIMENT, OF COURSE.
REGARDLESS OF YOUR MOTIVE...
...IT'S A SIGN OF YOUR STRENGTH OF WILL. THAT'S WHY I DECIDED TO TELL YOU ABOUT IT.
I CANNOT ESCAPE FROM THIS PRISON...
MY ONLY HOPE IS THAT HIS STORY'S TRUE...
NOT THAT I WANT TO ACTUALLY LIVE IN THIS "NARAKA" PLACE.

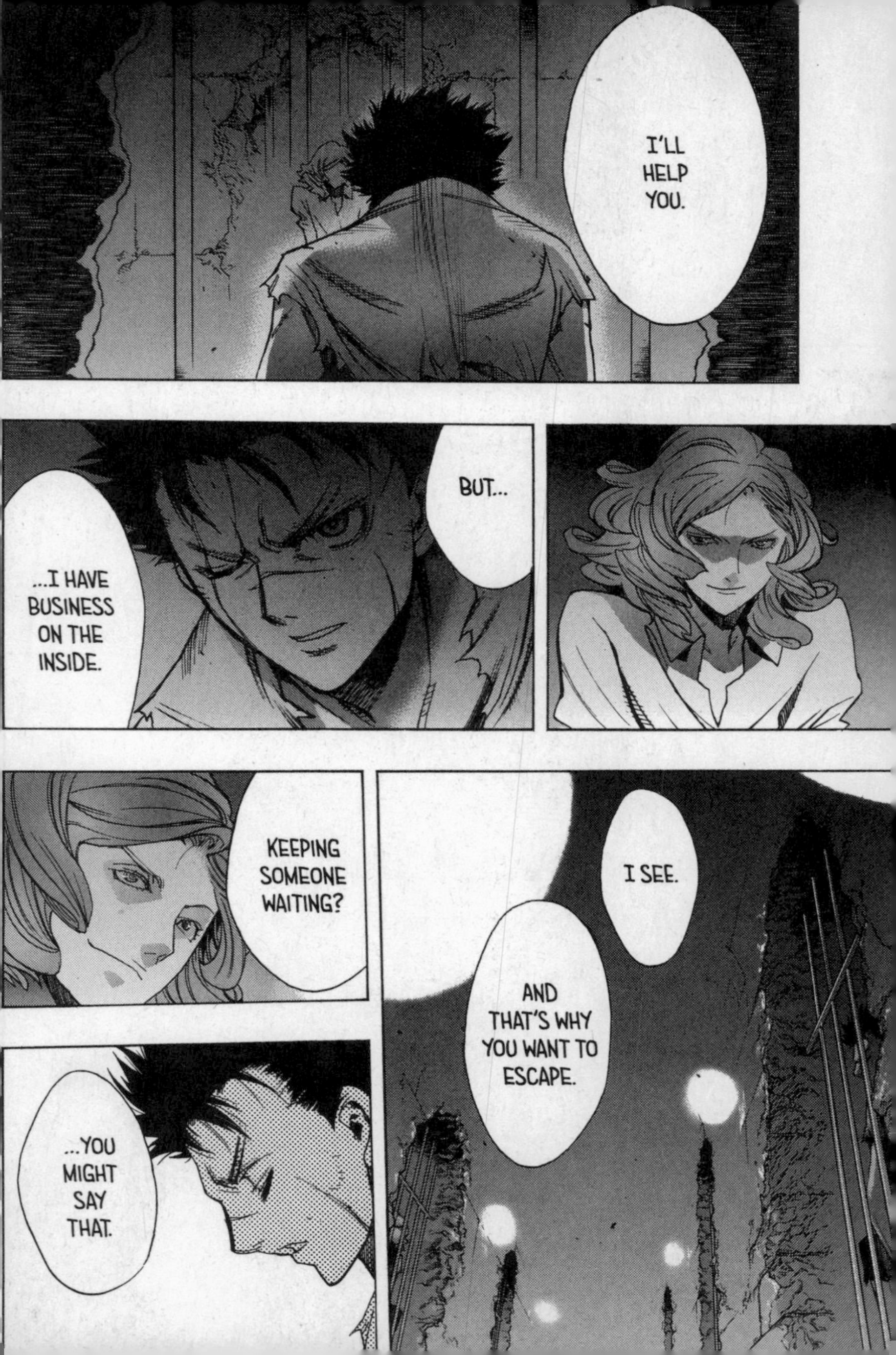
I'LL HELP YOU.
BUT...
...I HAVE BUSINESS ON THE INSIDE.
I SEE.
AND THAT'S WHY YOU WANT TO ESCAPE.
KEEPING SOMEONE WAITING?
...YOU MIGHT SAY THAT.

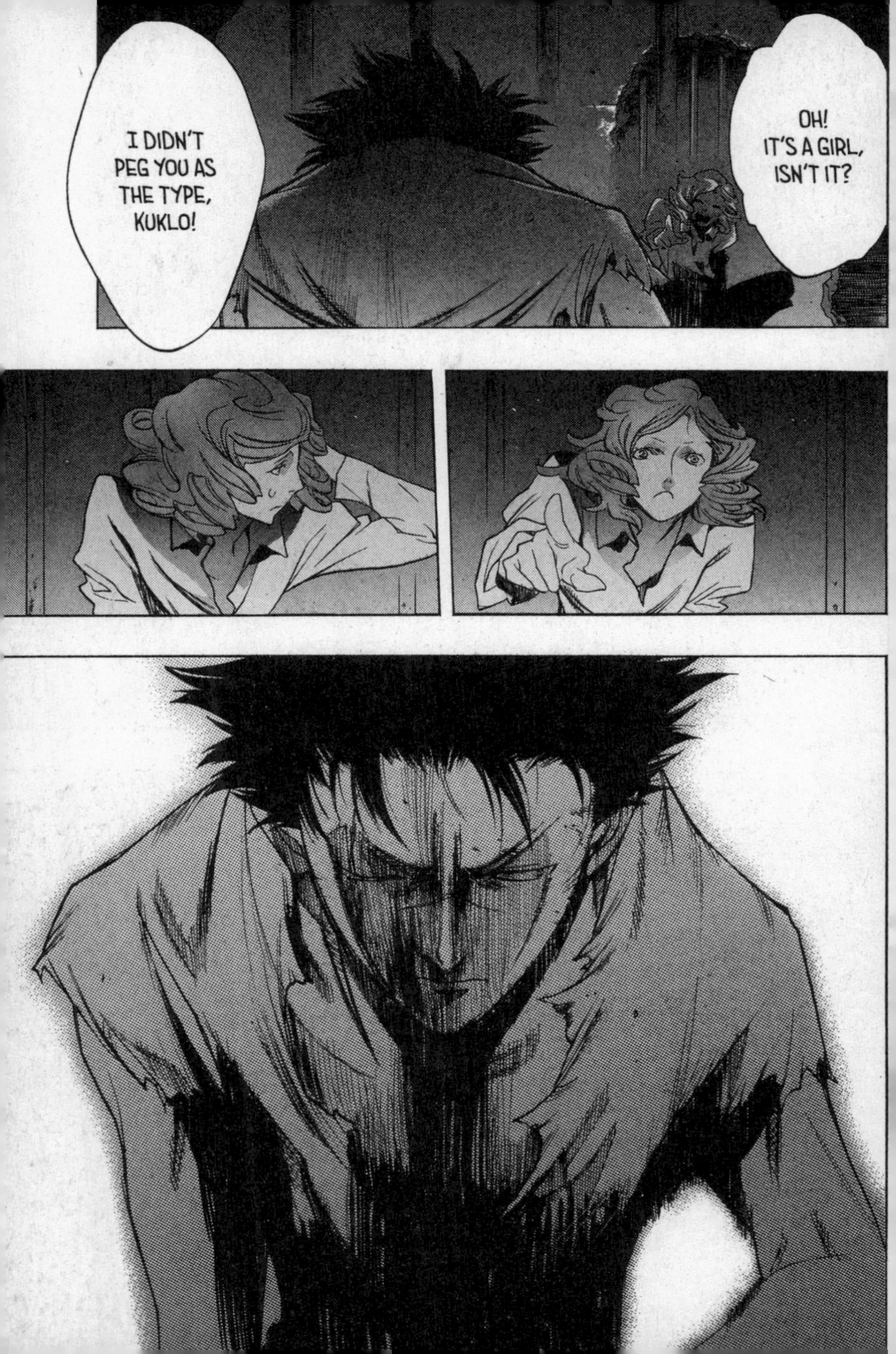
OH! IT'S A GIRL, ISN'T IT?
I DIDN'T PEG YOU AS THE TYPE, KUKLO!

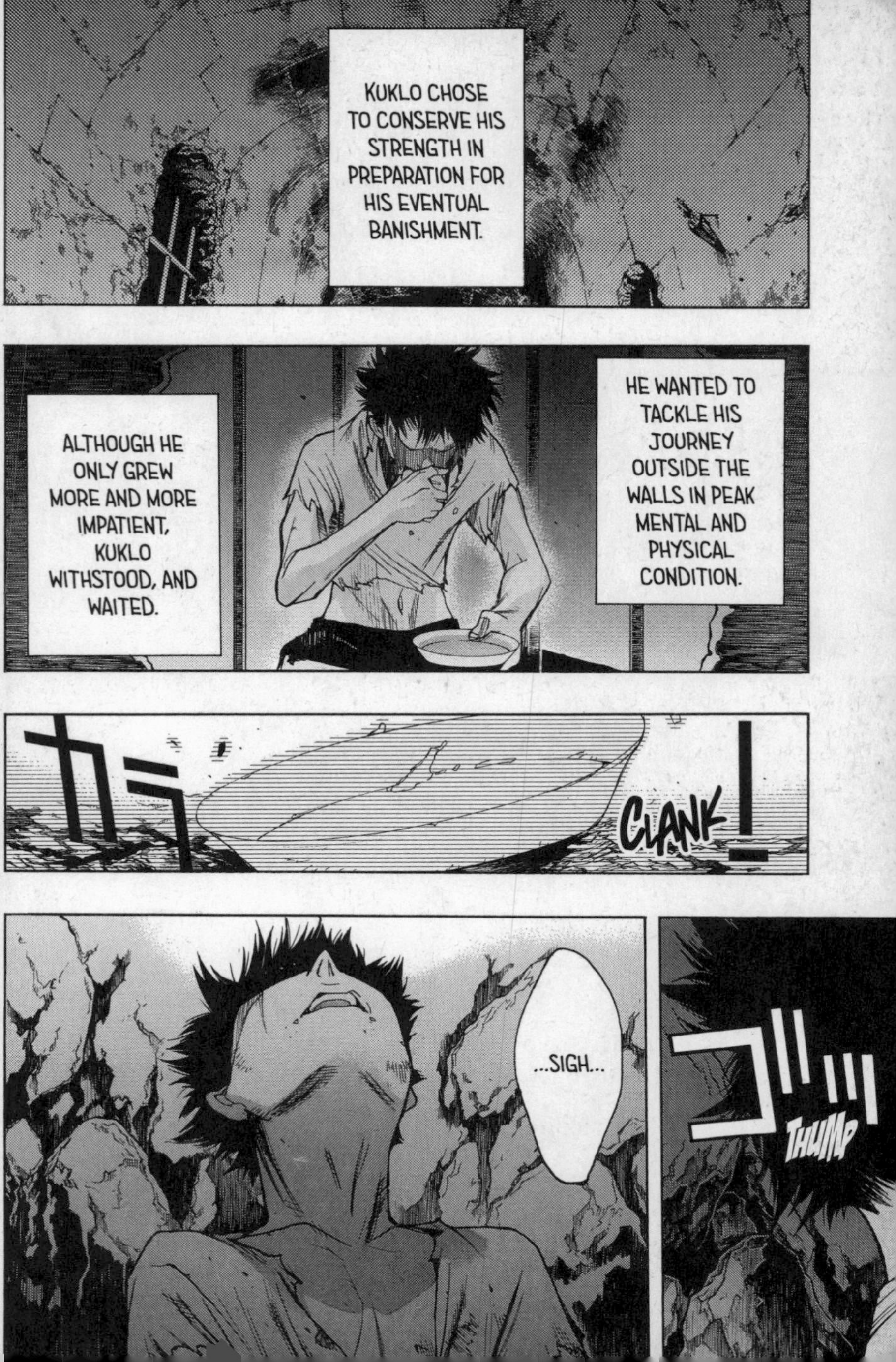
KUKLO CHOSE TO CONSERVE HIS STRENGTH IN PREPARATION FOR HIS EVENTUAL BANISHMENT.
HE WANTED TO TACKLE HIS JOURNEY OUTSIDE THE WALLS IN PEAK MENTAL AND PHYSICAL CONDITION.
ALTHOUGH HE ONLY GREW MORE AND MORE IMPATIENT, KUKLO WITHSTOOD, AND WAITED.
CLANK
カラ
ゴッ
THUMP
...SIGH...

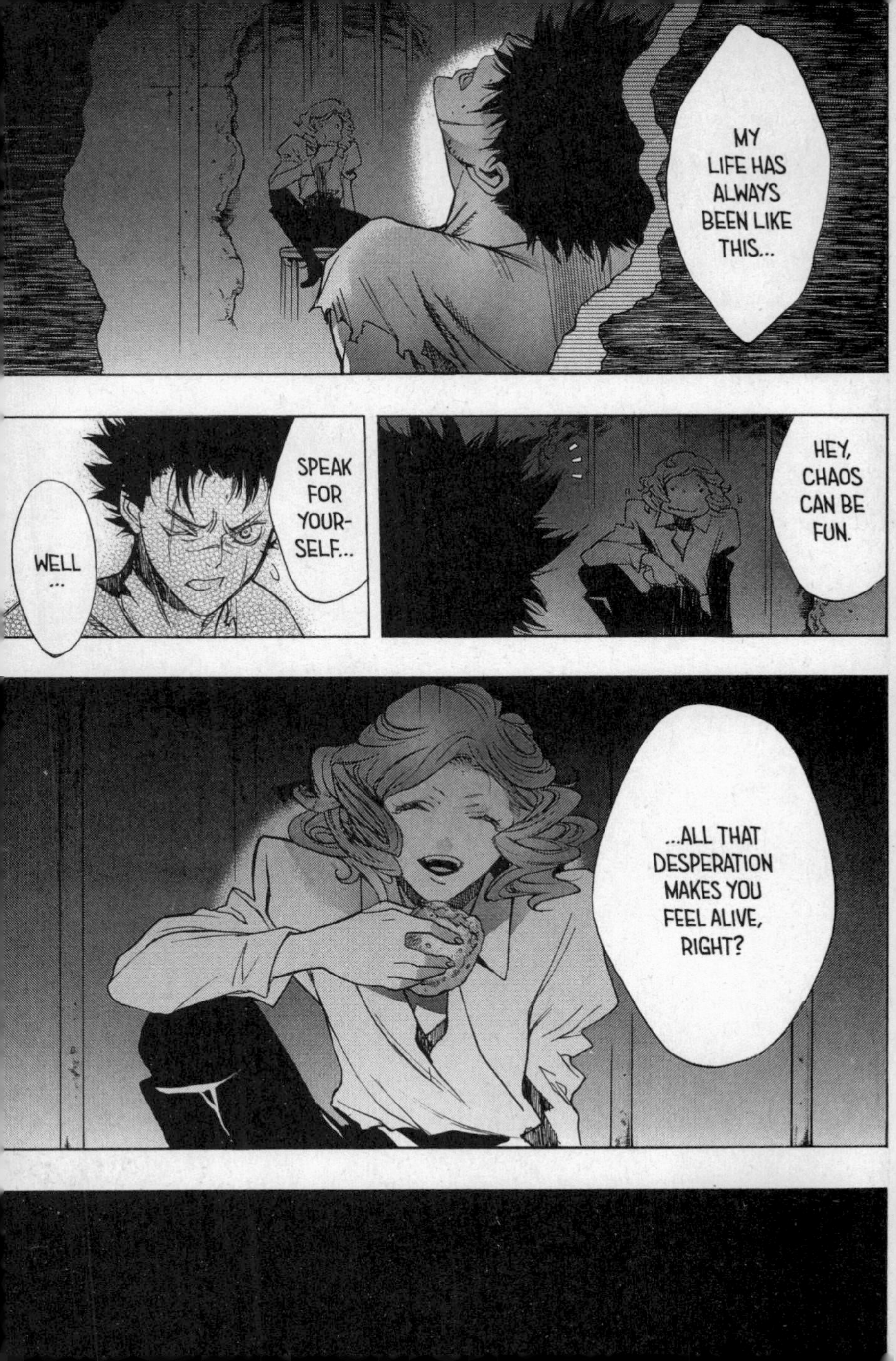
MY LIFE HAS ALWAYS BEEN LIKE THIS...
HEY, CHAOS CAN BE FUN.
SPEAK FOR YOUR-SELF...
WELL...
...ALL THAT DESPERATION MAKES YOU FEEL ALIVE, RIGHT?

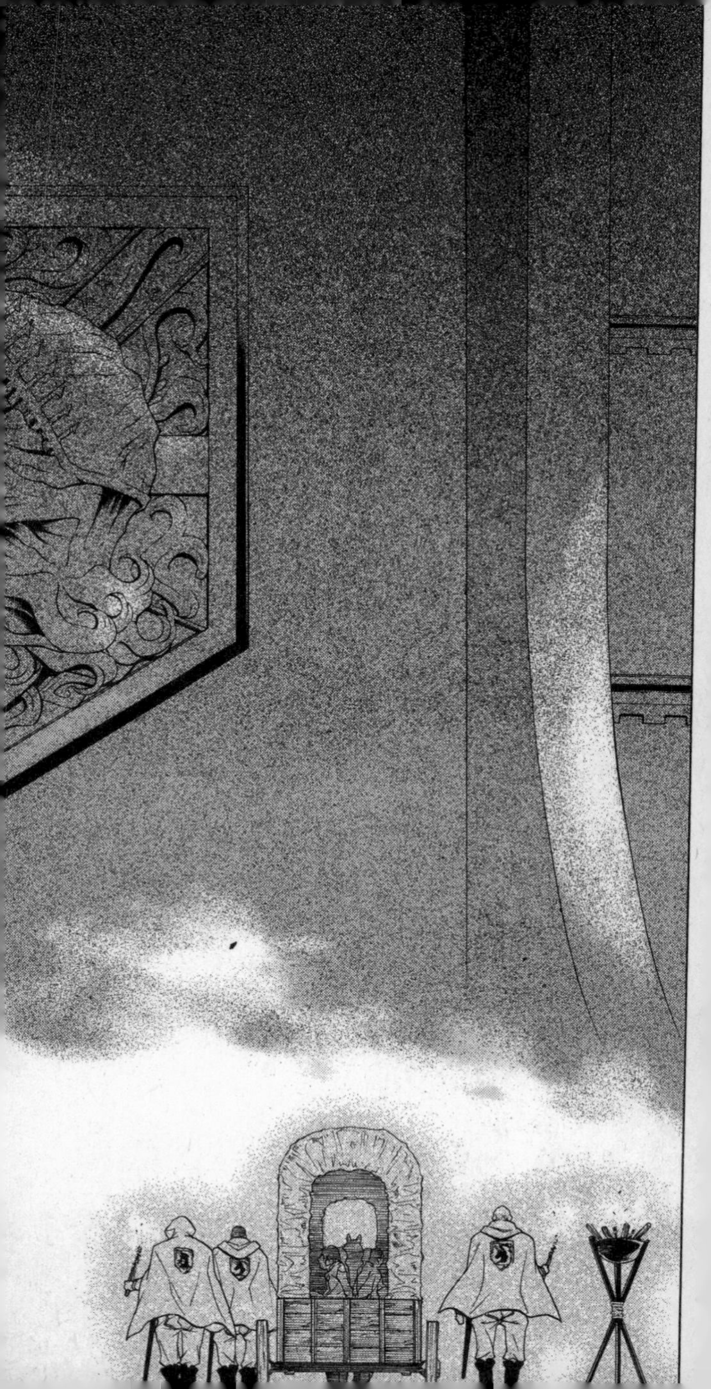

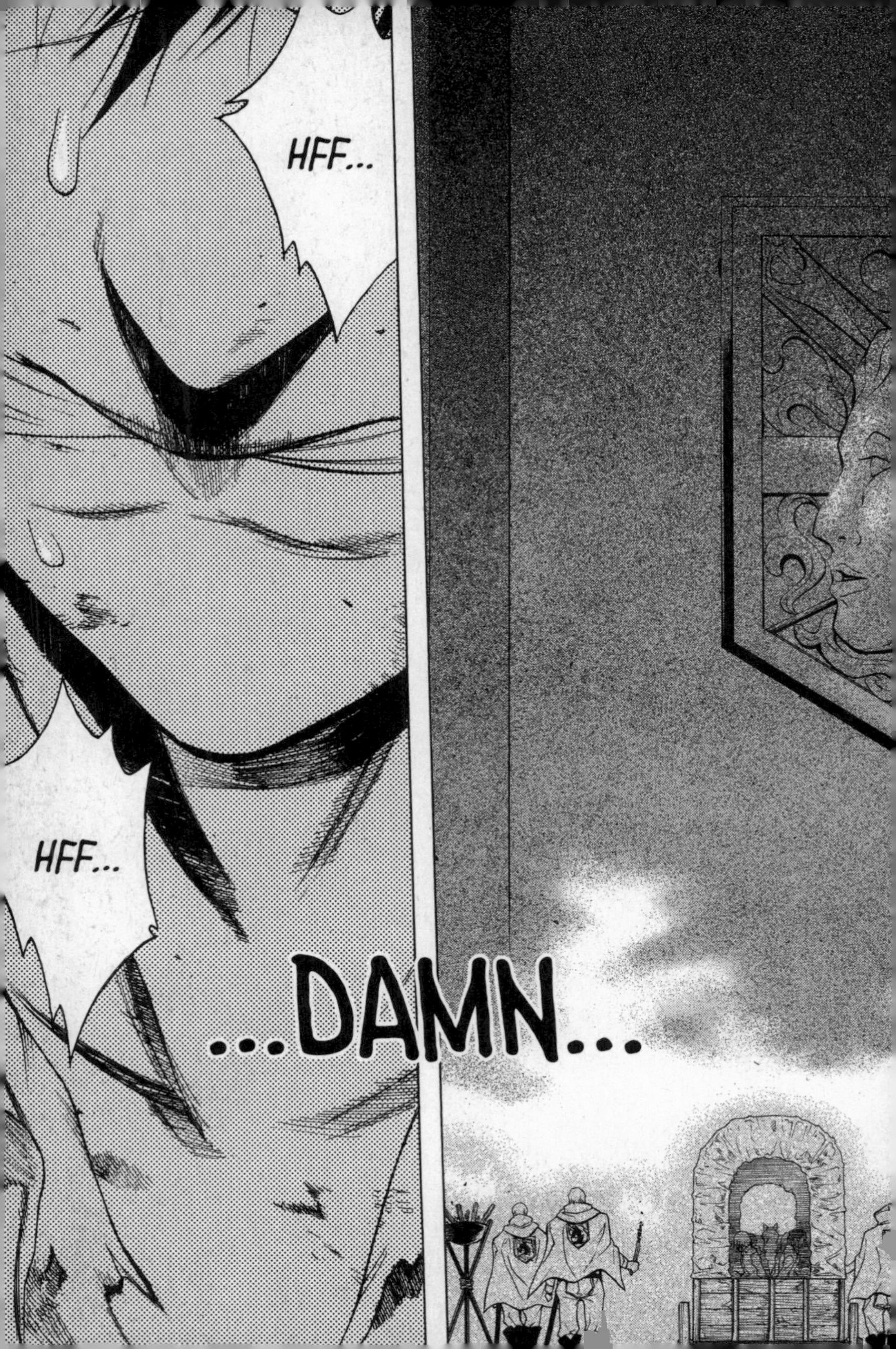
HFF...
HFF...
...DAMN...

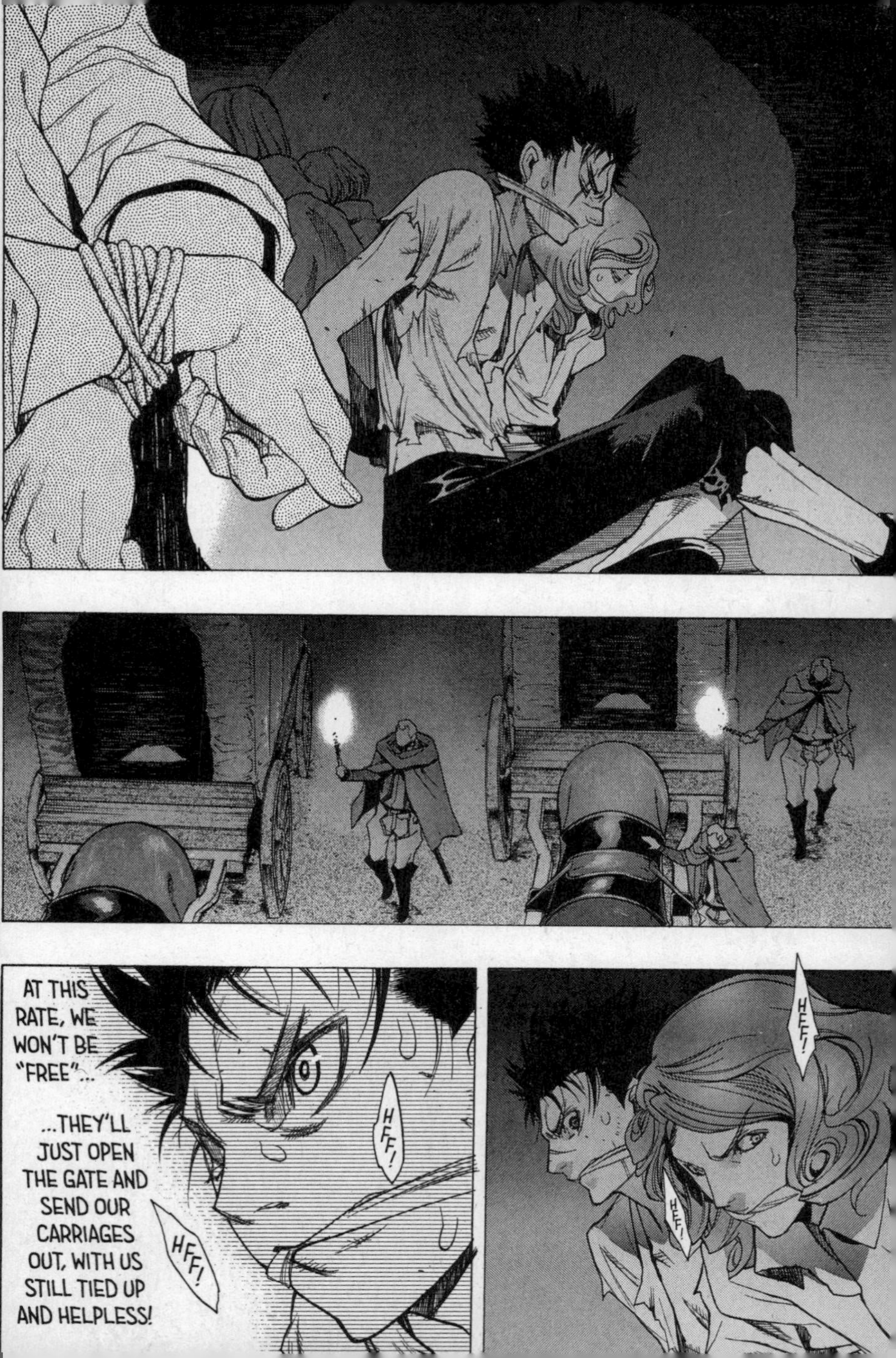
HFF!
HFF!
AT THIS RATE, WE WON'T BE "FREE"...
...THEY'LL JUST OPEN THE GATE AND SEND OUR CARRIAGES OUT, WITH US STILL TIED UP AND HELPLESS!
HFF!
HFF!

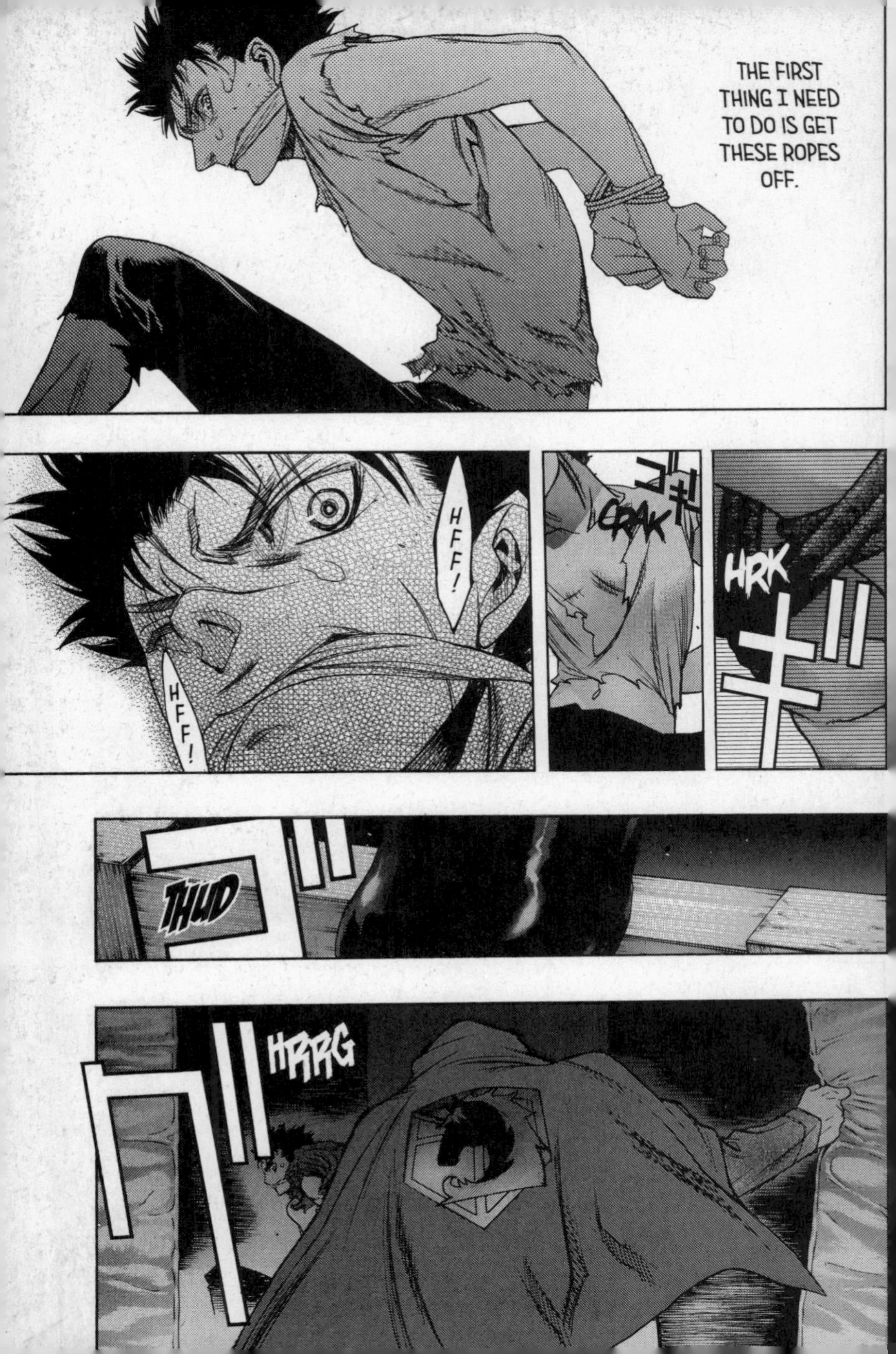

THE FIRST THING I NEED TO DO IS GET THESE ROPES OFF.
HRK
CRAK
HFF!
HFF!
THUD
HRRG

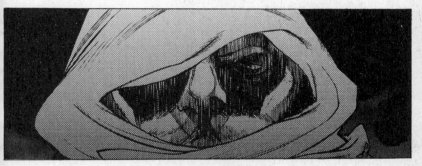

...SHIT!

HEE!

CREAK

GRRG

CREAK

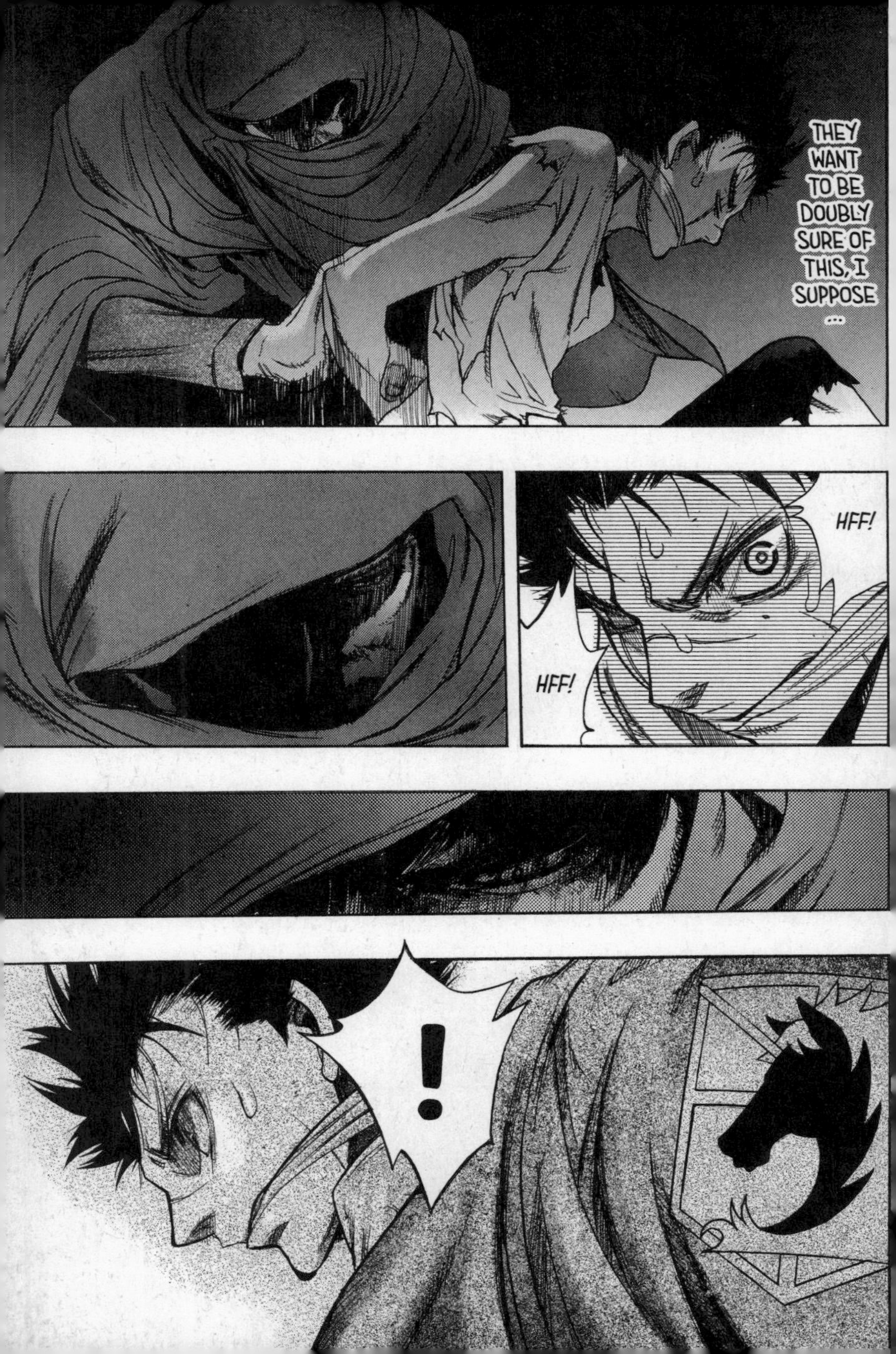
THEY WANT TO BE DOUBLY SURE OF THIS, I SUPPOSE ...
HFF!
HFF!
!

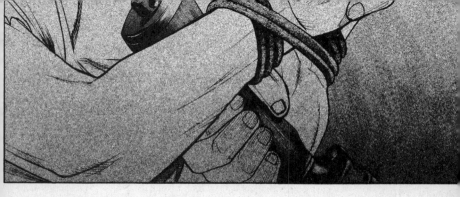

THE
KNIFE...
?!!

CREAK ‡!!

SPIN

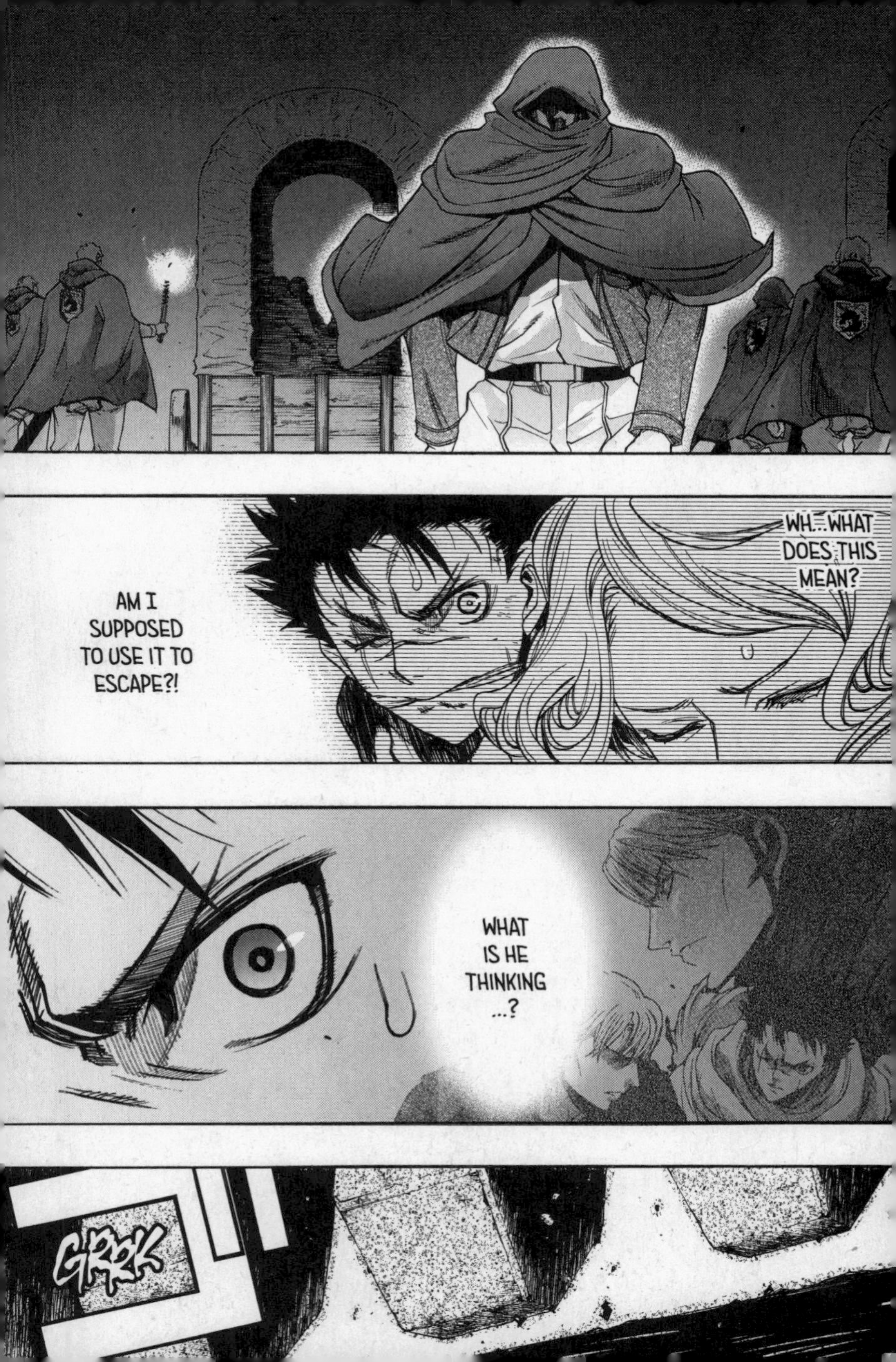
WH...WHAT DOES THIS MEAN?
AM I SUPPOSED TO USE IT TO ESCAPE?!
WHAT IS HE THINKING ...?
GROK

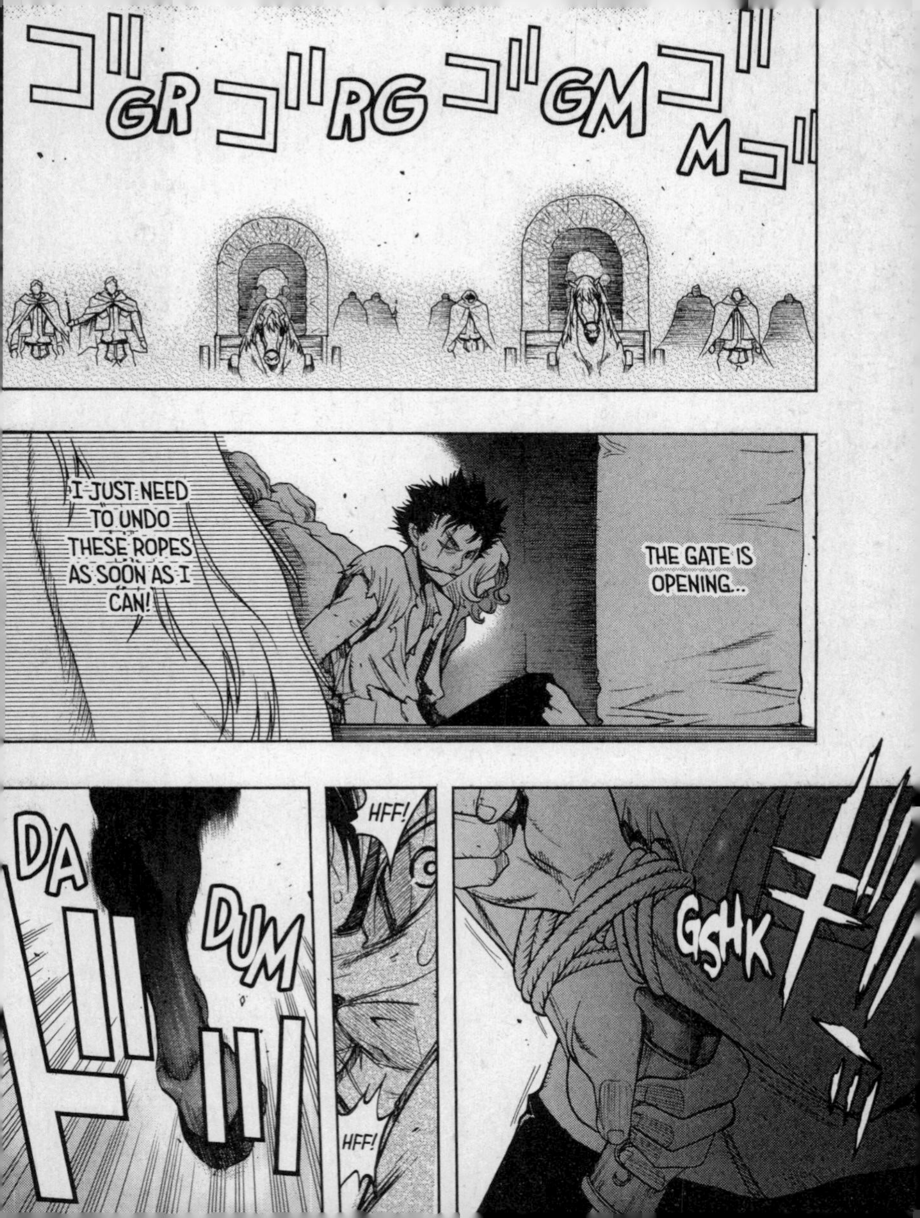
GRRGGMM
THE GATE IS OPENING...
I JUST NEED TO UNDO THESE ROPES AS SOON AS I CAN!
GSHK
HFF!
HFF!
DA DUM

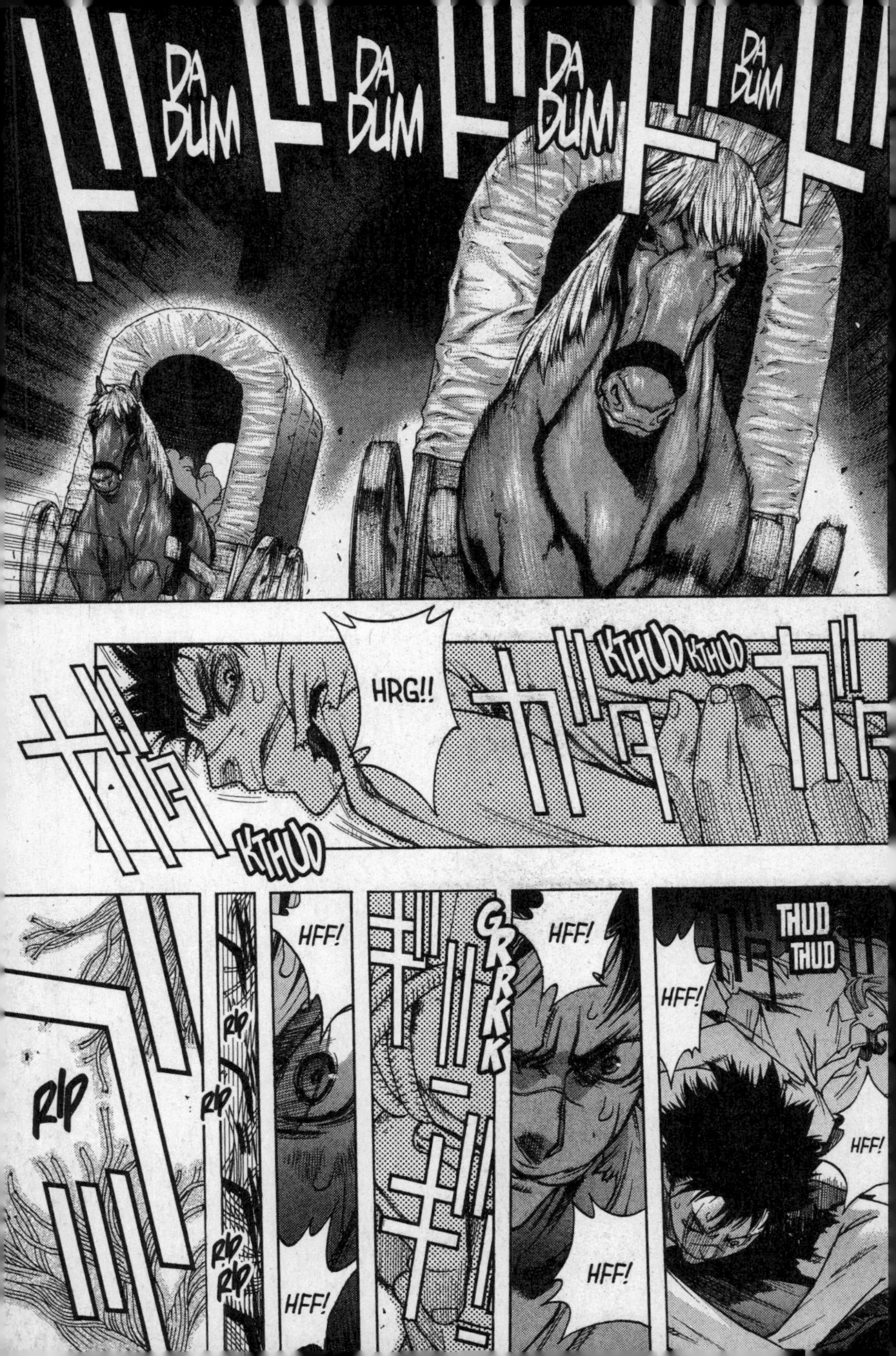
DA DUM
DA DUM
DA DUM
DA DUM
KTHUD KTHUD
HRG!!
KTHUD
THUD THUD
HFF!
HFF!
HFF!
HFF!
GRRKK
HFF!
HFF!
RIP
RIP
RIP RIP
RIP

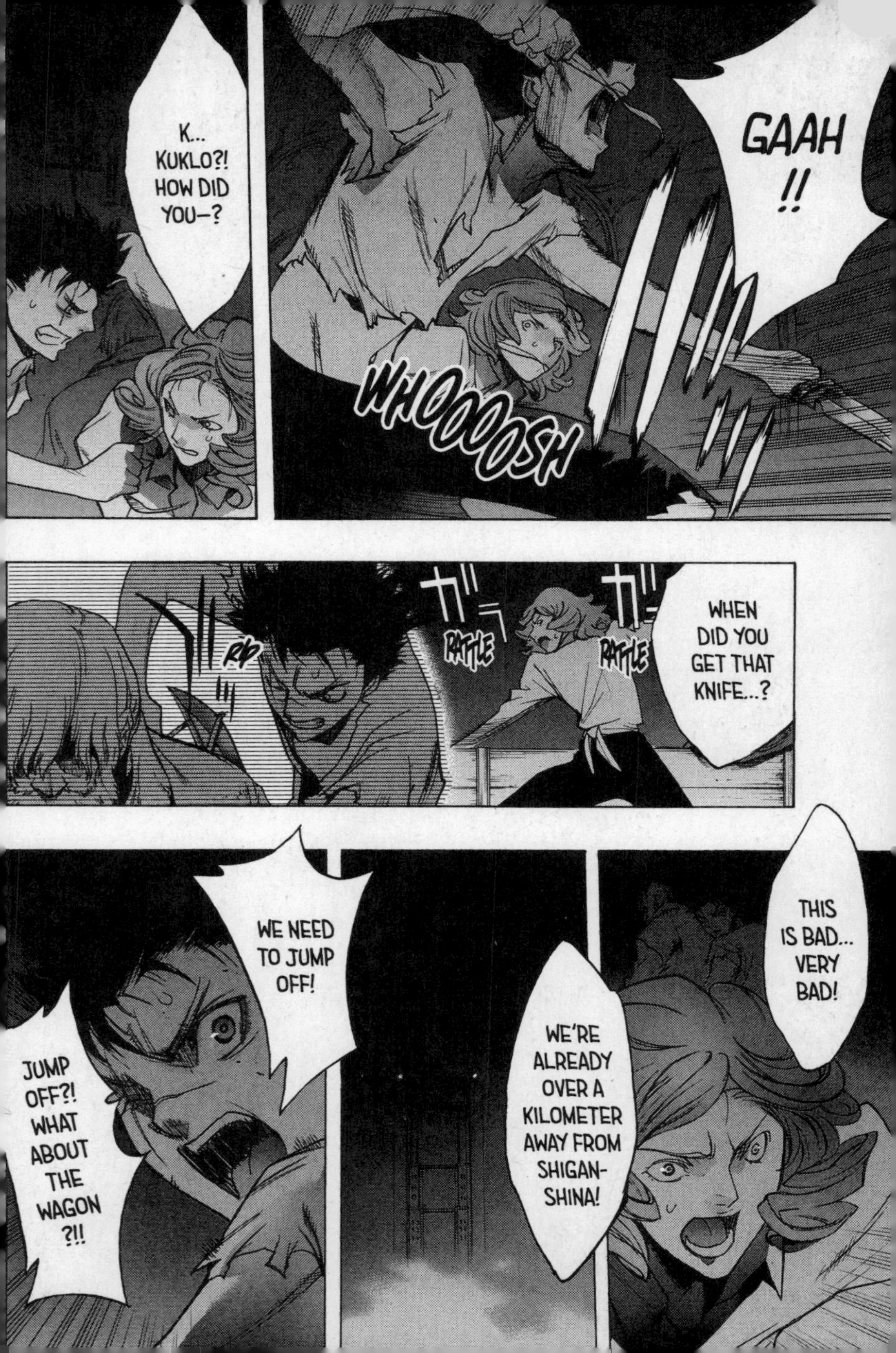
GAAH!!
WHOOOOOSH
K... KUKLO?! HOW DID YOU—?
WHEN DID YOU GET THAT KNIFE...?
RATTLE
RATTLE
RIP
THIS IS BAD... VERY BAD!
WE'RE ALREADY OVER A KILOMETER AWAY FROM SHIGAN-SHINA!
WE NEED TO JUMP OFF!
JUMP OFF?! WHAT ABOUT THE WAGON?!!

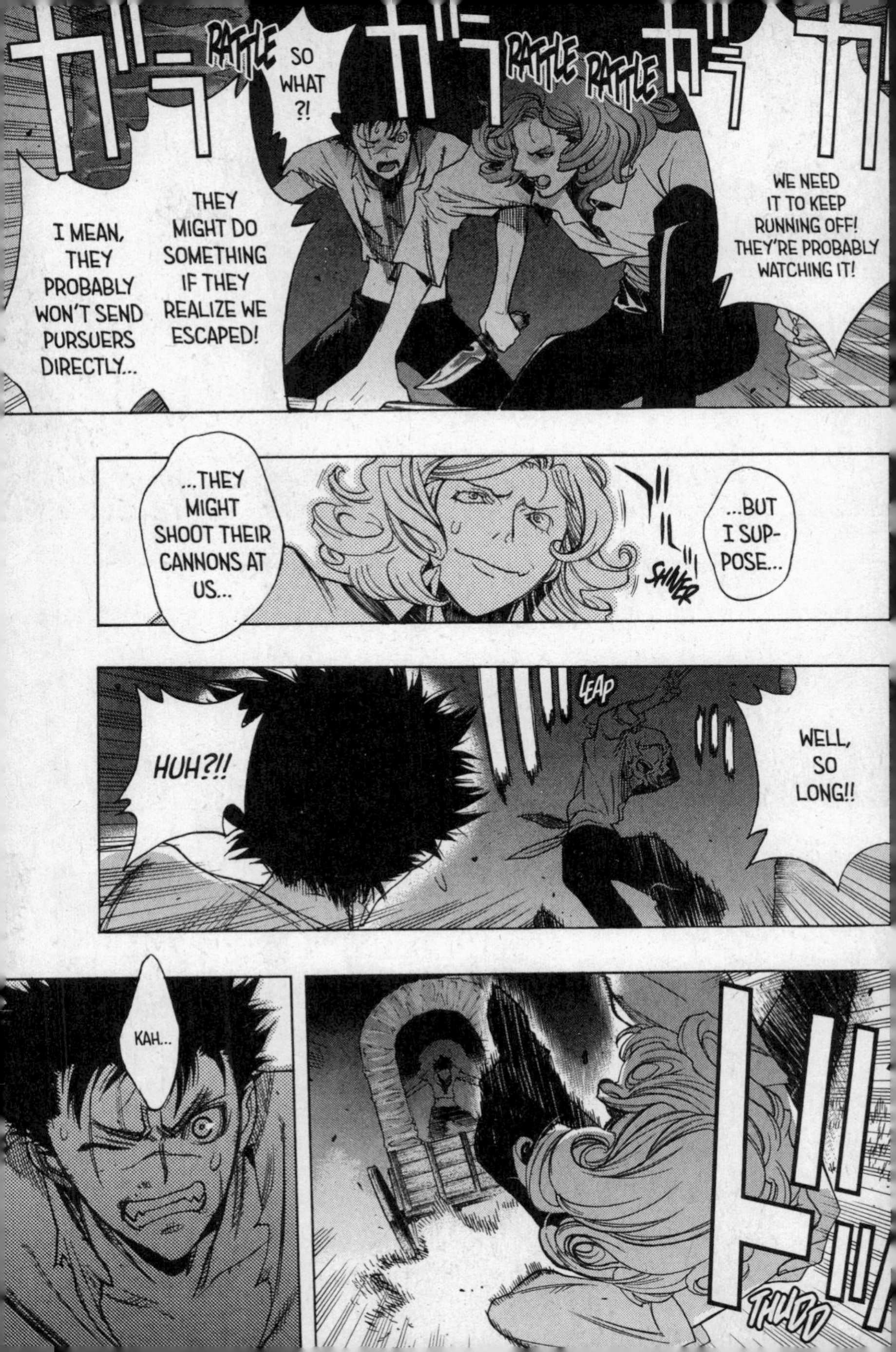
RATTLE
RATTLE
WE NEED IT TO KEEP RUNNING OFF! THEY'RE PROBABLY WATCHING IT!
RATTLE
SO WHAT?!
THEY MIGHT DO SOMETHING IF THEY REALIZE WE ESCAPED!
I MEAN, THEY PROBABLY WON'T SEND PURSUERS DIRECTLY...
...BUT I SUPPOSE...
SHIVER
...THEY MIGHT SHOOT THEIR CANNONS AT US...
WELL, SO LONG!!
LEAP
HUH?!!
THUDD
KAH...

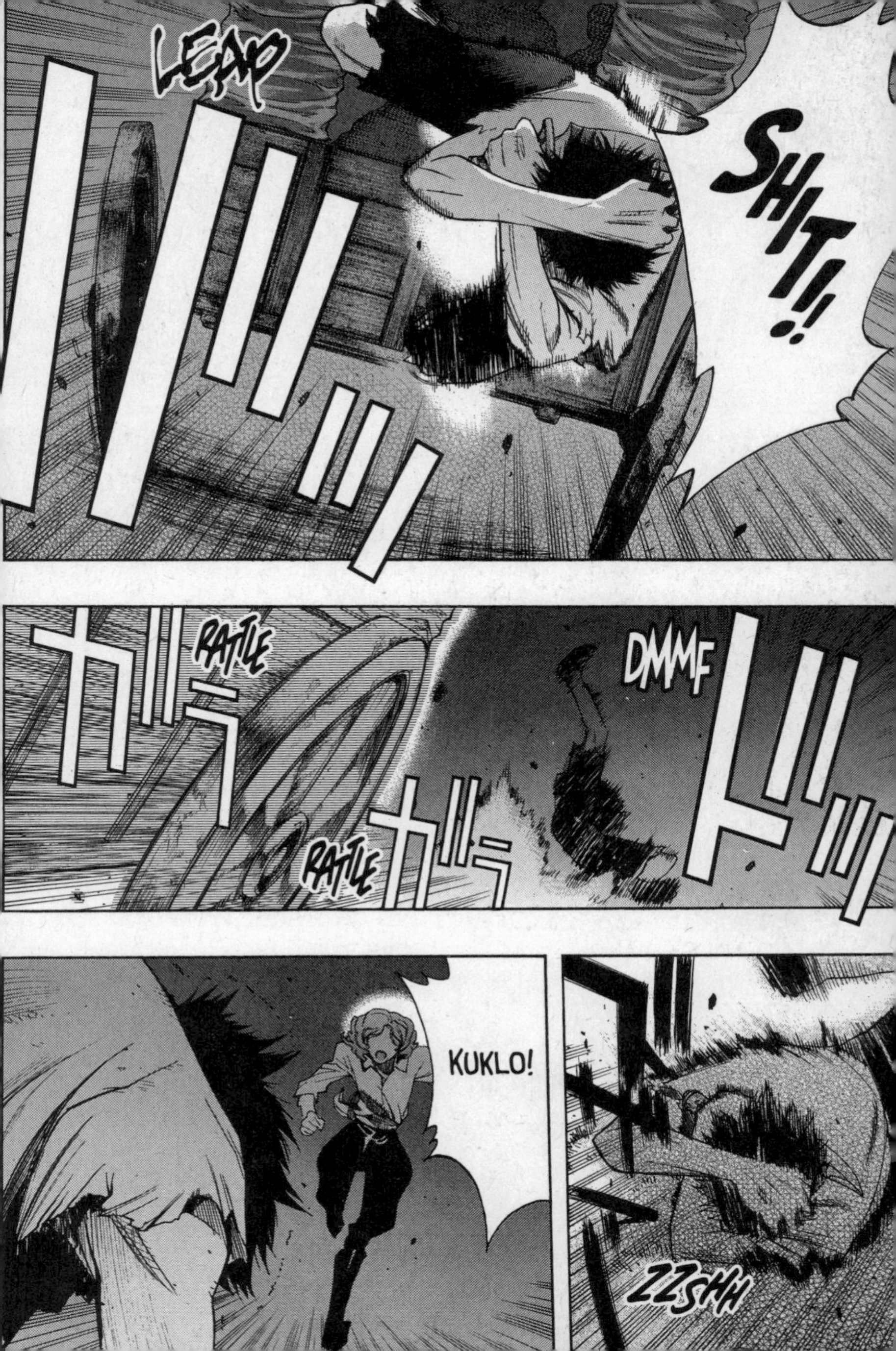
SHIT!!
LEAP
DMMF
ドッ
ガラ
RATTLE
ガラ
RATTLE
ZZSHH
KUKLO!

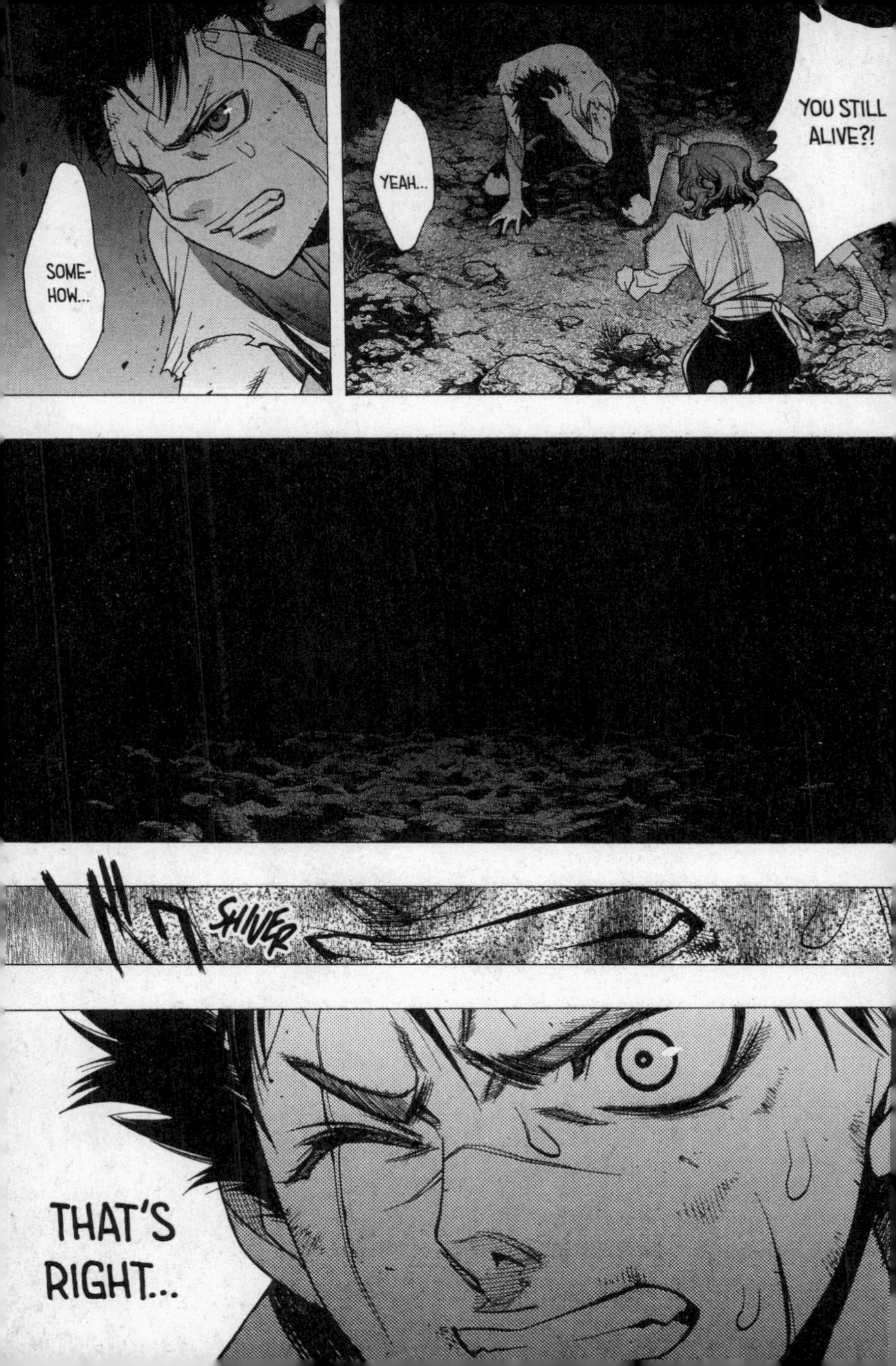
YOU STILL ALIVE?!
YEAH...
SOME-HOW...
SHIVER
THAT'S RIGHT...

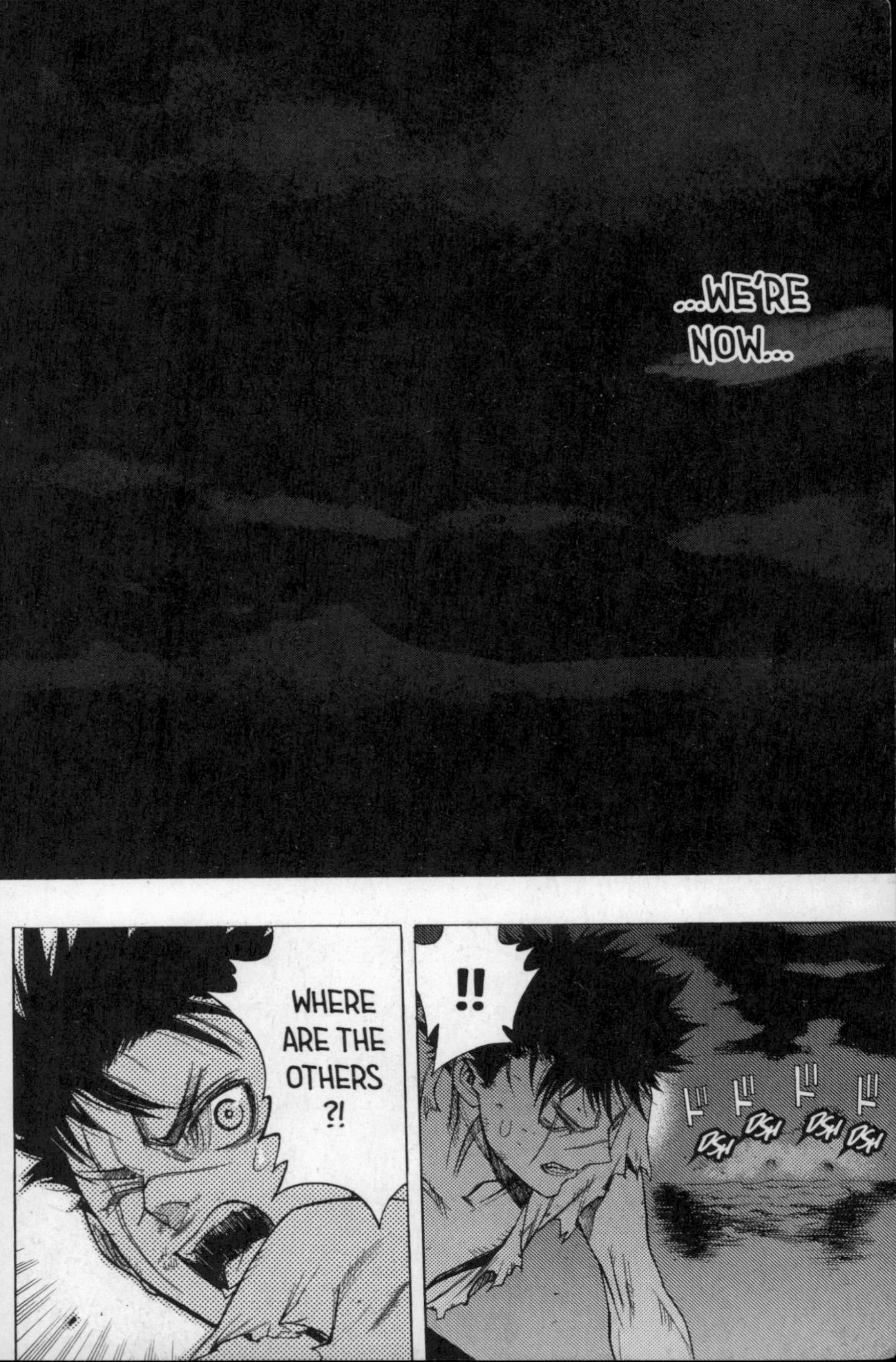
...WE'RE NOW...
!!
ドドドド
DSH DSH DSH DSH
WHERE ARE THE OTHERS ?!

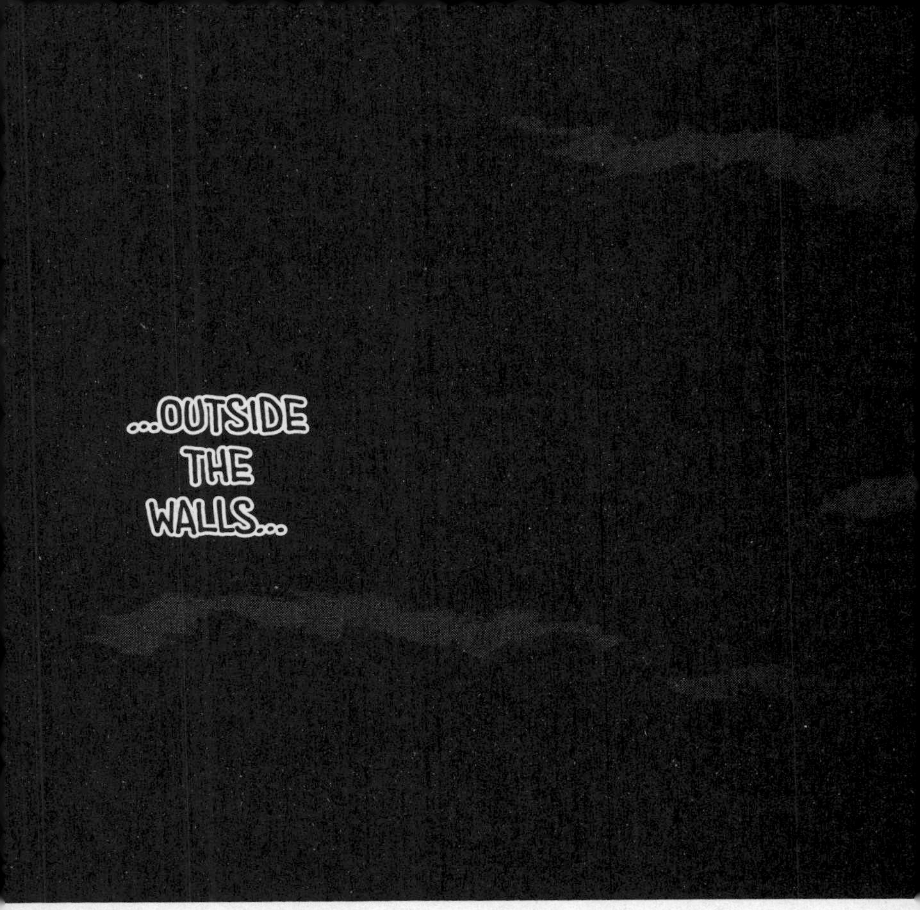
...OUTSIDE THE WALLS...
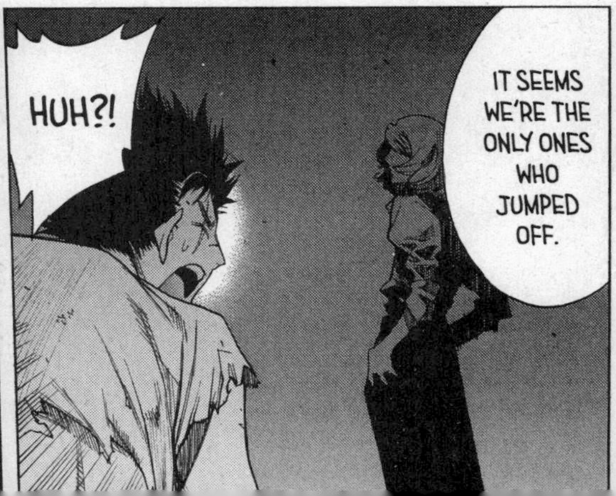
IT SEEMS WE'RE THE ONLY ONES WHO JUMPED OFF.
HUH?!
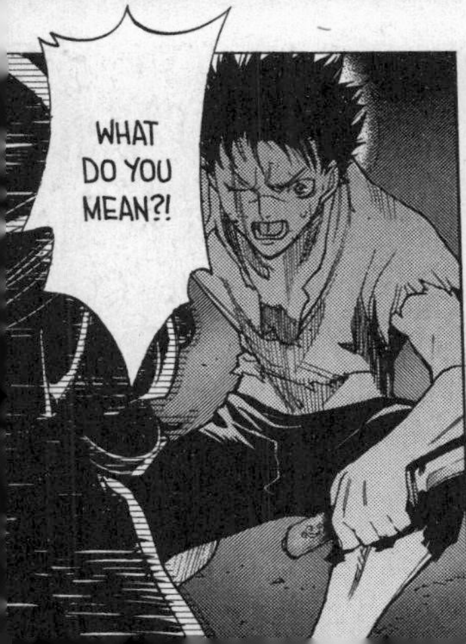
WHAT DO YOU MEAN?!

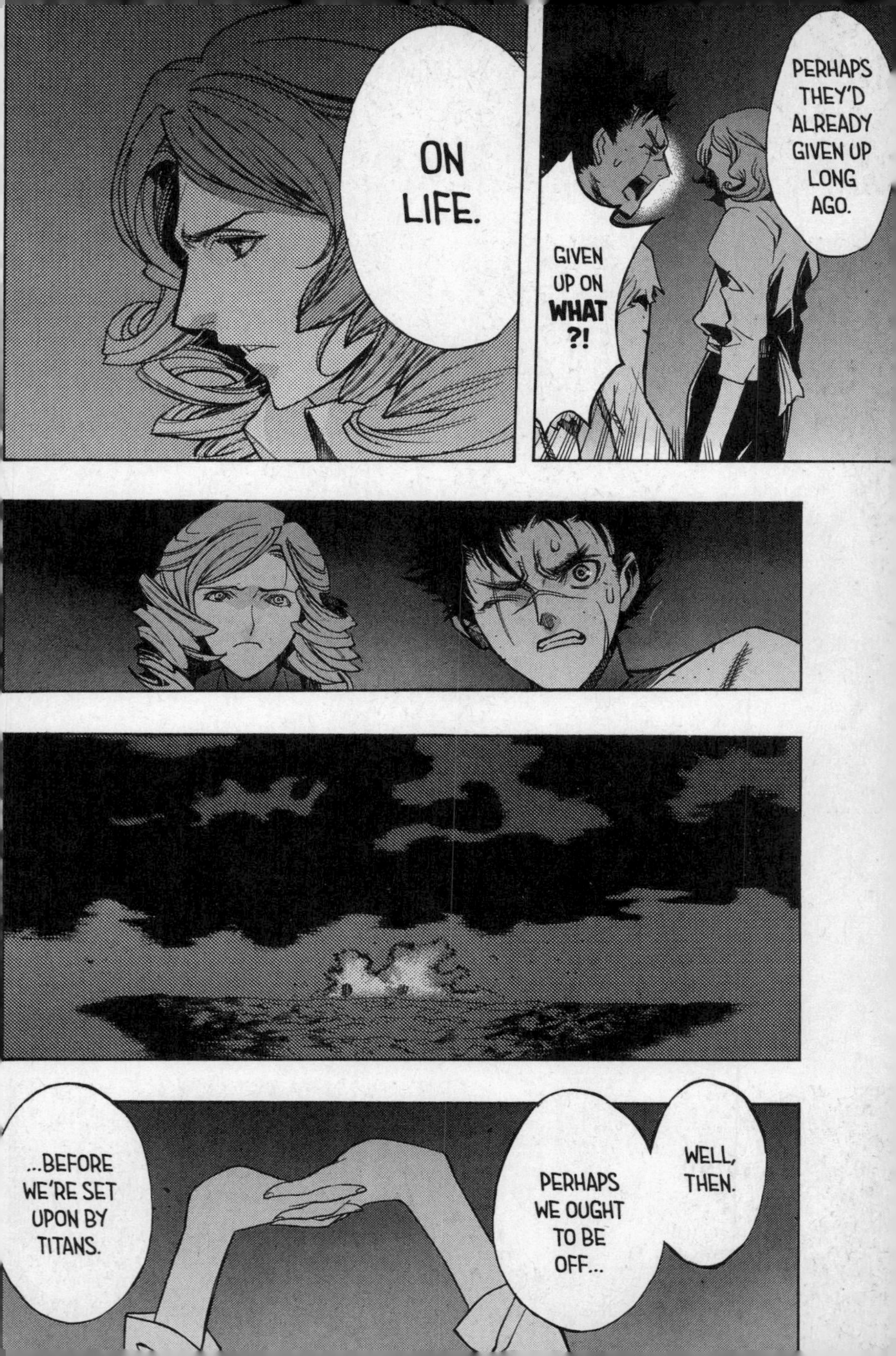
PERHAPS THEY'D ALREADY GIVEN UP LONG AGO.
GIVEN UP ON WHAT?!
ON LIFE.
WELL, THEN.
PERHAPS WE OUGHT TO BE OFF...
...BEFORE WE'RE SET UPON BY TITANS.

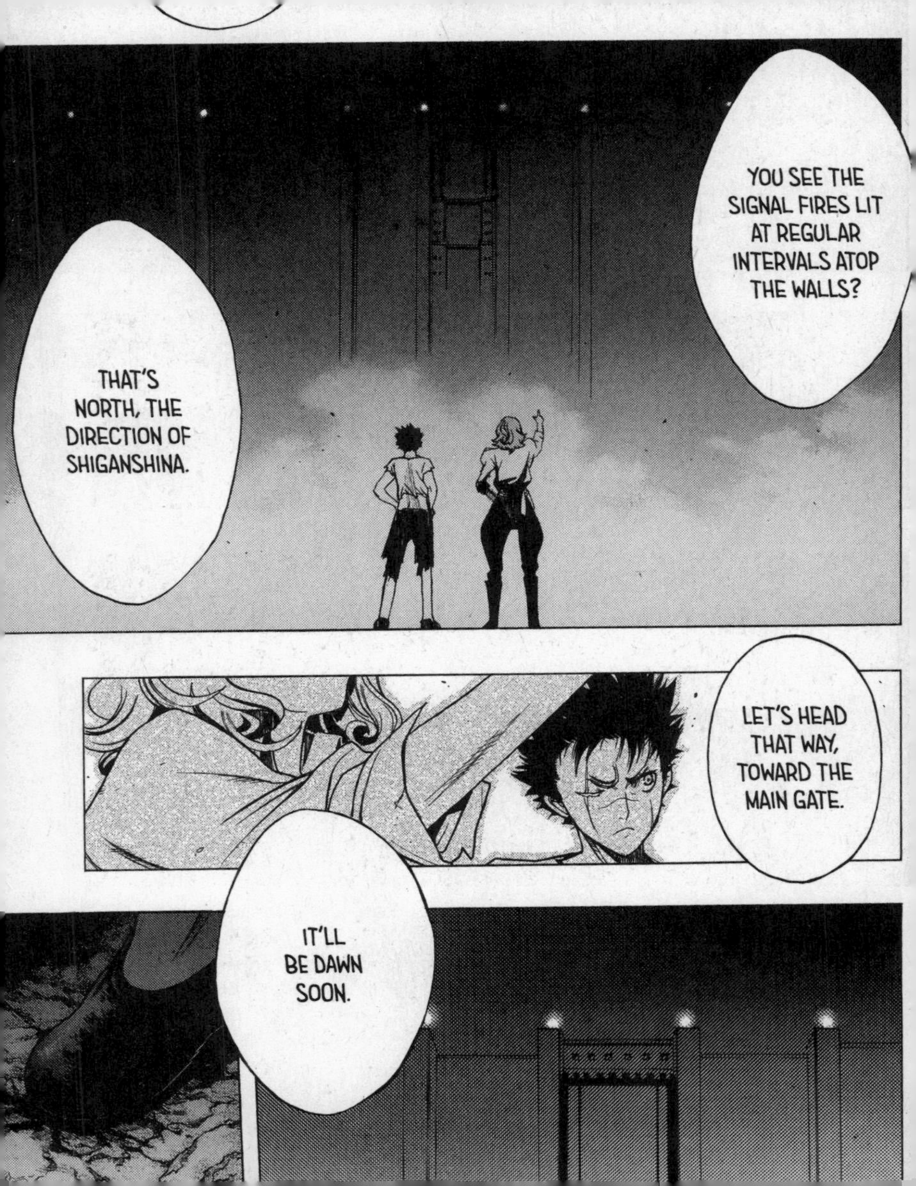
YOU SEE THE SIGNAL FIRES LIT AT REGULAR INTERVALS ATOP THE WALLS?
THAT'S NORTH, THE DIRECTION OF SHIGANSHINA.
LET'S HEAD THAT WAY, TOWARD THE MAIN GATE.
IT'LL BE DAWN SOON.

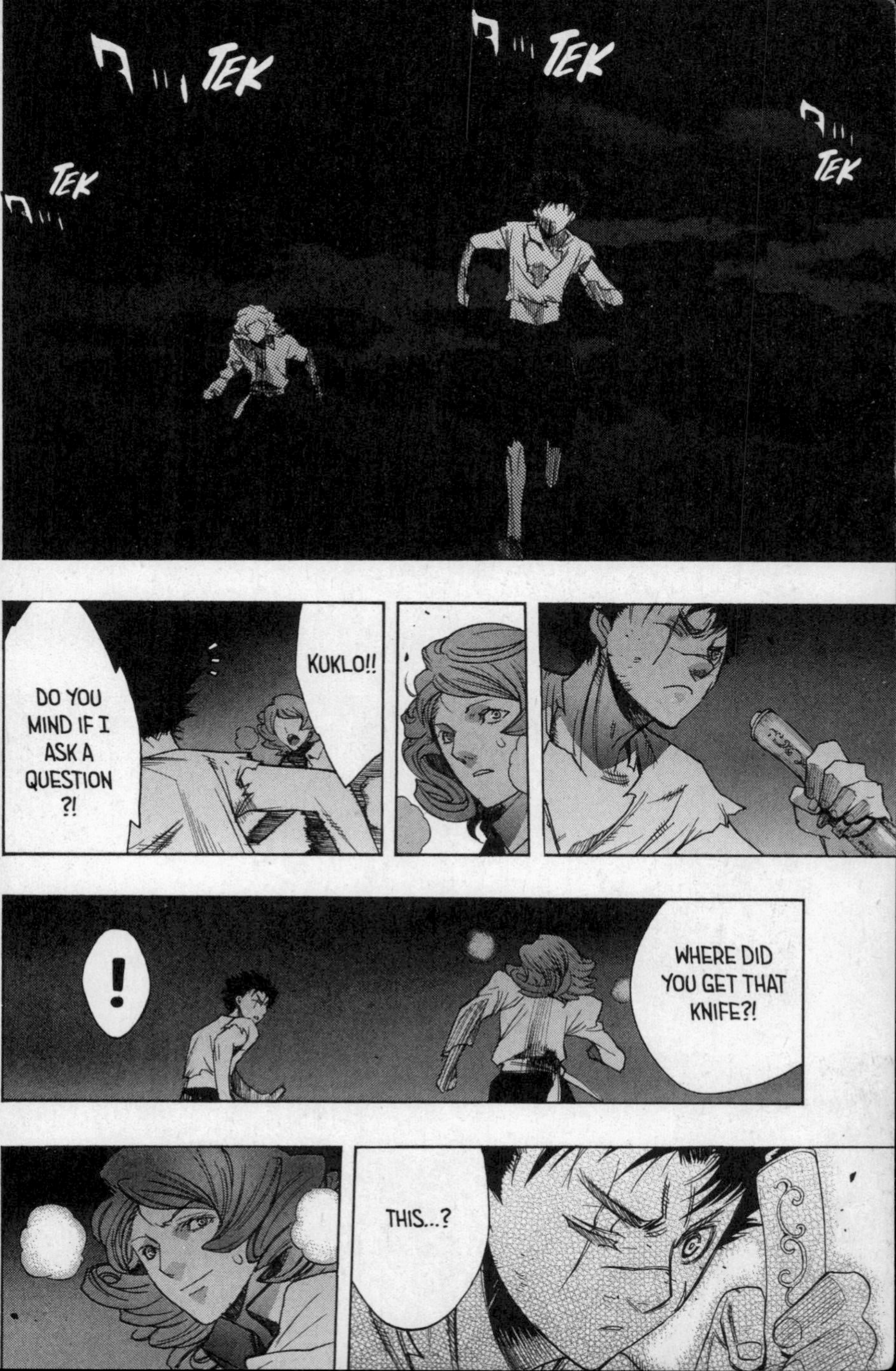
TEK
TEK
TEK
TEK
KUKLO!!
DO YOU MIND IF I ASK A QUESTION ?!
WHERE DID YOU GET THAT KNIFE?!
!
THIS...?

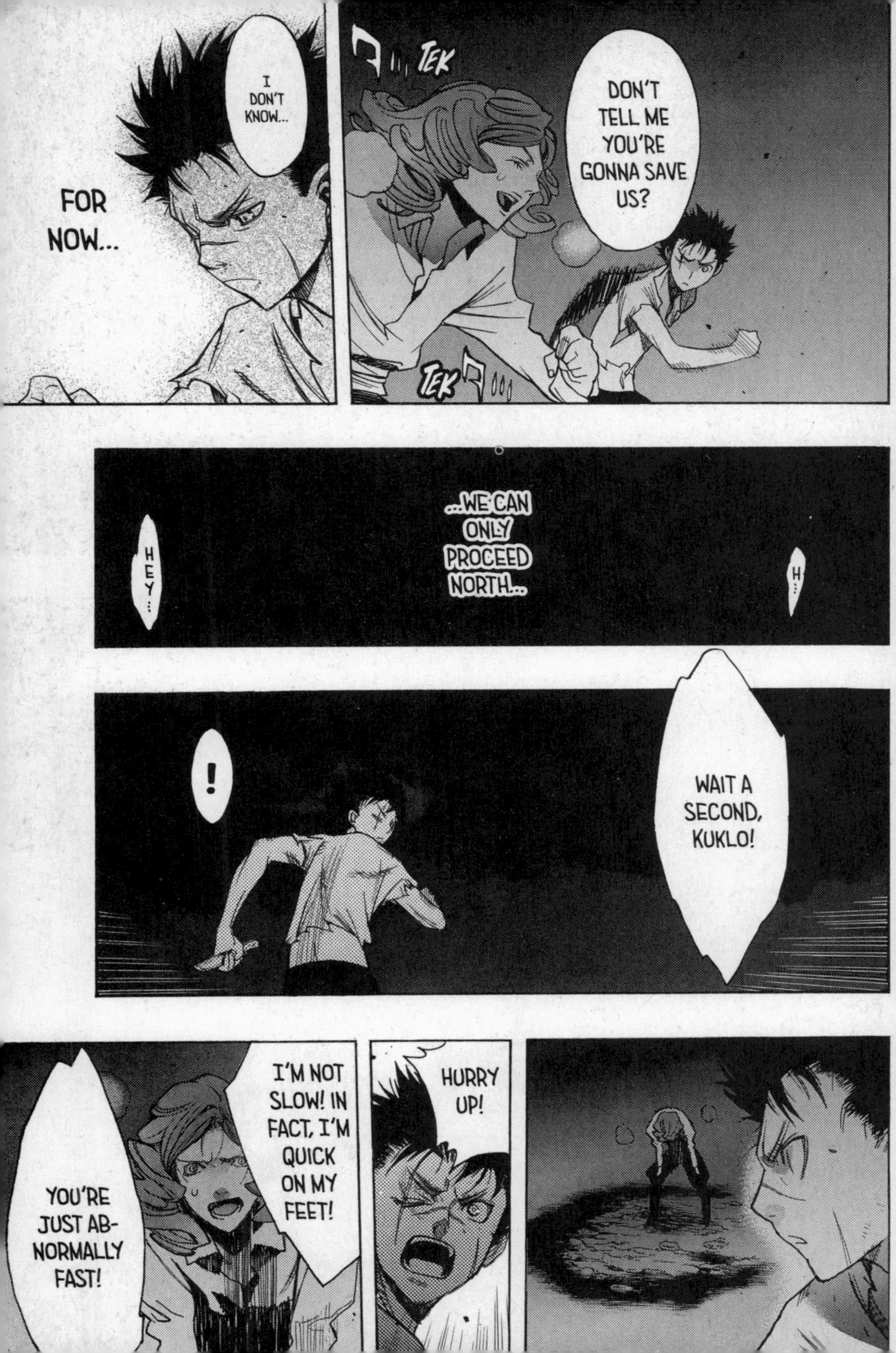
TEK
DON'T TELL ME YOU'RE GONNA SAVE US?
TEK
I DON'T KNOW...
FOR NOW...
...WE CAN ONLY PROCEED NORTH...
H...
HEY...
WAIT A SECOND, KUKLO!
!
HURRY UP!
I'M NOT SLOW! IN FACT, I'M QUICK ON MY FEET!
YOU'RE JUST AB-NORMALLY FAST!

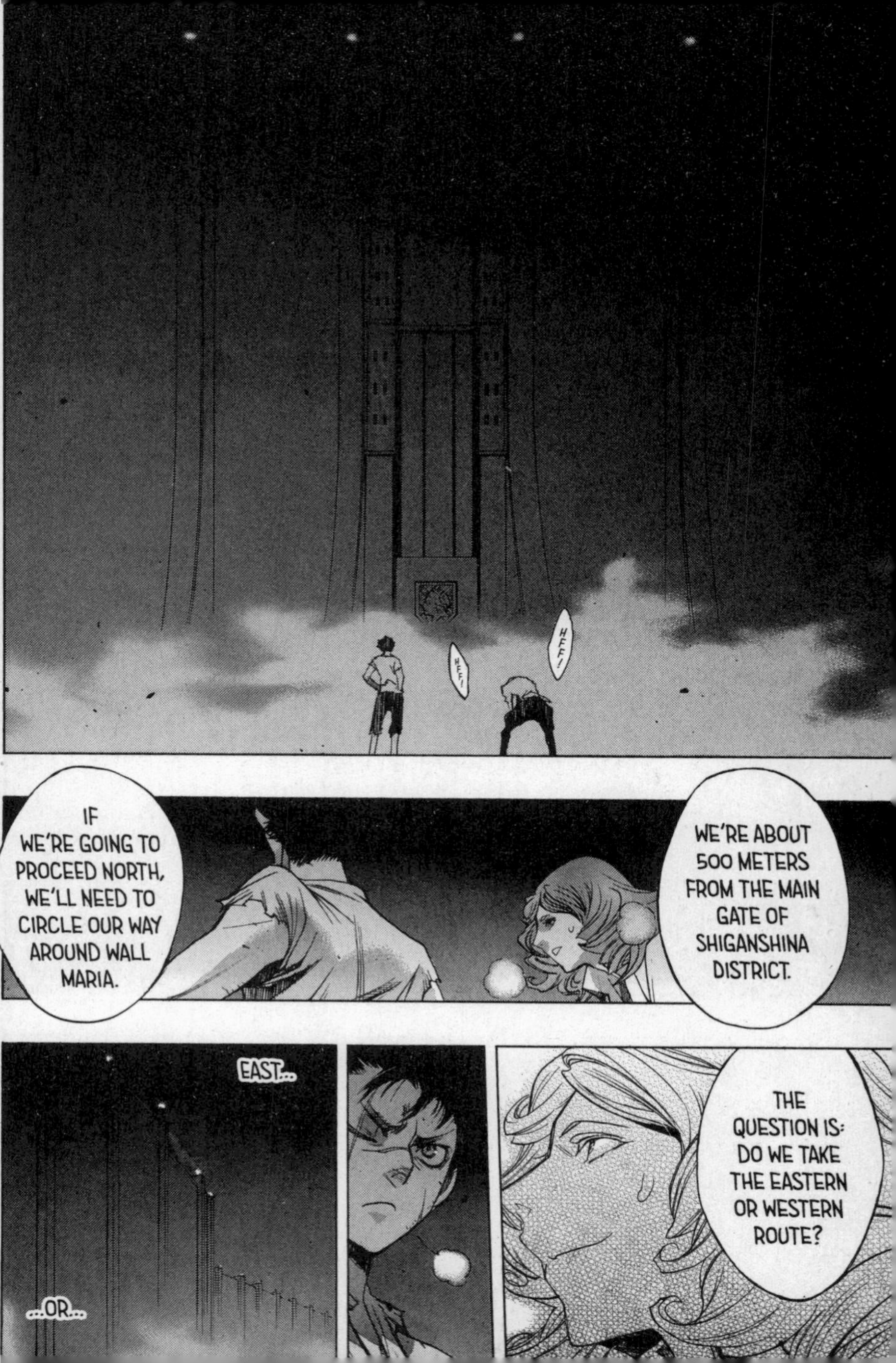
HFF!
HFF!
WE'RE ABOUT 500 METERS FROM THE MAIN GATE OF SHIGANSHINA DISTRICT.
IF WE'RE GOING TO PROCEED NORTH, WE'LL NEED TO CIRCLE OUR WAY AROUND WALL MARIA.
THE QUESTION IS: DO WE TAKE THE EASTERN OR WESTERN ROUTE?
EAST...
...OR...

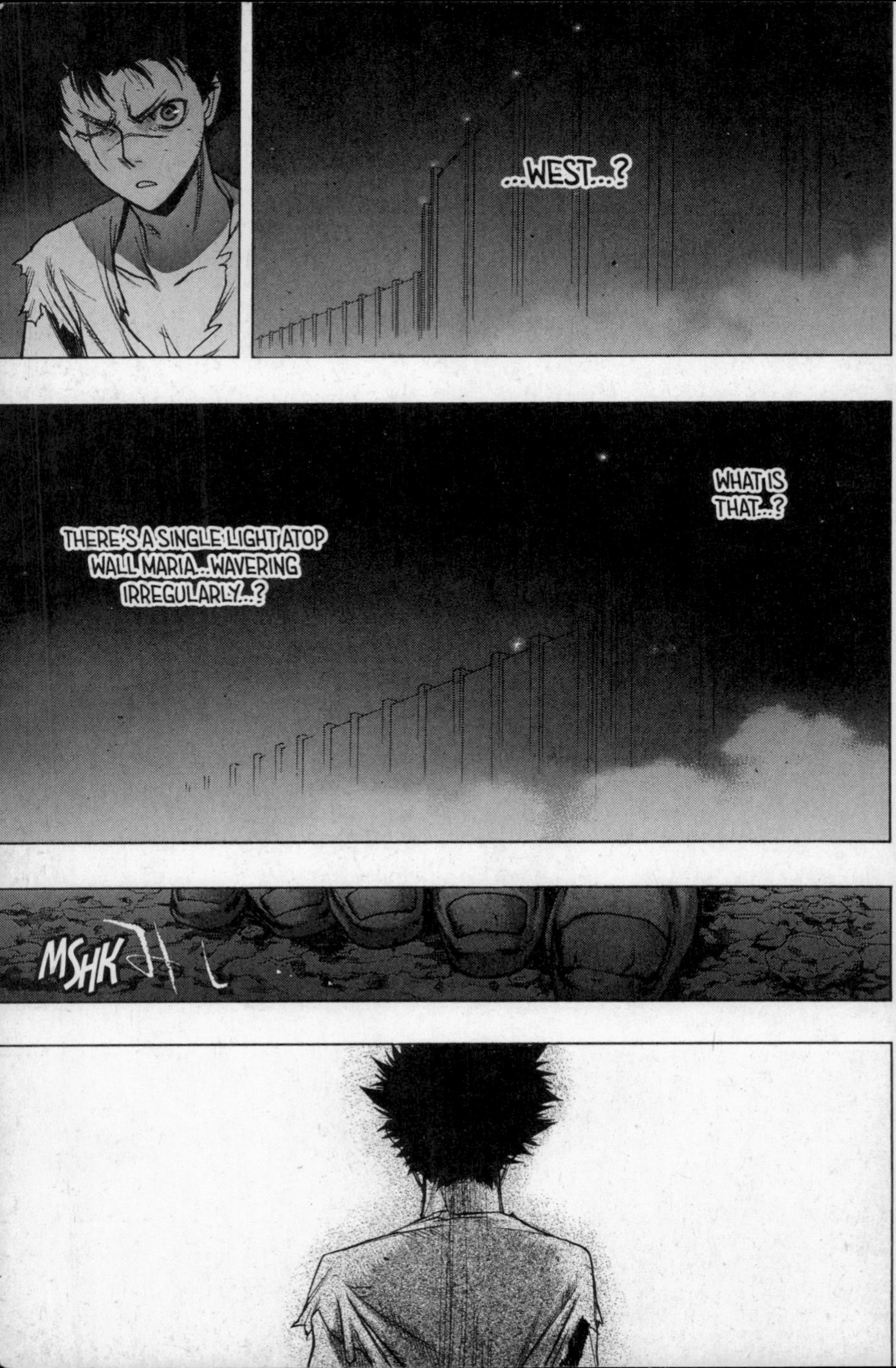
...WEST...?
WHAT IS THAT...?
THERE'S A SINGLE LIGHT ATOP WALL MARIA...WAVERING IRREGULARLY...?
MSHK

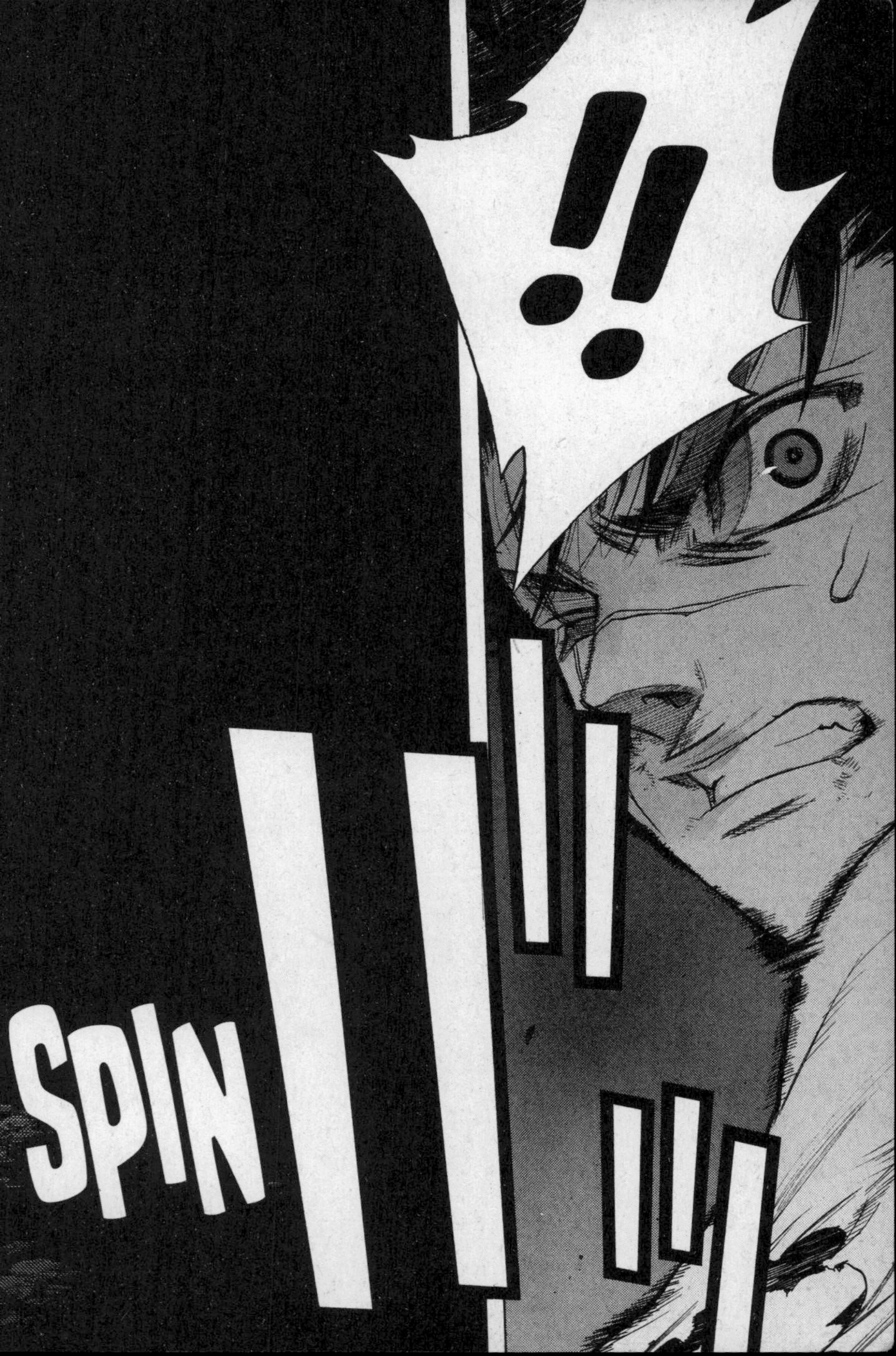
!!
SPIN

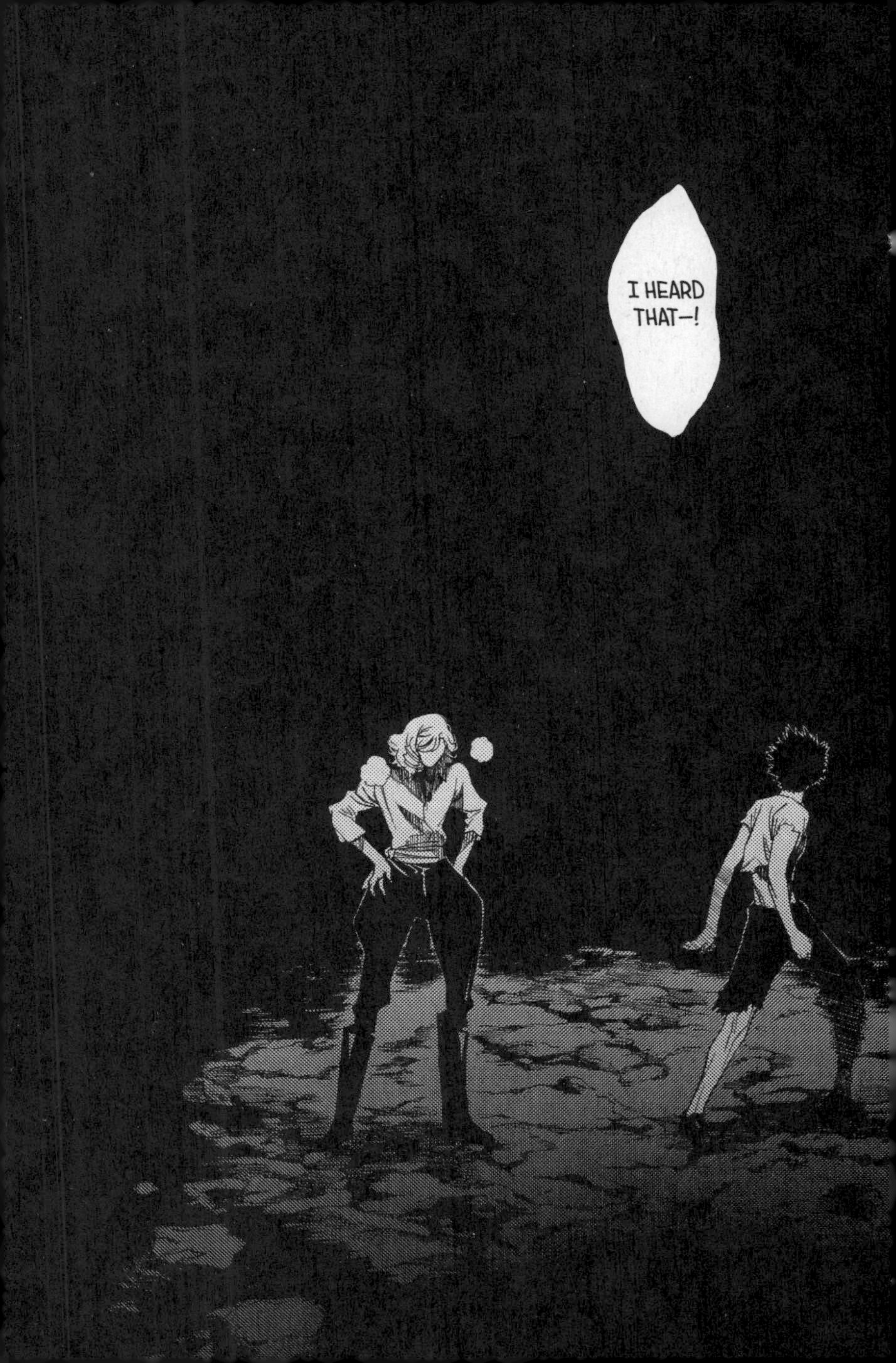
I HEARD THAT—!

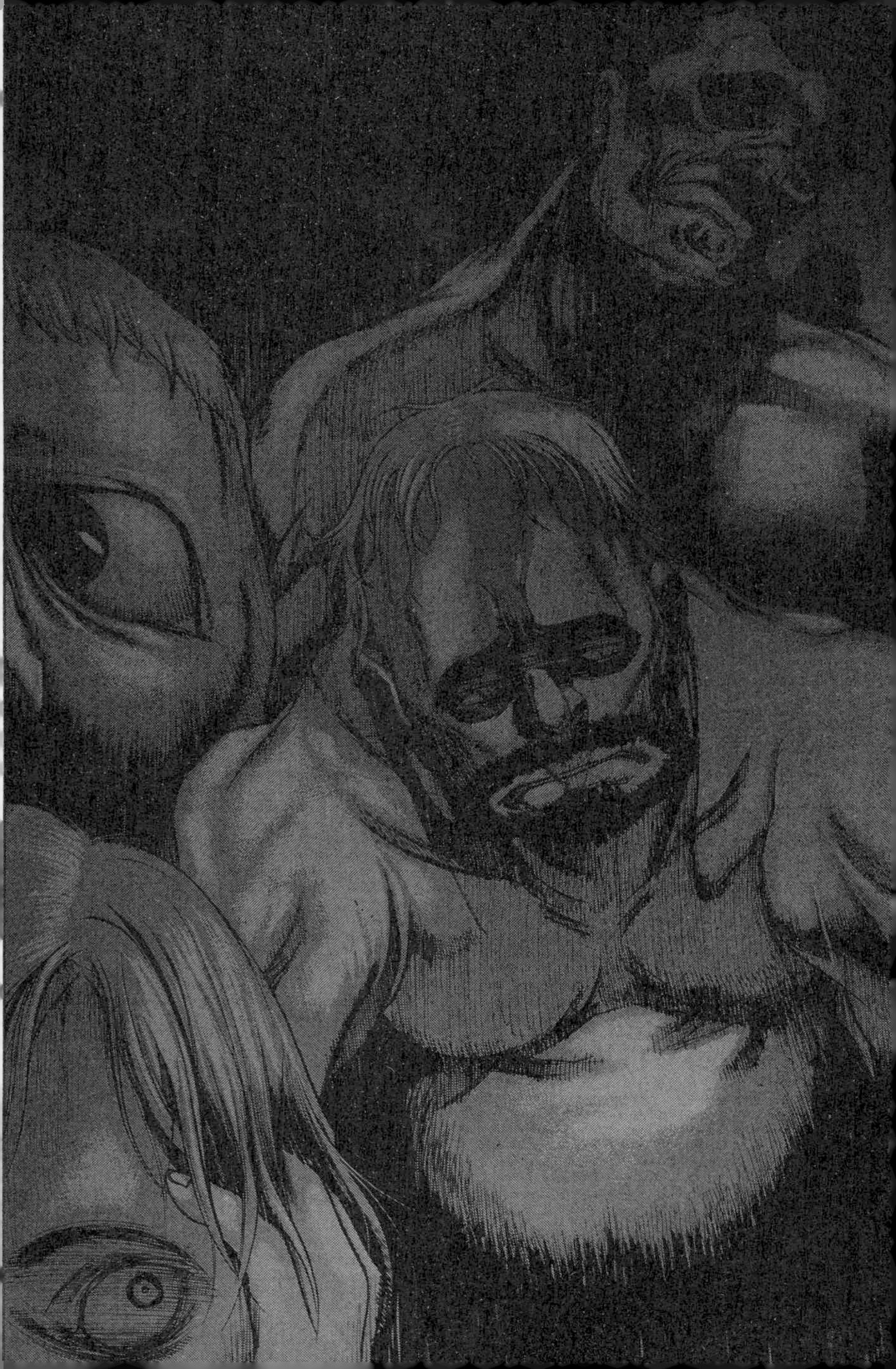

Chapter 11: Serendipity Behind Bars END

ATTACK
on TITAN
BEFORE THE FALL

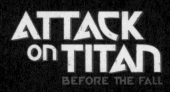

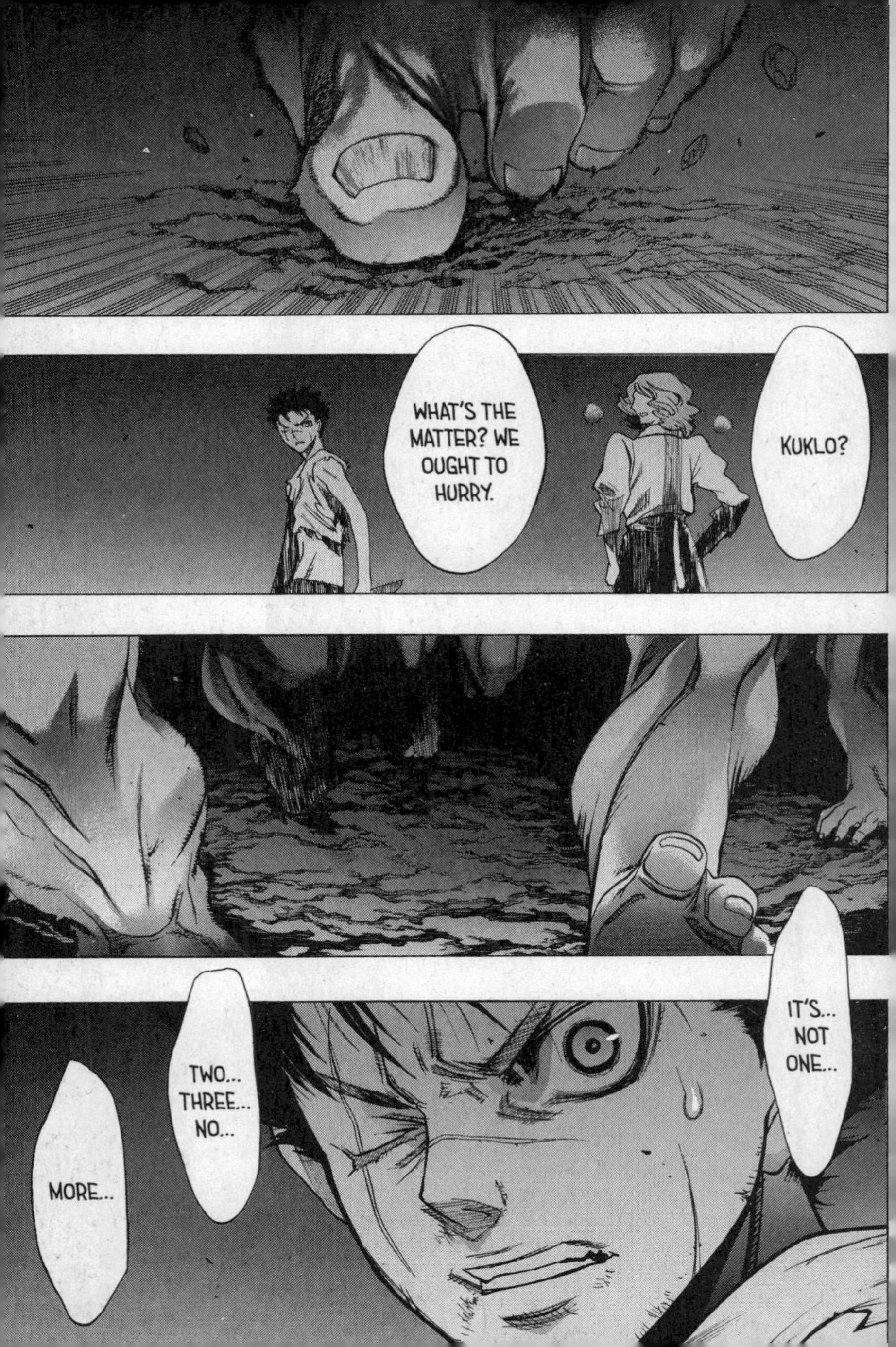
KUKLO?
WHAT'S THE MATTER? WE OUGHT TO HURRY.
IT'S... NOT ONE...
TWO... THREE... NO...
MORE...

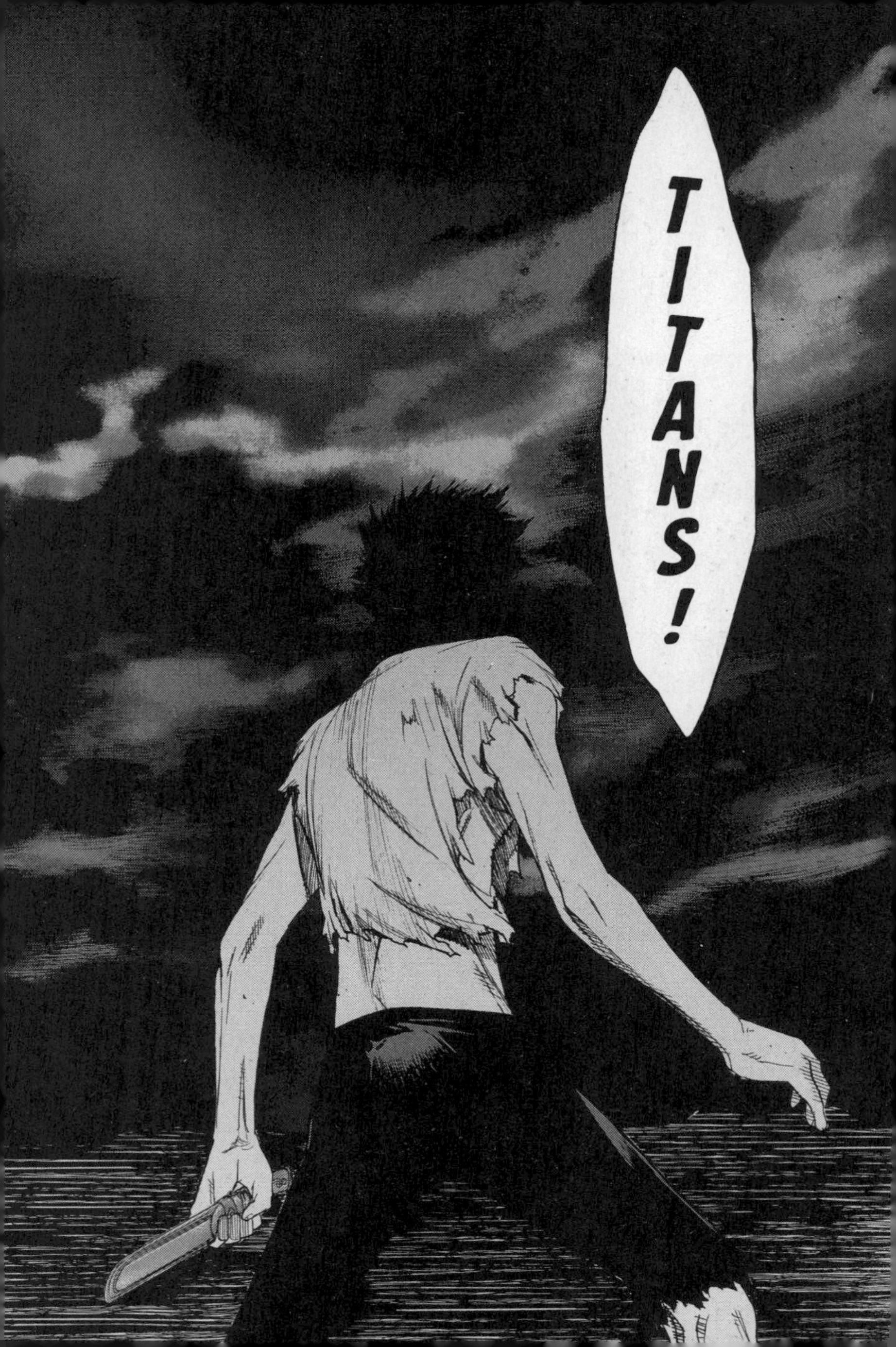
TITANS!

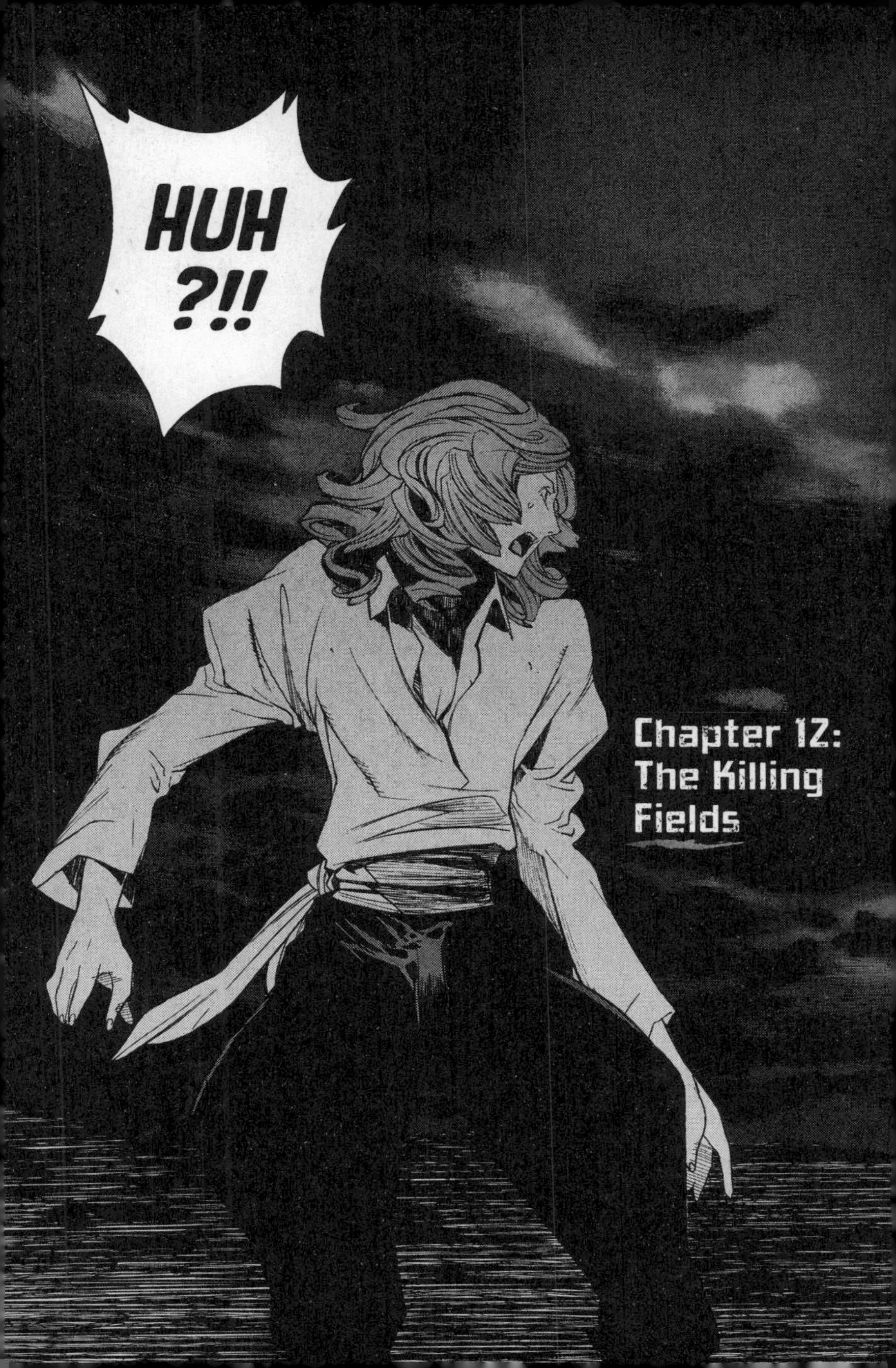

Chapter 12: The Killing Fields

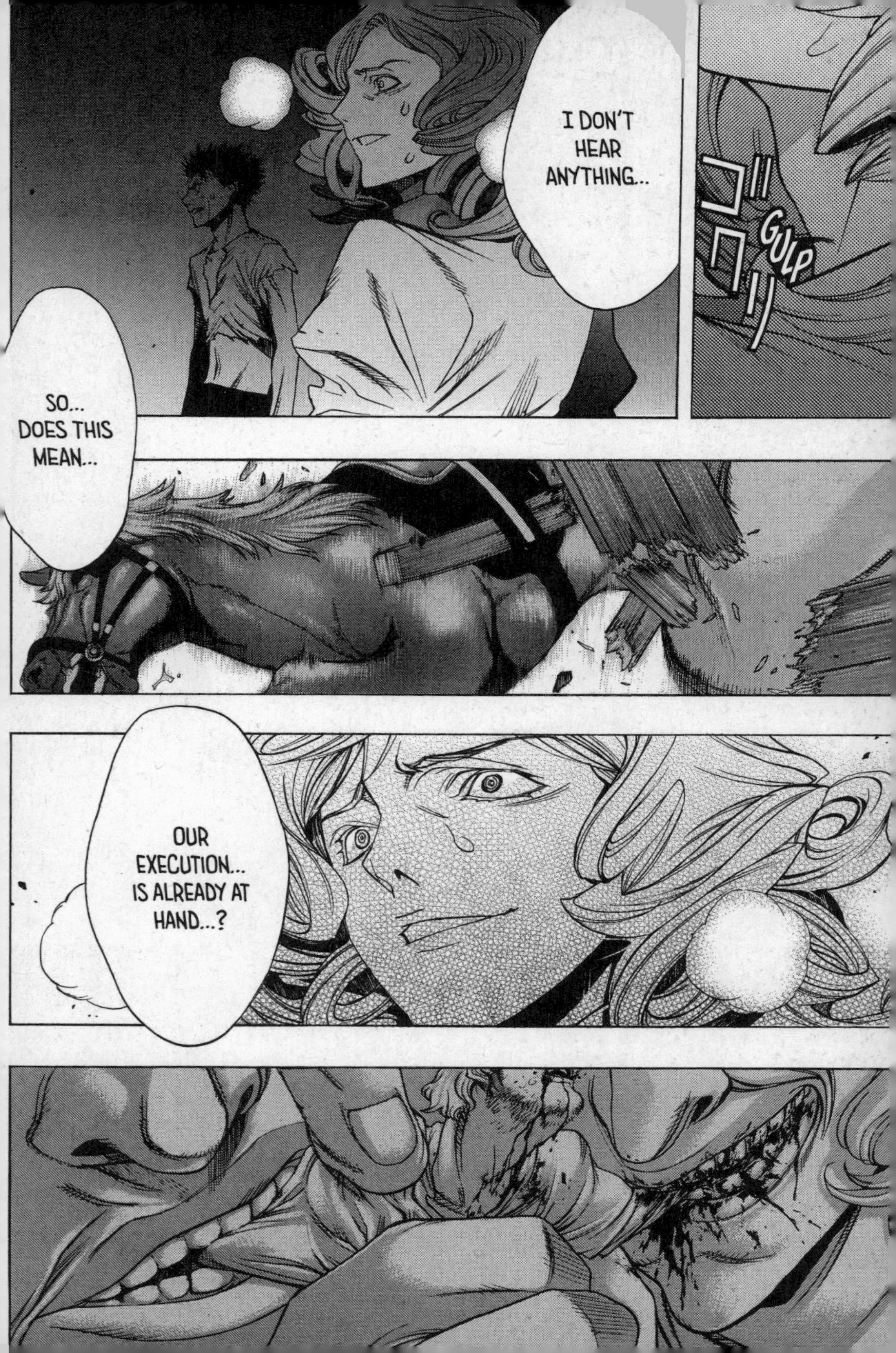
GULP
I DON'T HEAR ANYTHING...
SO... DOES THIS MEAN...
OUR EXECUTION... IS ALREADY AT HAND...?

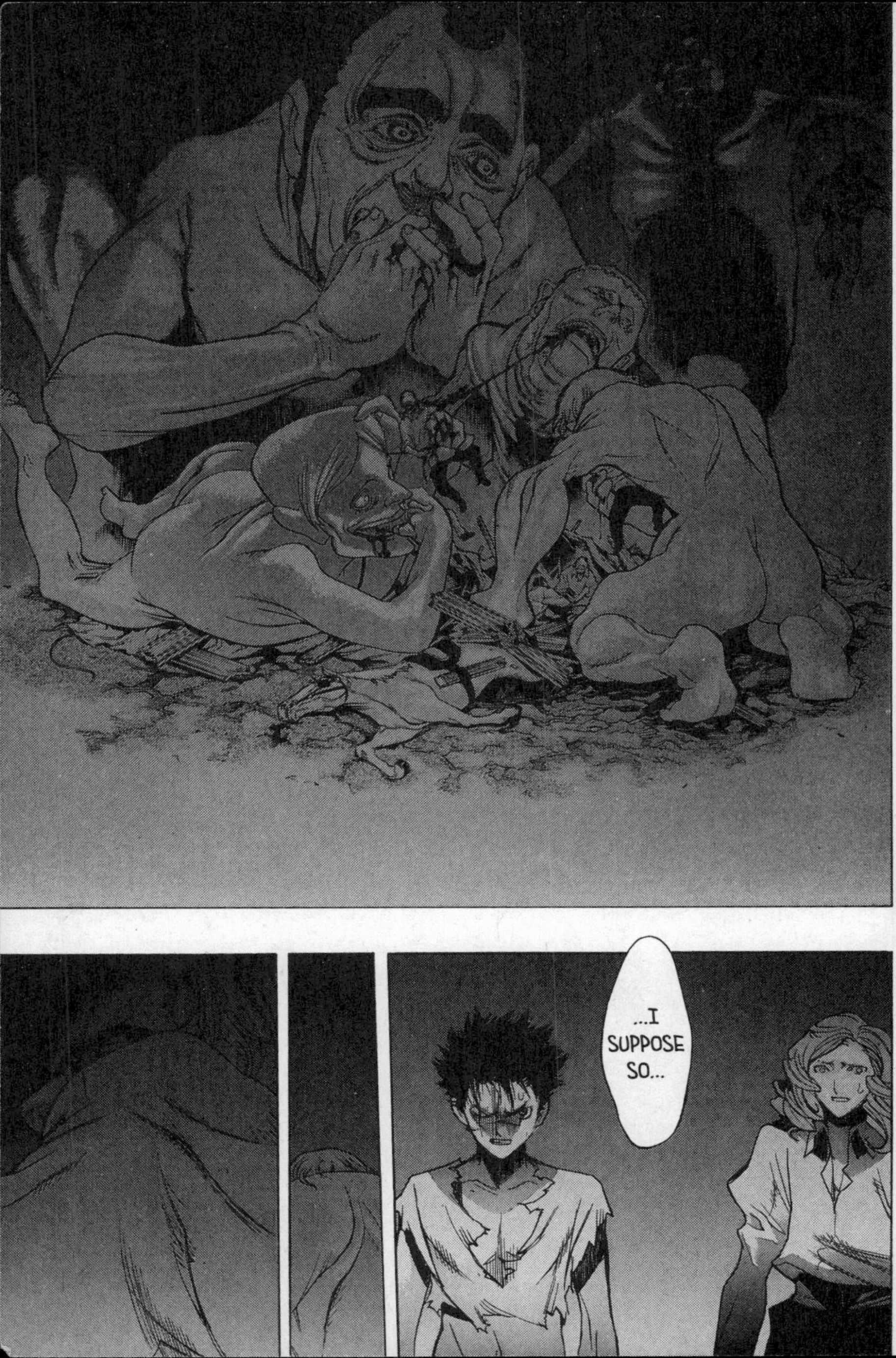
...I SUPPOSE SO...

....!

HERE THEY COME!

WHUD

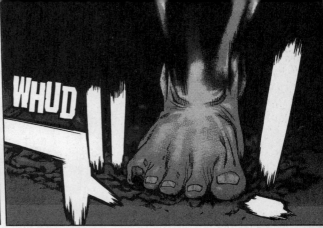

THEY'RE APPROACHING NOW!!

CARDINA!

!

WE'VE GOT TO GO!

Y-YOU'RE KIDDING, RIGHT?!

THIS WAY!! **WEST!!**

NOT THAT WAY!

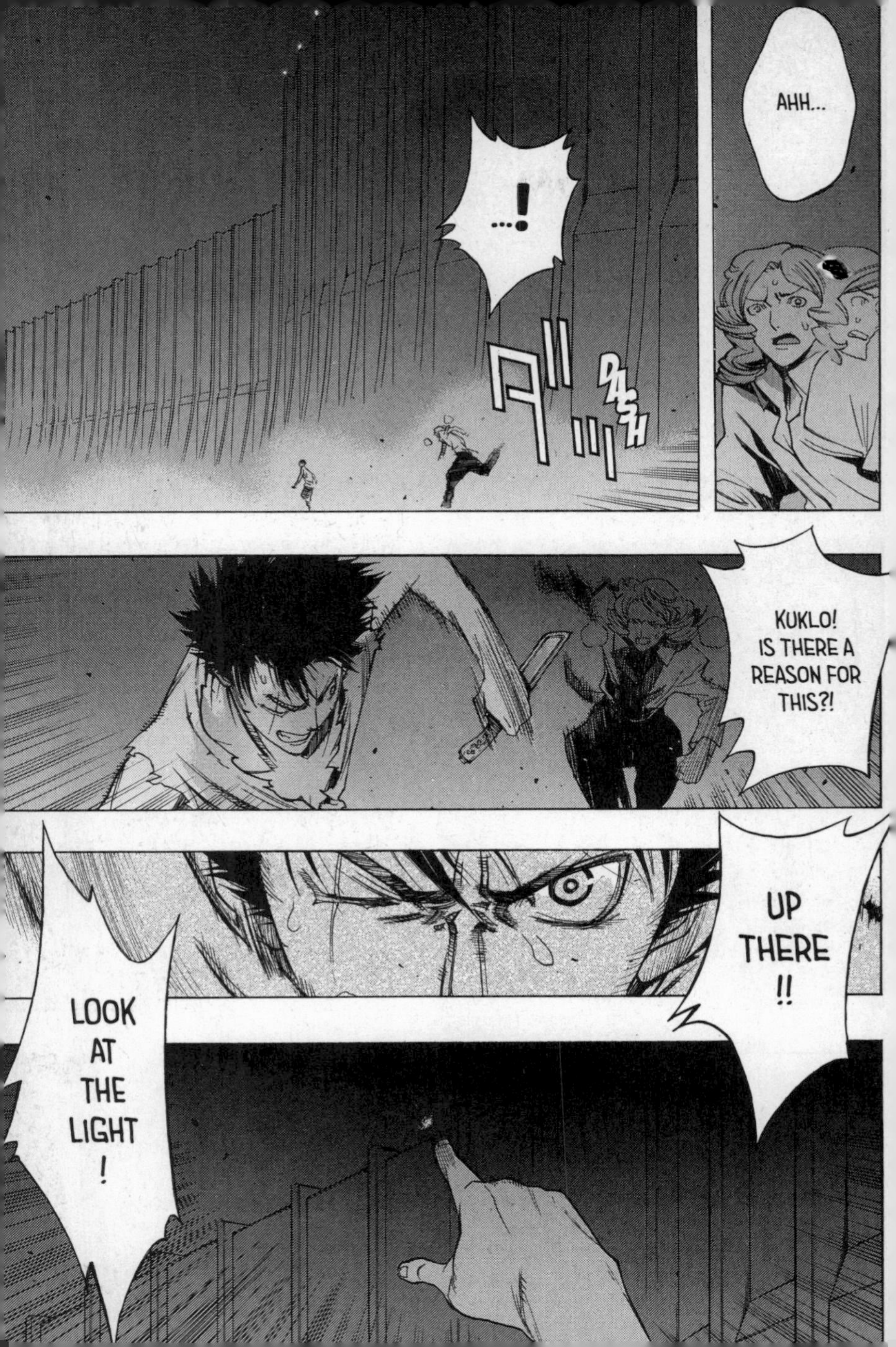
AHH...
...!
DASH
KUKLO! IS THERE A REASON FOR THIS?!
UP THERE !!
LOOK AT THE LIGHT !

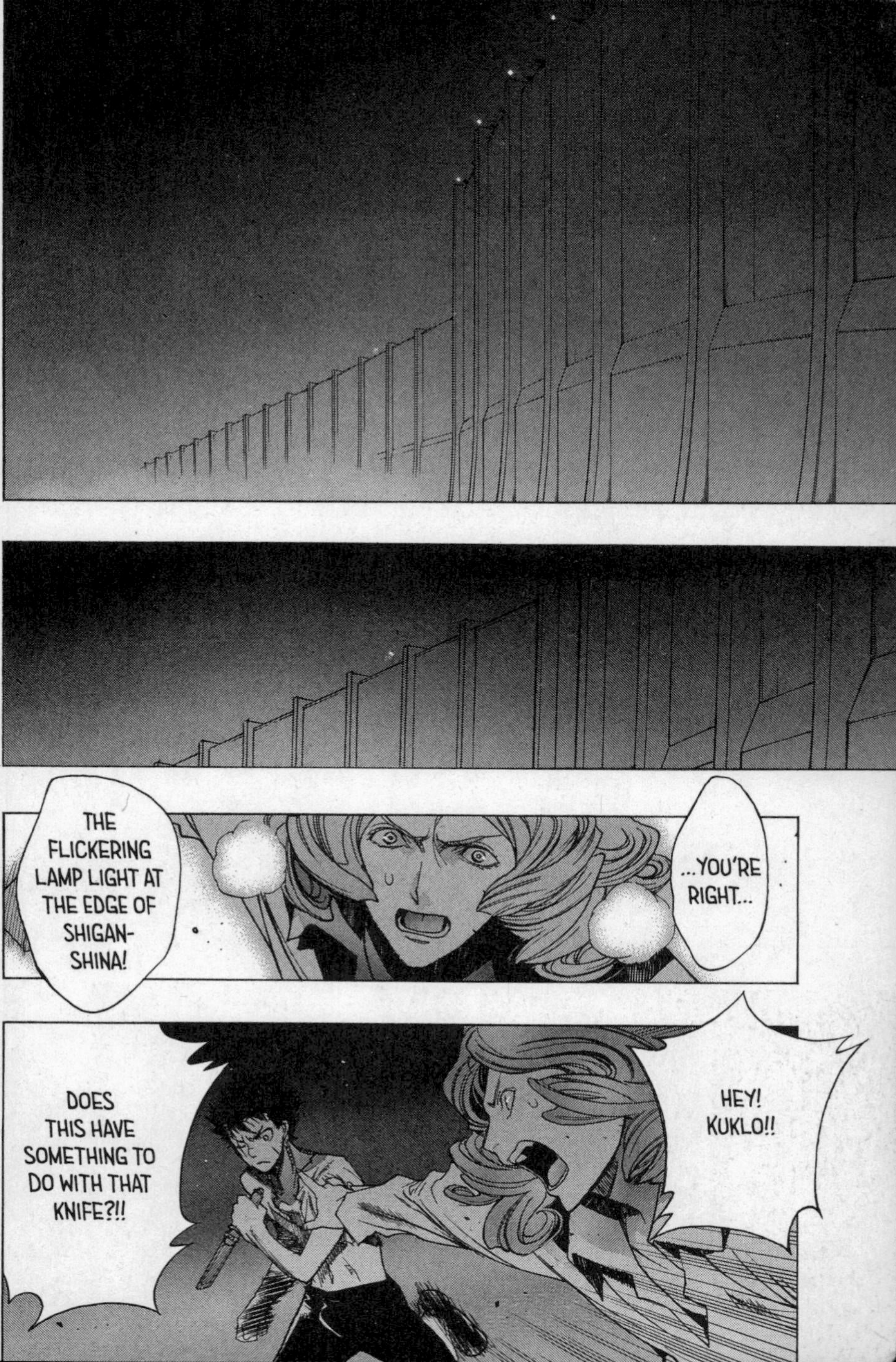
...YOU'RE RIGHT...
THE FLICKERING LAMP LIGHT AT THE EDGE OF SHIGAN-SHINA!
HEY! KUKLO!!
DOES THIS HAVE SOMETHING TO DO WITH THAT KNIFE?!!

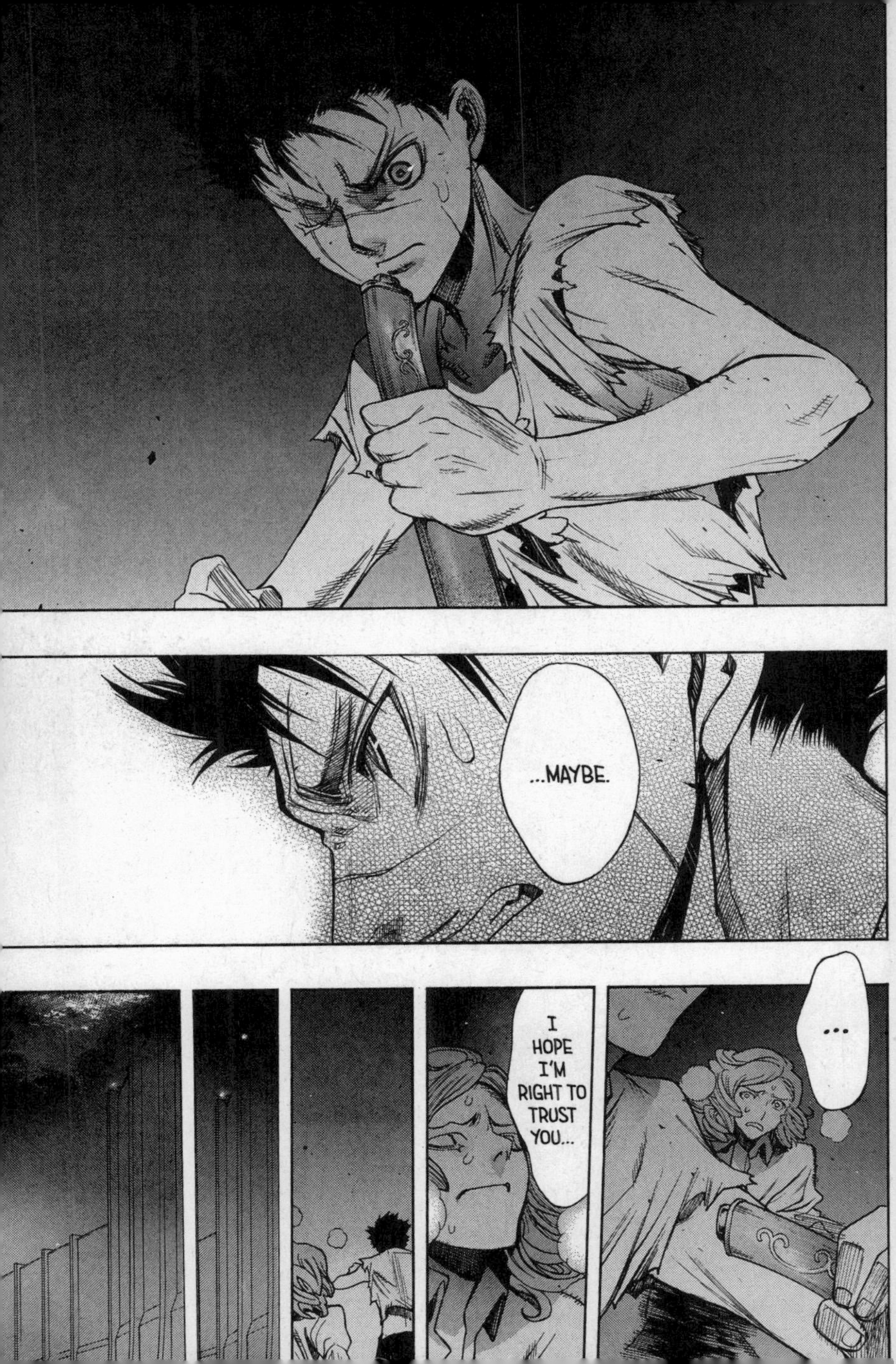
...MAYBE.
...
I HOPE I'M RIGHT TO TRUST YOU...

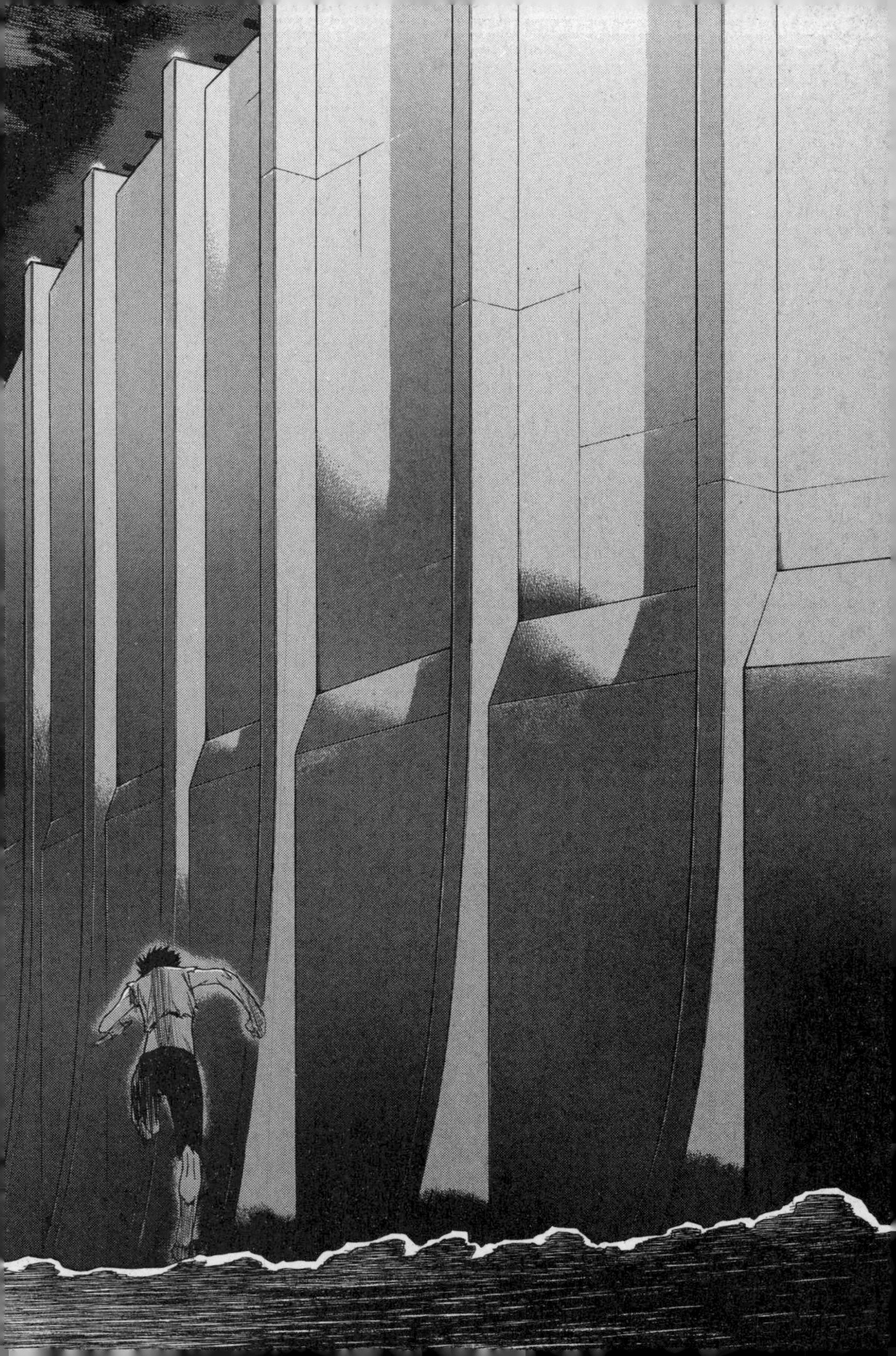

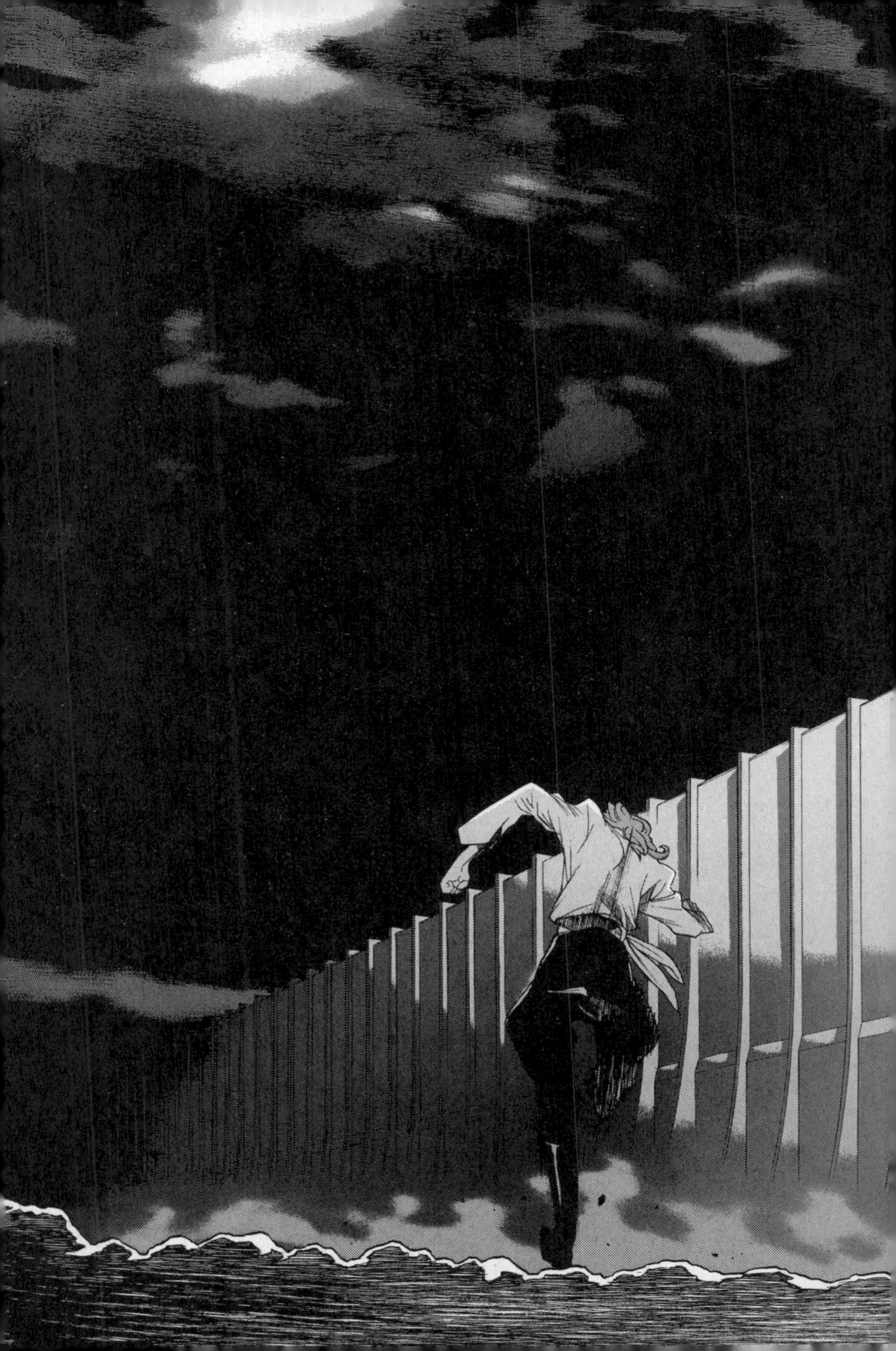

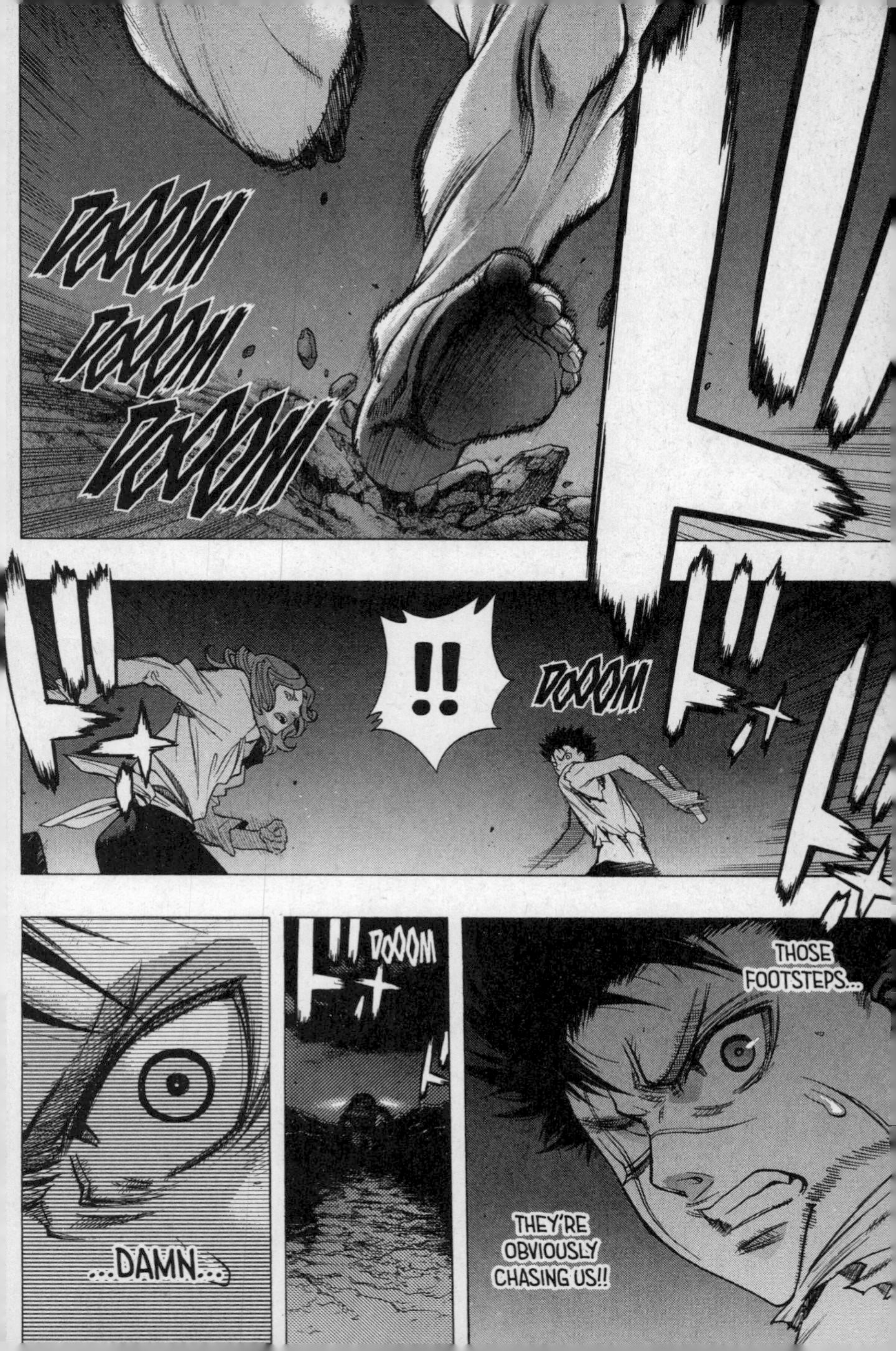
DOOOM
DOOOM
DOOOM
DOOOM
!!
THOSE FOOTSTEPS...
THEY'RE OBVIOUSLY CHASING US!!
DOOOM
...DAMN...

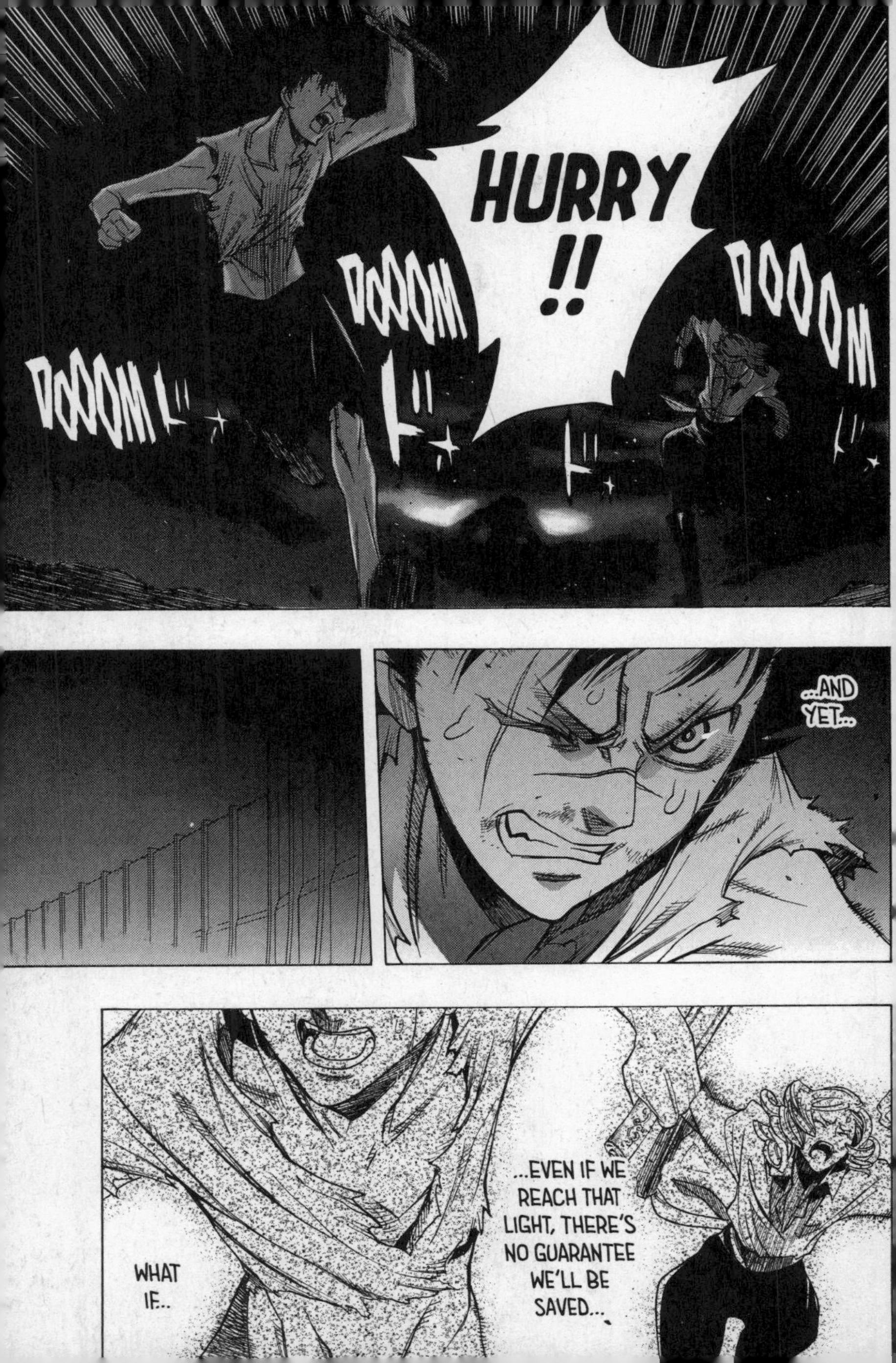

HURRY!!
DOOOM!!
DOOOM!!
DOOOM!!
...AND YET...
...EVEN IF WE REACH THAT LIGHT, THERE'S NO GUARANTEE WE'LL BE SAVED...
WHAT IF...

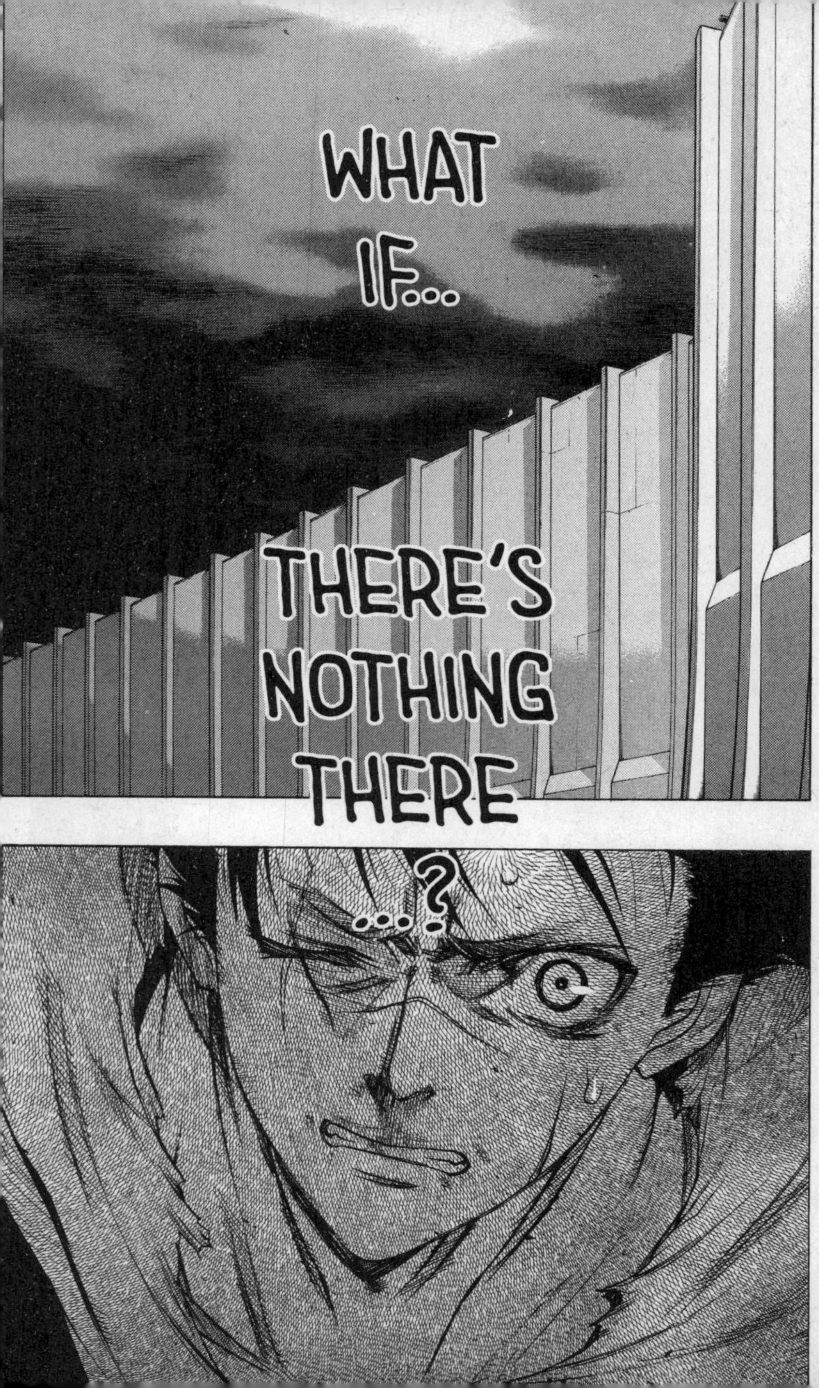
WHAT IF...
THERE'S NOTHING THERE
...?

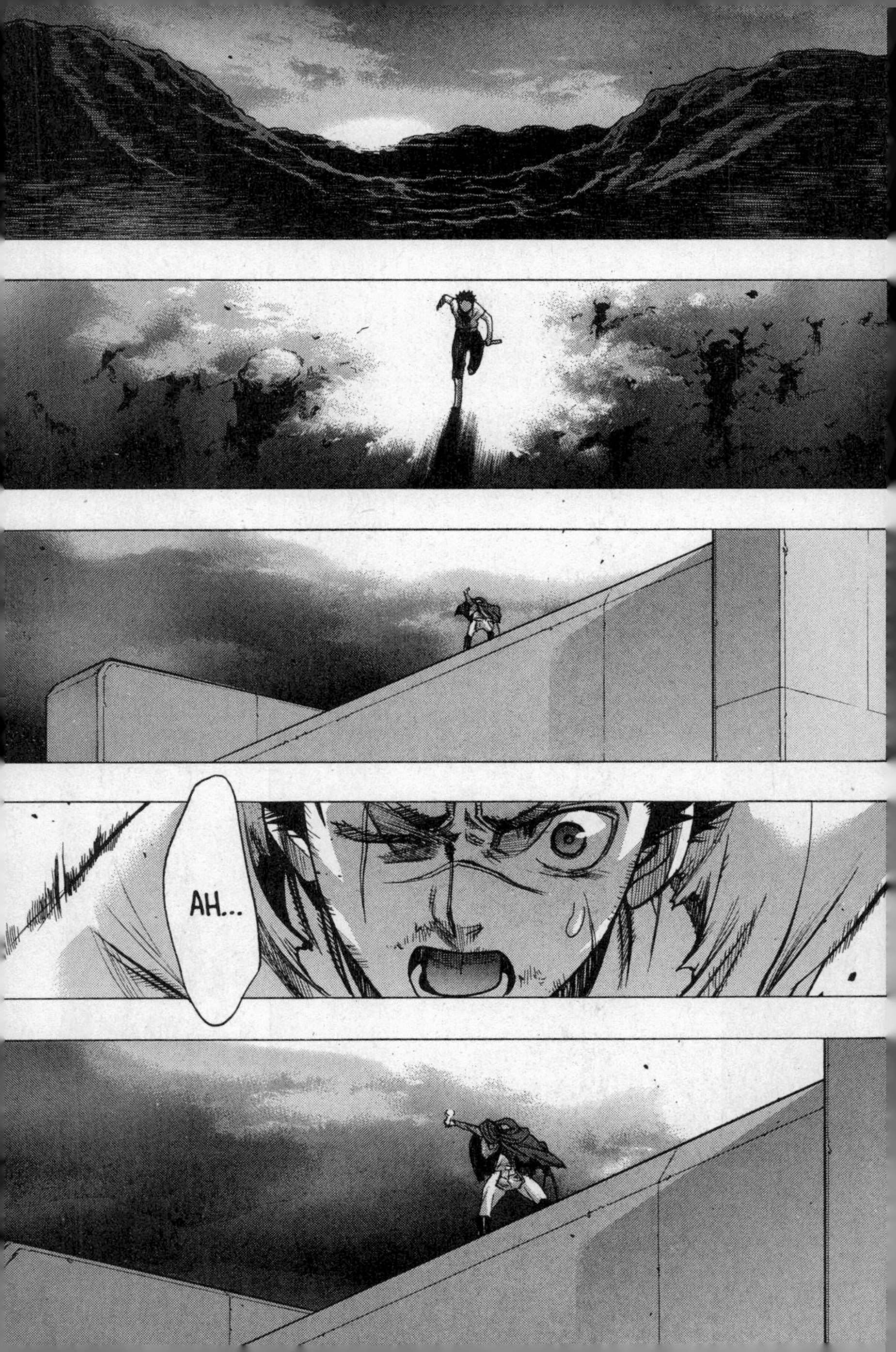
AH...

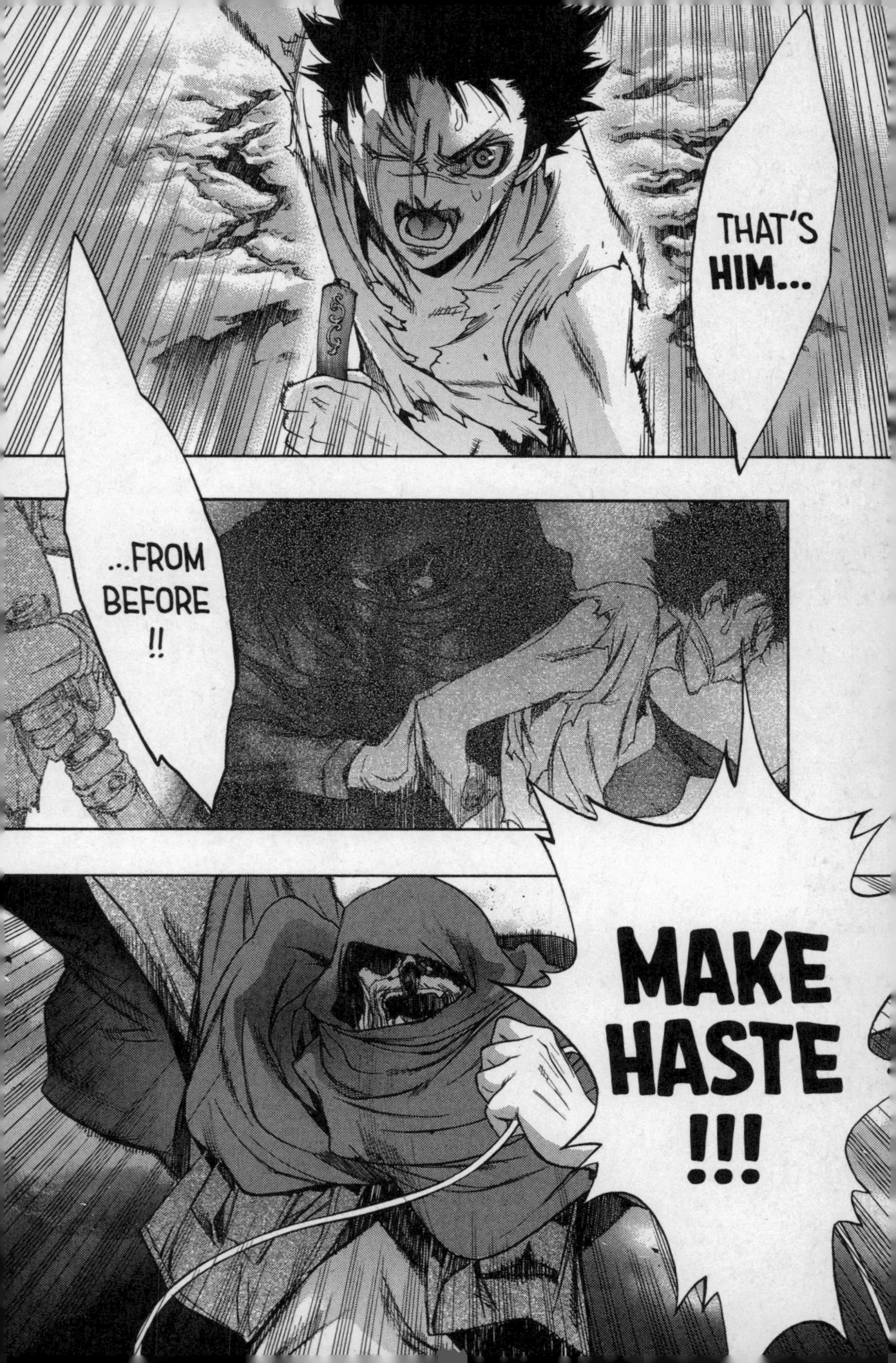

THAT'S HIM...
...FROM BEFORE !!
MAKE HASTE !!!

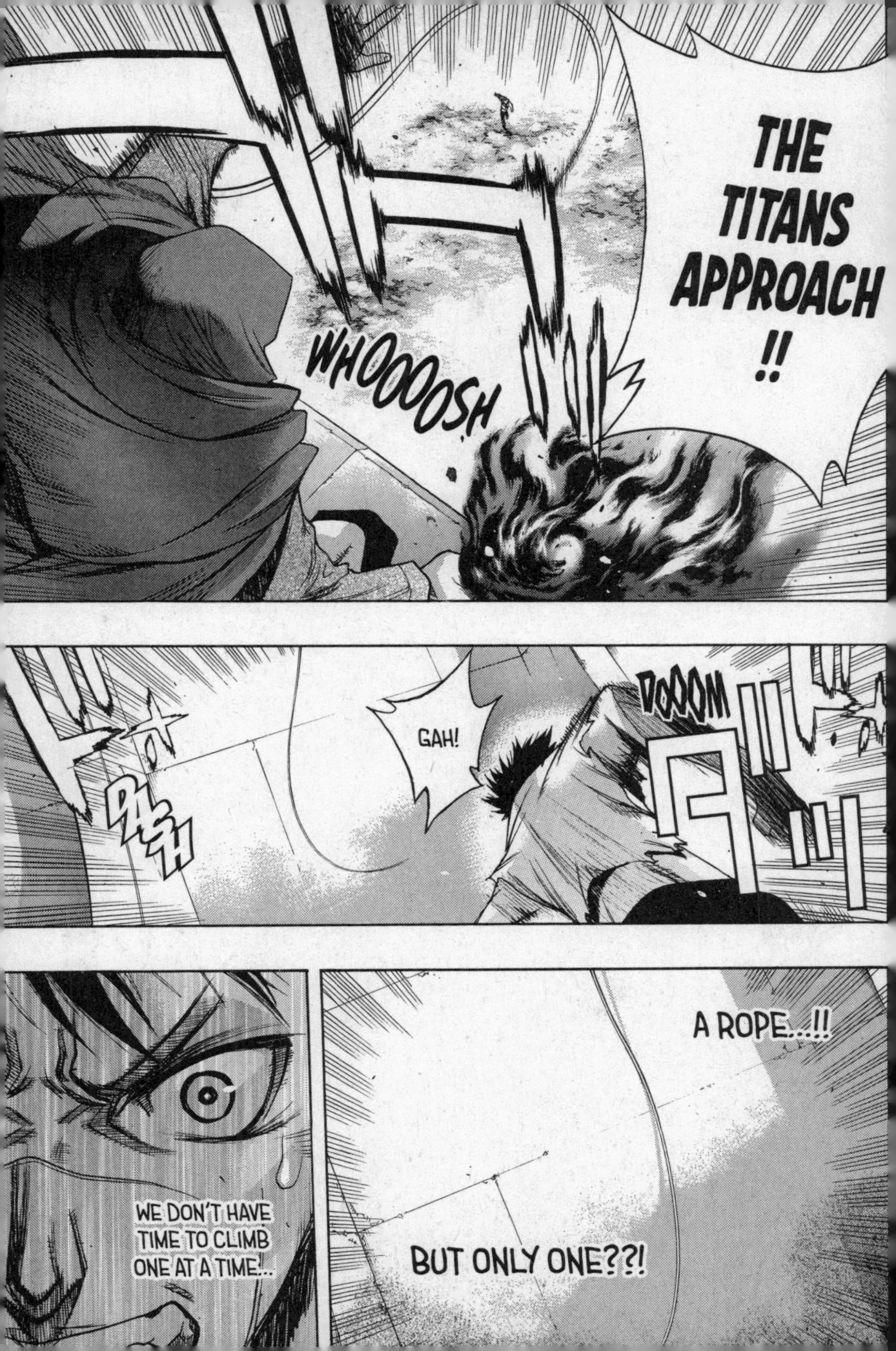
THE TITANS APPROACH !!
WHOOOOSH
DOOOM
GAH!
DASH
A ROPE...!!
BUT ONLY ONE??!
WE DON'T HAVE TIME TO CLIMB ONE AT A TIME...

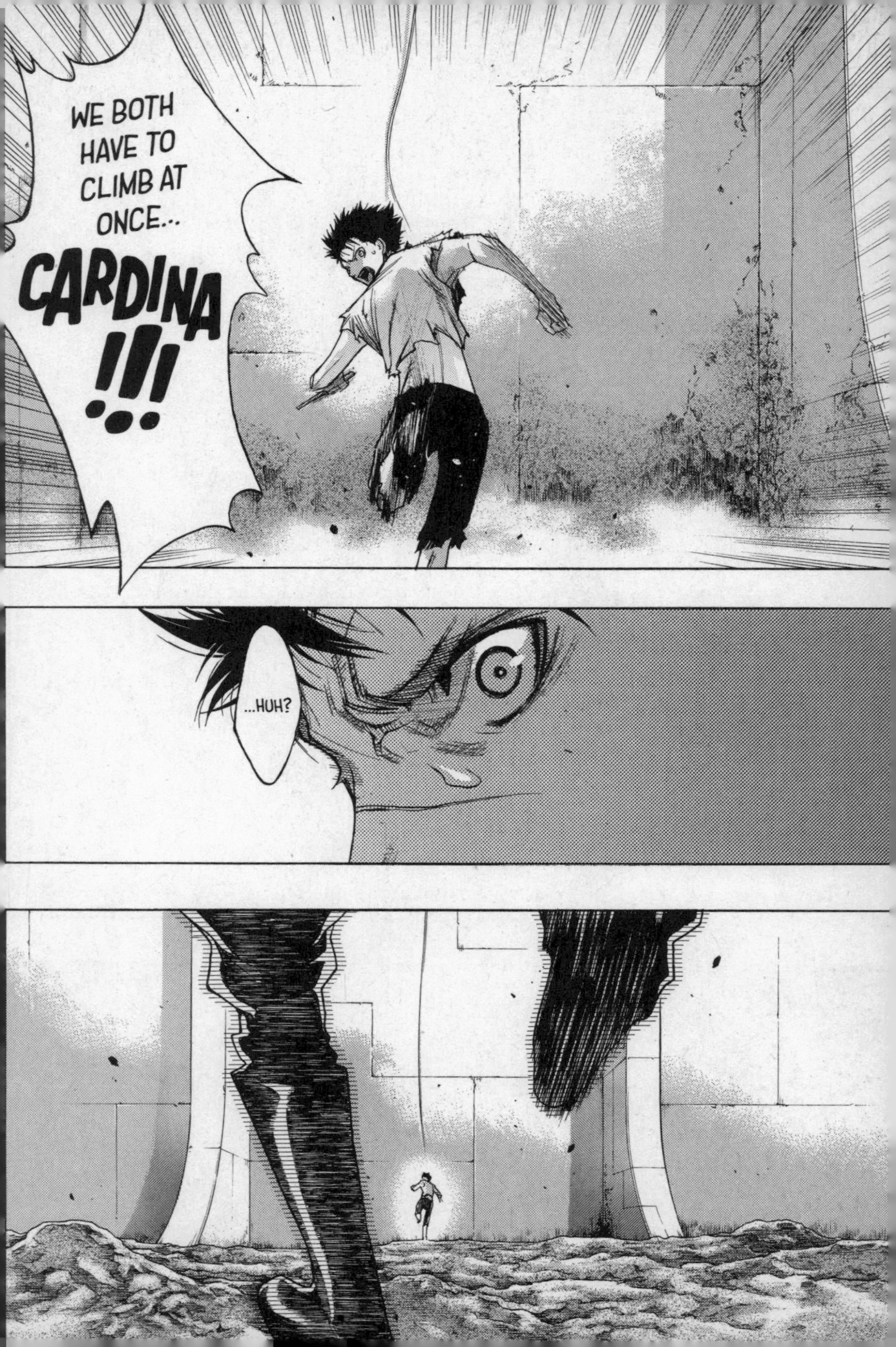
WE BOTH HAVE TO CLIMB AT ONCE...
CARDINA!!!
...HUH?

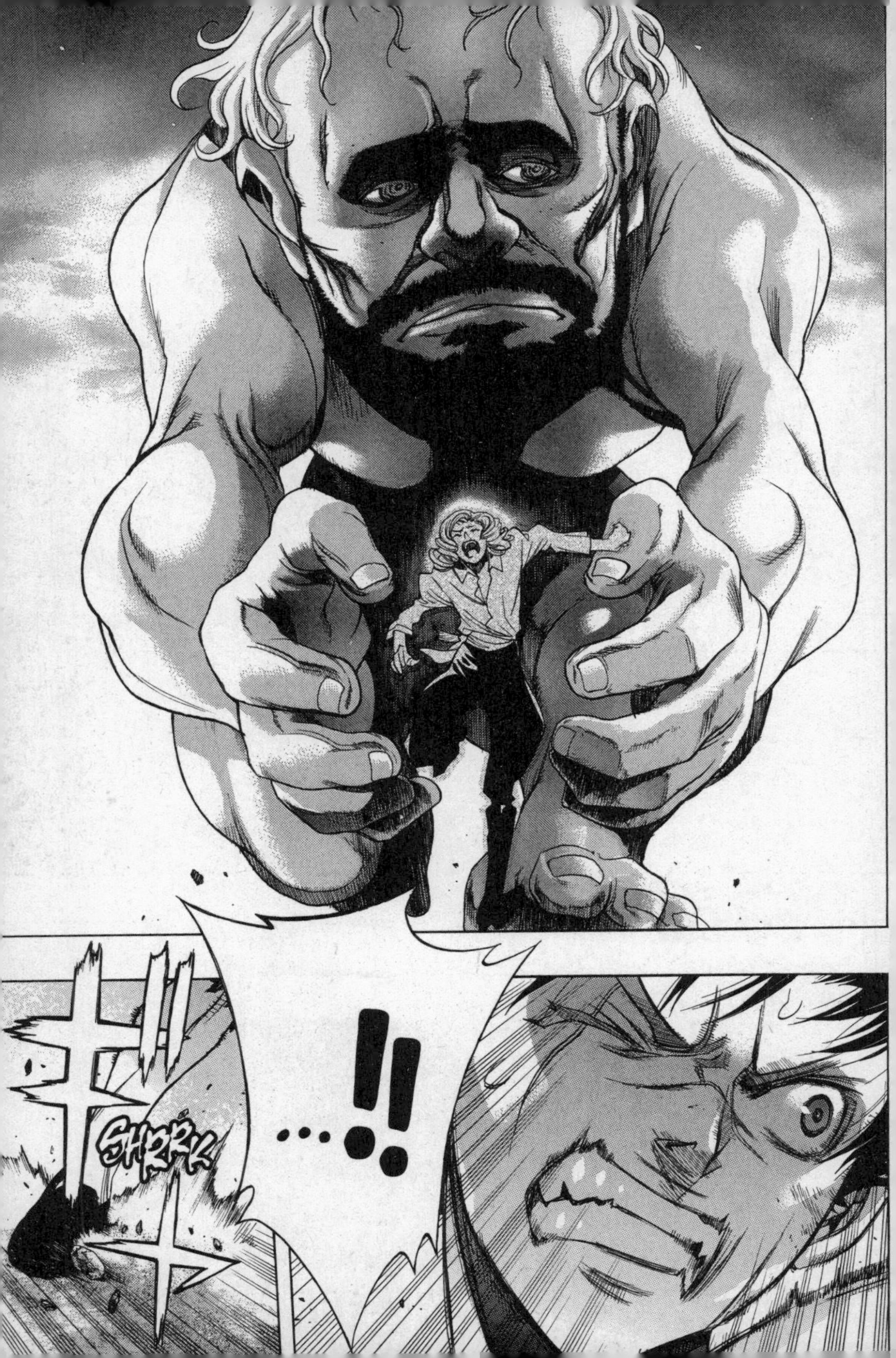

...!!
SHRRK

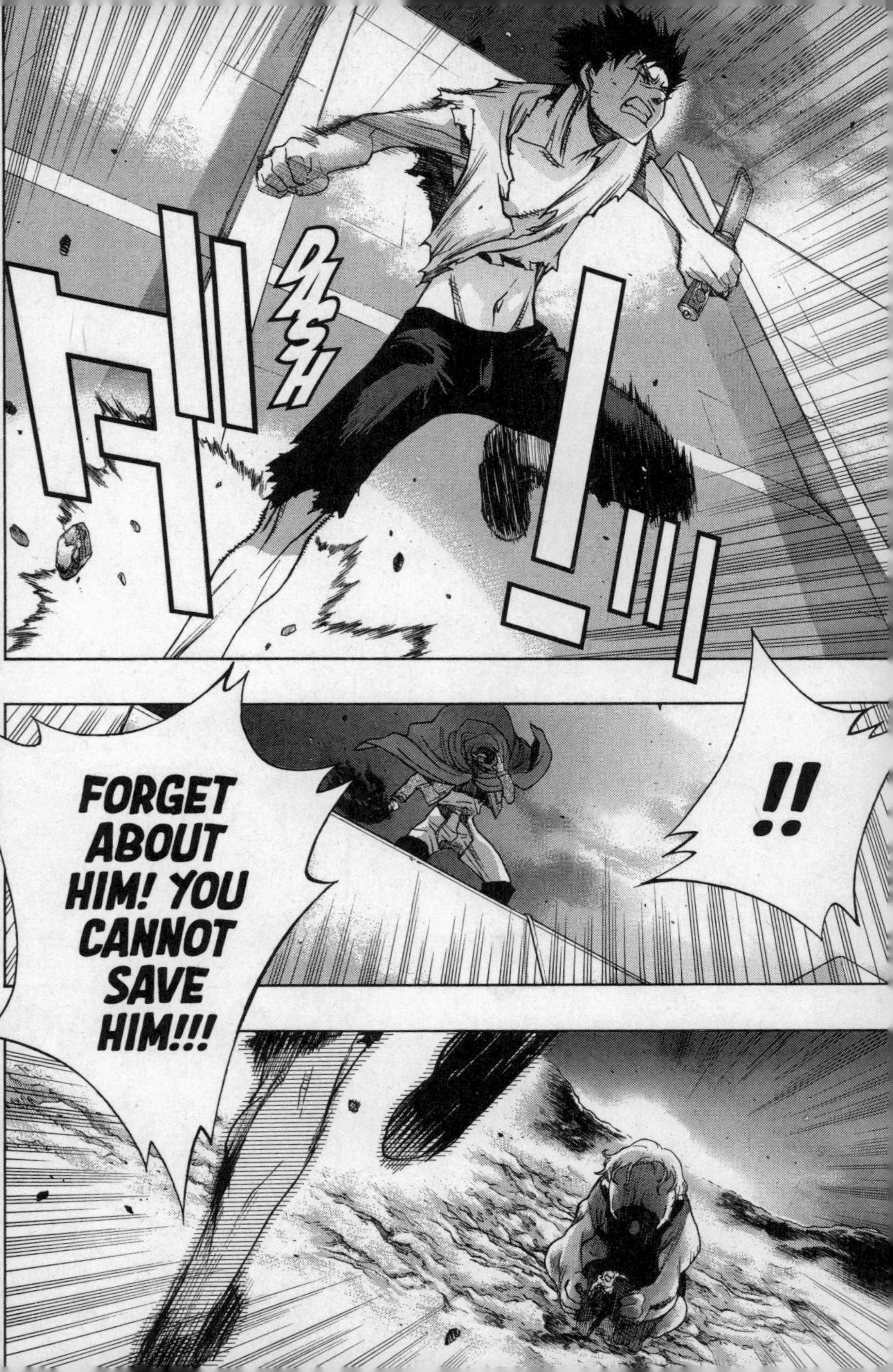
DASH
!!
FORGET ABOUT HIM! YOU CANNOT SAVE HIM!!!

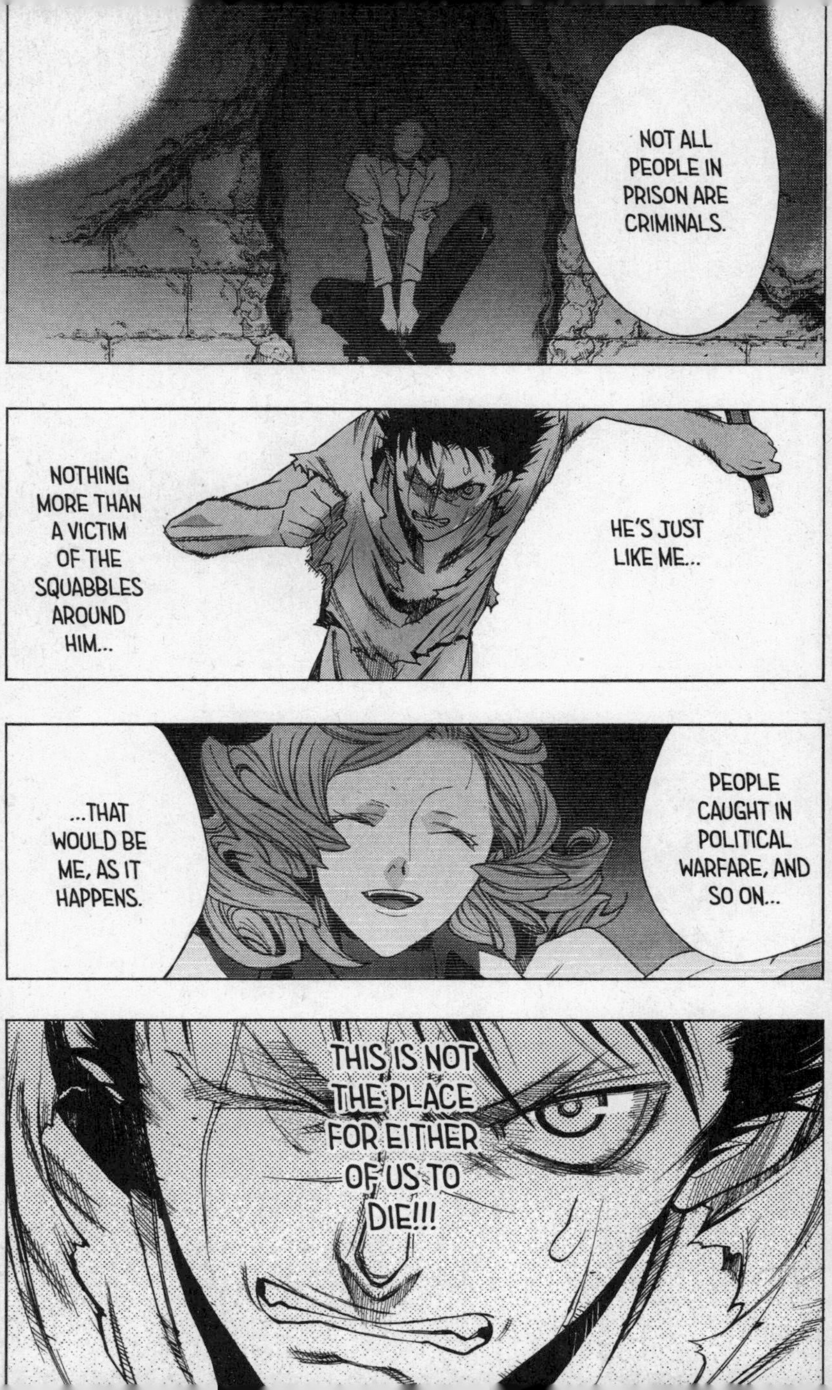
NOT ALL PEOPLE IN PRISON ARE CRIMINALS.
HE'S JUST LIKE ME...
NOTHING MORE THAN A VICTIM OF THE SQUABBLES AROUND HIM...
PEOPLE CAUGHT IN POLITICAL WARFARE, AND SO ON...
...THAT WOULD BE ME, AS IT HAPPENS.
THIS IS NOT THE PLACE FOR EITHER OF US TO DIE!!!

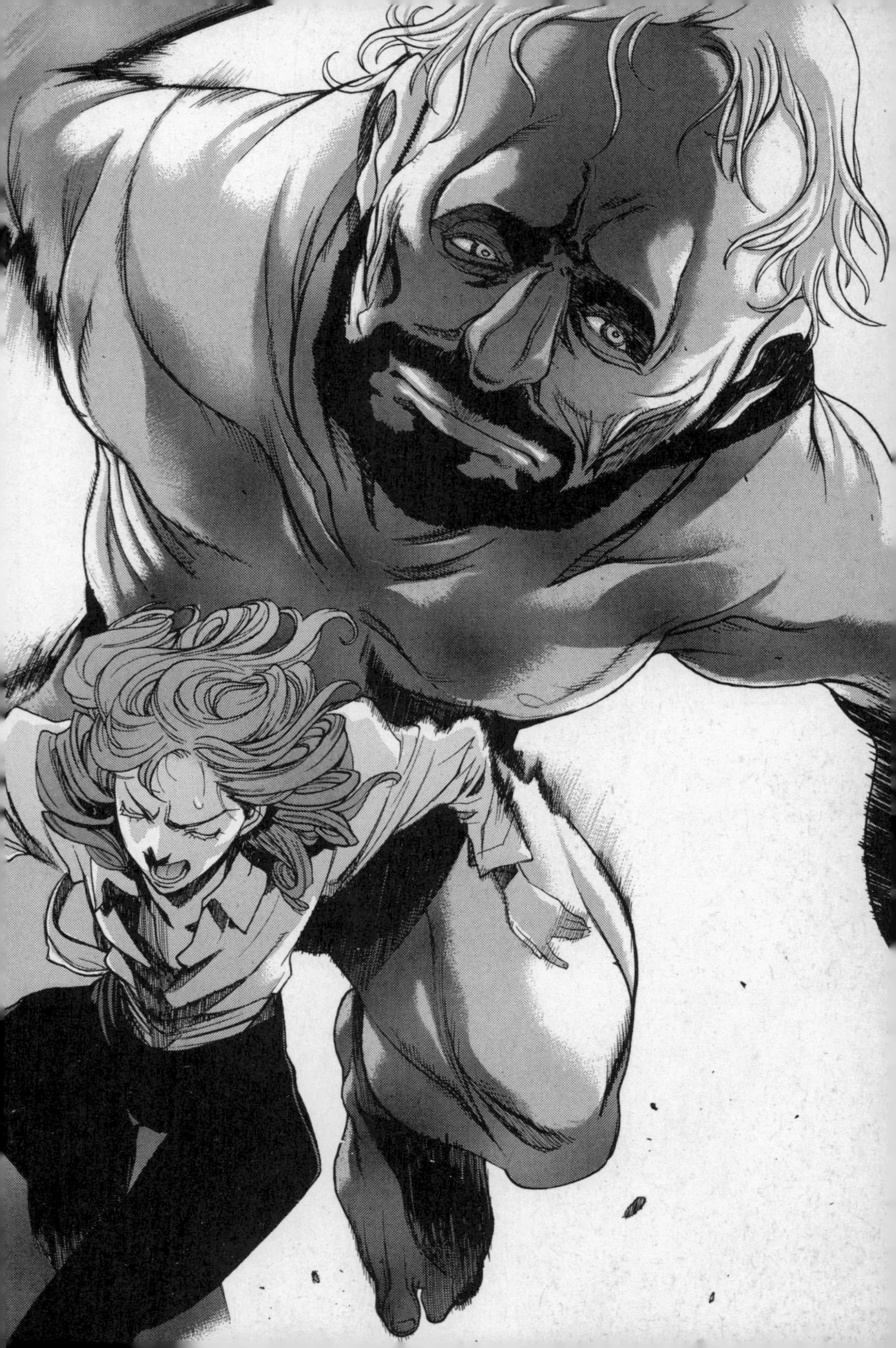

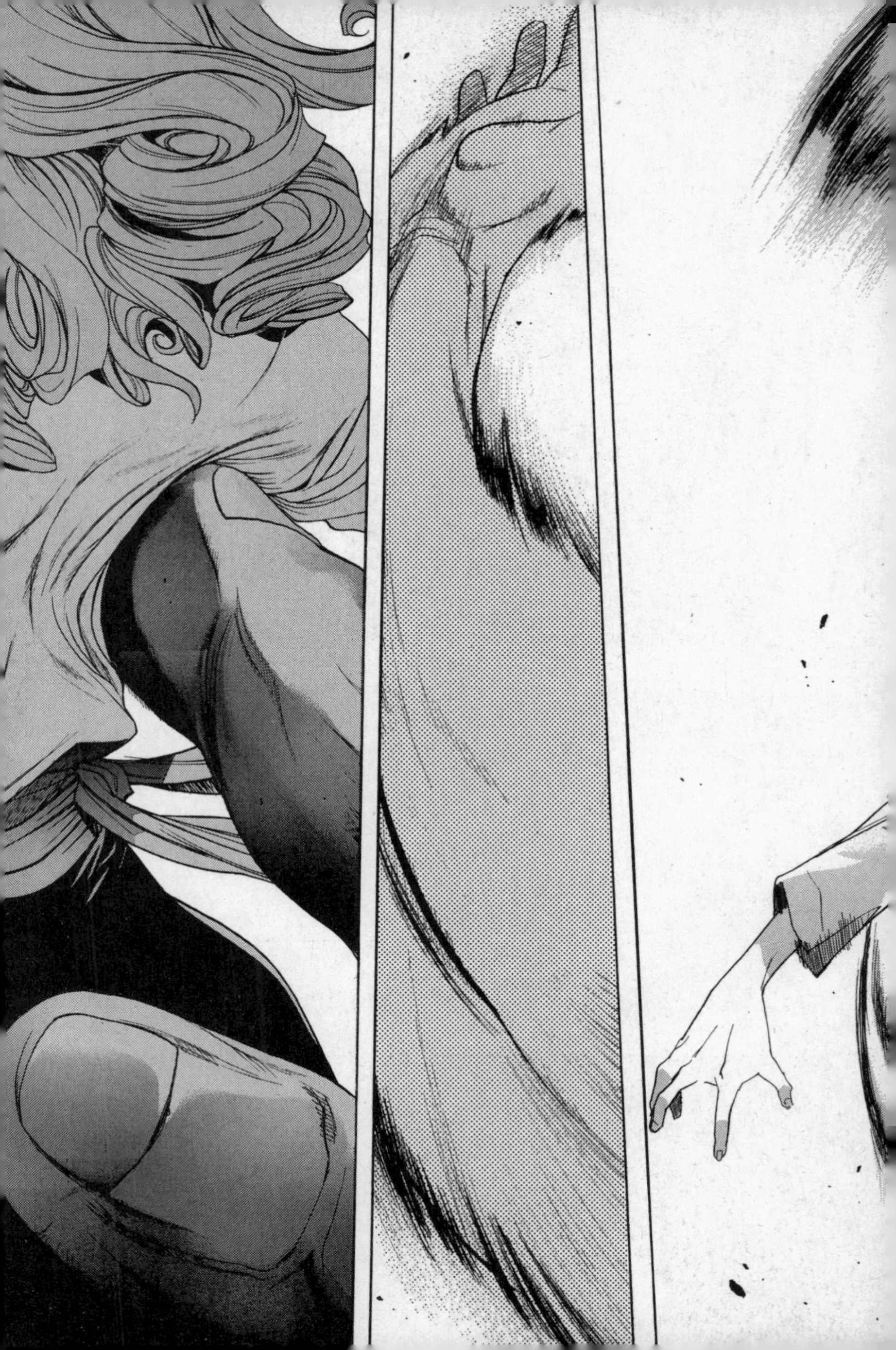

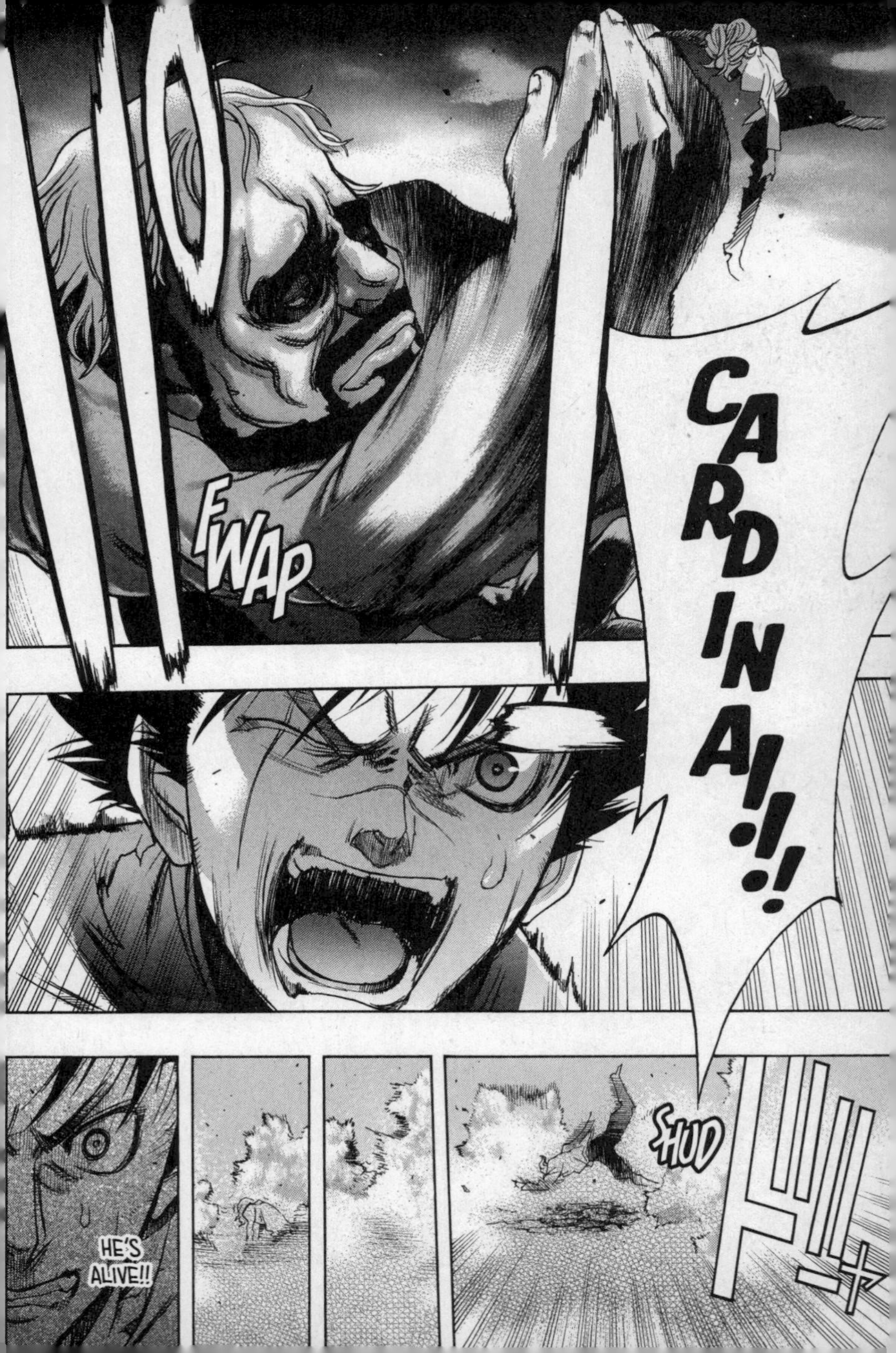
FWAP
CARDINA!!!
SHUD
HE'S ALIVE!!

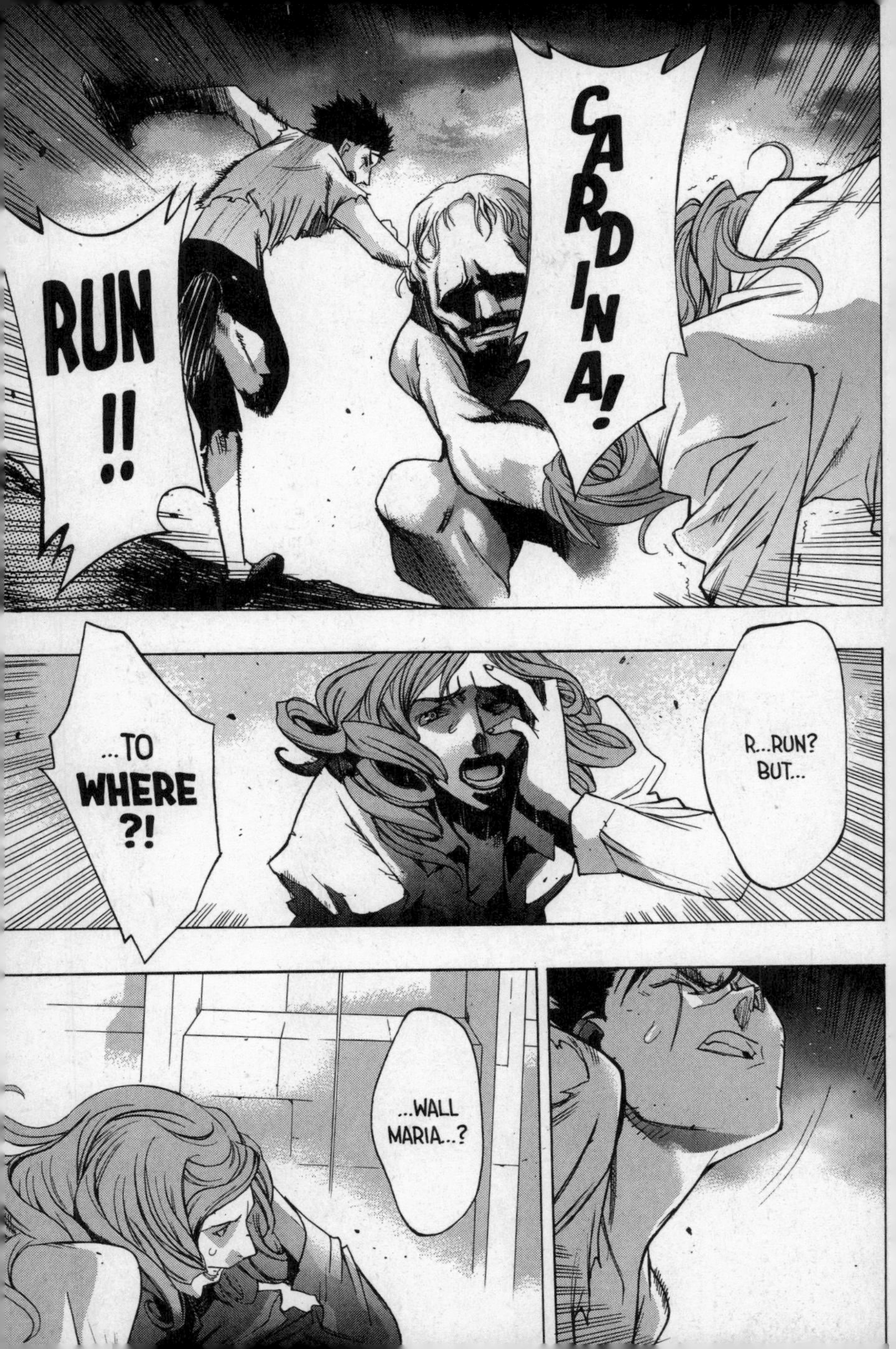
CARDINA!
RUN!!
R...RUN? BUT...
...TO WHERE?!
...WALL MARIA...?

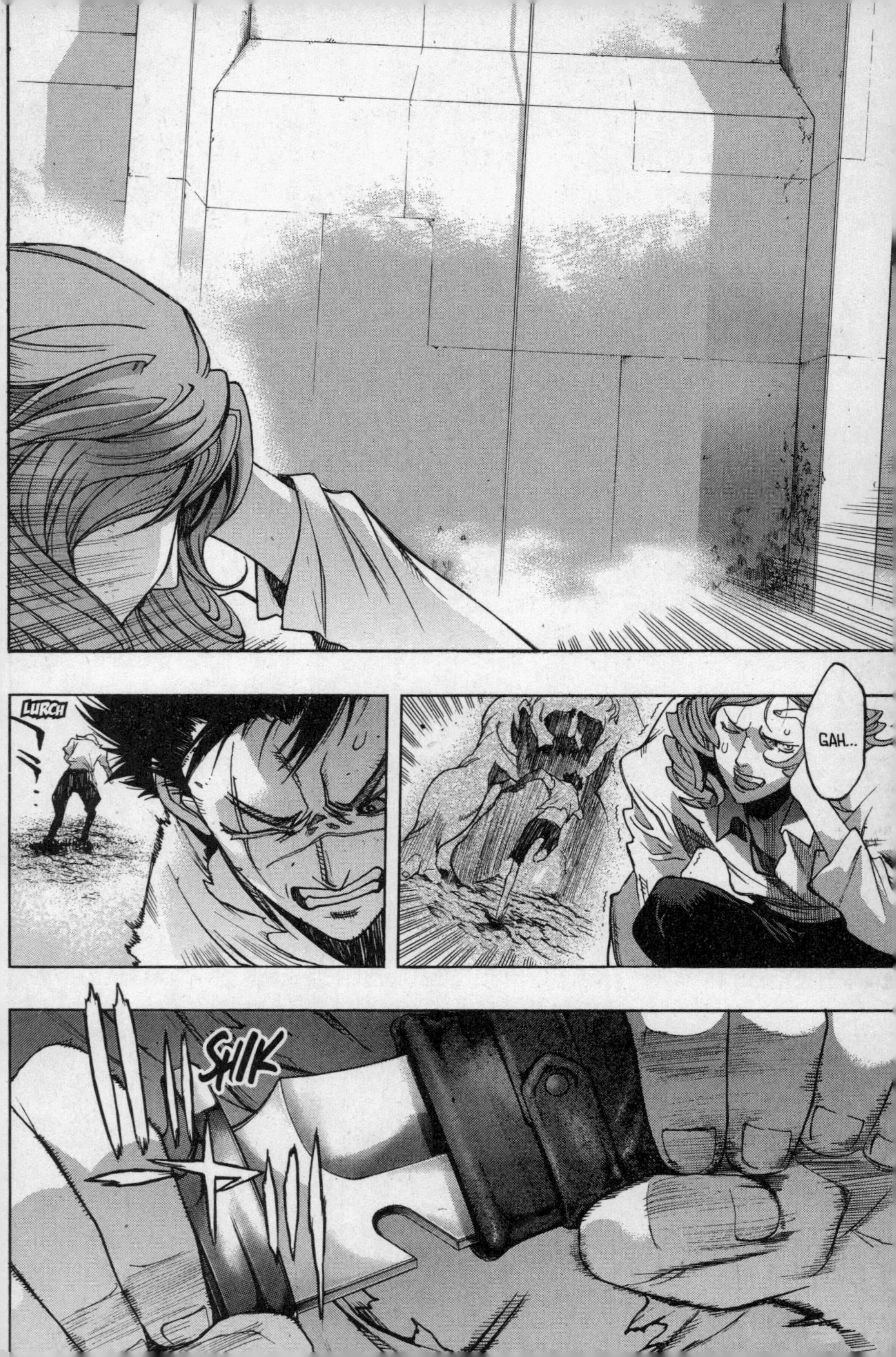
GAH...
LURCH
SHIK

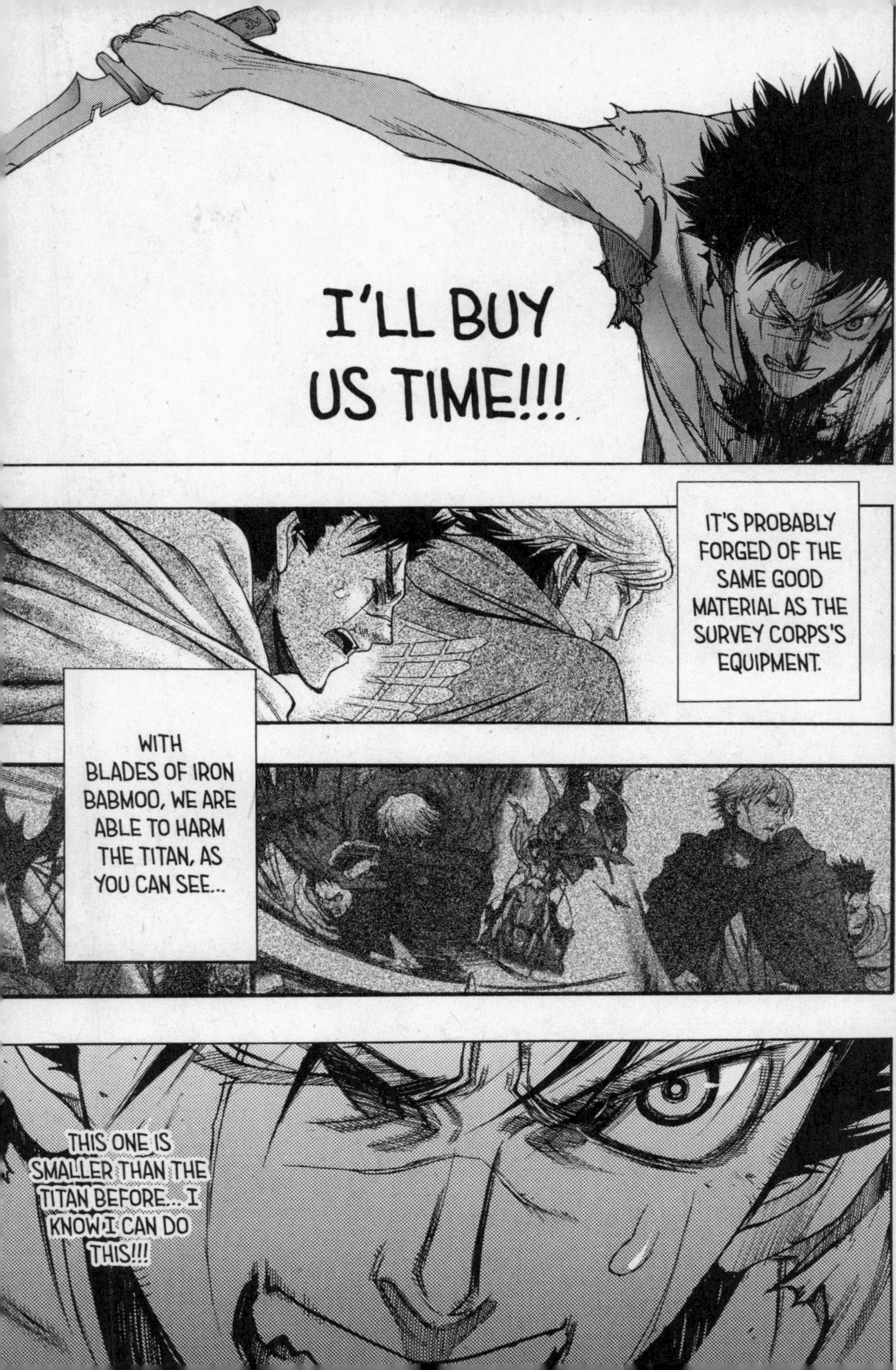
I'LL BUY US TIME!!!
IT'S PROBABLY FORGED OF THE SAME GOOD MATERIAL AS THE SURVEY CORPS'S EQUIPMENT.
WITH BLADES OF IRON BABMOO, WE ARE ABLE TO HARM THE TITAN, AS YOU CAN SEE...
THIS ONE IS SMALLER THAN THE TITAN BEFORE... I KNOW I CAN DO THIS!!!

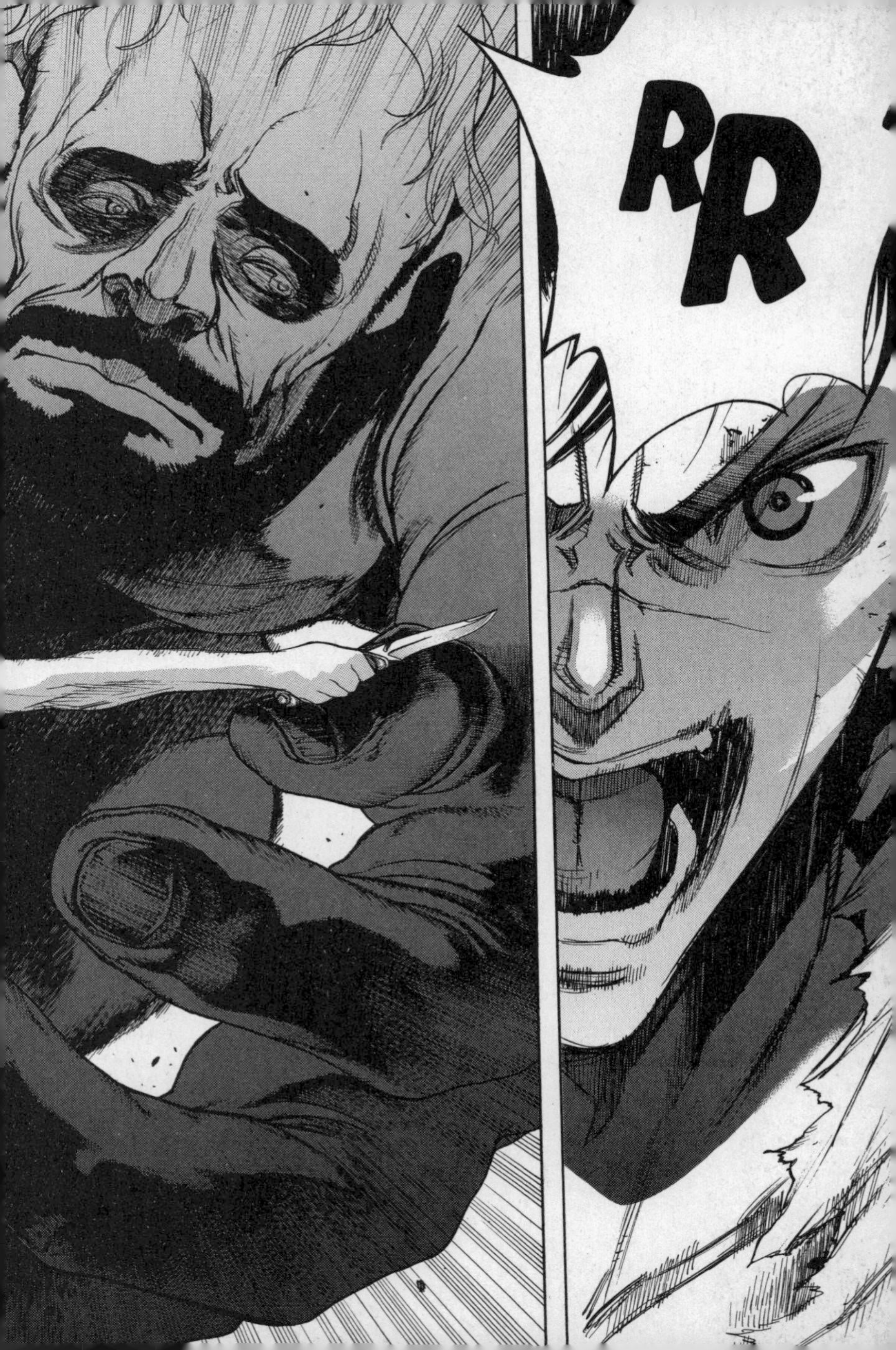
RR

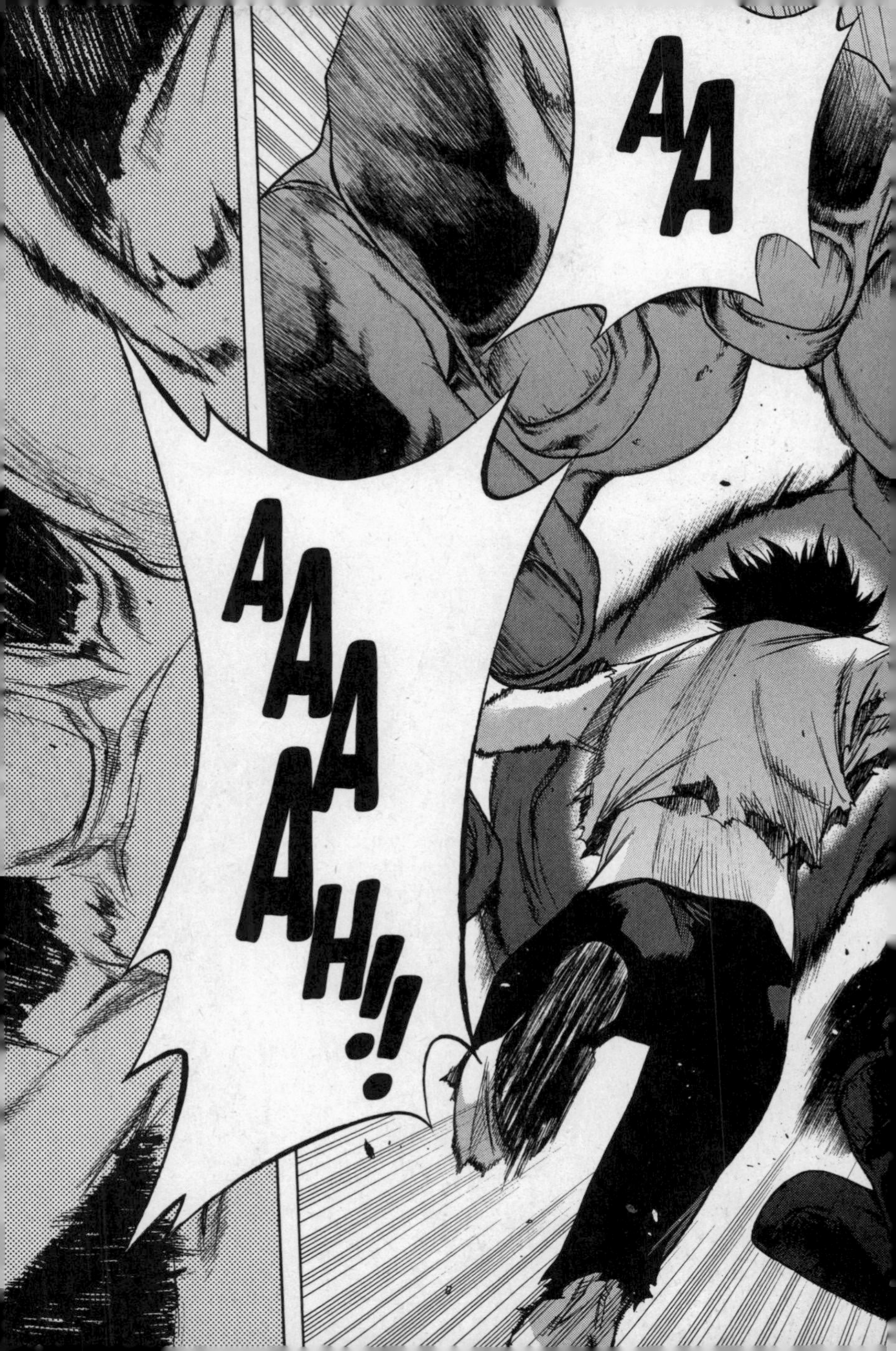
AA
AAAAAH!!

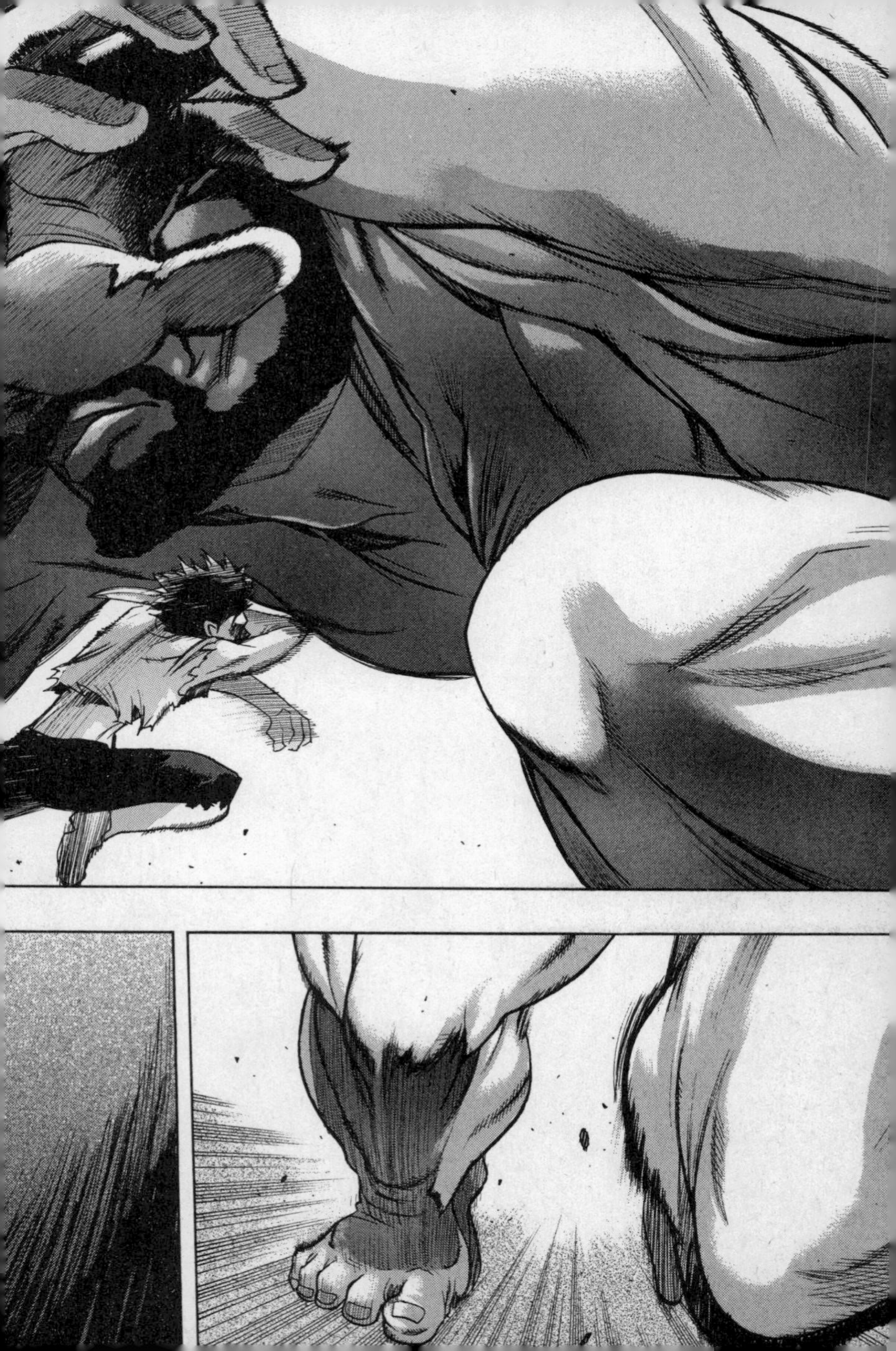

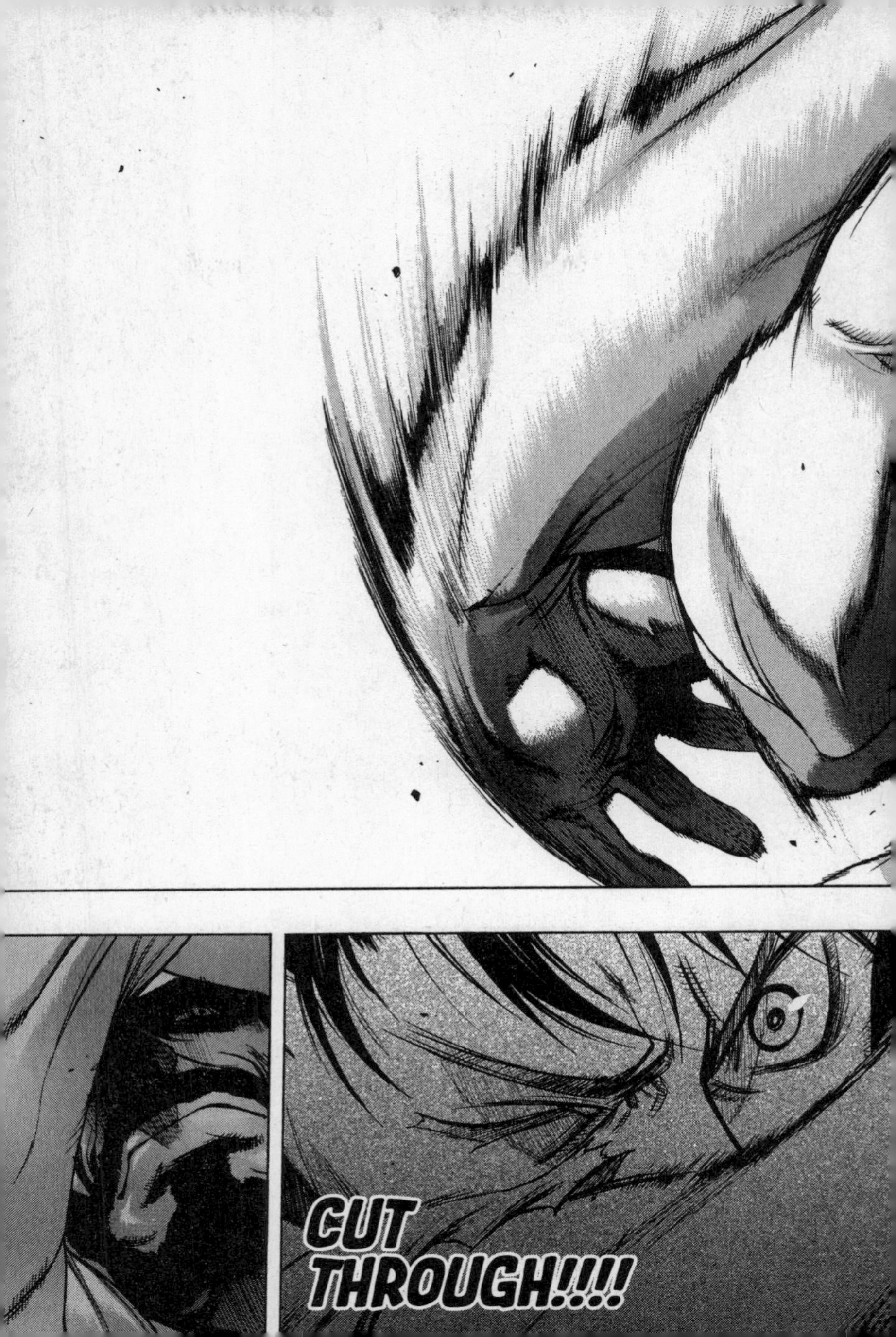
CUT THROUGH!!!!

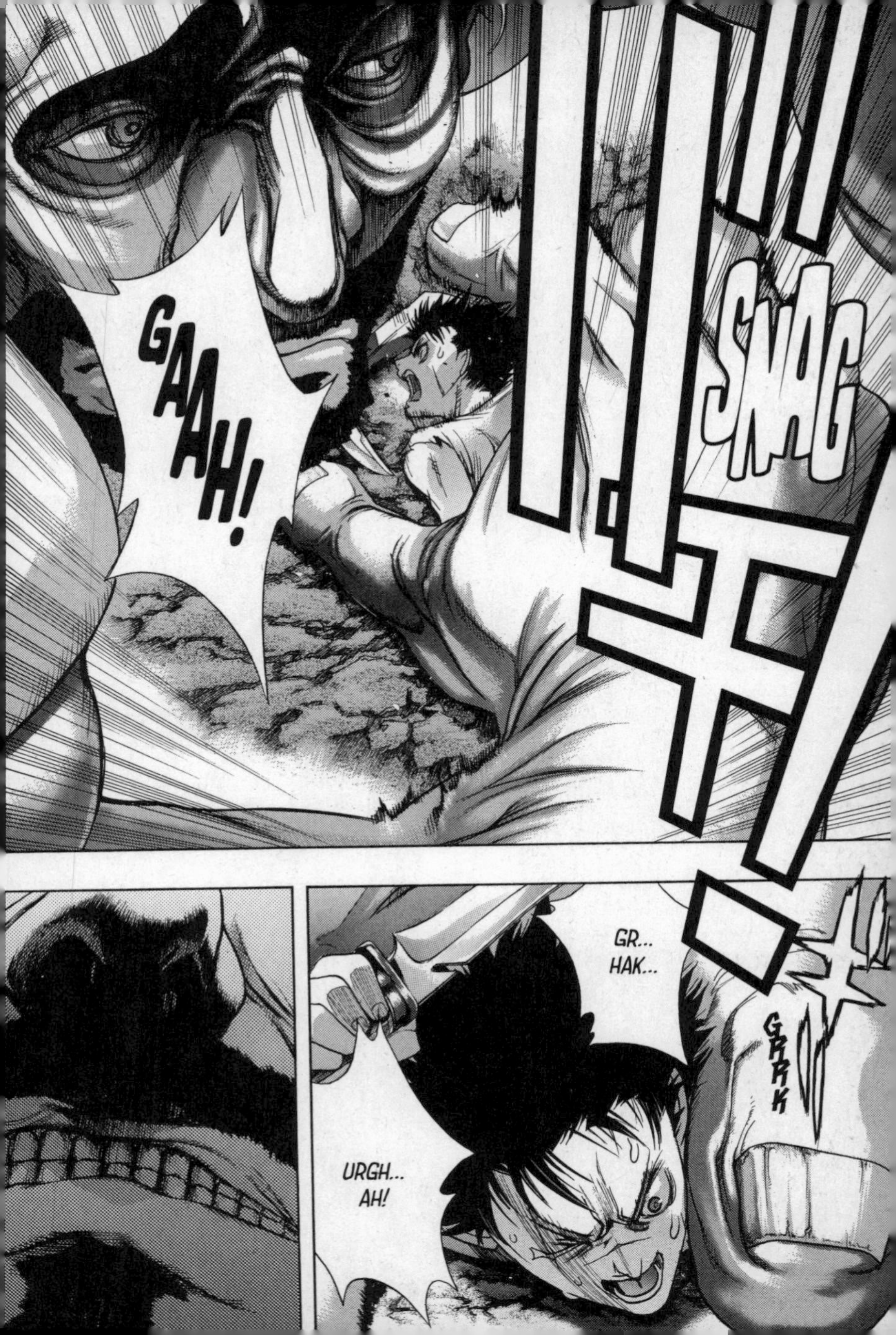
SNAG
GAAH!
GRRK
GR... HAK...
URGH... AH!

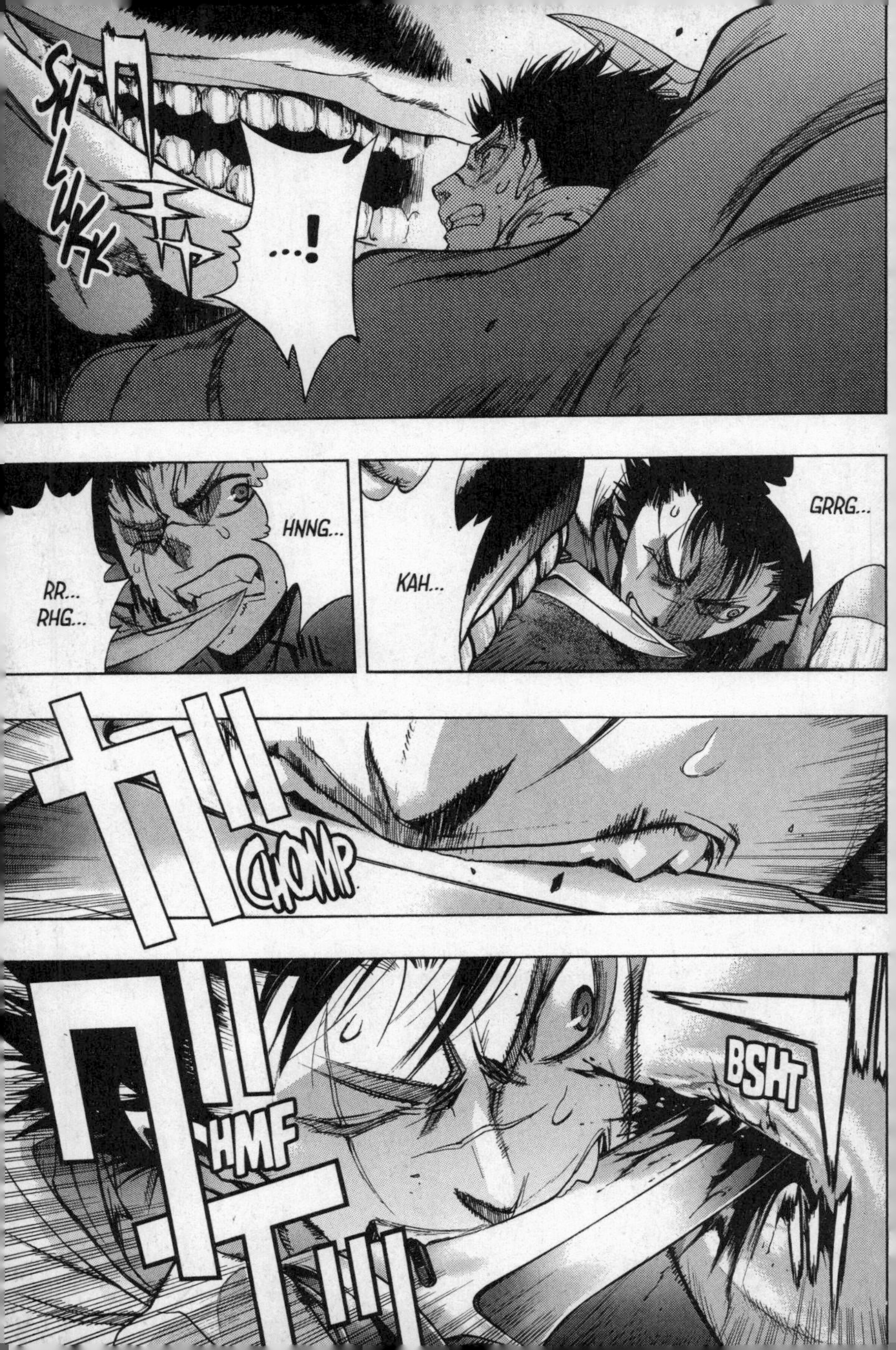
...!
SHLLUKK
GRRG...
KAH...
HNNG...
RR... RHG...
CHOMP
BSHT
HMF

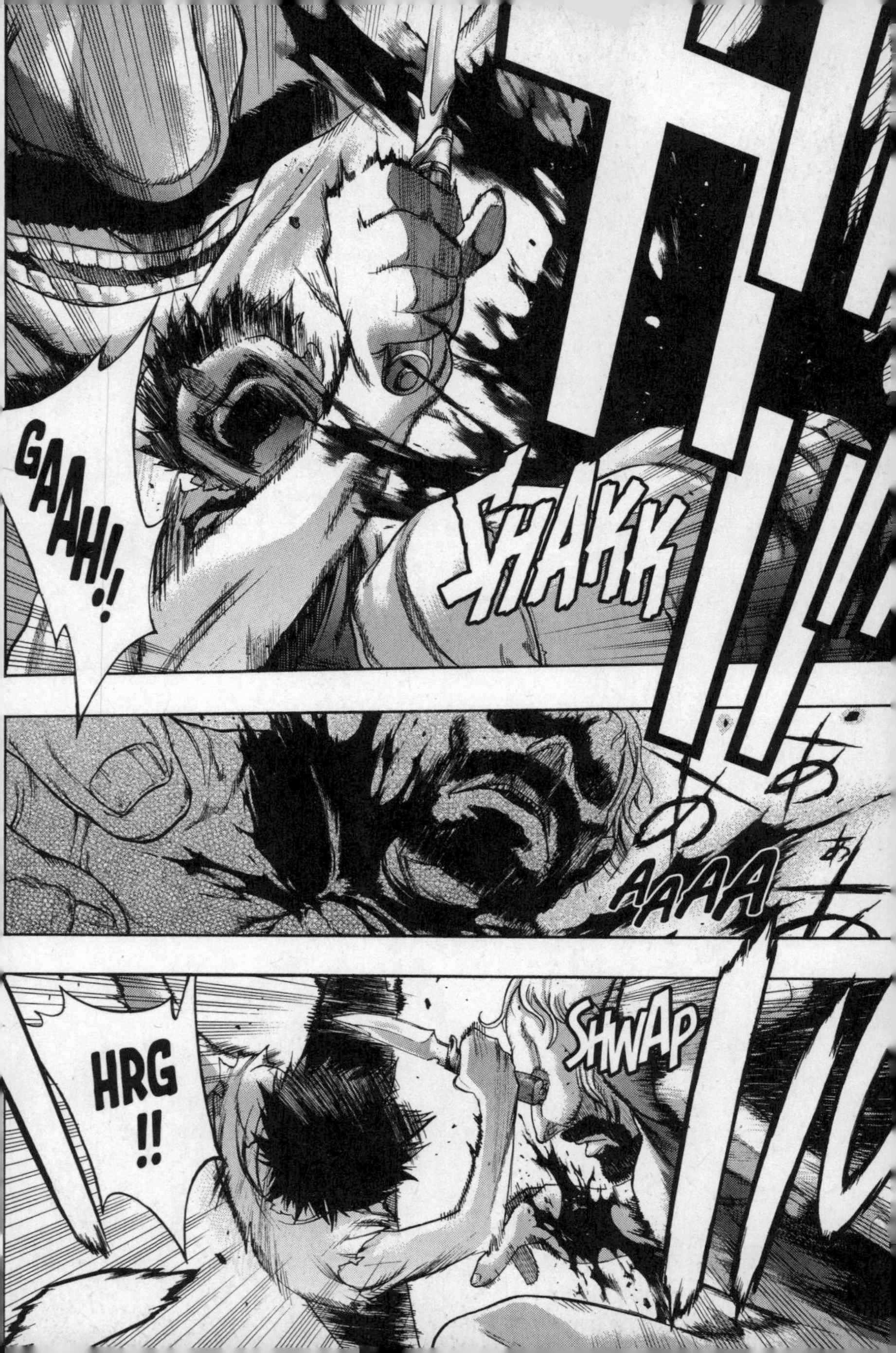
SHAKK
GAAH!!
AAAA
SHWAP
HRG !!

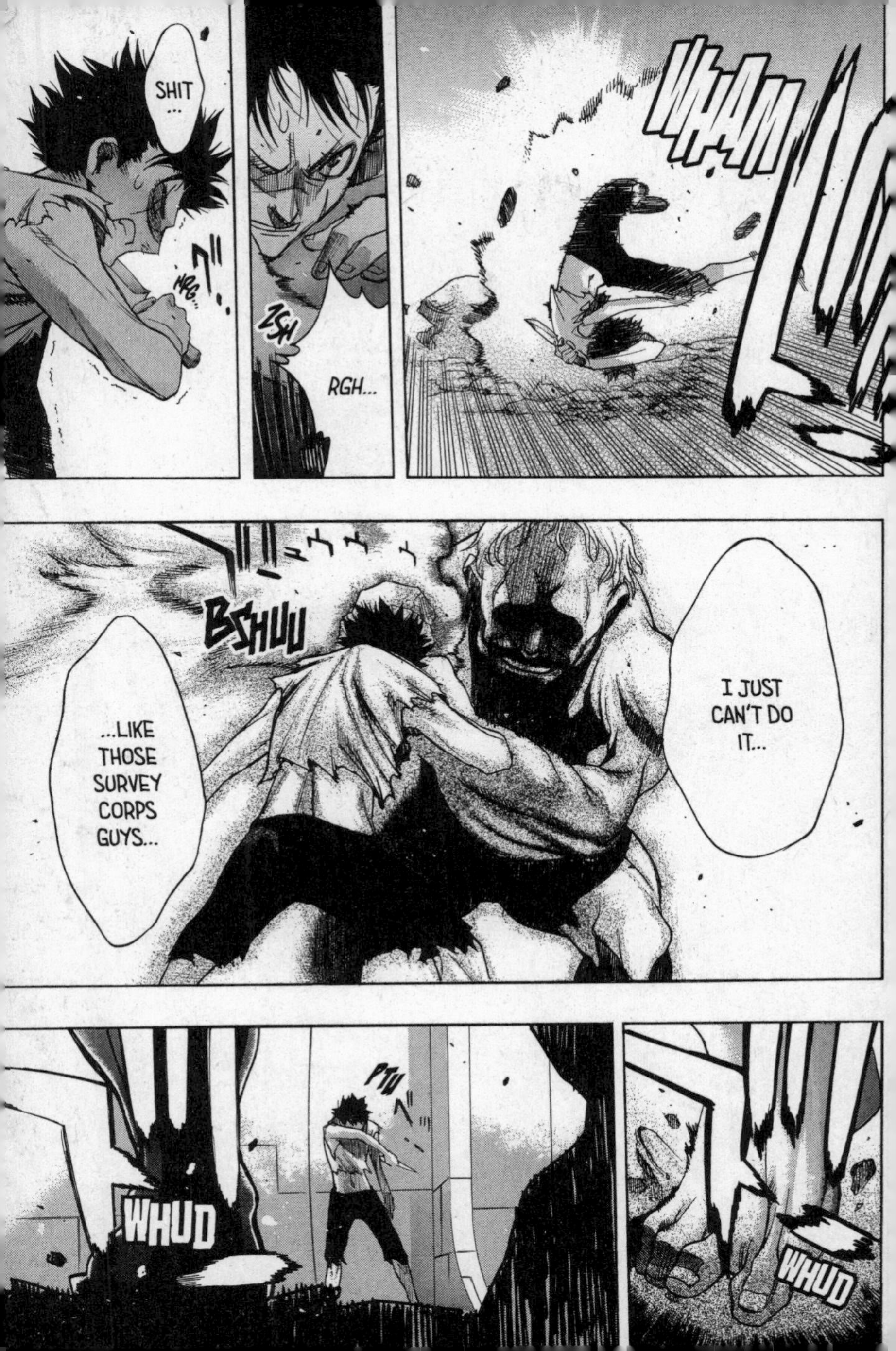
WHAM
ZSH
RGH...
SHIT...
NRG...
I JUST CAN'T DO IT...
BSHUU
...LIKE THOSE SURVEY CORPS GUYS...
WHUD
PTU
WHUD

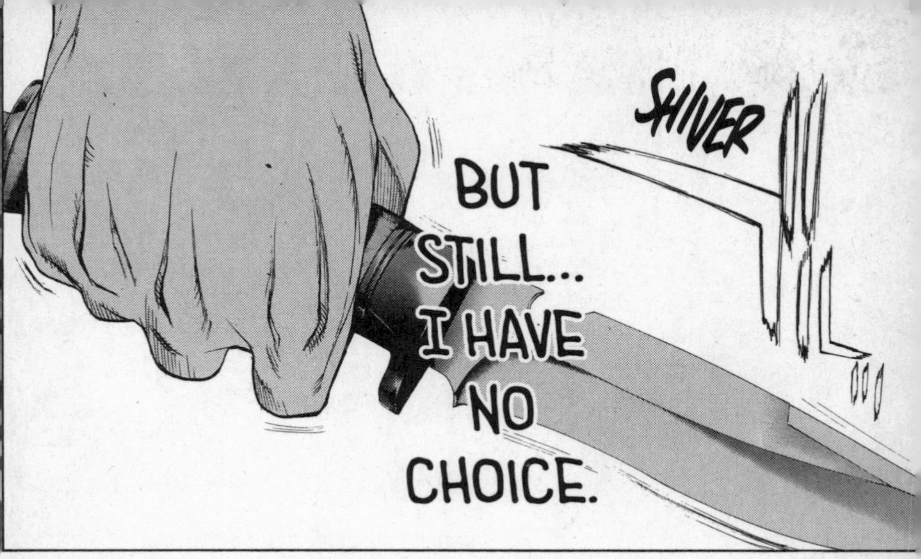
SHIVER
BUT STILL... I HAVE NO CHOICE.
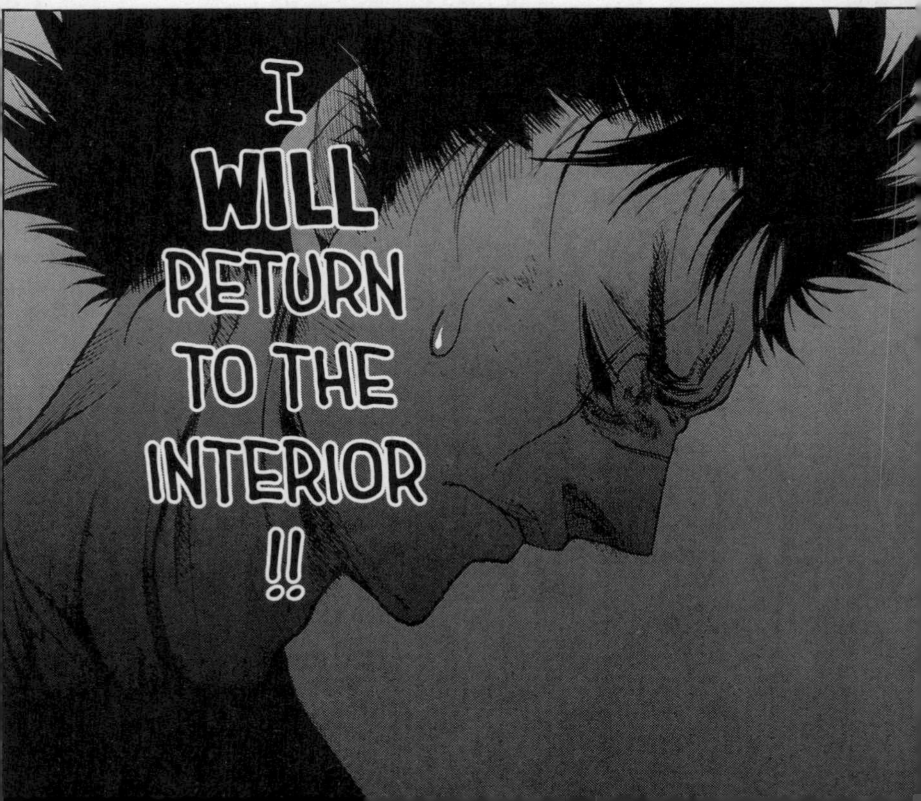
I WILL RETURN TO THE INTERIOR !!

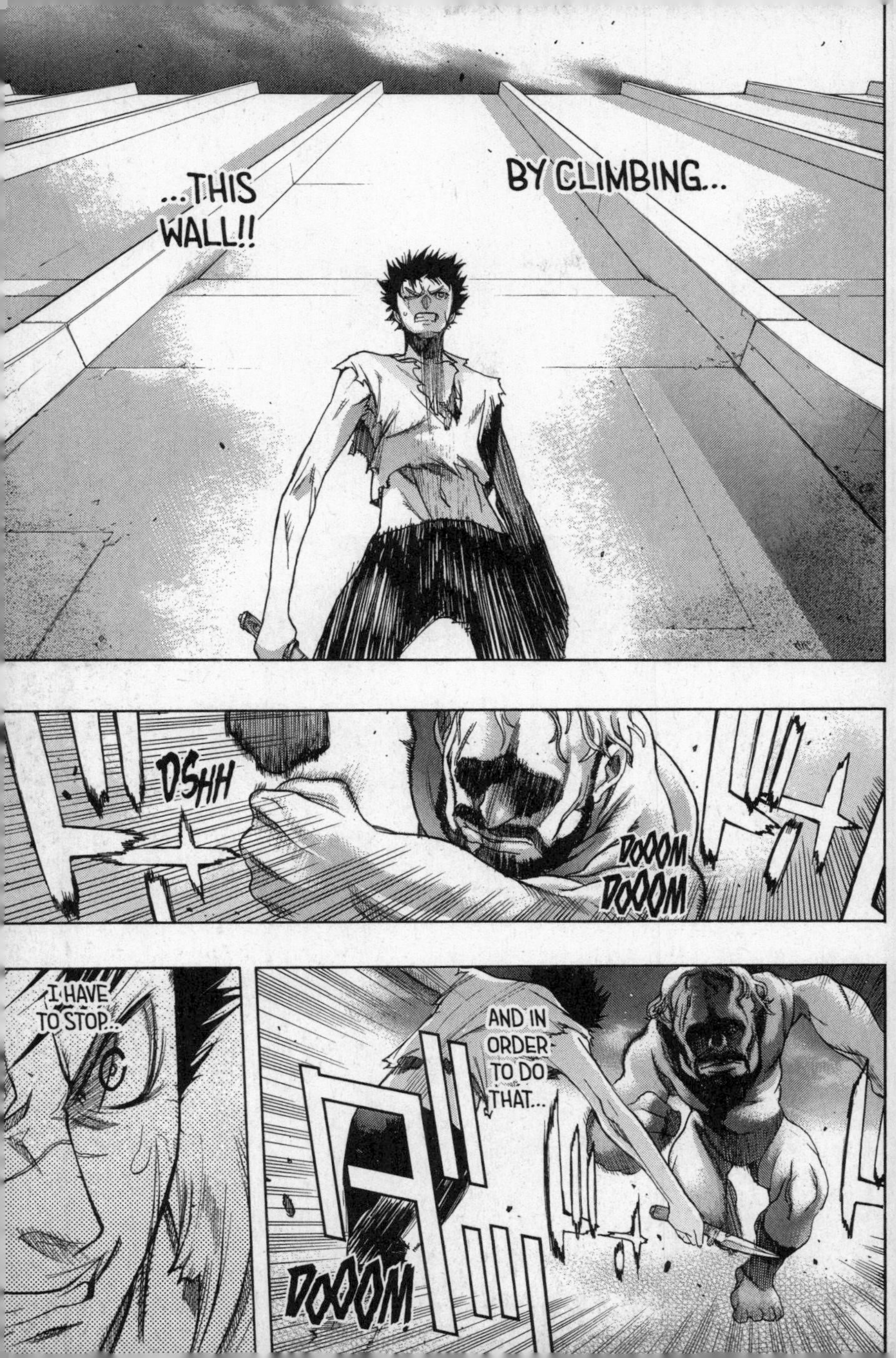
BY CLIMBING...
...THIS WALL!!
DOOOM DOOOM
DSHH
AND IN ORDER TO DO THAT...
DOOOM
I HAVE TO STOP...

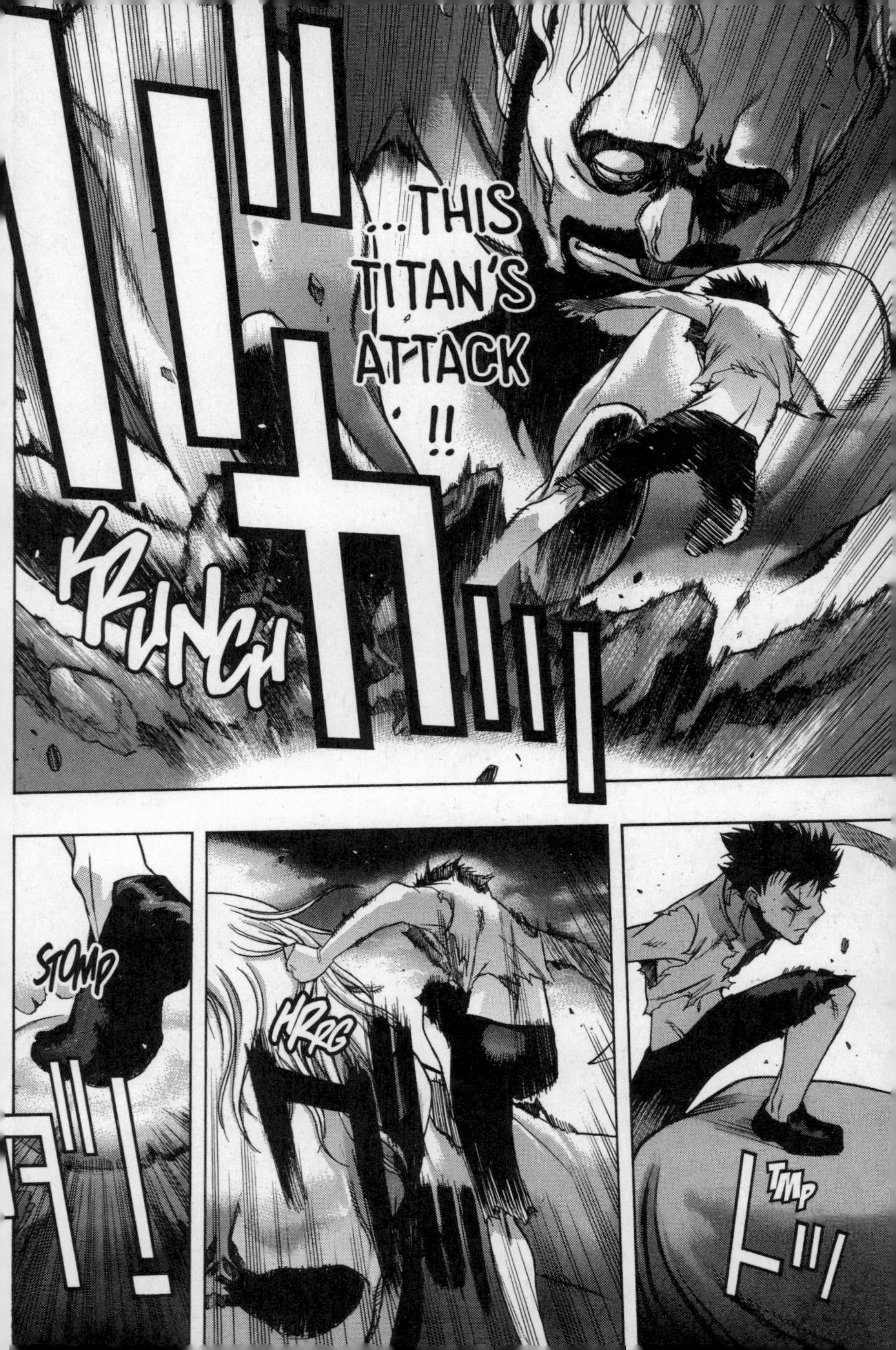
...THIS TITAN'S ATTACK !!
KRUNCH
TMP
HRRG
STOMP

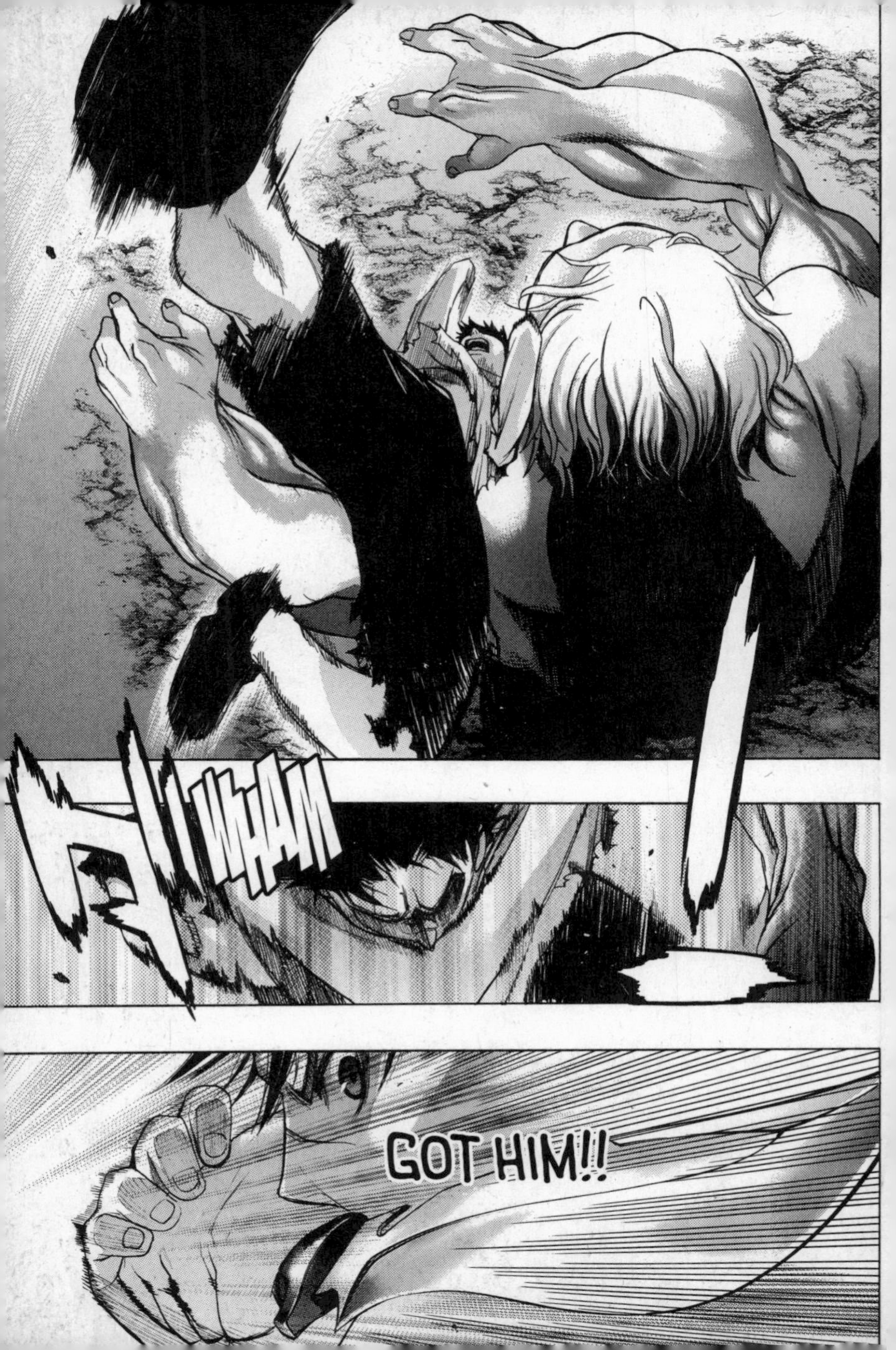
WHAM
GOT HIM!!

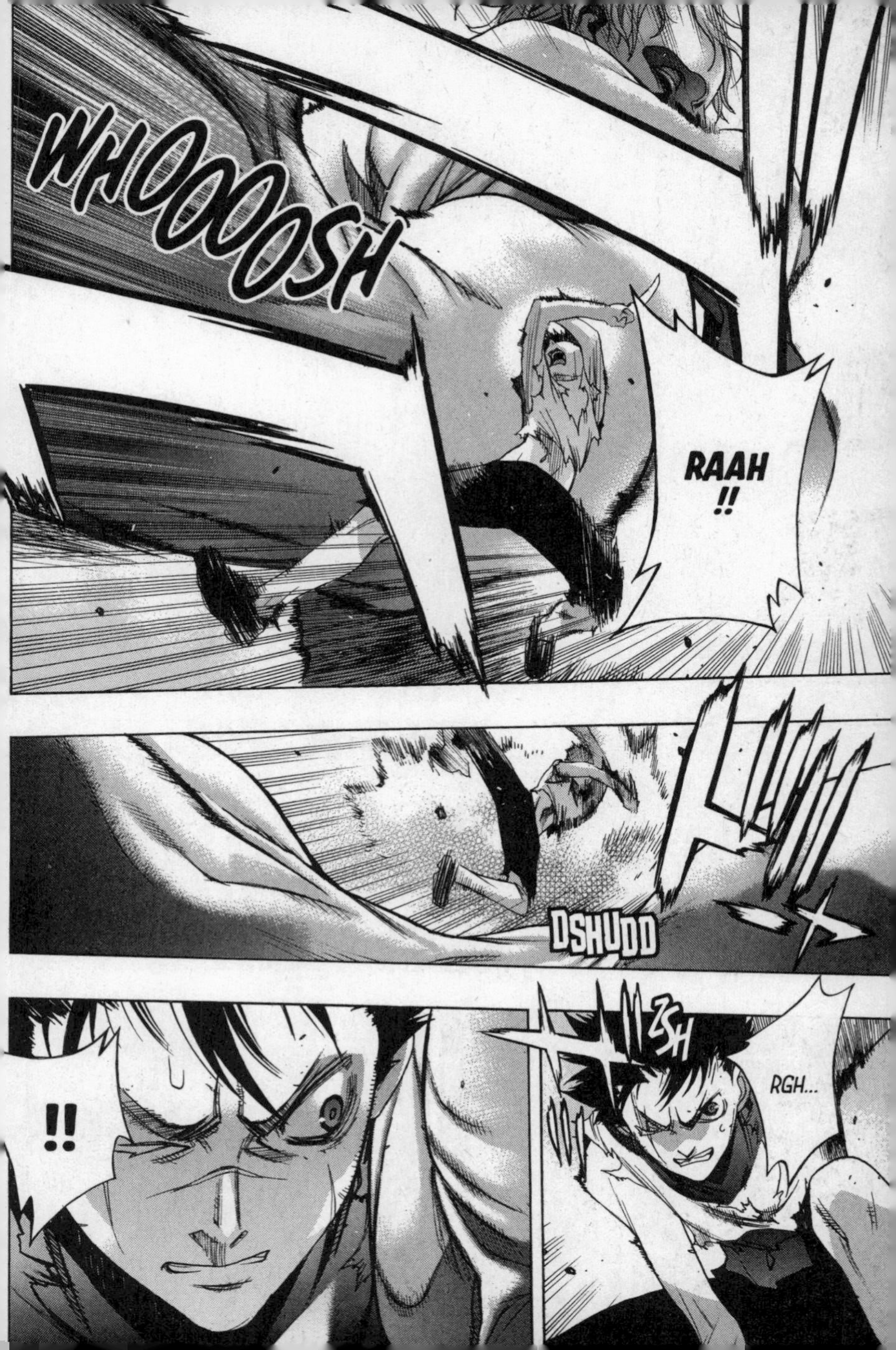
WHOOOOSH
RAAH!!
DSHUDD
ZSH
RGH...
!!

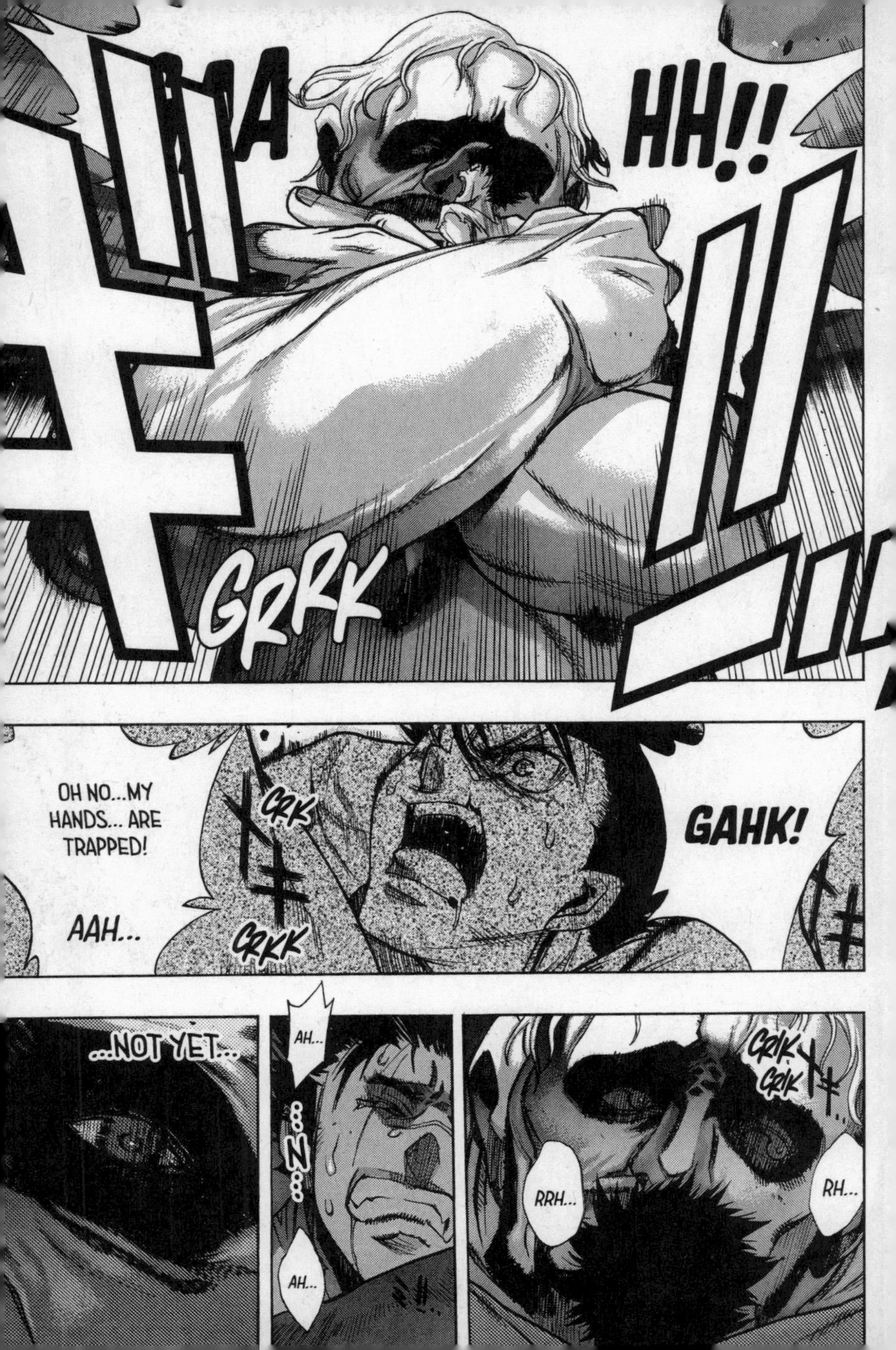
A
HH!!
GRRK
GAHK!
OH NO...MY HANDS... ARE TRAPPED!
CRK
CRKK
AAH...
CRIK CRIK
RH...
RRH...
AH...
...N...
AH...
...NOT YET...

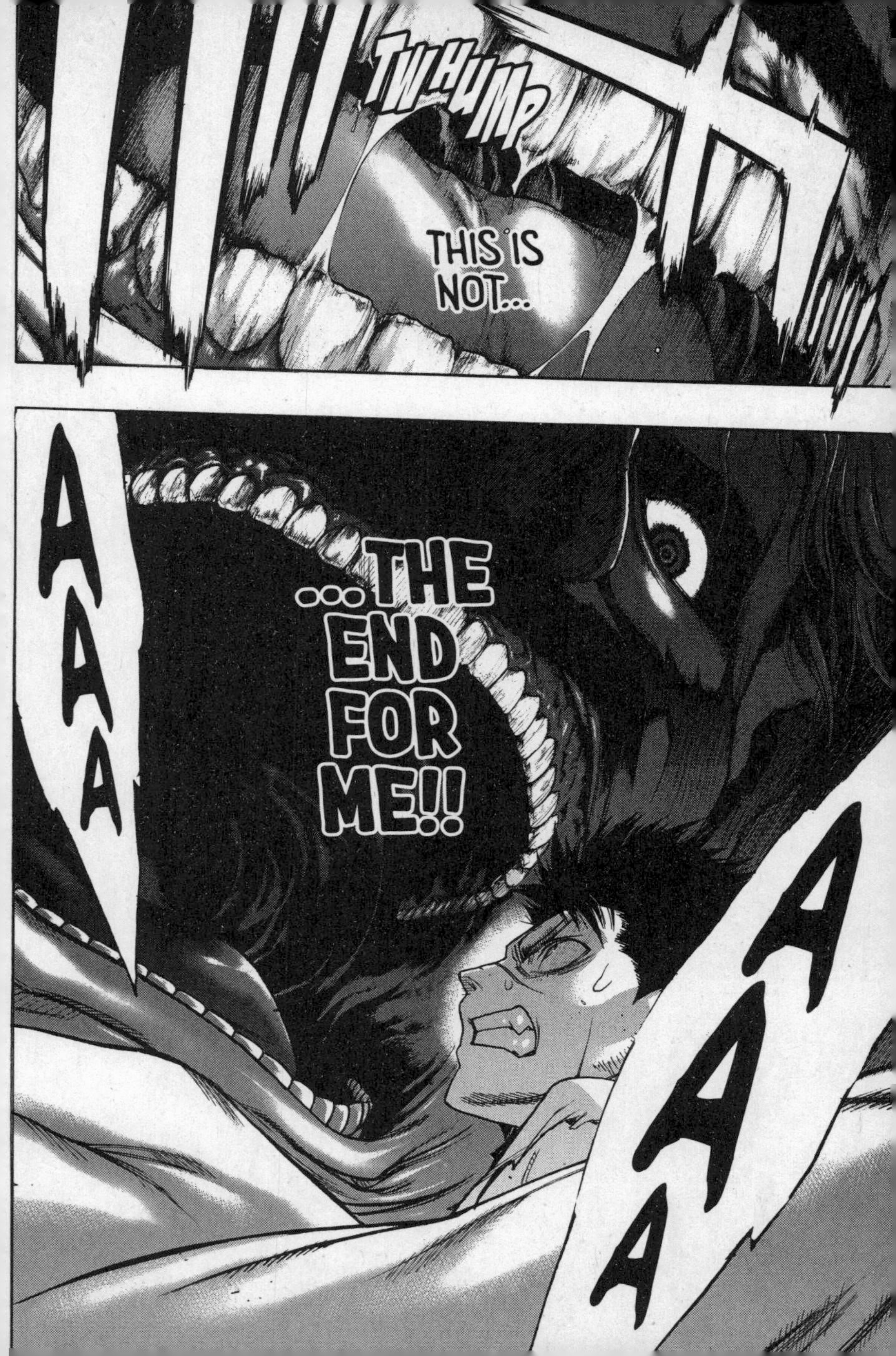
TWHUMP
THIS IS NOT...
AAAA
...THE END FOR ME!!
AAAA

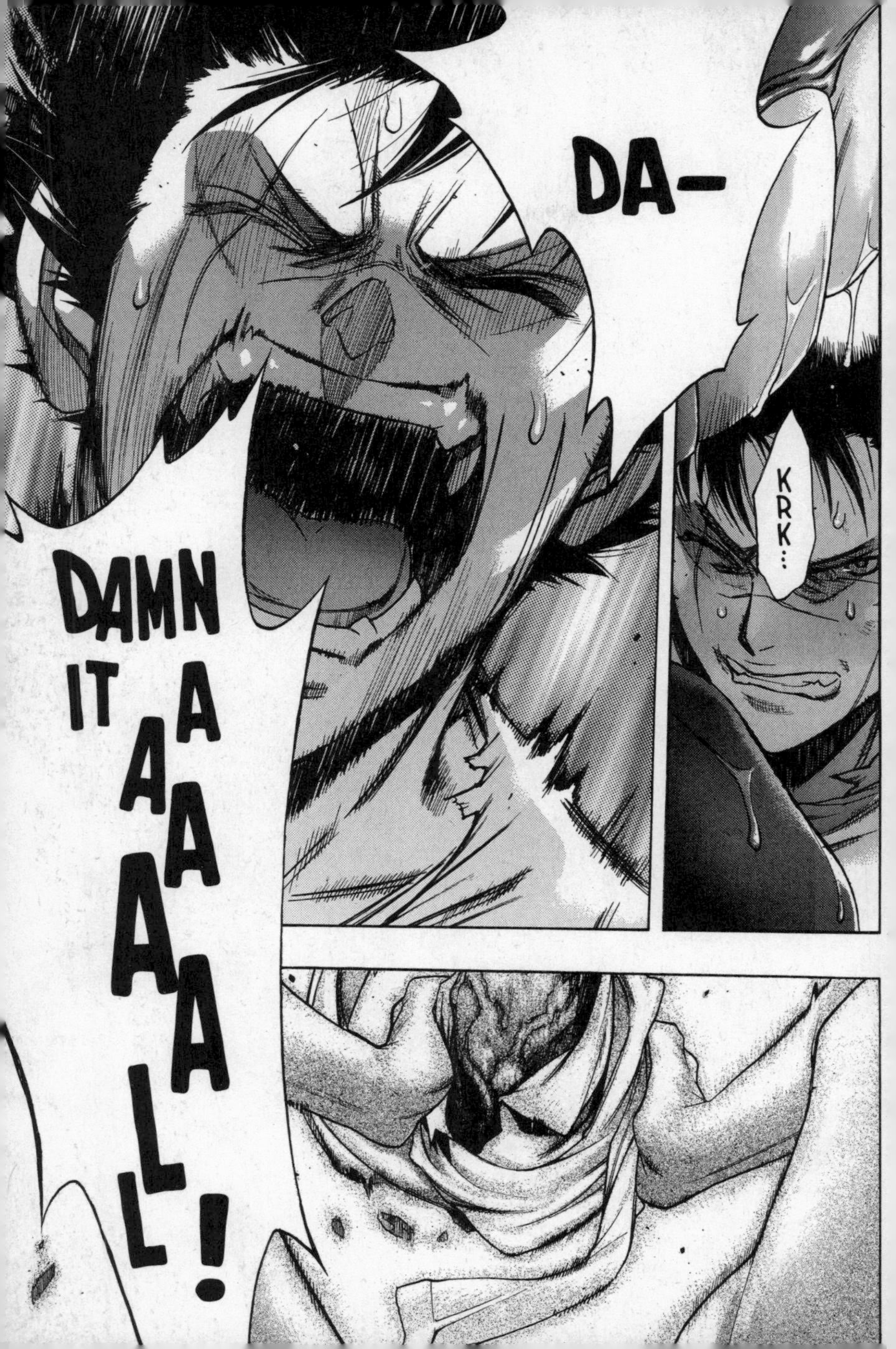
DA-
KRK...
DAMN IT AAAAALL!

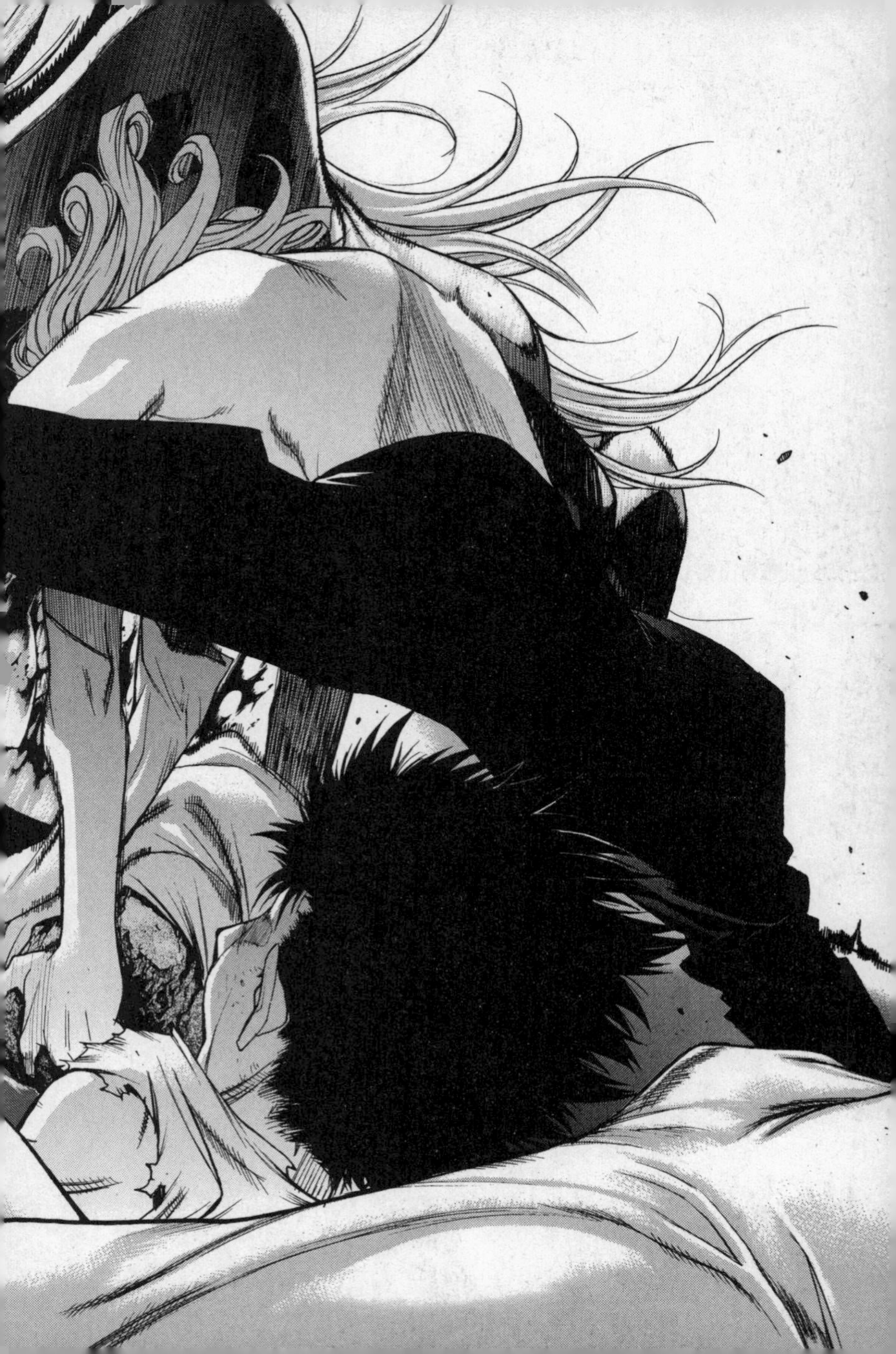

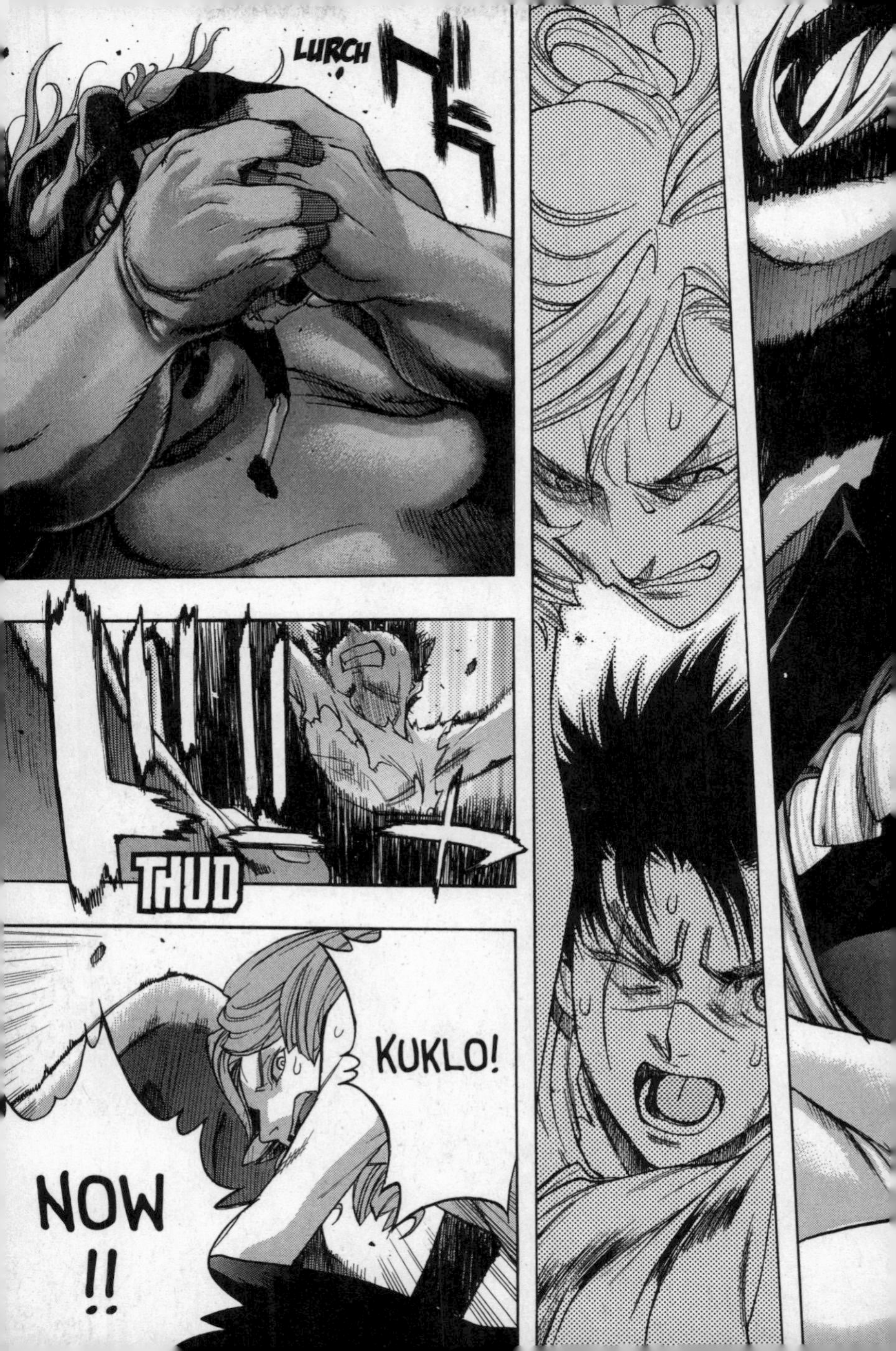
LURCH
THUD
KUKLO!
NOW !!

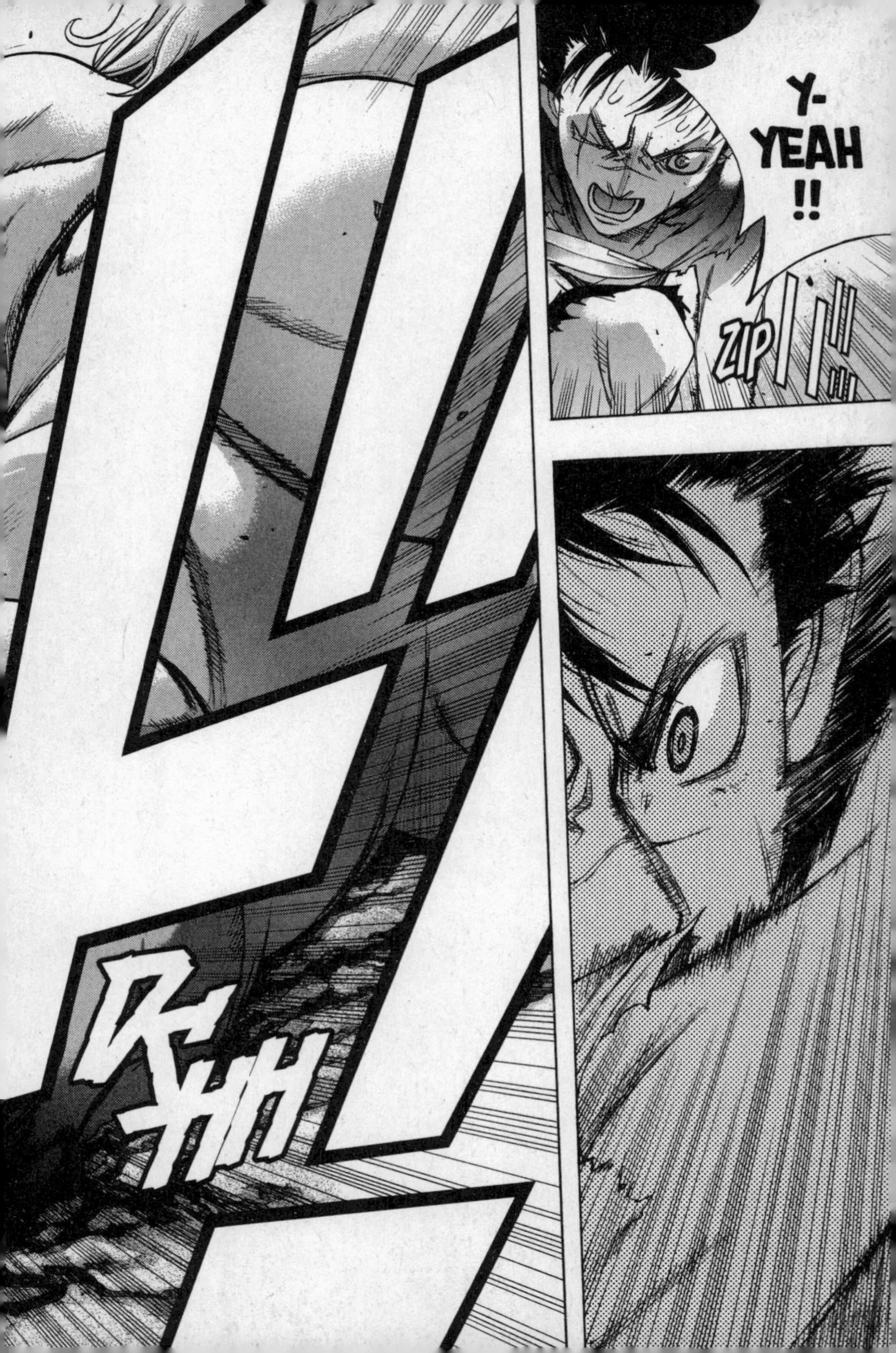
Y-YEAH!!
ZIP

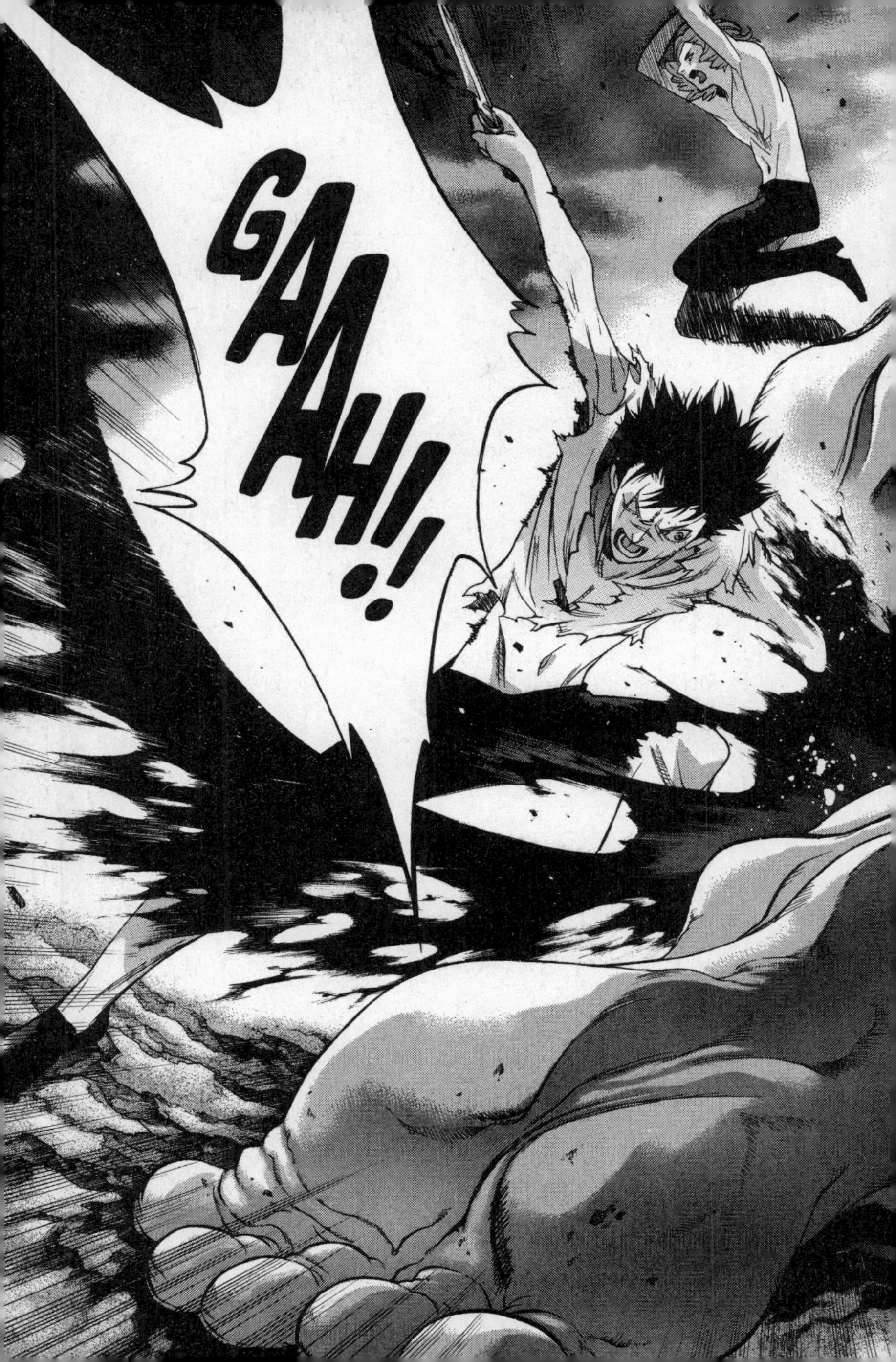
GAAH!!

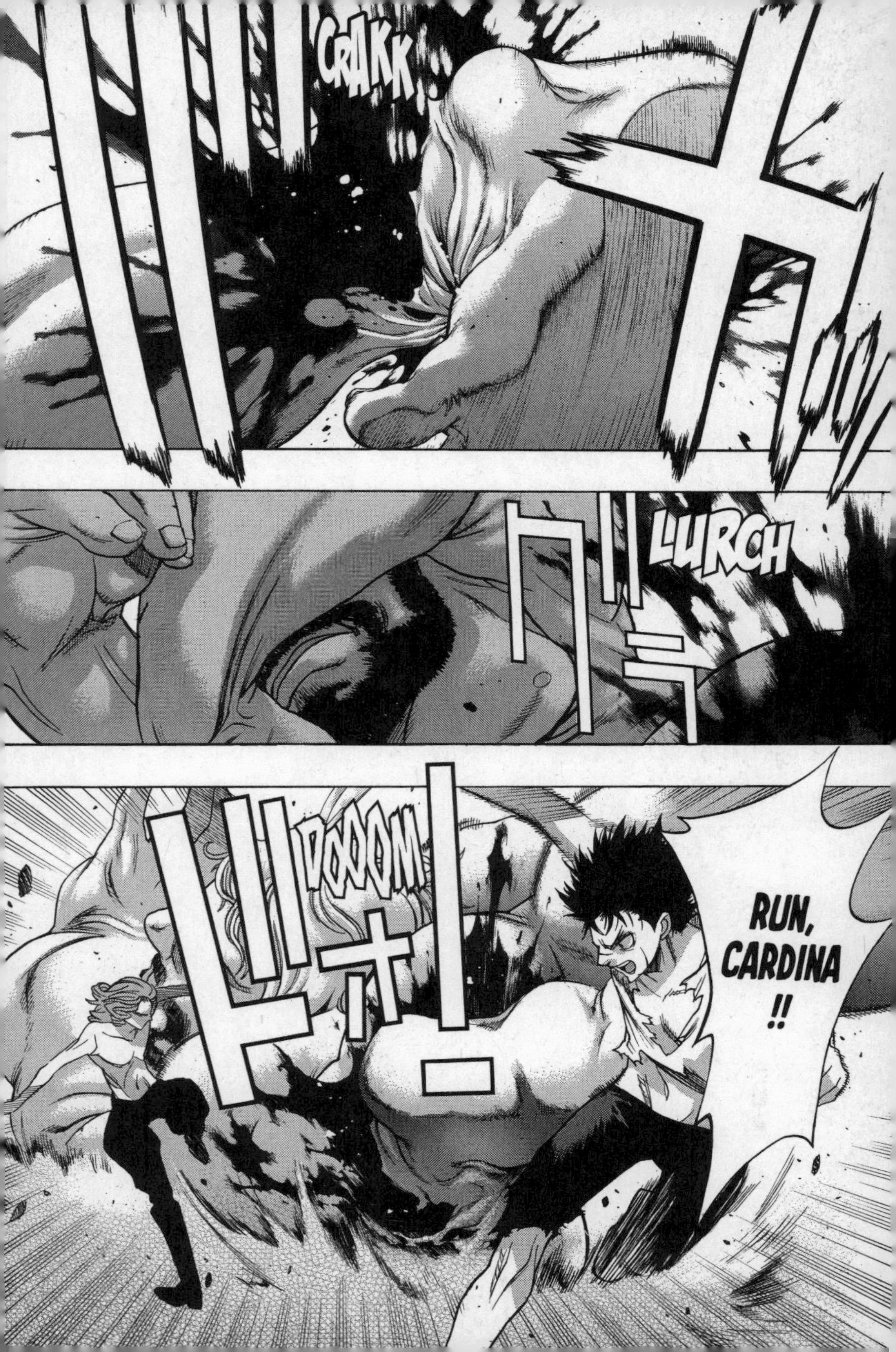

CRAKK
LURCH
RUN, CARDINA !!
DOOOM

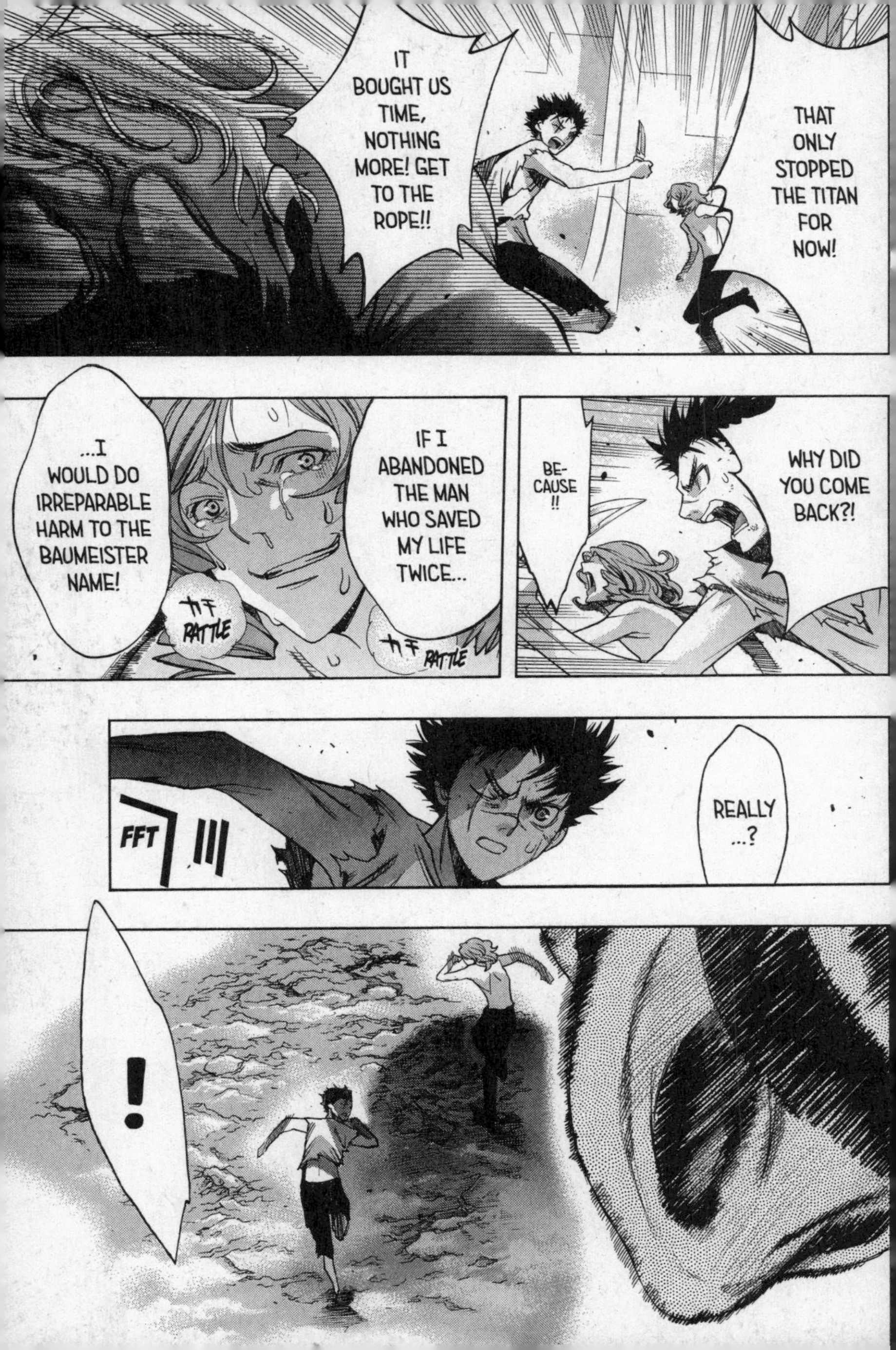
THAT ONLY STOPPED THE TITAN FOR NOW!
IT BOUGHT US TIME, NOTHING MORE! GET TO THE ROPE!!
WHY DID YOU COME BACK?!
BE-CAUSE !!
IF I ABANDONED THE MAN WHO SAVED MY LIFE TWICE...
カチ RATTLE
...I WOULD DO IRREPARABLE HARM TO THE BAUMEISTER NAME!
カチ RATTLE
REALLY ...?
FFT
!

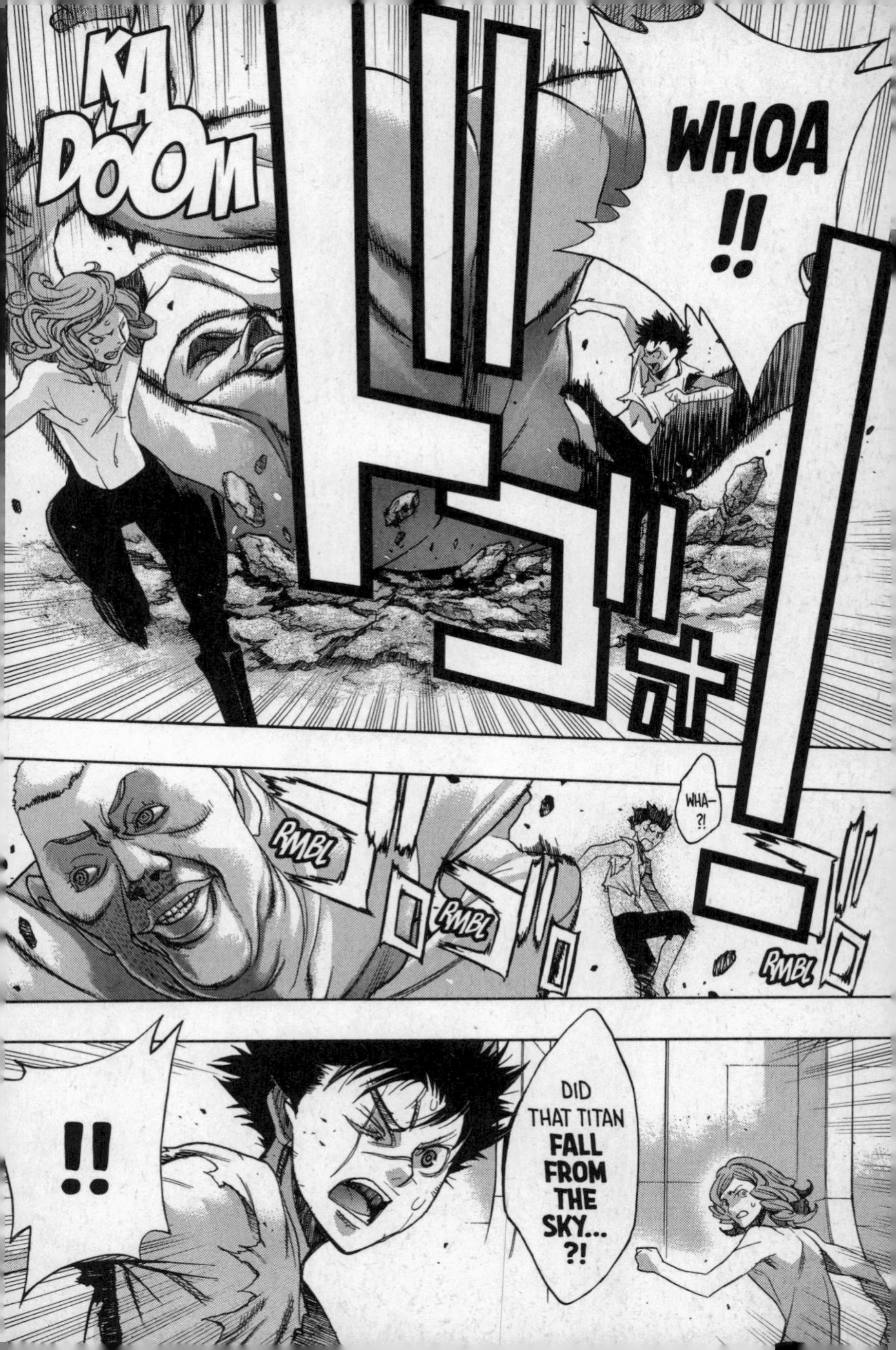
WHOA !!
KA DOOM
WHA— ?!
RMBL
RMBL
RMBL
DID THAT TITAN FALL FROM THE SKY... ?!
!!

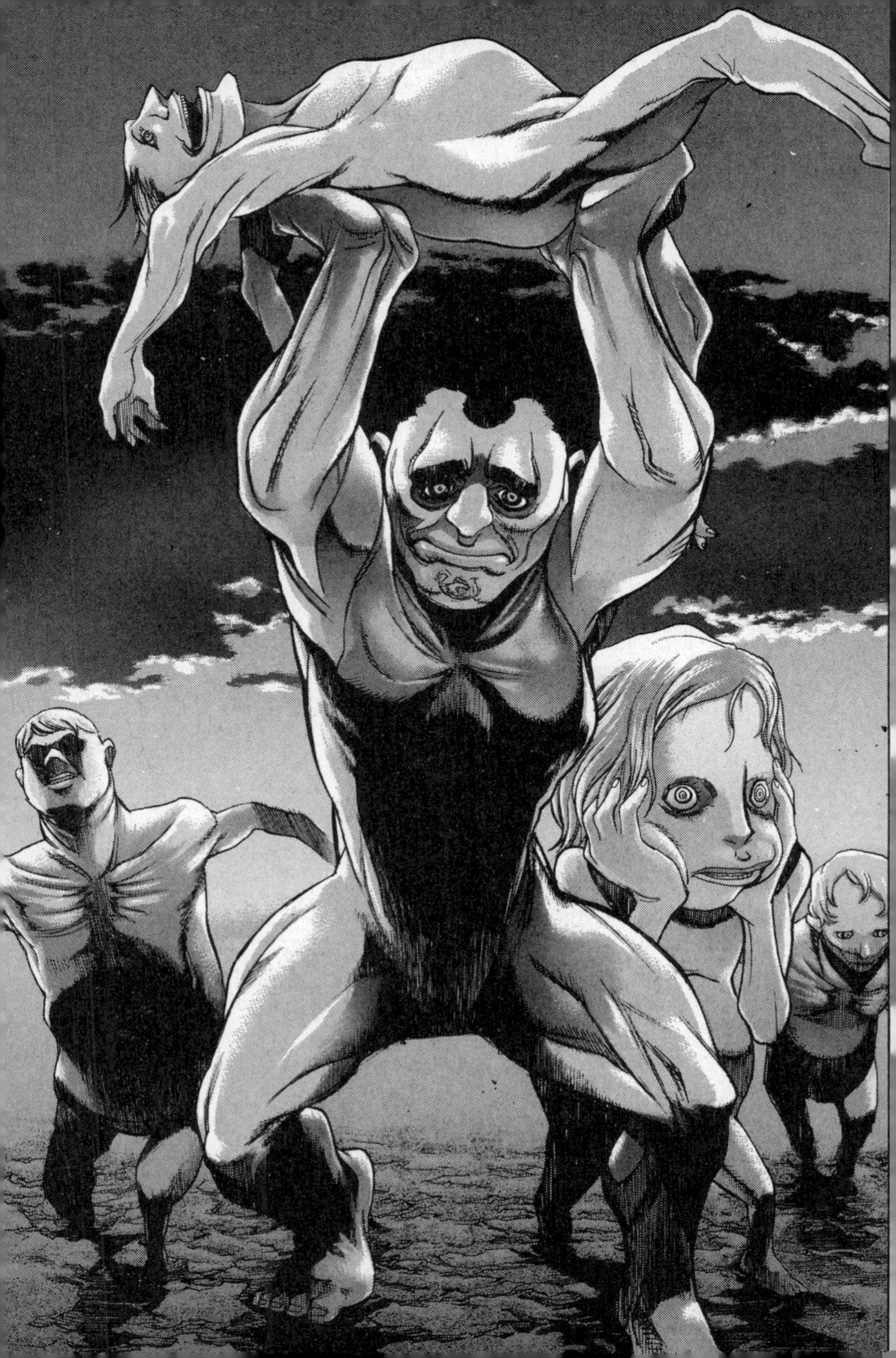

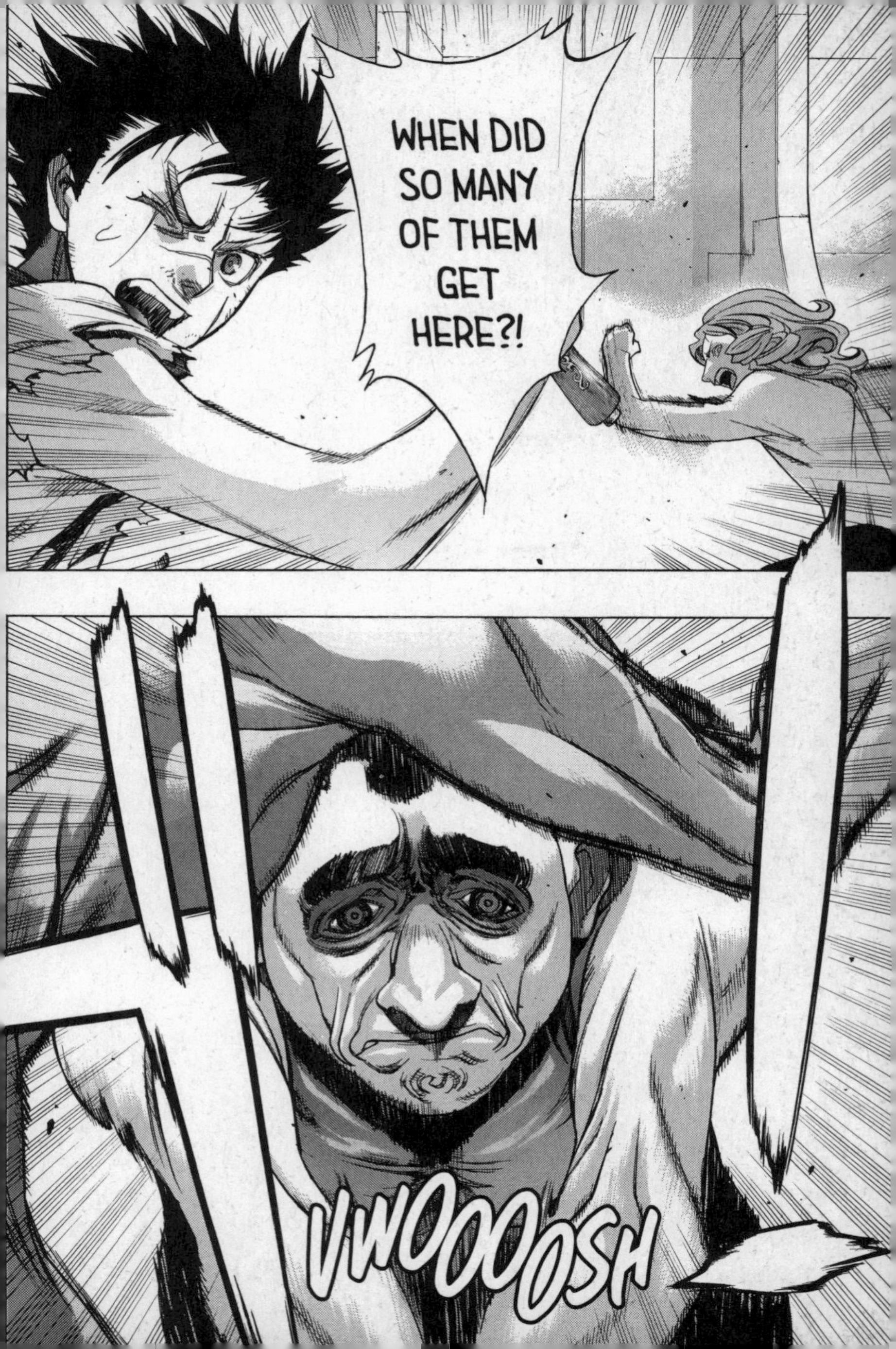
WHEN DID SO MANY OF THEM GET HERE?!
VWOOOOSH

Chapter 12: The Killing Fields END

ATTACK
on TITAN
BEFORE THE FALL

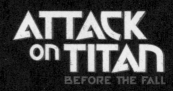

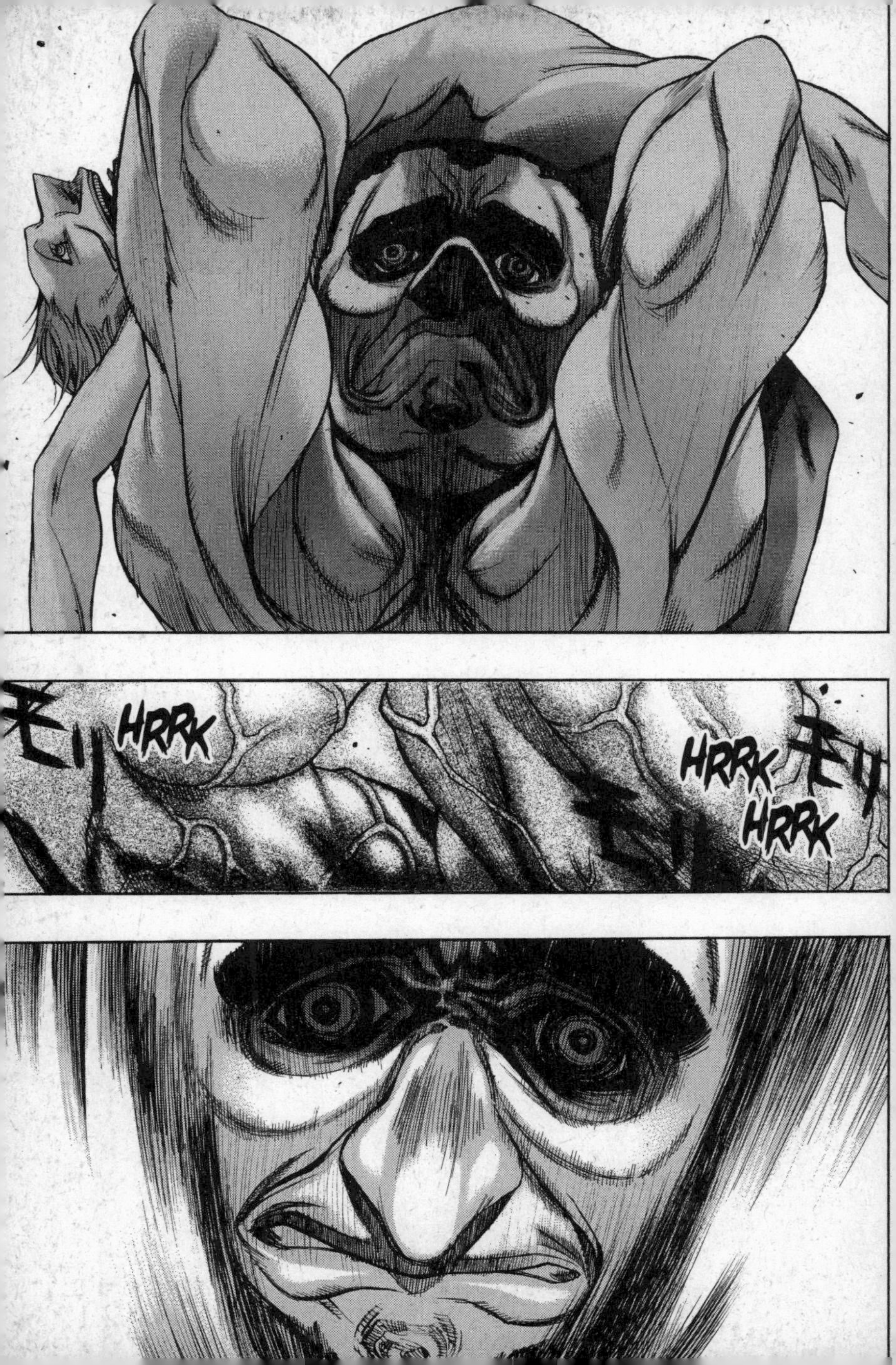
HRRK
HRRK
HRRK

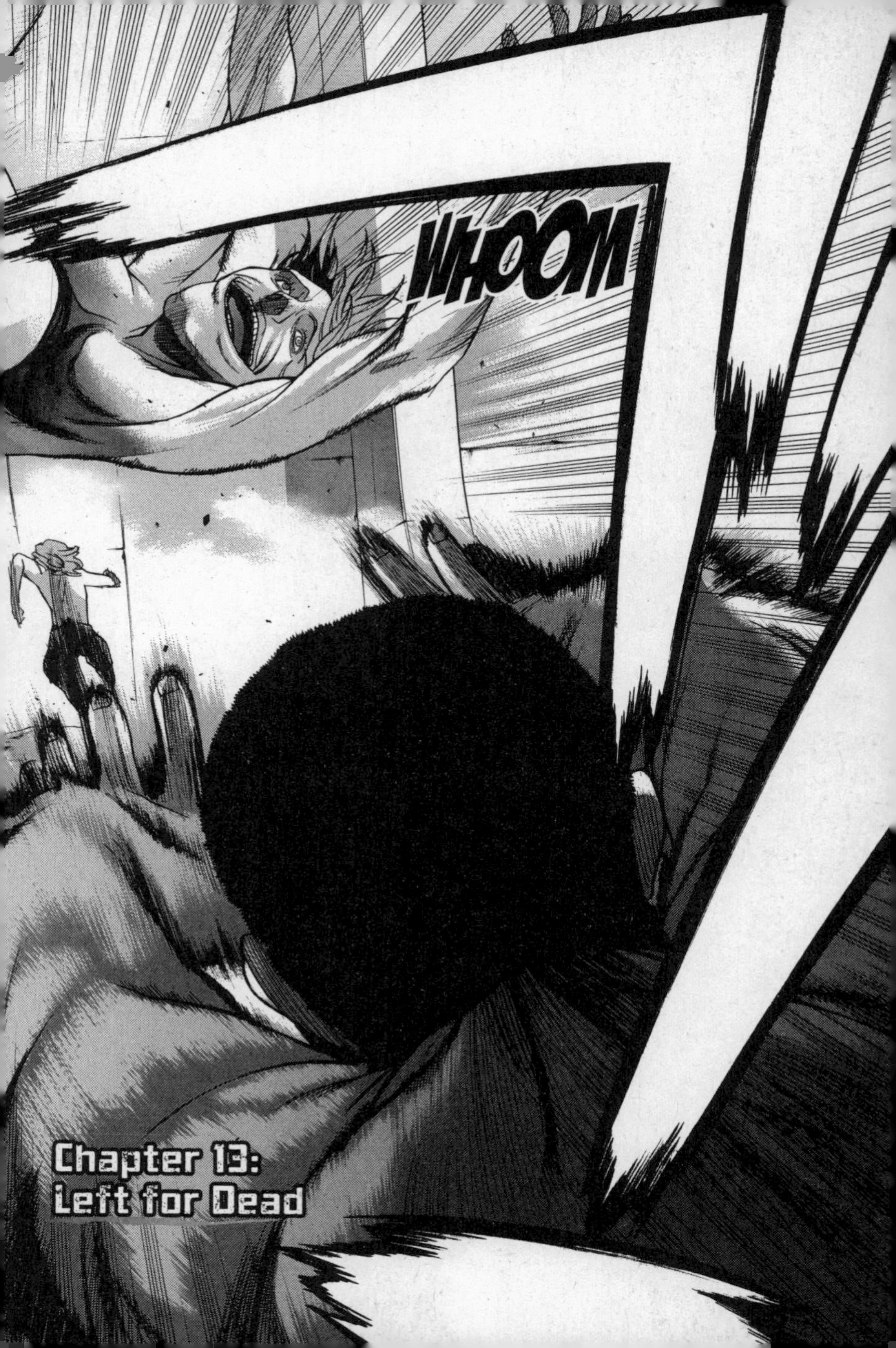
WHOOM
Chapter 13:
Left for Dead

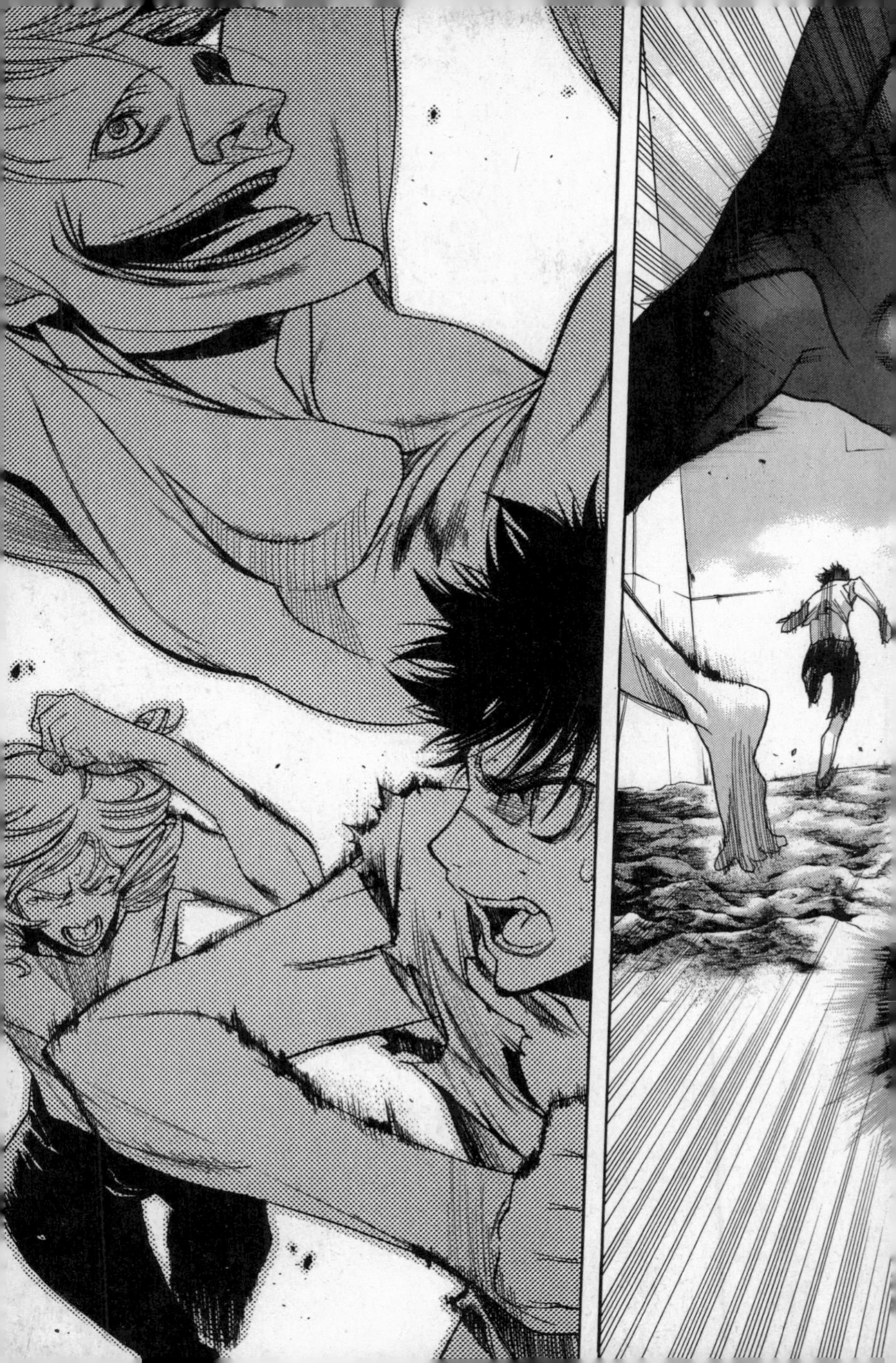

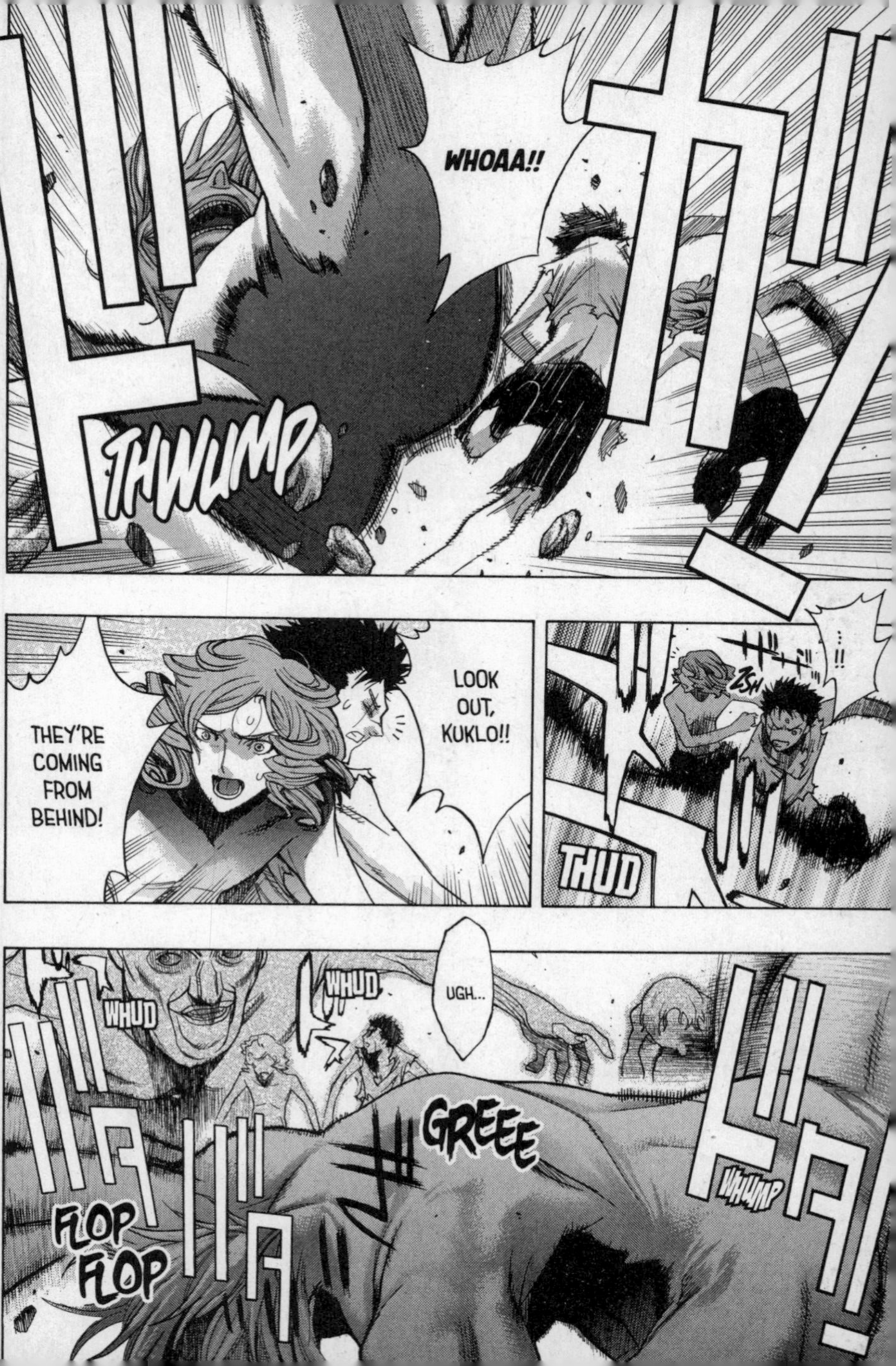
WHOAA!!
THWUMP
...!!
ZSH
THUD
LOOK OUT, KUKLO!!
THEY'RE COMING FROM BEHIND!
UGH...
WHUMP
WHUD
GREEE
WHUD
FLOP FLOP

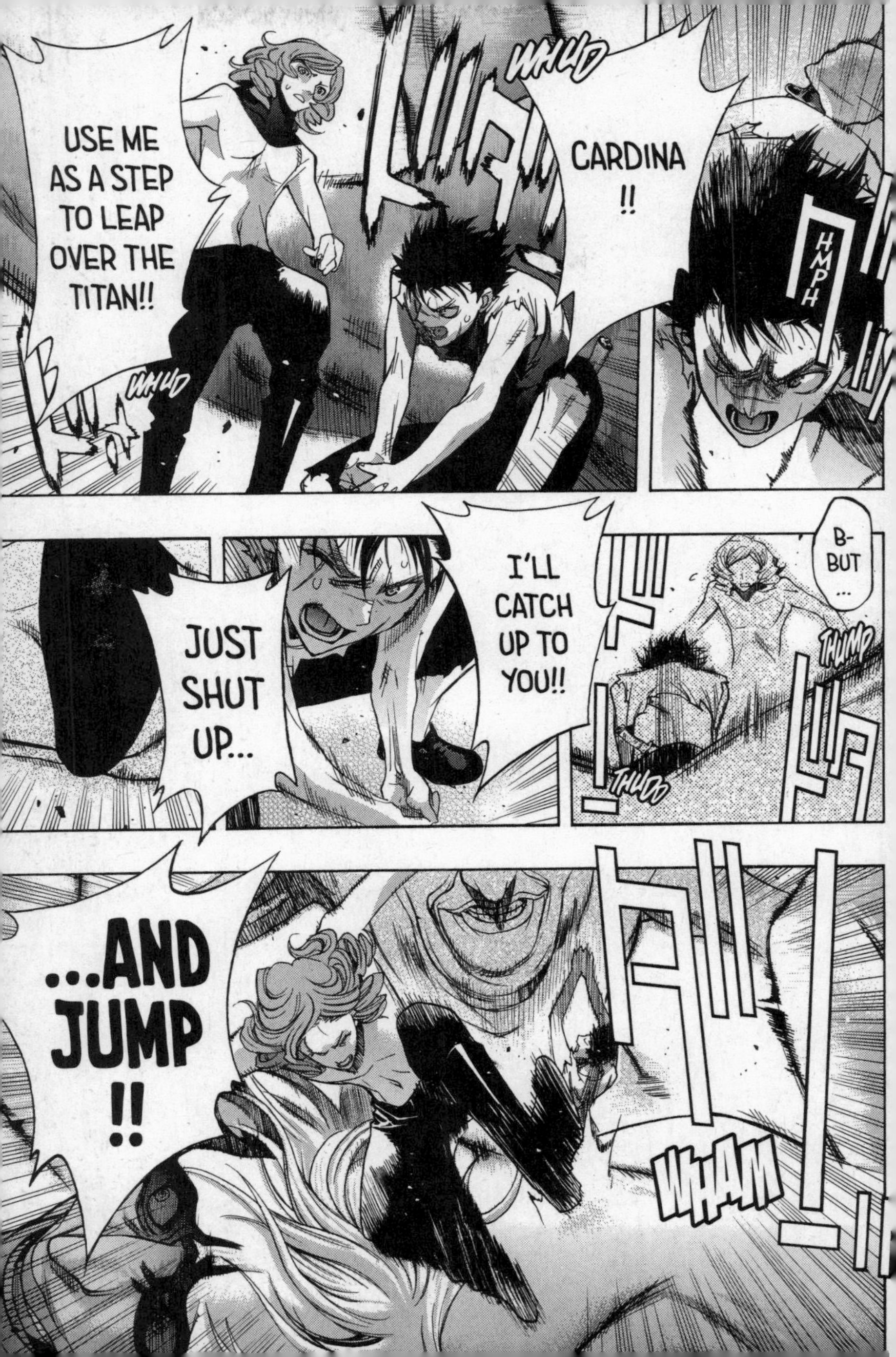
HMPH
WHUD
CARDINA!!
USE ME AS A STEP TO LEAP OVER THE TITAN!!
WHUD
B-BUT...
THUMP
THUD
I'LL CATCH UP TO YOU!!
JUST SHUT UP...
WHAM
...AND JUMP!!

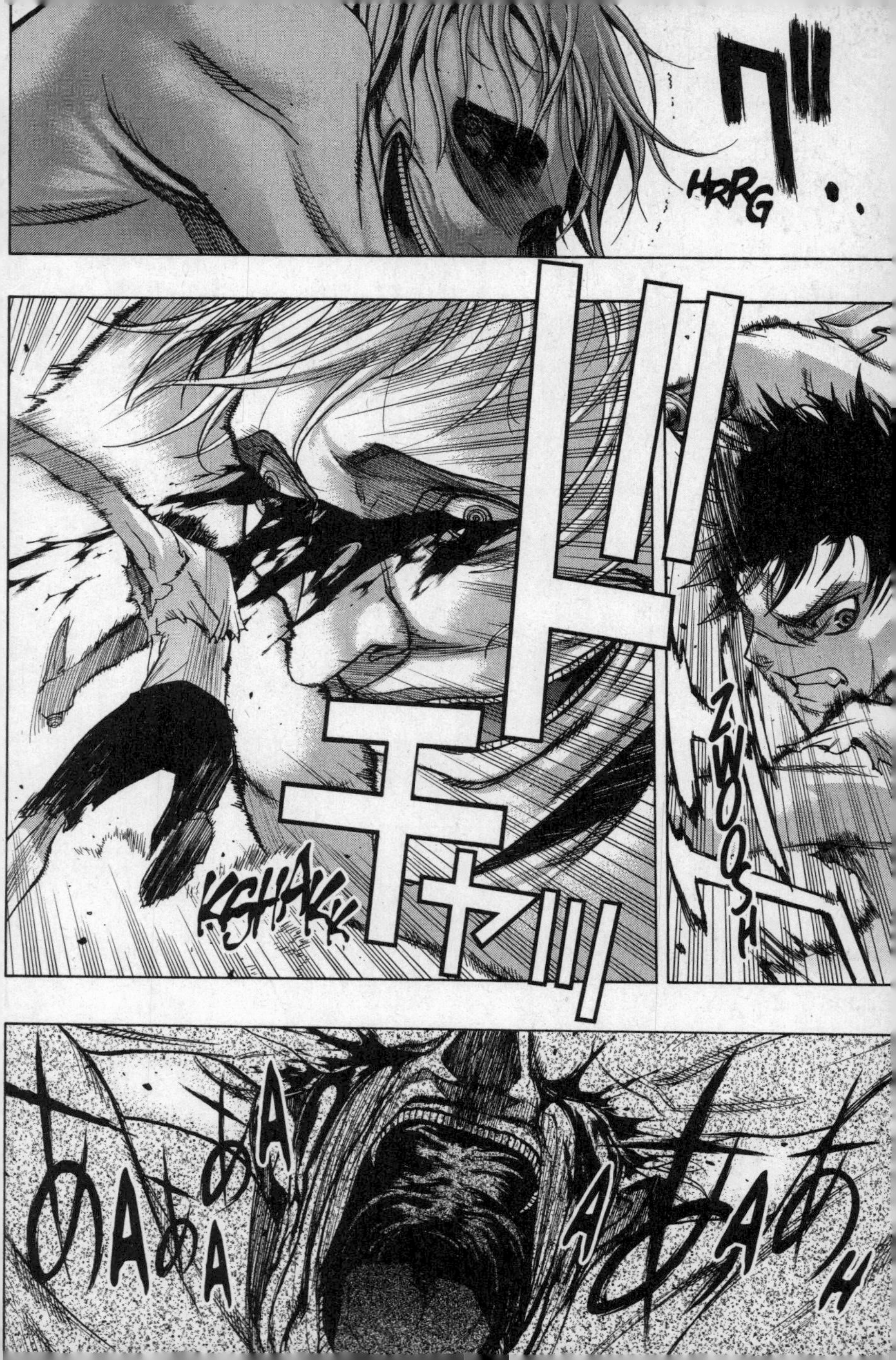
HRRG
ZWOOSH
KSHAAK!!
AAAAAAH

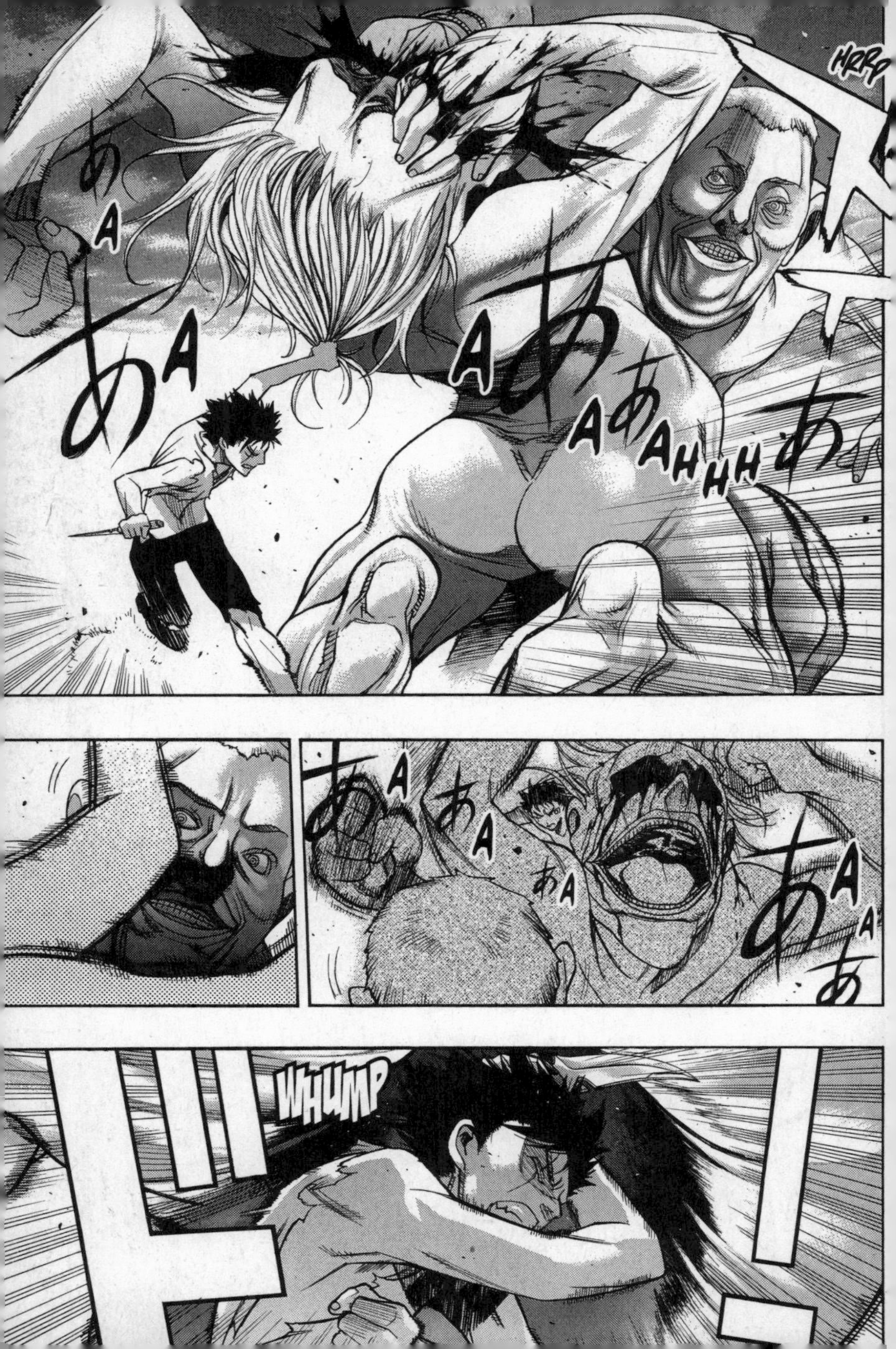
HRRG
あA
あA
あA
Aあ
あA
AHHHH
あ
あA
あA
あA
あA
A
あ
WHUMP

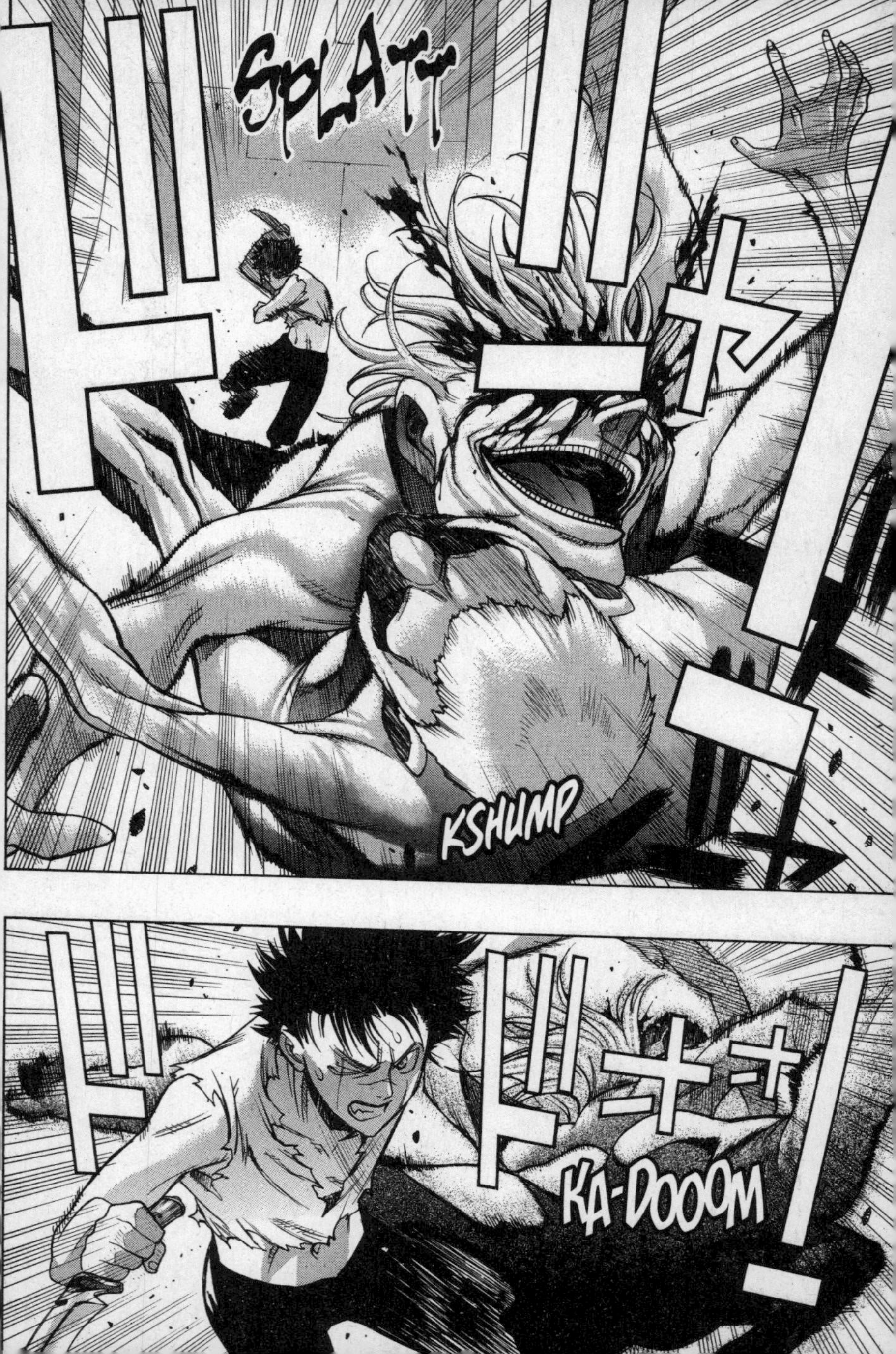
SPLATT
KSHUMP
KA-DOOOM

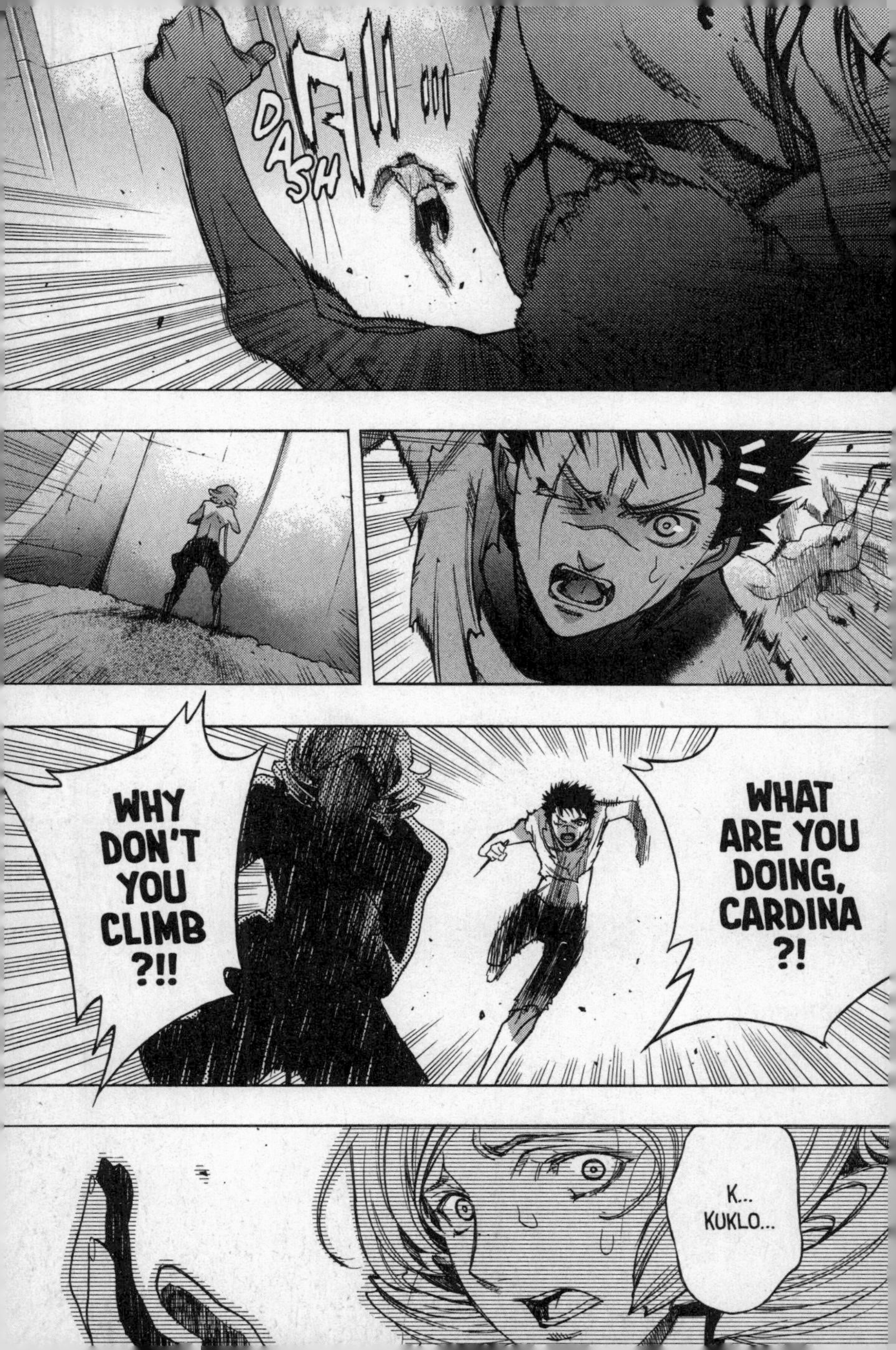
DASH
WHAT ARE YOU DOING, CARDINA ?!
WHY DON'T YOU CLIMB ?!!
K... KUKLO...

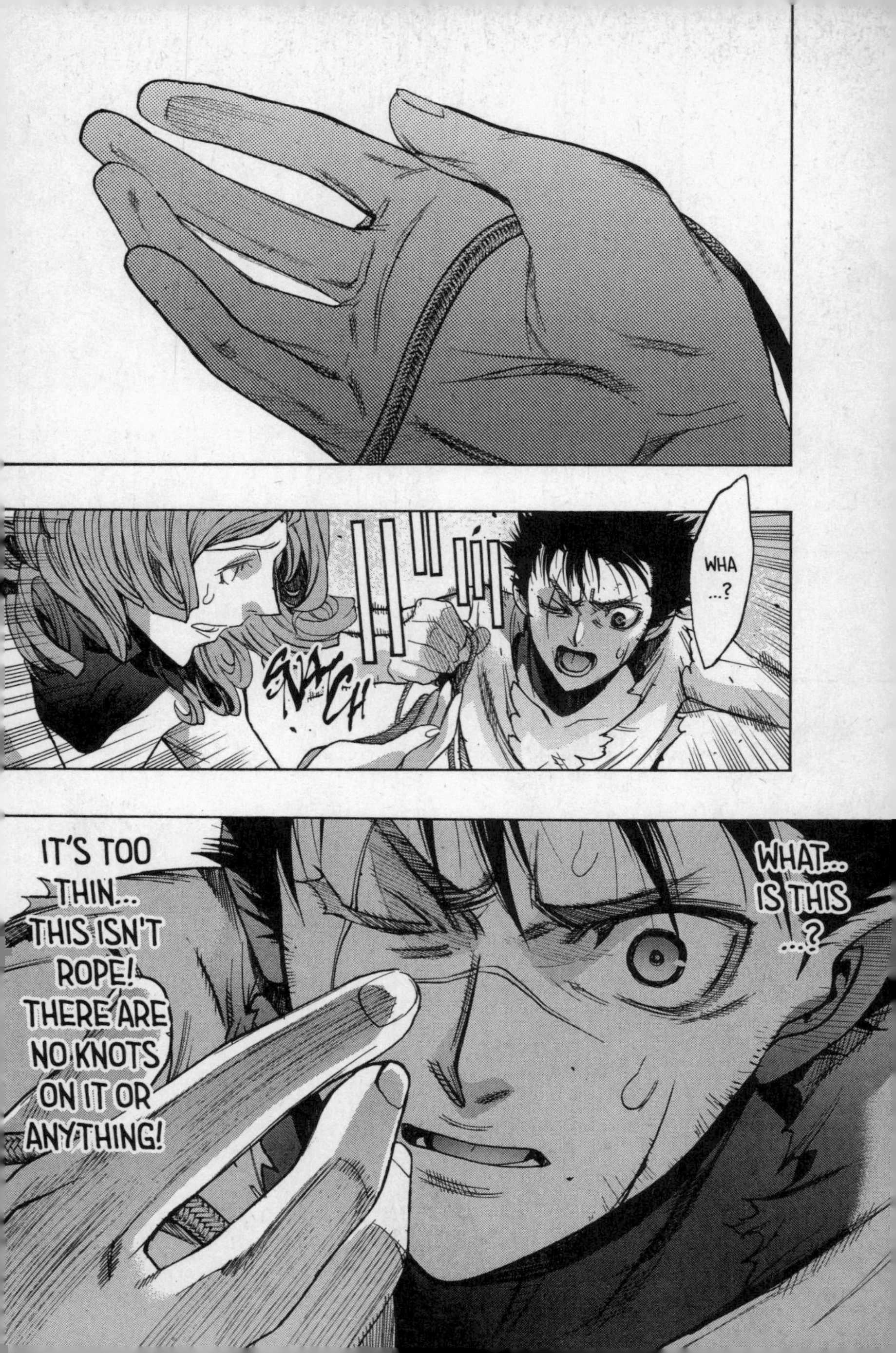
WHA ...?
WHAT... IS THIS ...?
IT'S TOO THIN... THIS ISN'T ROPE! THERE ARE NO KNOTS ON IT OR ANYTHING!

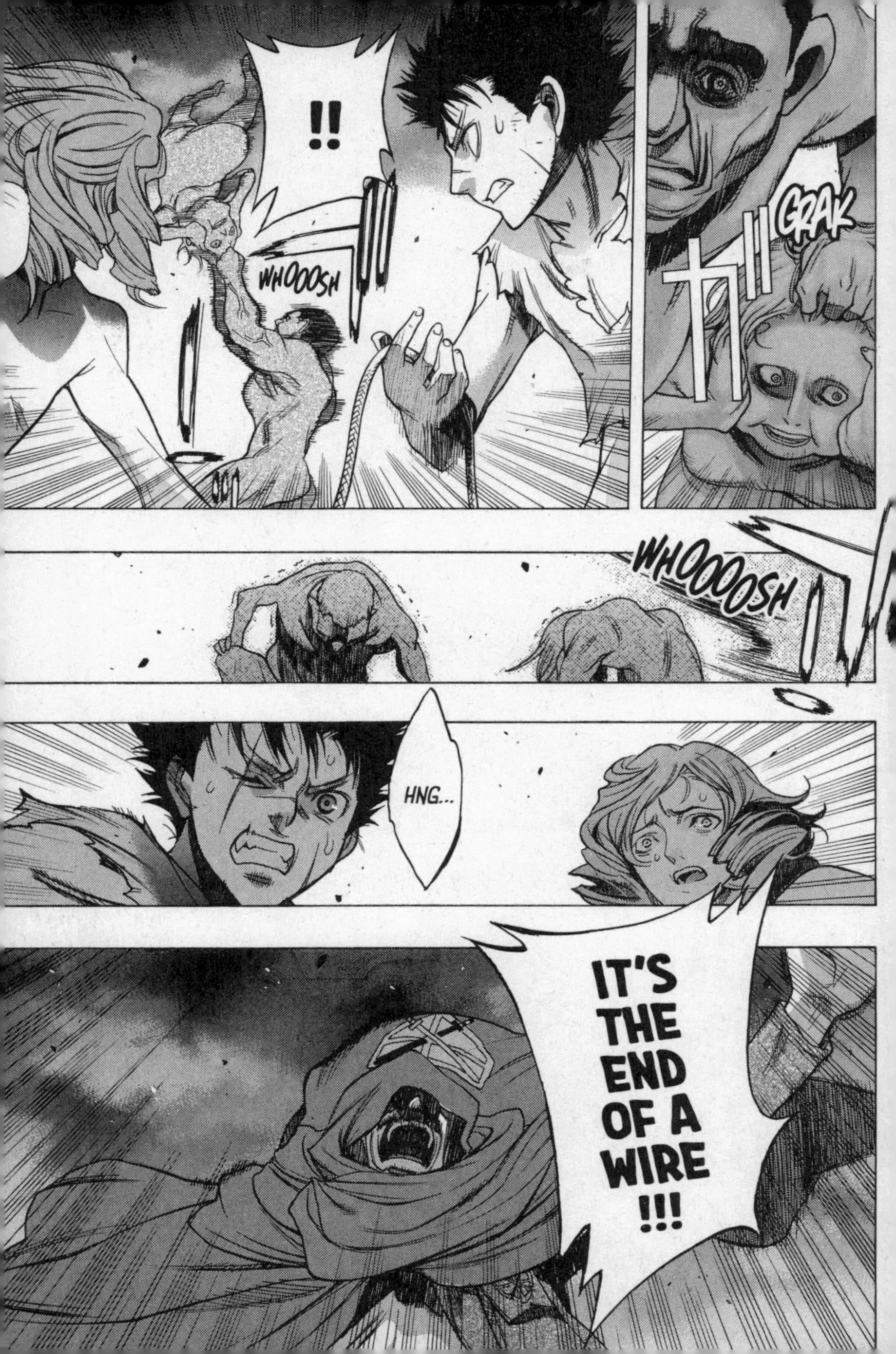
GRAK
!!
WHOOOSH
WHOOOOSH
HNG...
IT'S THE END OF A WIRE!!!

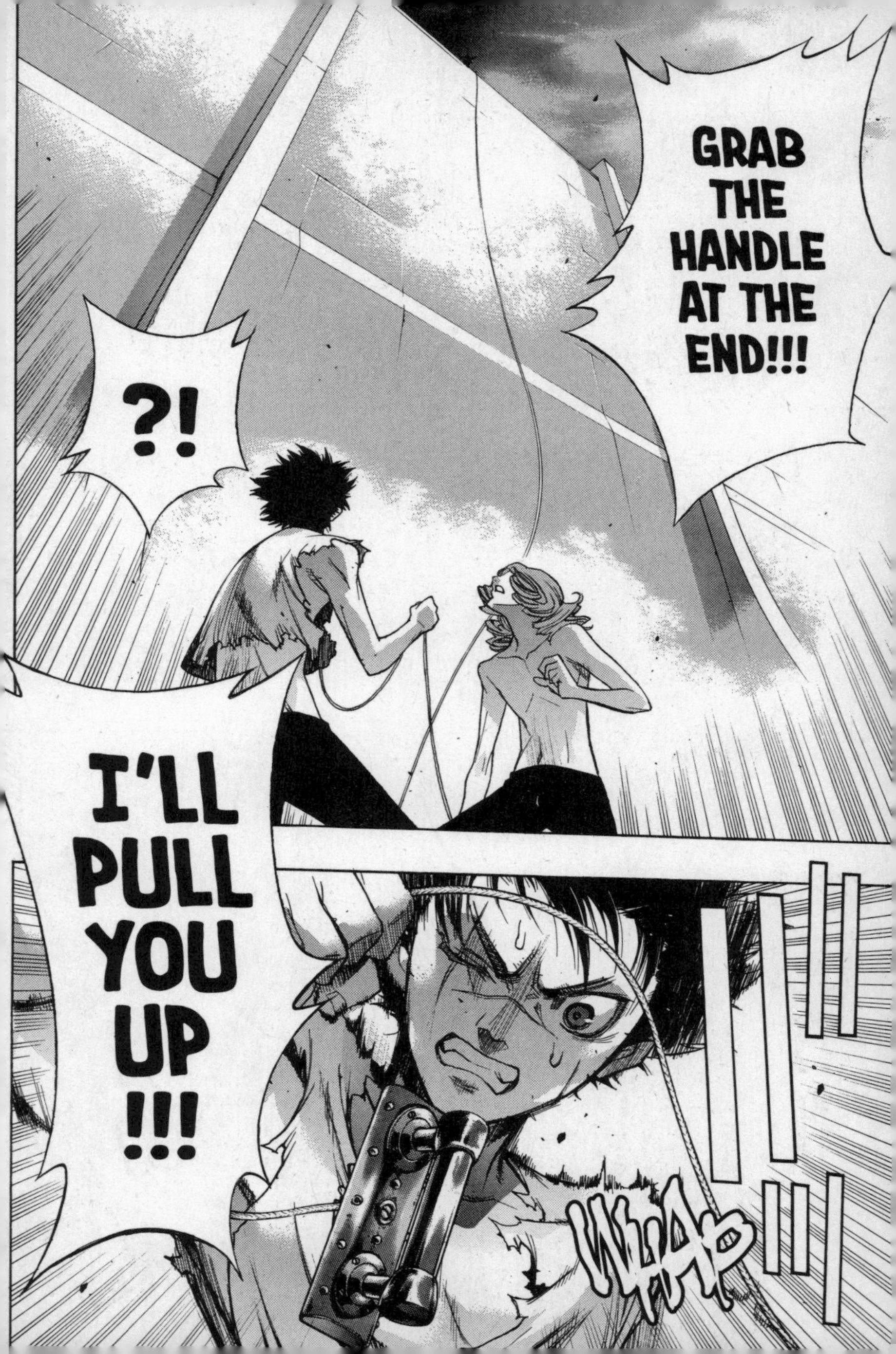
GRAB THE HANDLE AT THE END!!!
?!
I'LL PULL YOU UP!!!
WHAP

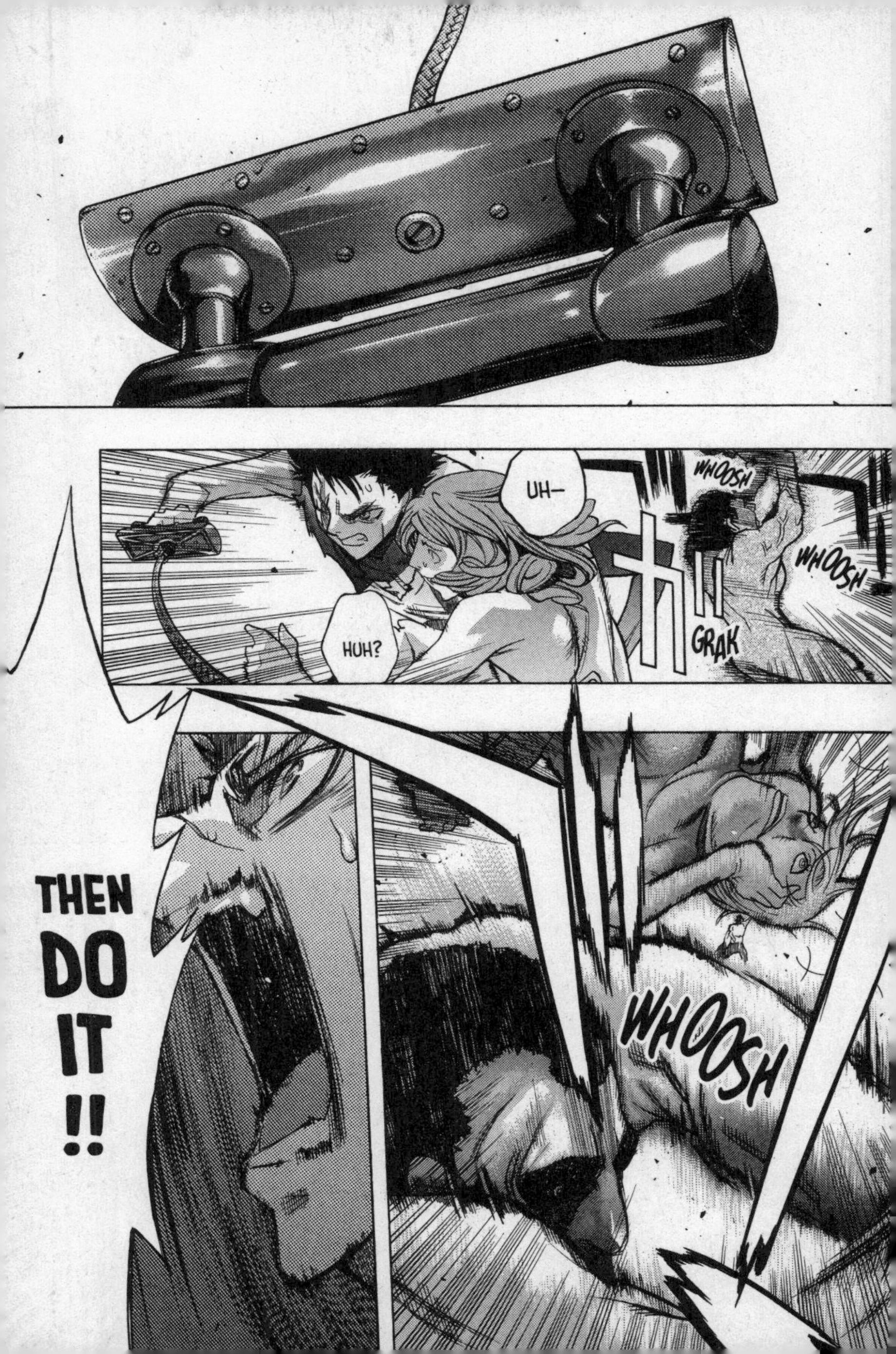
WHOOSH
WHOOSH
GRAK
UH–
HUH?
WHOOSH
THEN DO IT!!

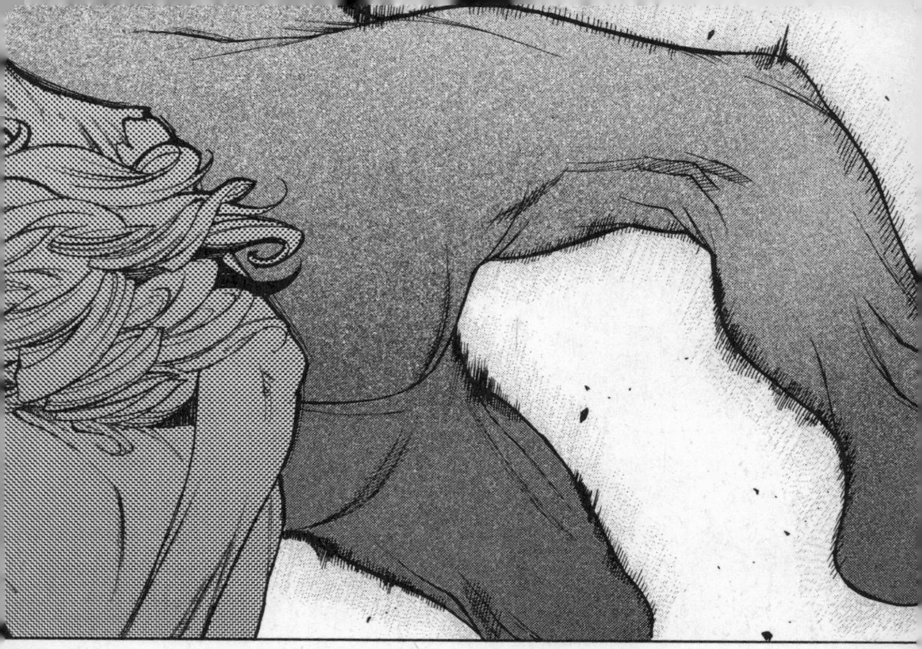
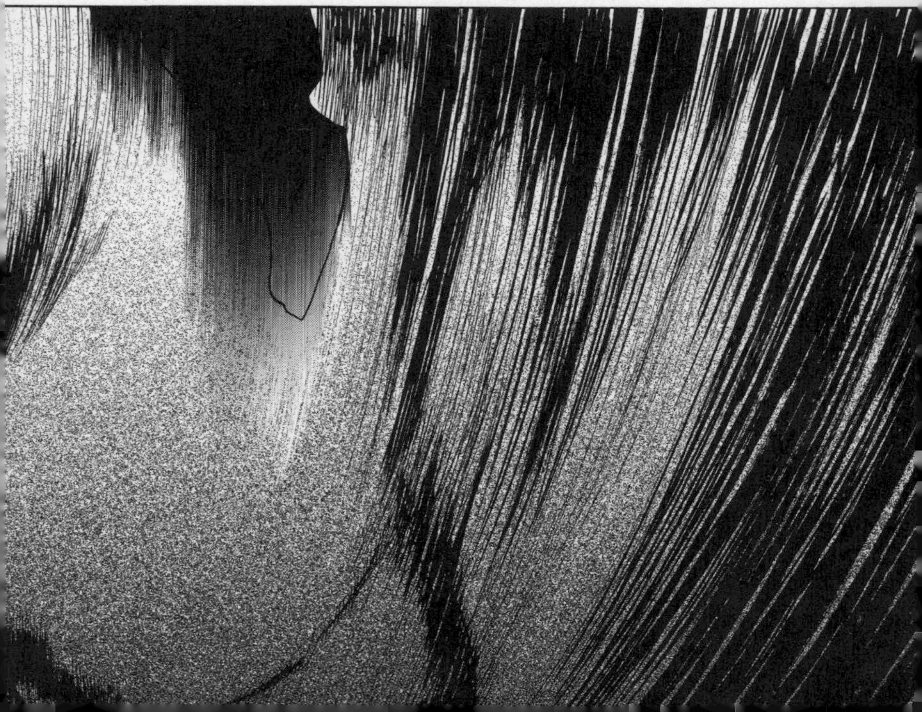

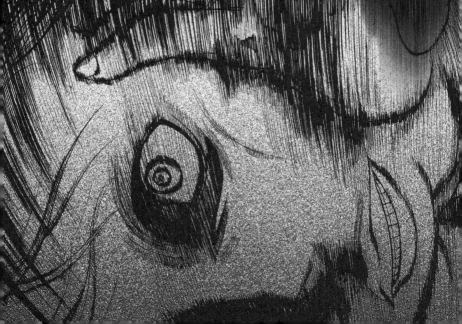

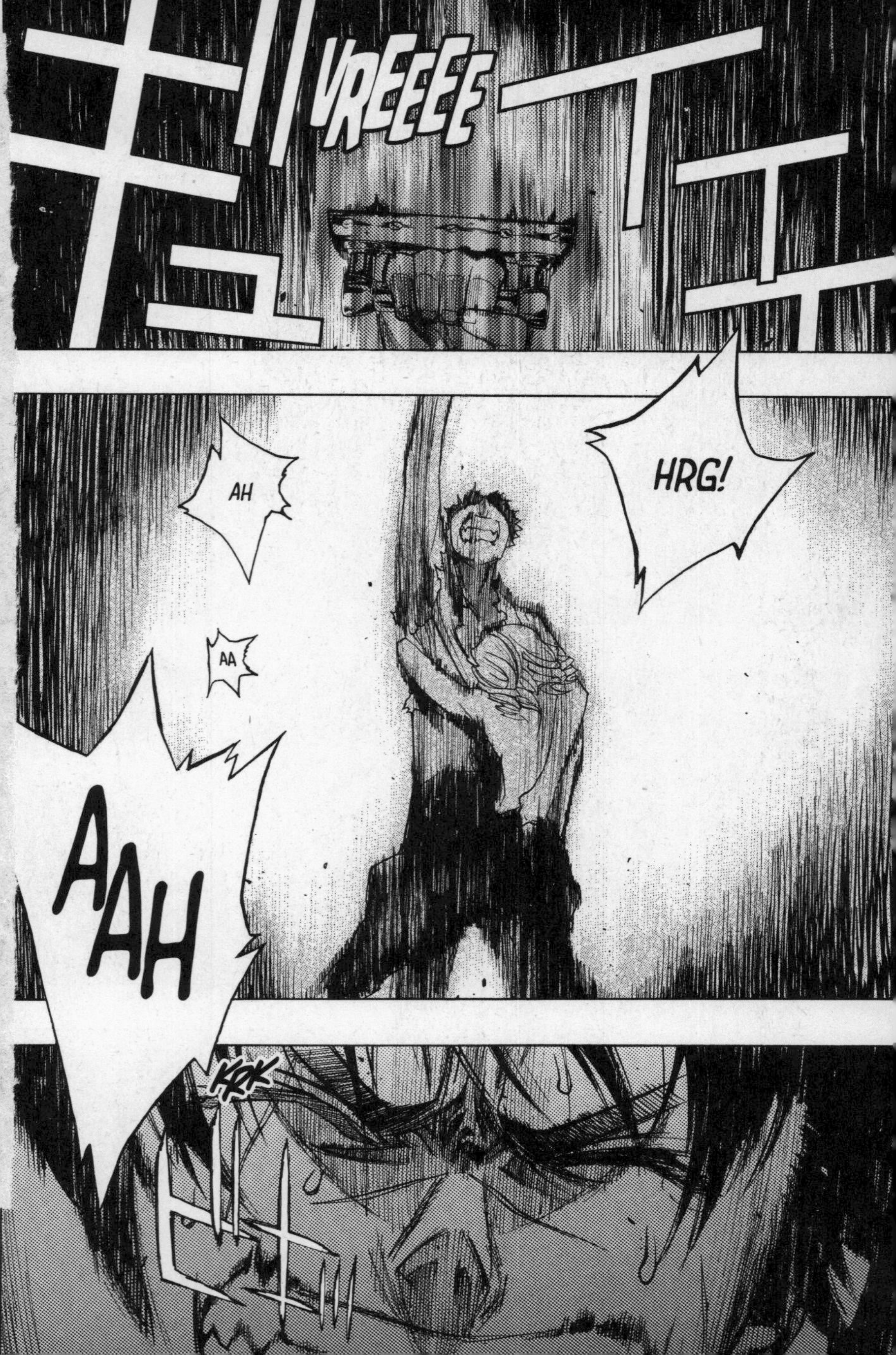
VREEEE
HRG!
AH
AA
AAH
KRK

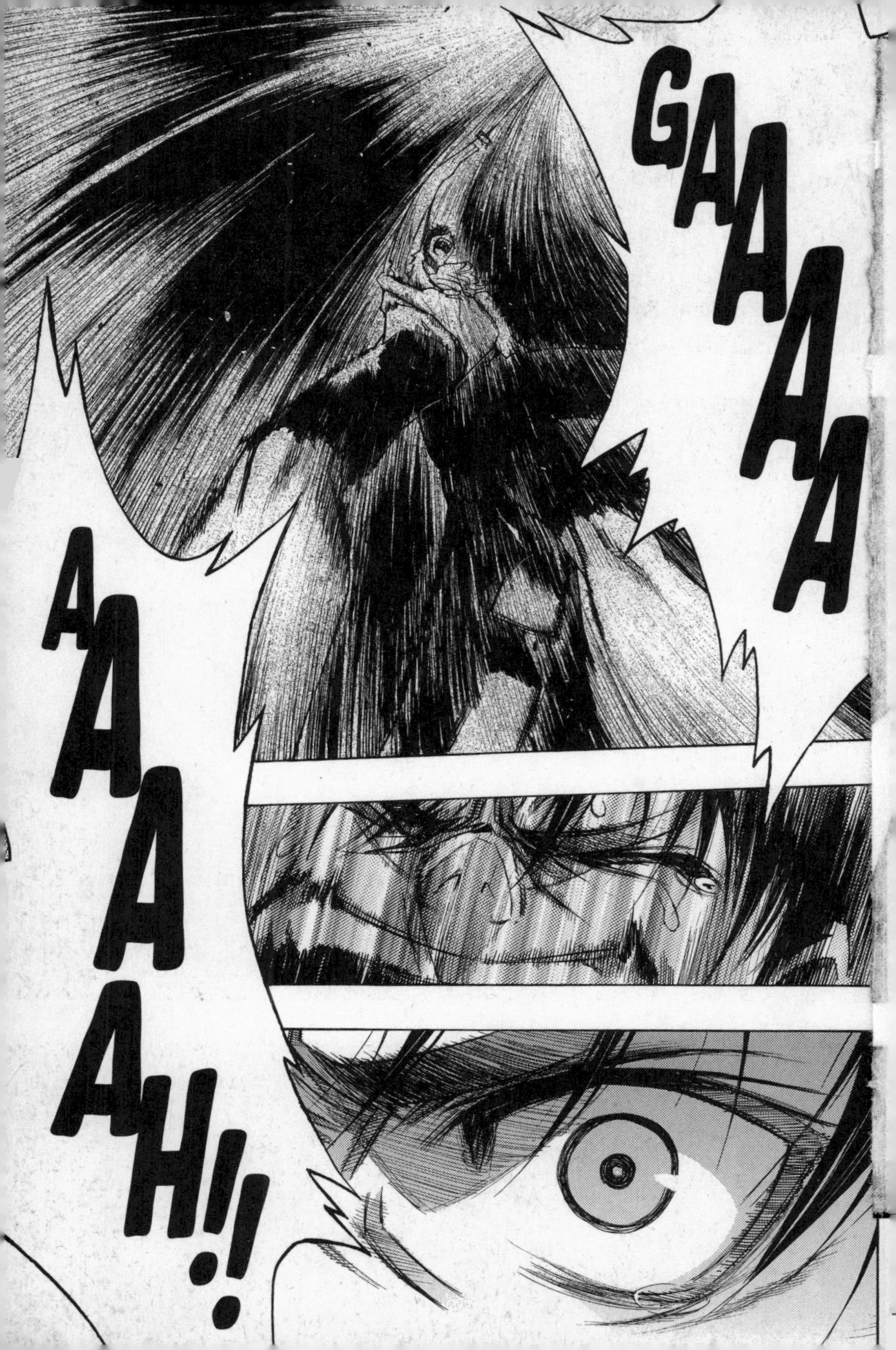
GAAAAAA
AAAAAAH!!

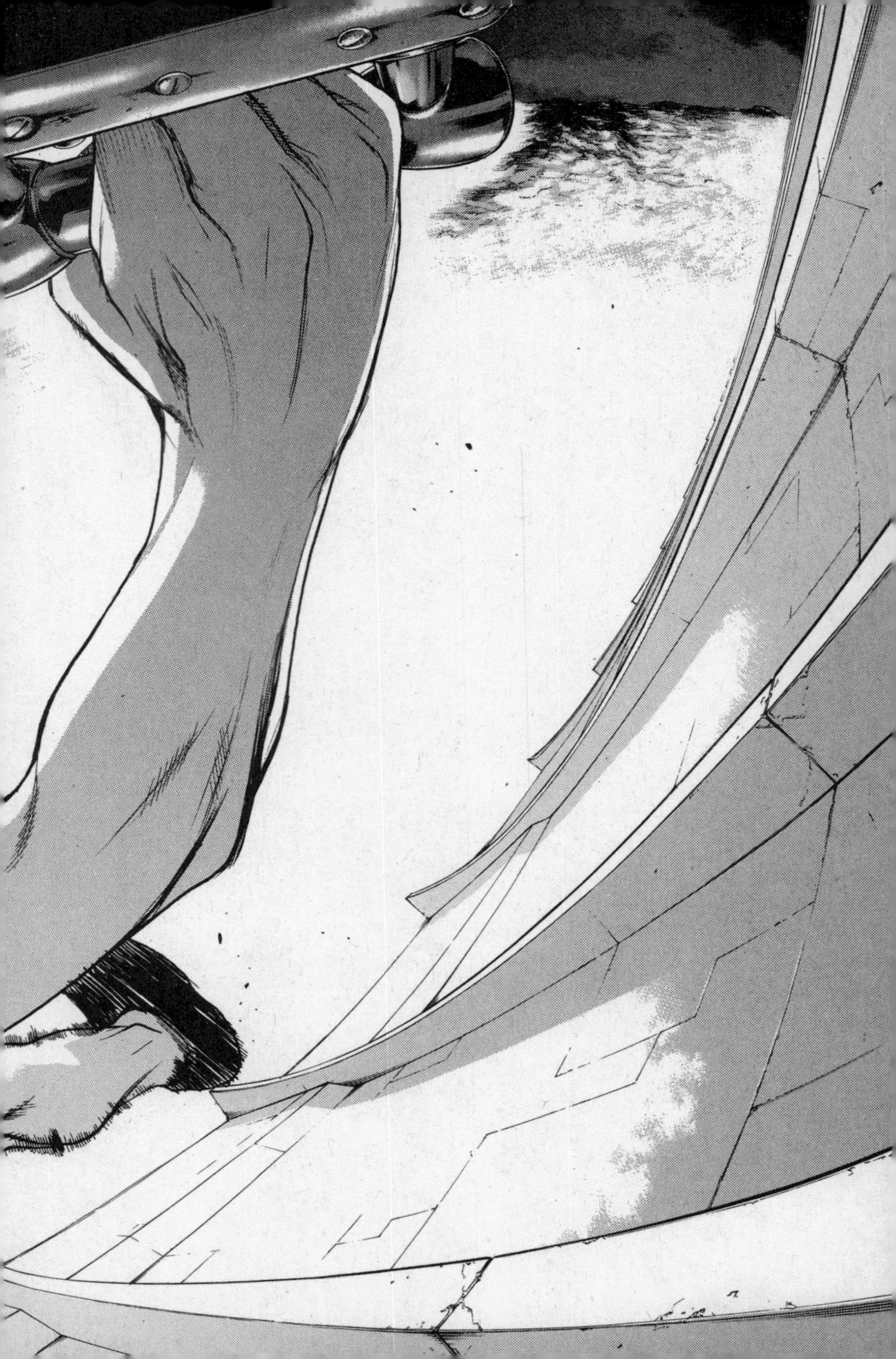

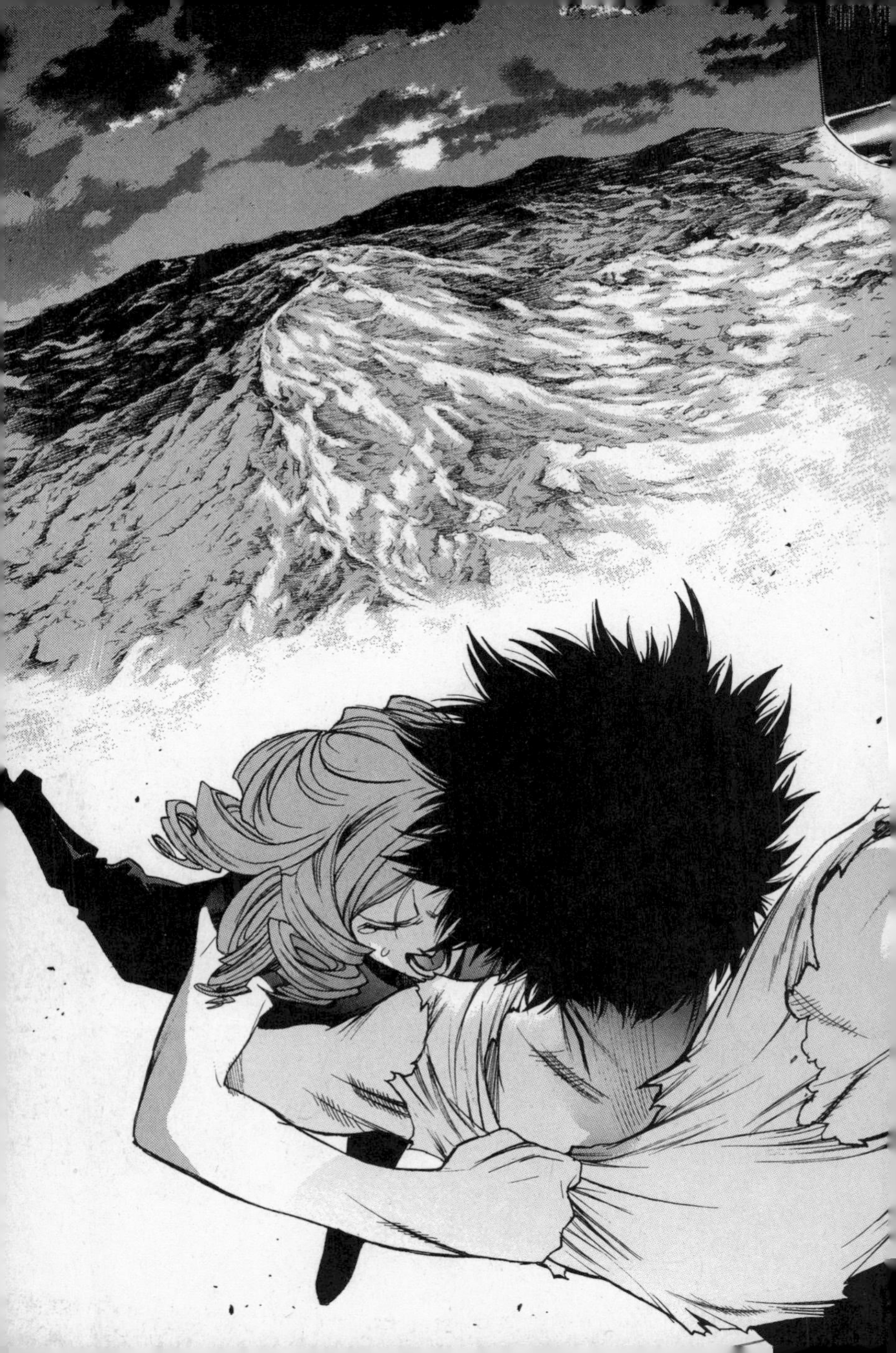

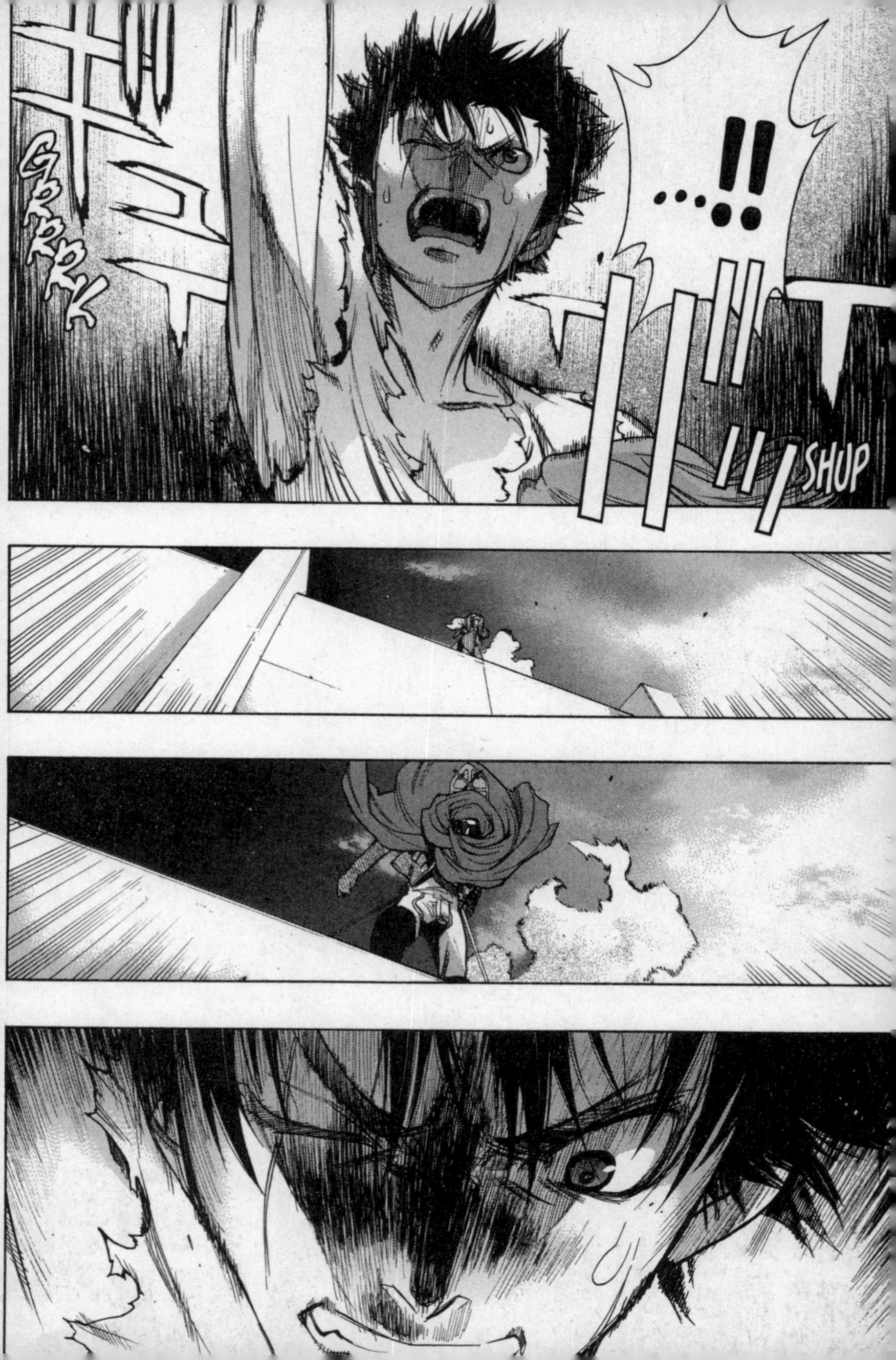

...!!
SHUP
GRRRRK

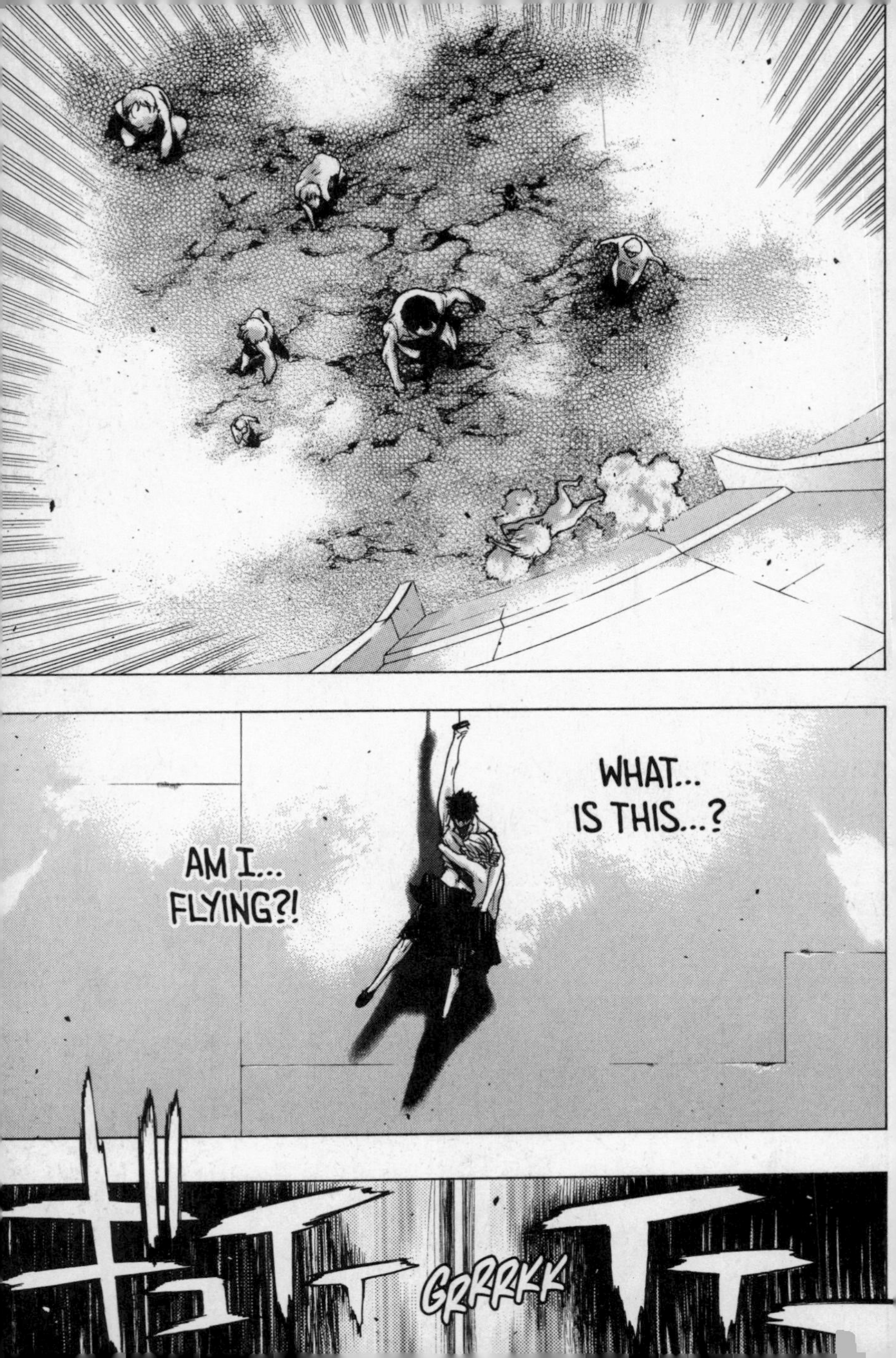
WHAT... IS THIS...?
AM I... FLYING?!
GRRRKK

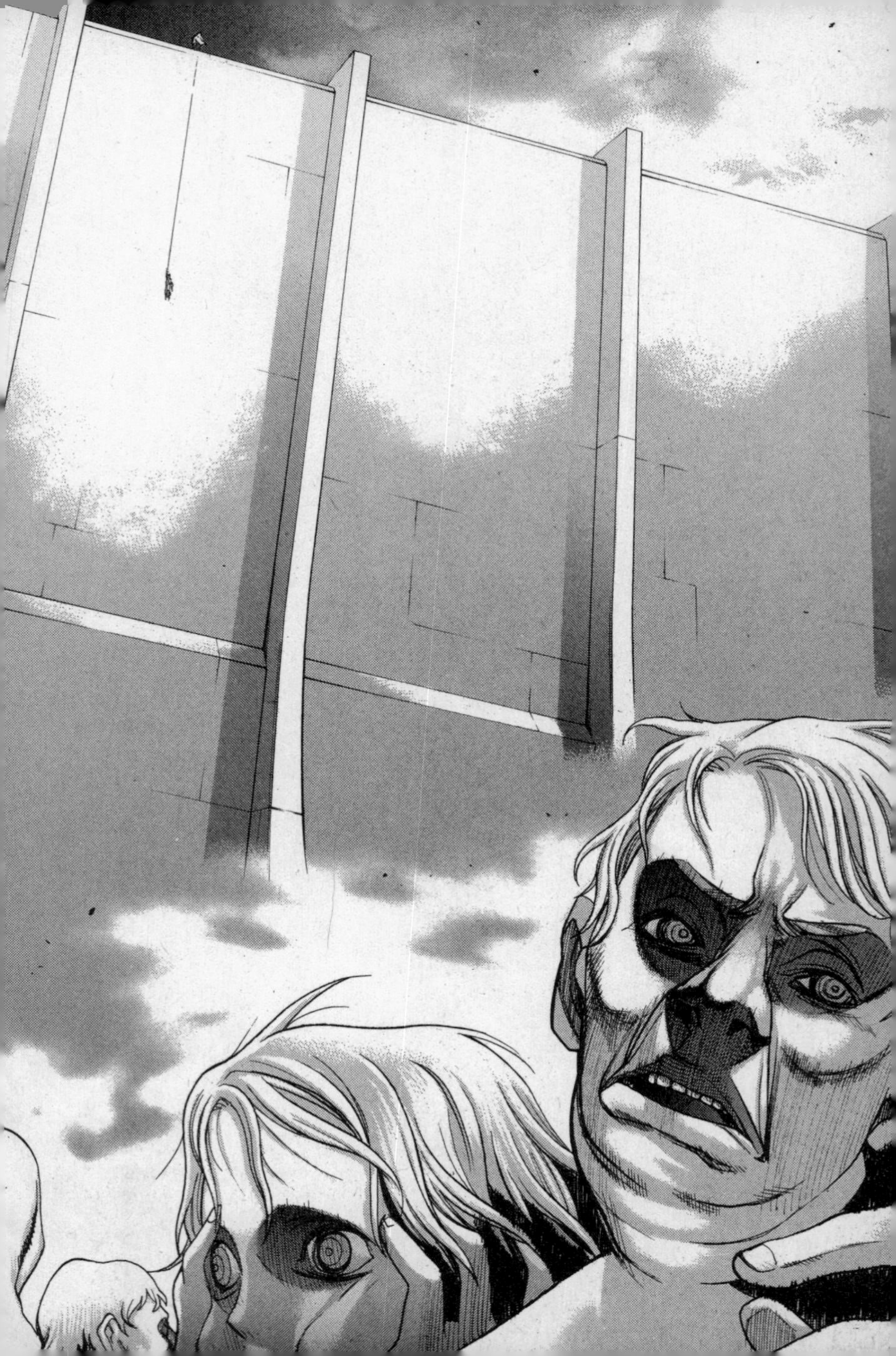

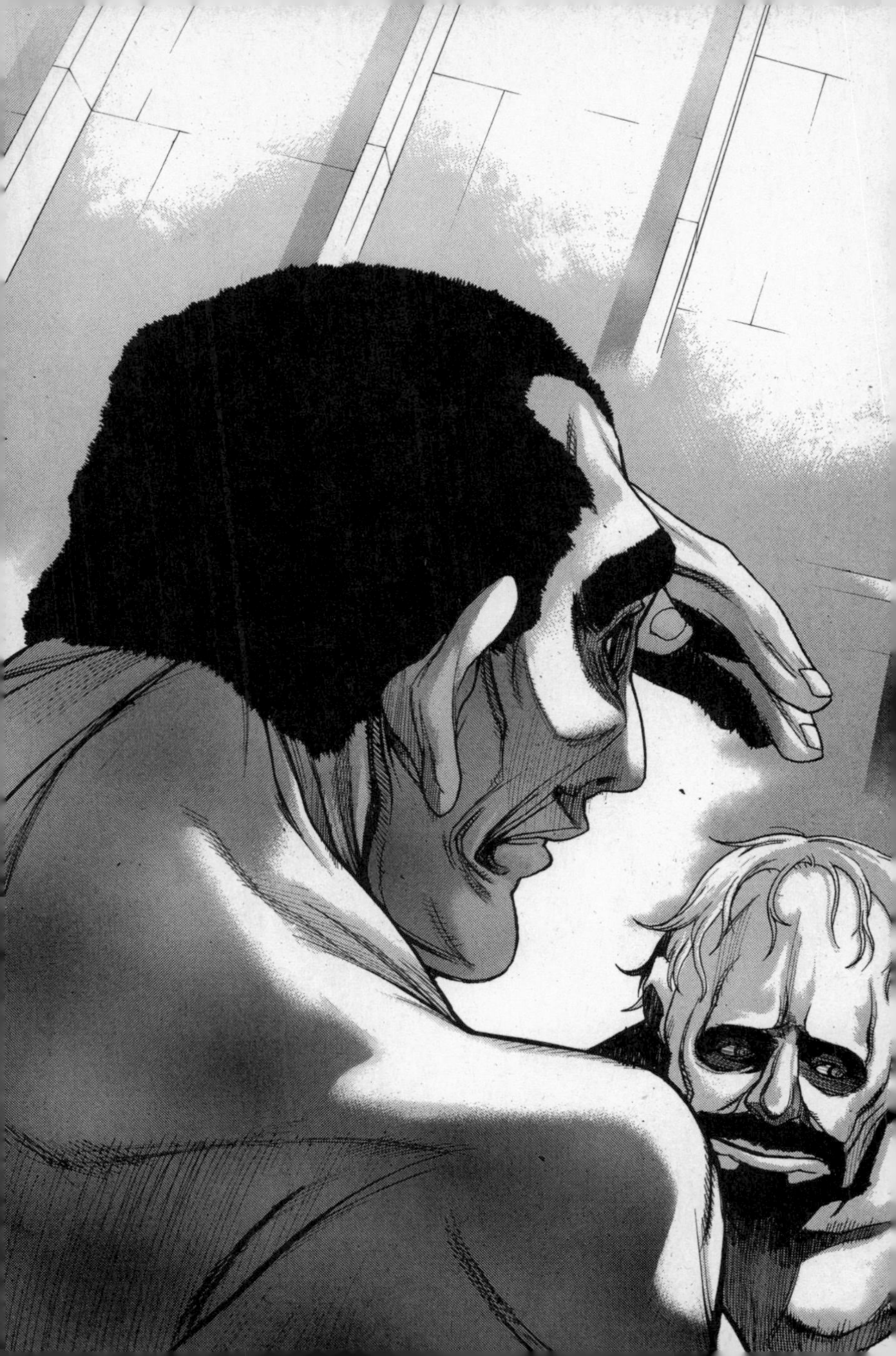

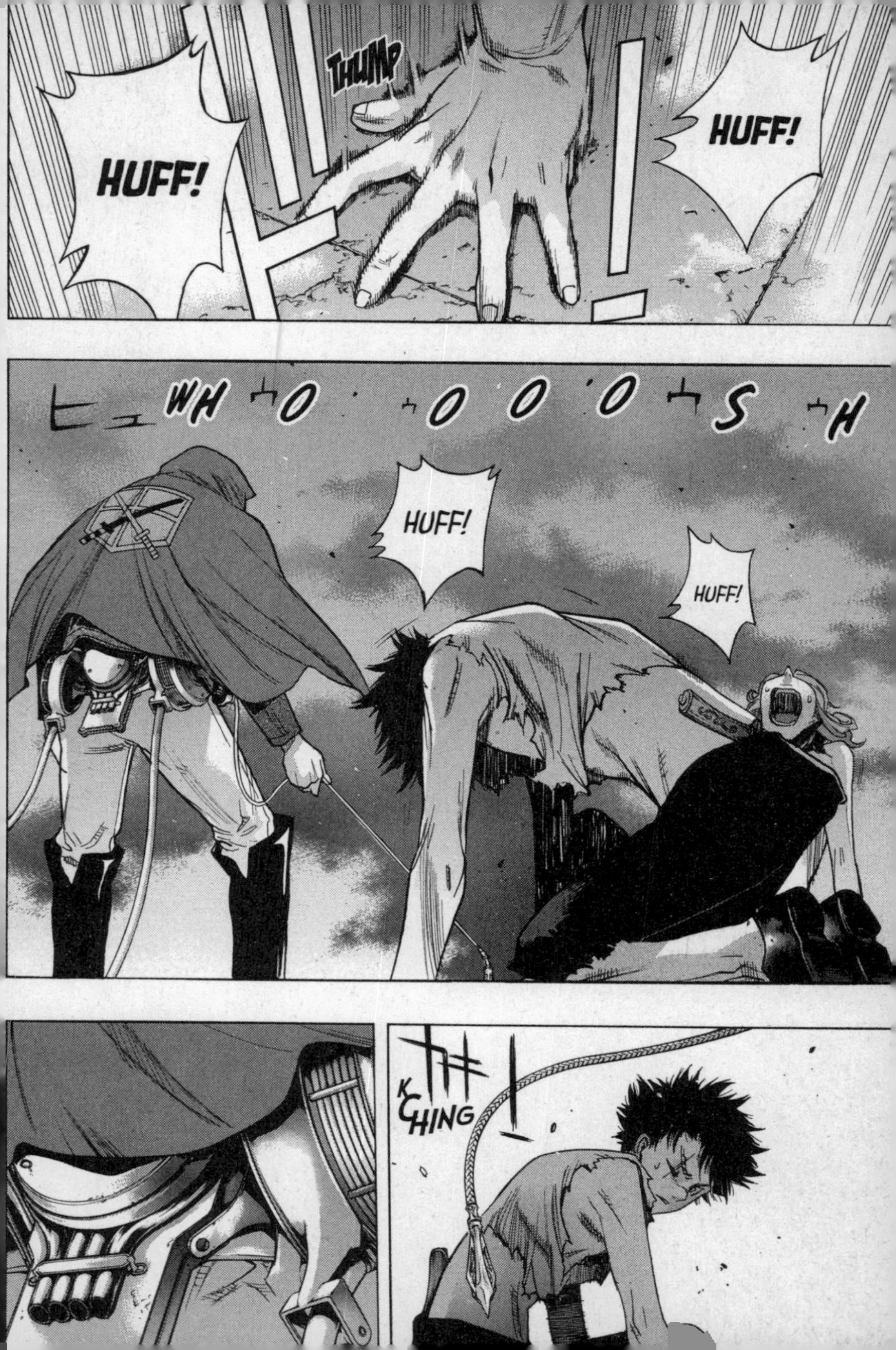

HUFF!
THUMP
HUFF!
WHOOOOSH
HUFF!
HUFF!
K'CHING

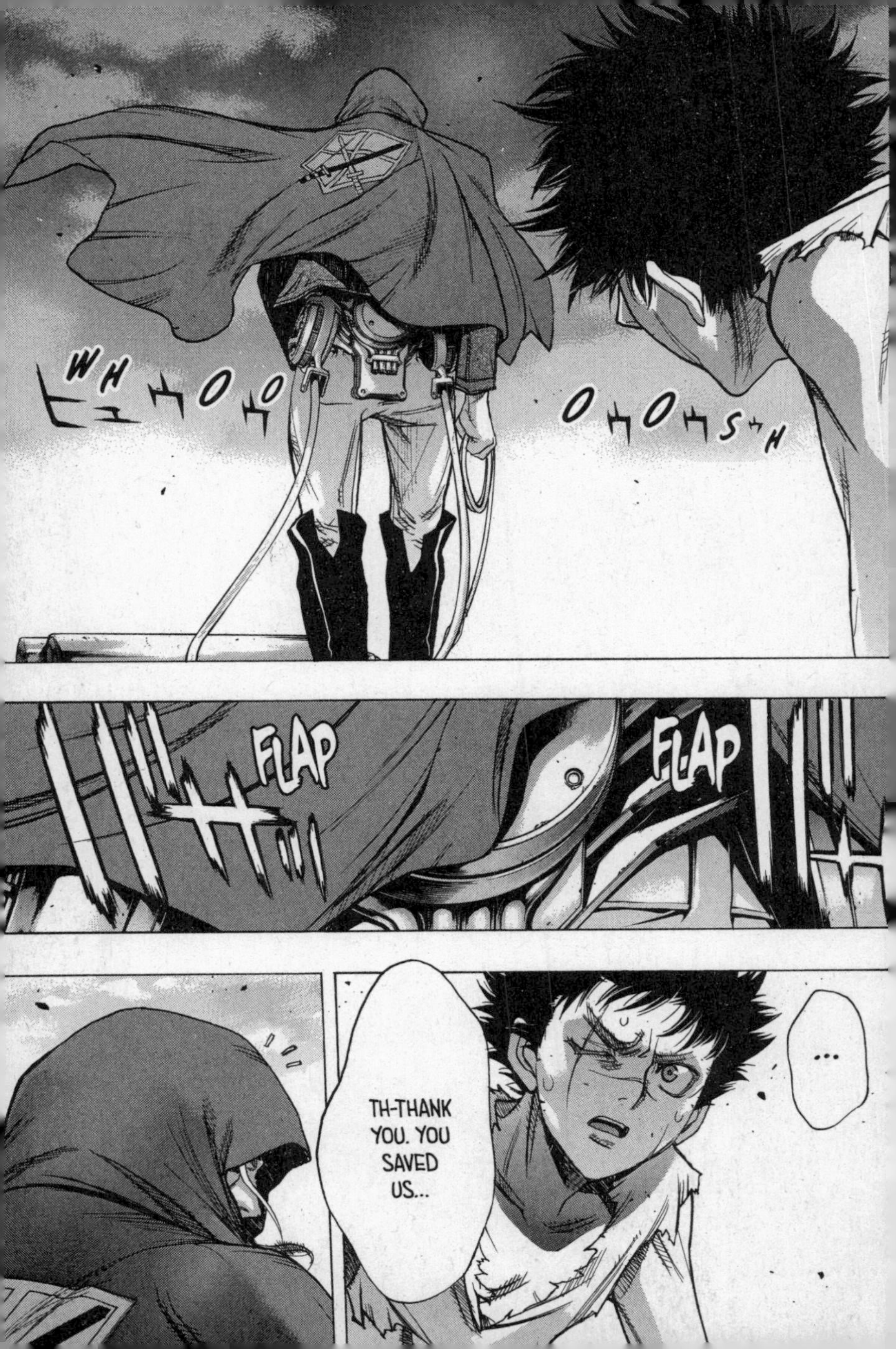
WHOOO OOOSH
FLAP
FLAP
...
TH-THANK YOU. YOU SAVED US...

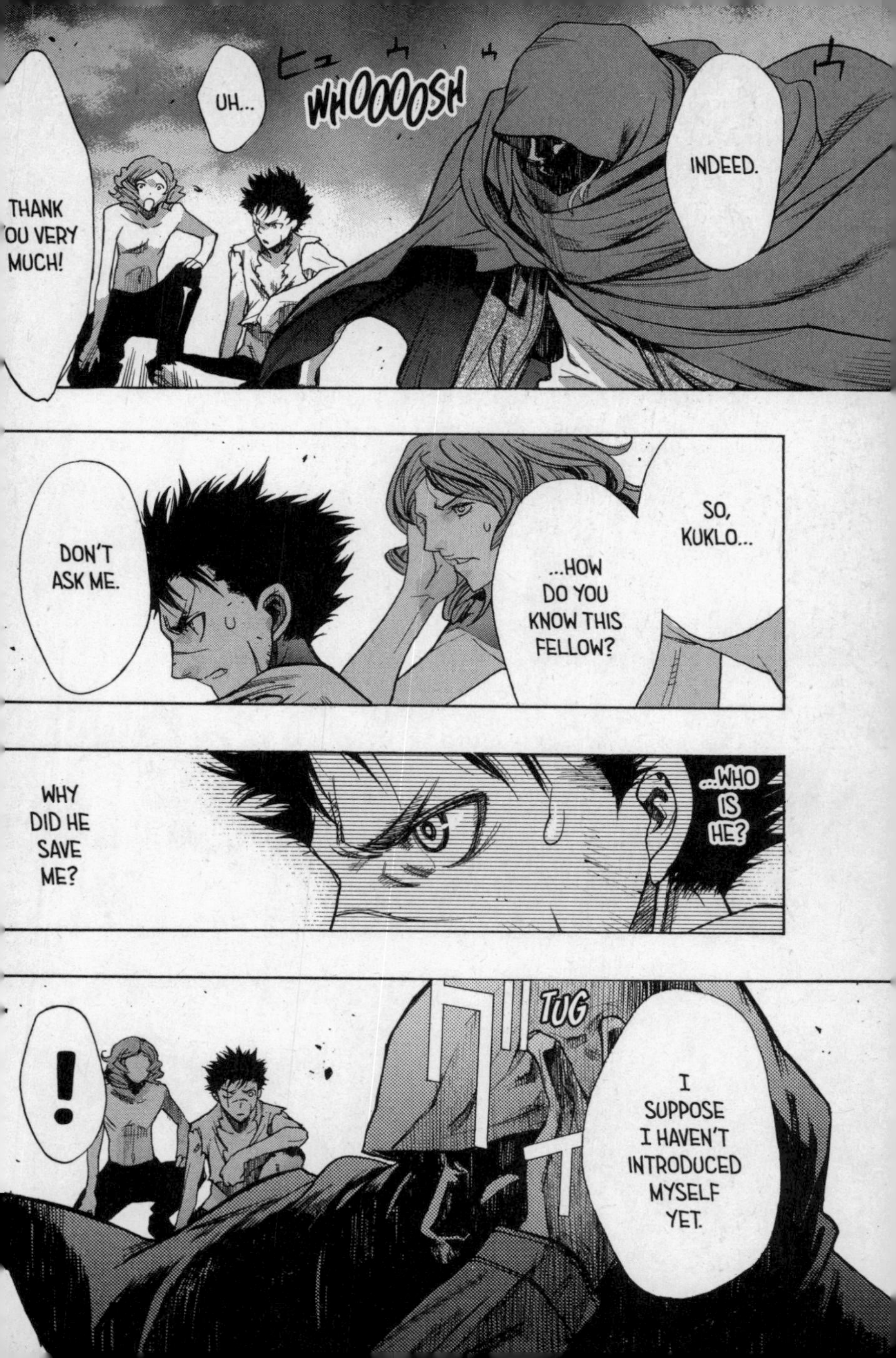
INDEED.
WHOOOOSH
UH...
THANK OU VERY MUCH!
SO, KUKLO...
...HOW DO YOU KNOW THIS FELLOW?
DON'T ASK ME.
...WHO IS HE?
WHY DID HE SAVE ME?
I SUPPOSE I HAVEN'T INTRODUCED MYSELF YET.
TUG
!

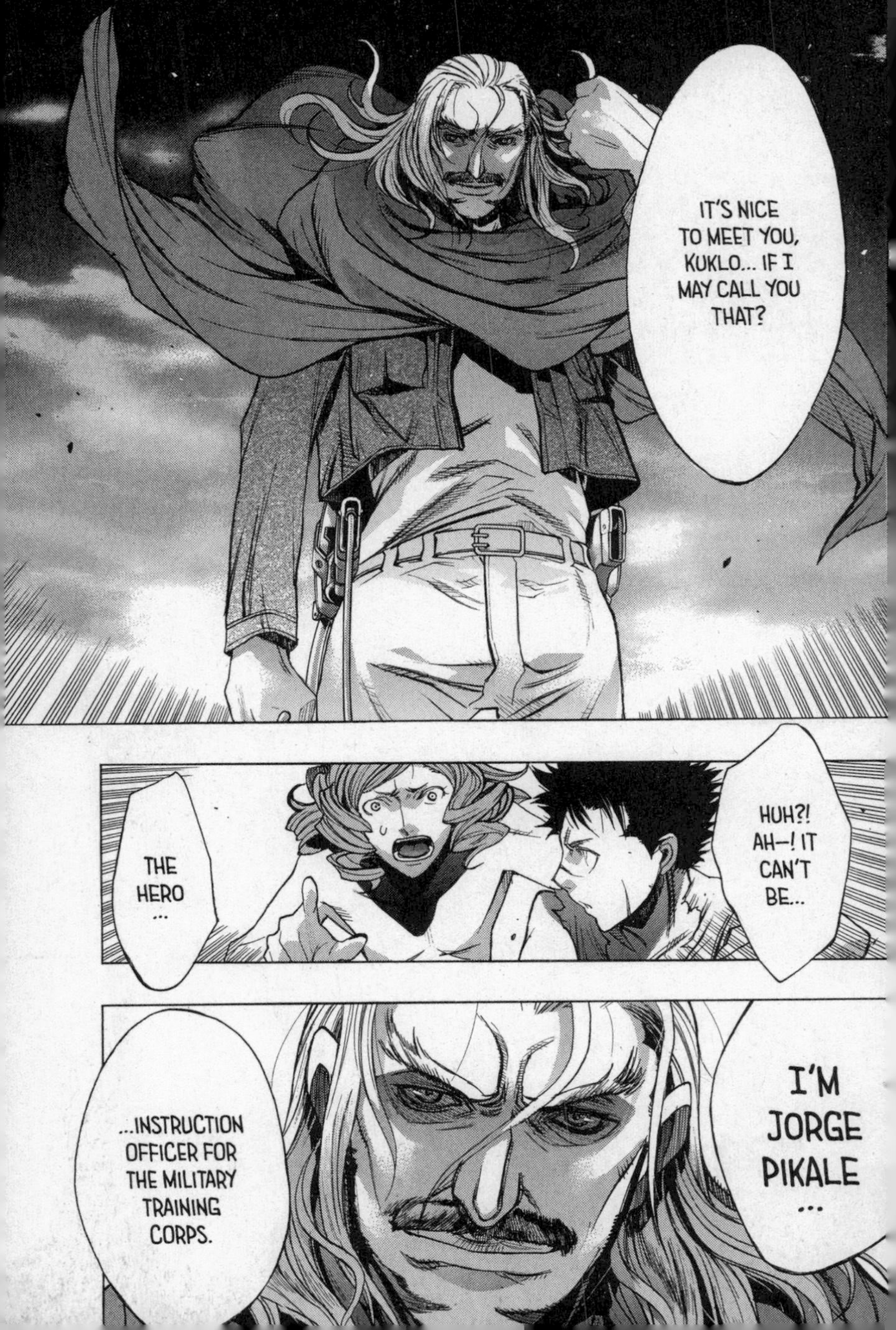
IT'S NICE TO MEET YOU, KUKLO... IF I MAY CALL YOU THAT?
HUH?! AH—! IT CAN'T BE...
THE HERO ...
I'M JORGE PIKALE ...
...INSTRUCTION OFFICER FOR THE MILITARY TRAINING CORPS.

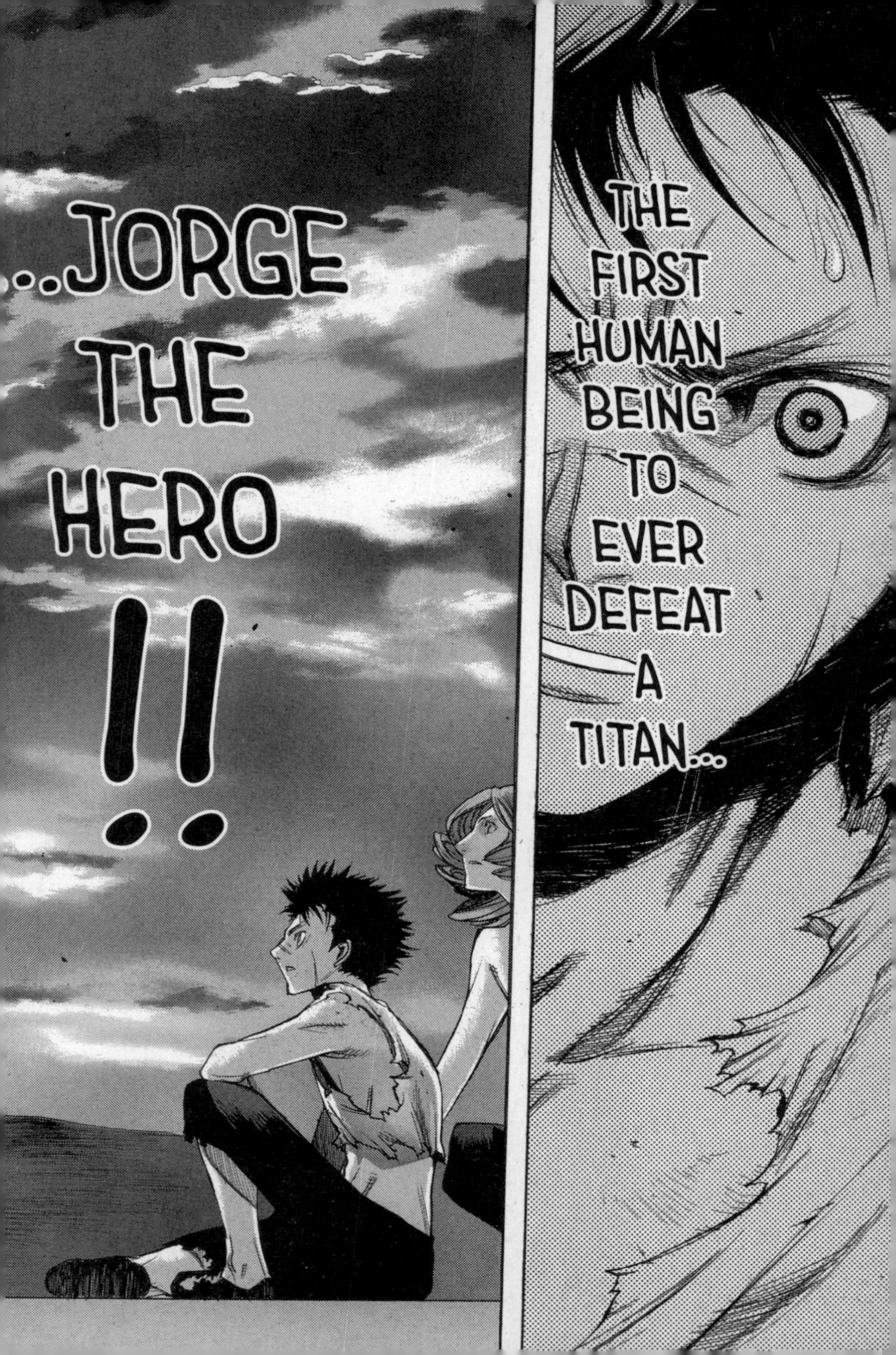
THE FIRST HUMAN BEING TO EVER DEFEAT A TITAN...
...JORGE THE HERO!!

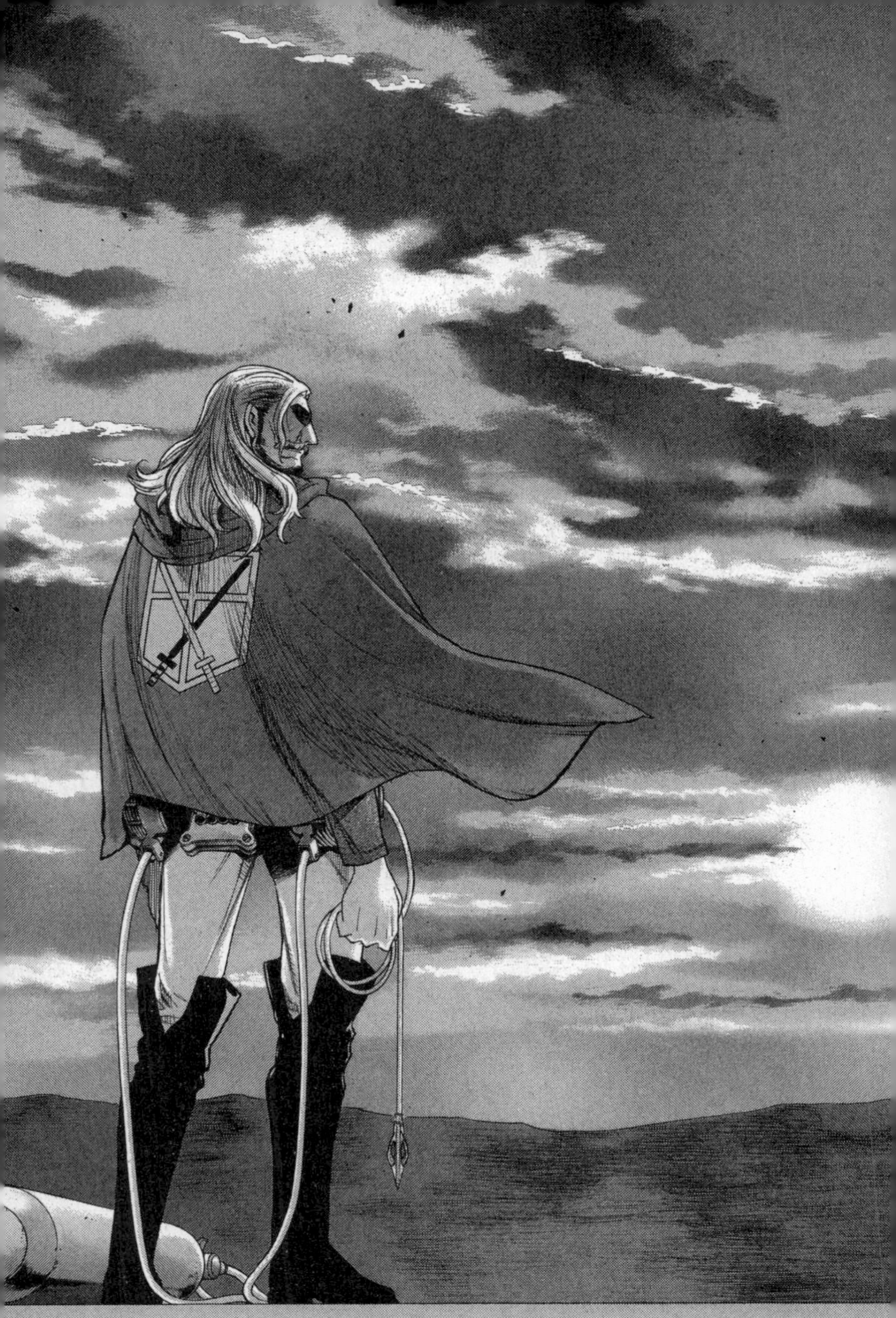

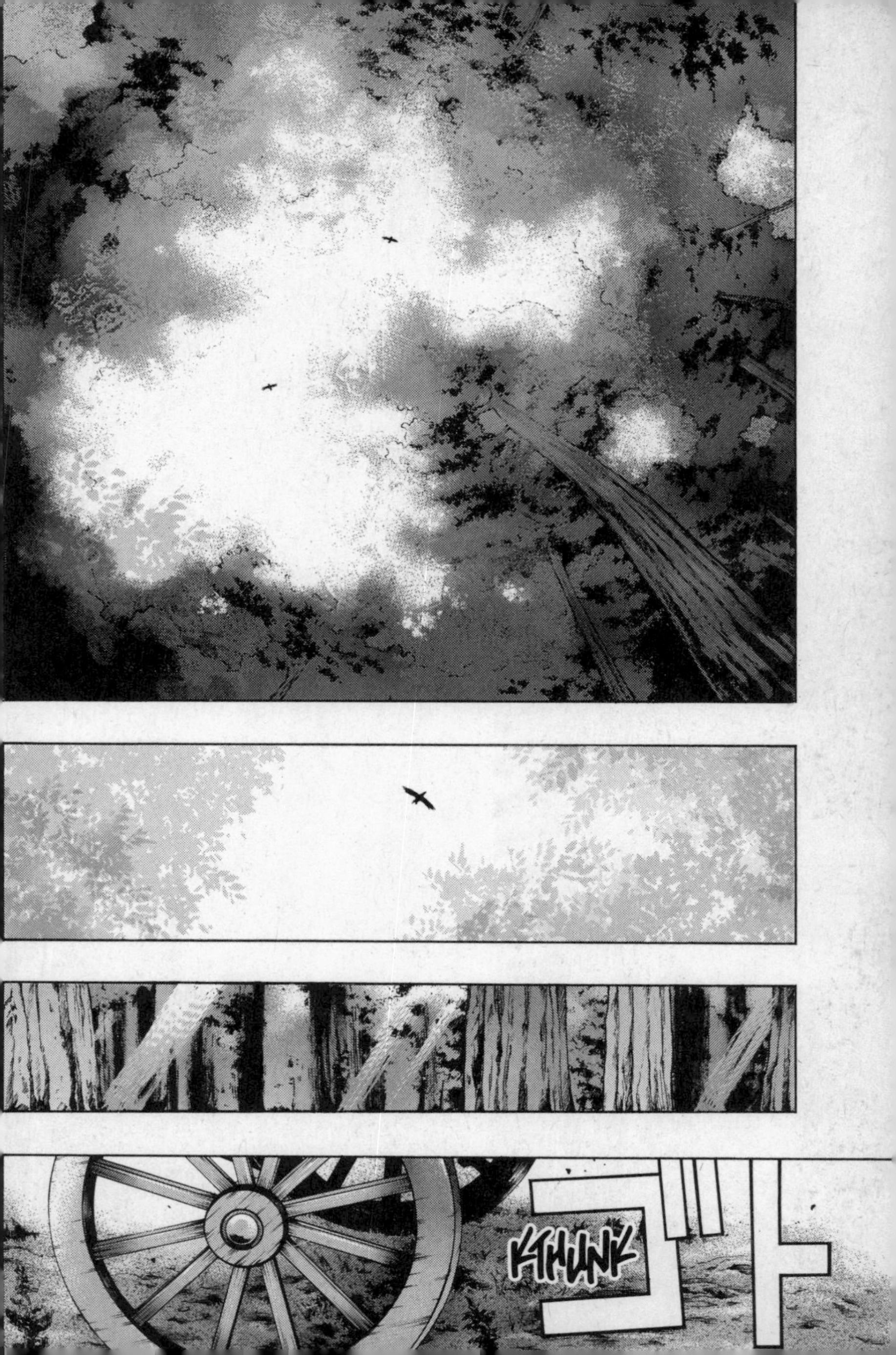
ゴト
KTHUNK

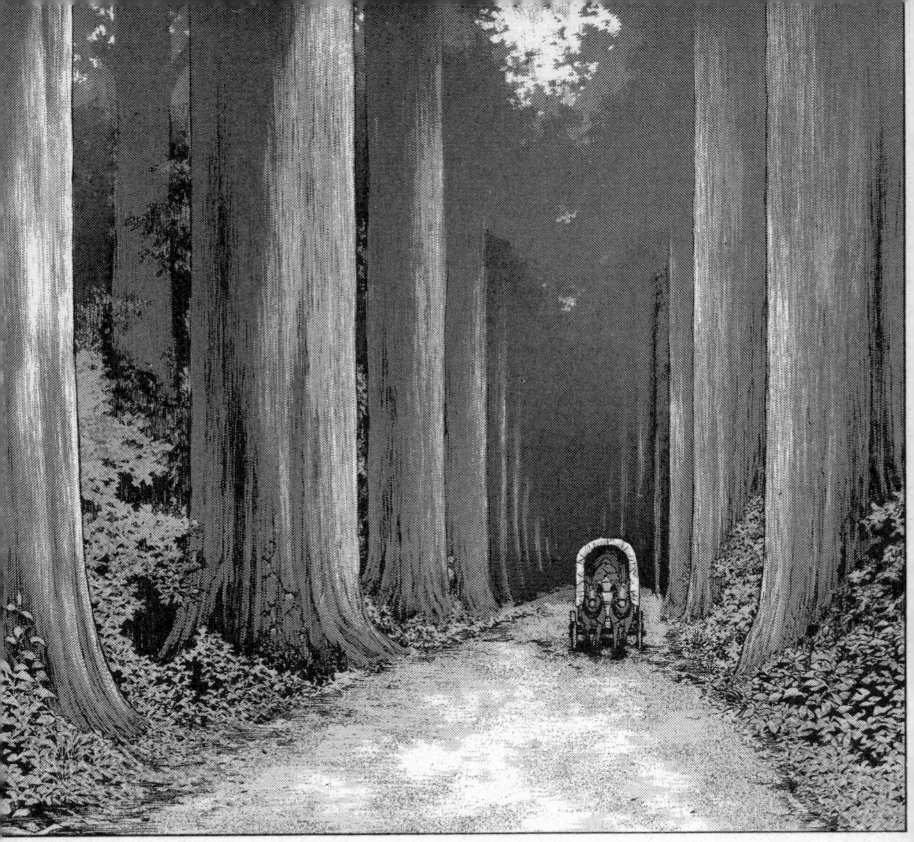

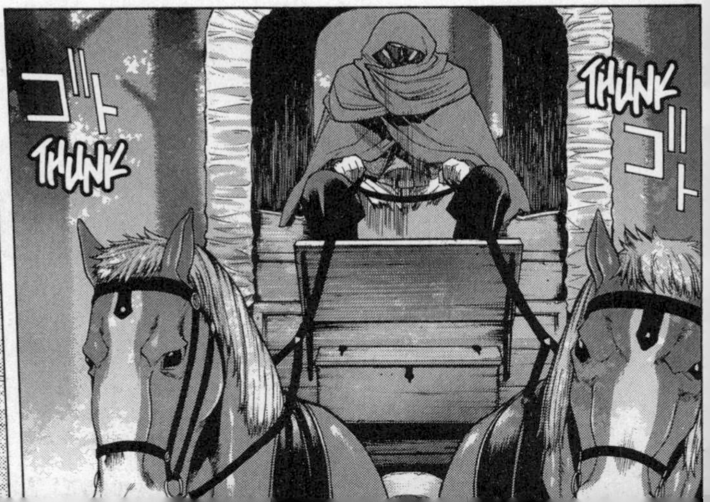
THUNK
ゴット
ゴット
THUNK

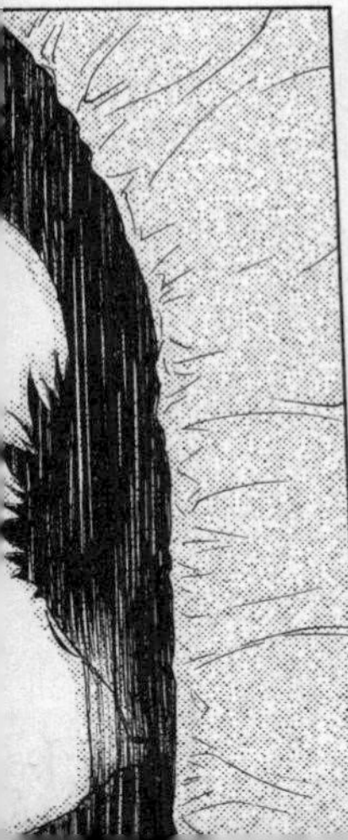

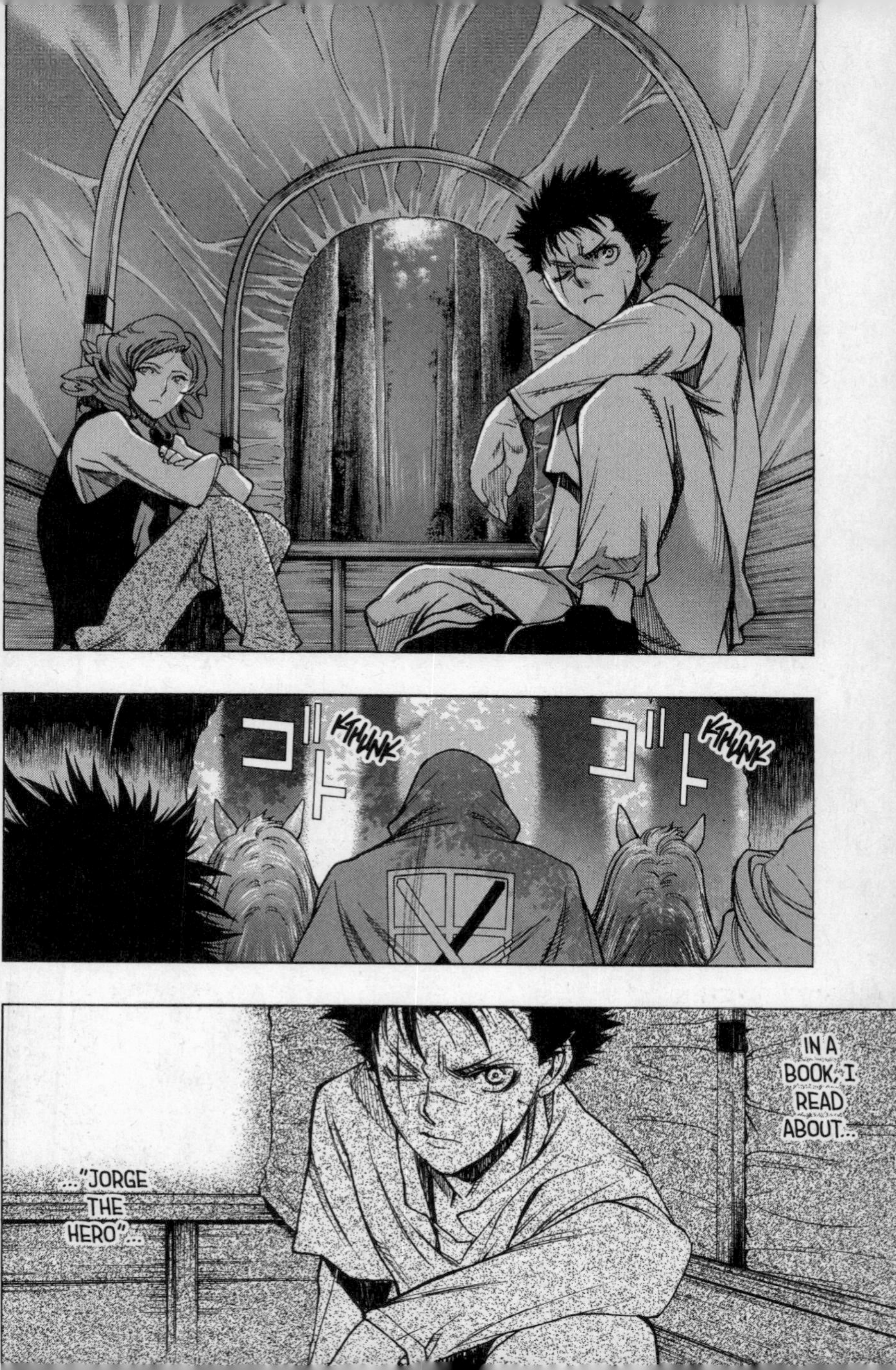
ゴト
KTHUNK
ゴト
KTHUNK
IN A BOOK, I READ ABOUT...
..."JORGE THE HERO"...

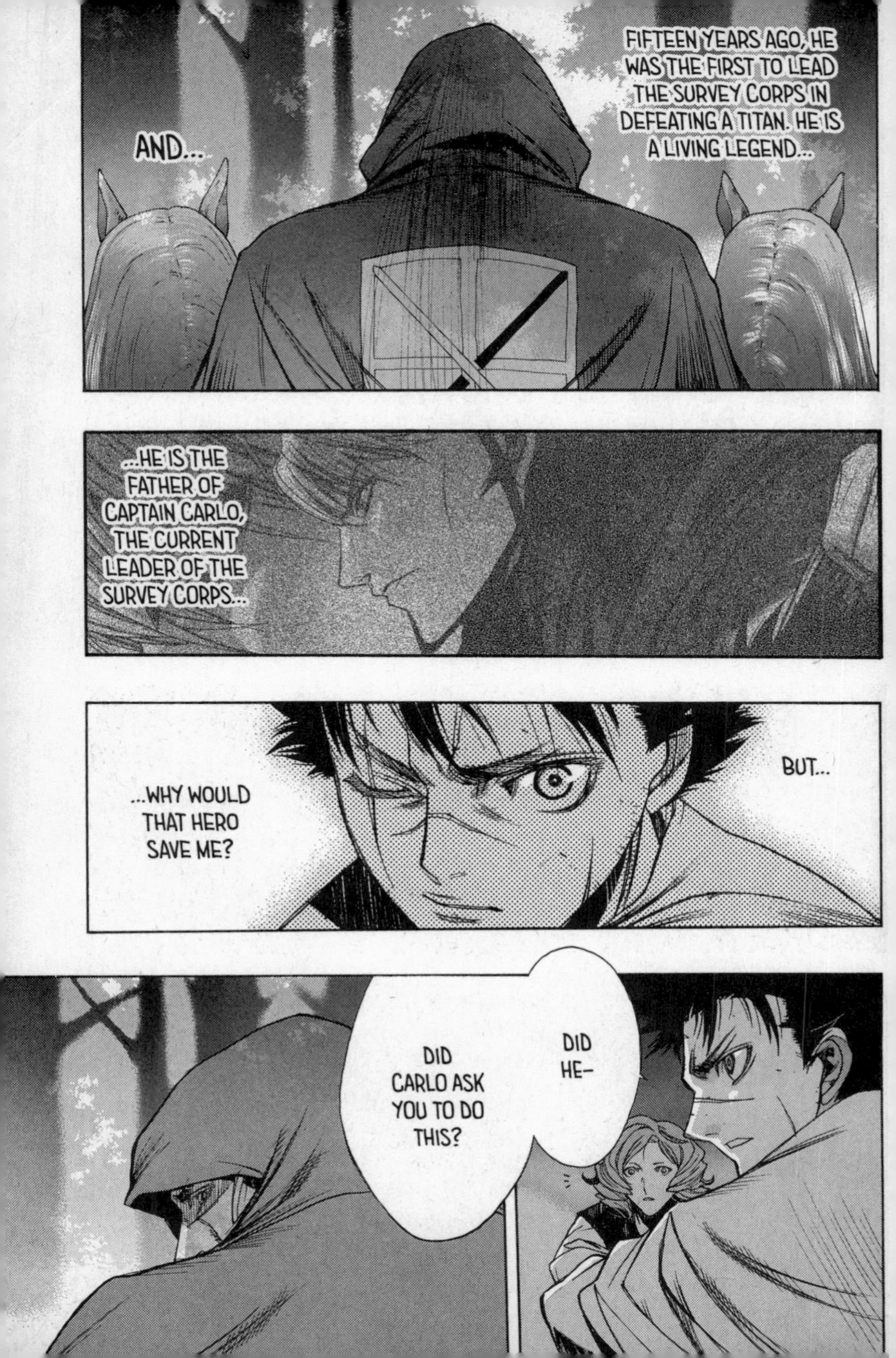
FIFTEEN YEARS AGO, HE WAS THE FIRST TO LEAD THE SURVEY CORPS IN DEFEATING A TITAN. HE IS A LIVING LEGEND...
AND...
...HE IS THE FATHER OF CAPTAIN CARLO, THE CURRENT LEADER OF THE SURVEY CORPS...
BUT...
...WHY WOULD THAT HERO SAVE ME?
DID HE-
DID CARLO ASK YOU TO DO THIS?

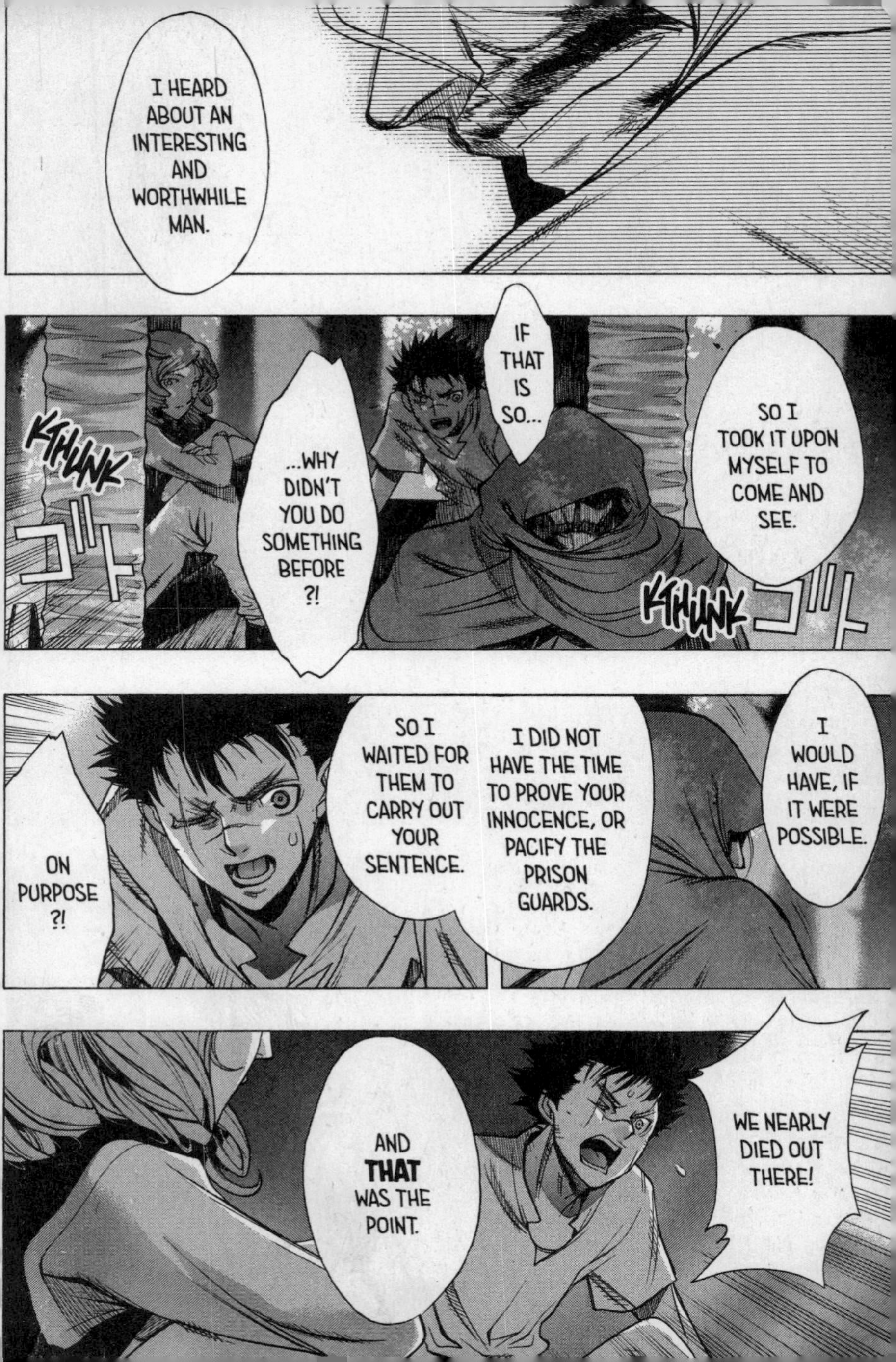
I HEARD ABOUT AN INTERESTING AND WORTHWHILE MAN.
SO I TOOK IT UPON MYSELF TO COME AND SEE.
KTHUNK
ゴット
IF THAT IS SO...
...WHY DIDN'T YOU DO SOMETHING BEFORE?!
KTHUNK
ゴット
I WOULD HAVE, IF IT WERE POSSIBLE.
I DID NOT HAVE THE TIME TO PROVE YOUR INNOCENCE, OR PACIFY THE PRISON GUARDS.
SO I WAITED FOR THEM TO CARRY OUT YOUR SENTENCE.
ON PURPOSE?!
WE NEARLY DIED OUT THERE!
AND **THAT** WAS THE POINT.

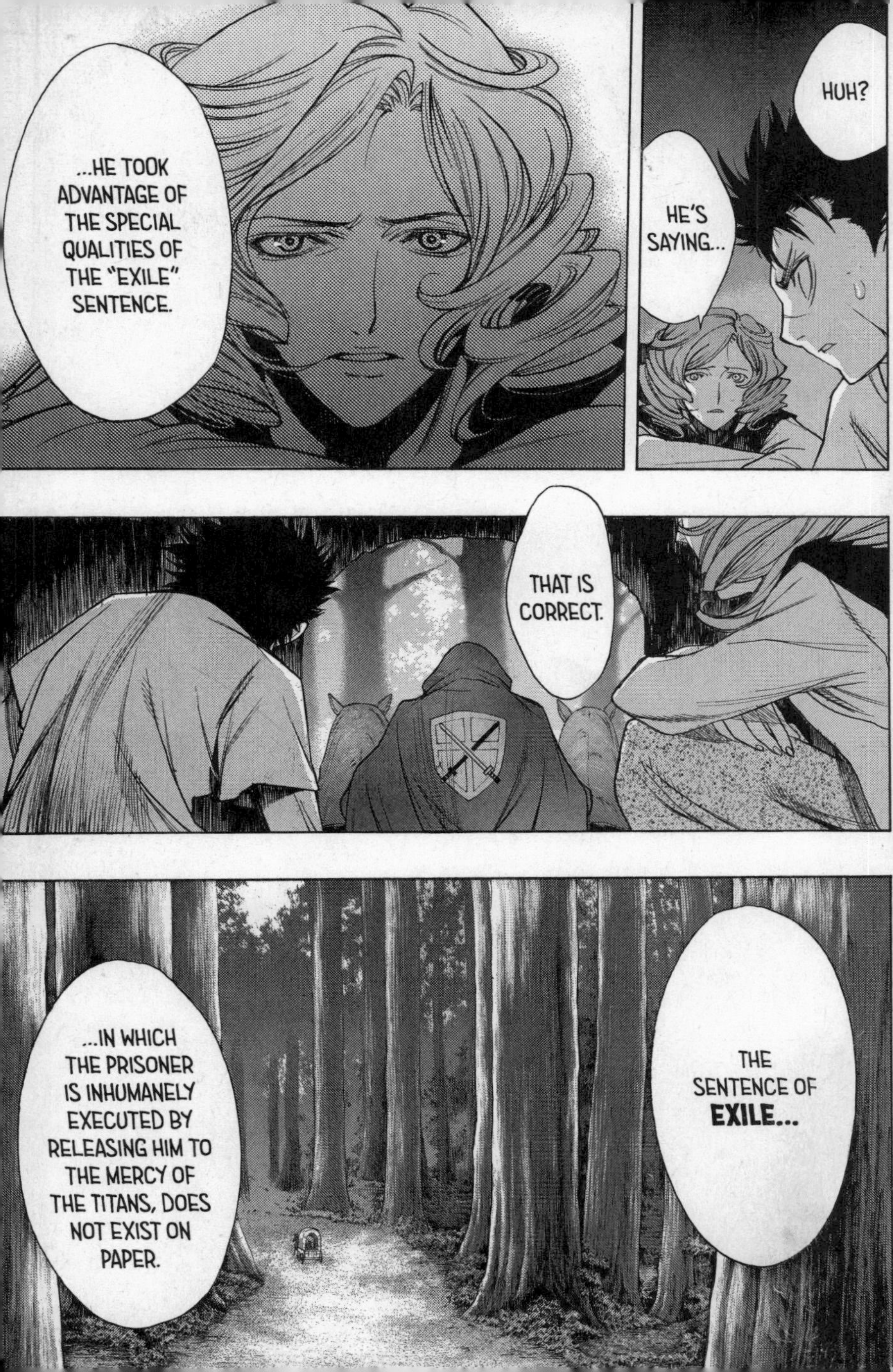
HUH?
HE'S SAYING...
...HE TOOK ADVANTAGE OF THE SPECIAL QUALITIES OF THE "EXILE" SENTENCE.
THAT IS CORRECT.
THE SENTENCE OF **EXILE...**
...IN WHICH THE PRISONER IS INHUMANELY EXECUTED BY RELEASING HIM TO THE MERCY OF THE TITANS, DOES NOT EXIST ON PAPER.

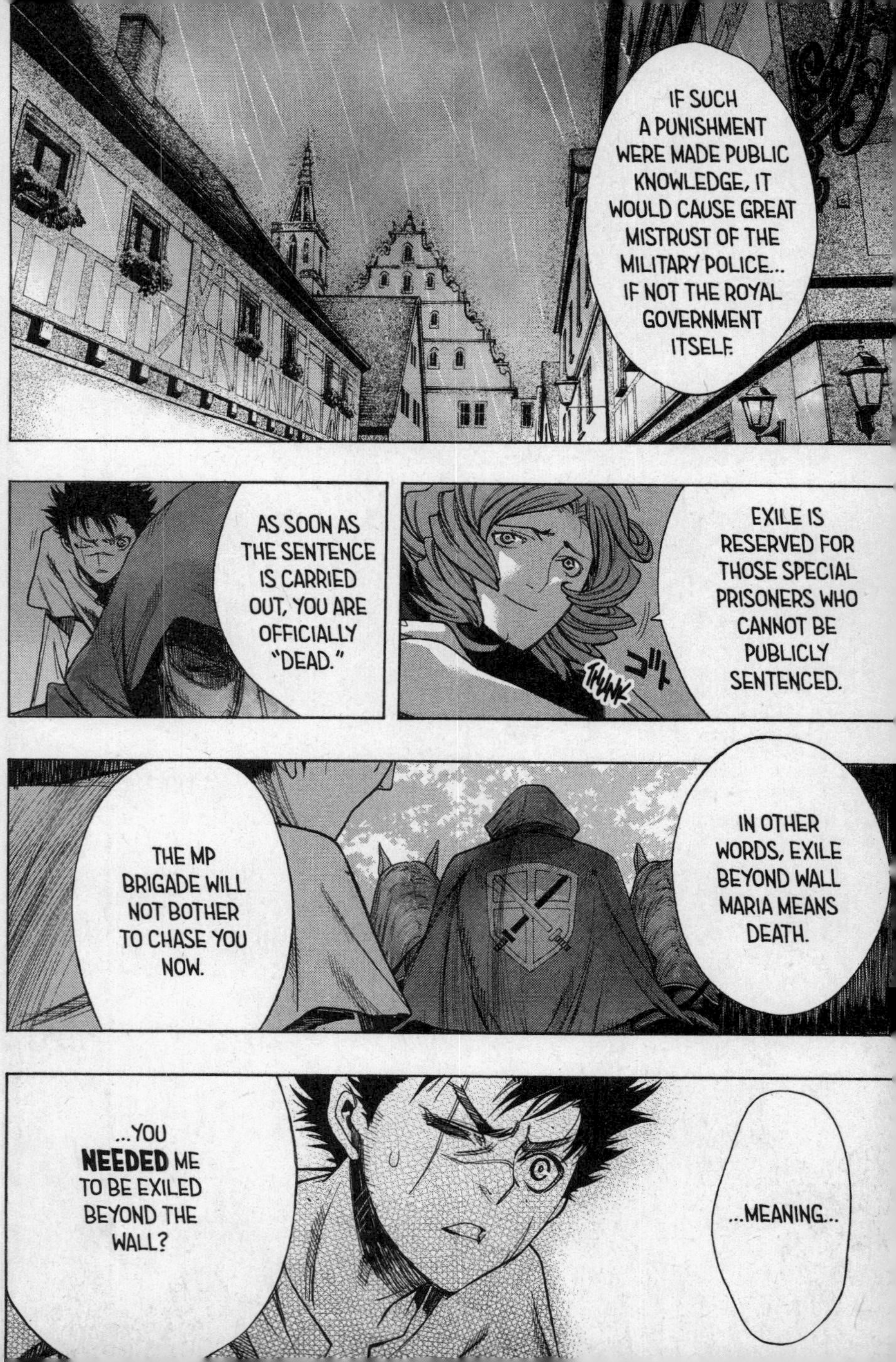
IF SUCH A PUNISHMENT WERE MADE PUBLIC KNOWLEDGE, IT WOULD CAUSE GREAT MISTRUST OF THE MILITARY POLICE... IF NOT THE ROYAL GOVERNMENT ITSELF.
EXILE IS RESERVED FOR THOSE SPECIAL PRISONERS WHO CANNOT BE PUBLICLY SENTENCED.
ゴッ THUNK
AS SOON AS THE SENTENCE IS CARRIED OUT, YOU ARE OFFICIALLY "DEAD."
IN OTHER WORDS, EXILE BEYOND WALL MARIA MEANS DEATH.
THE MP BRIGADE WILL NOT BOTHER TO CHASE YOU NOW.
...MEANING...
...YOU **NEEDED** ME TO BE EXILED BEYOND THE WALL?

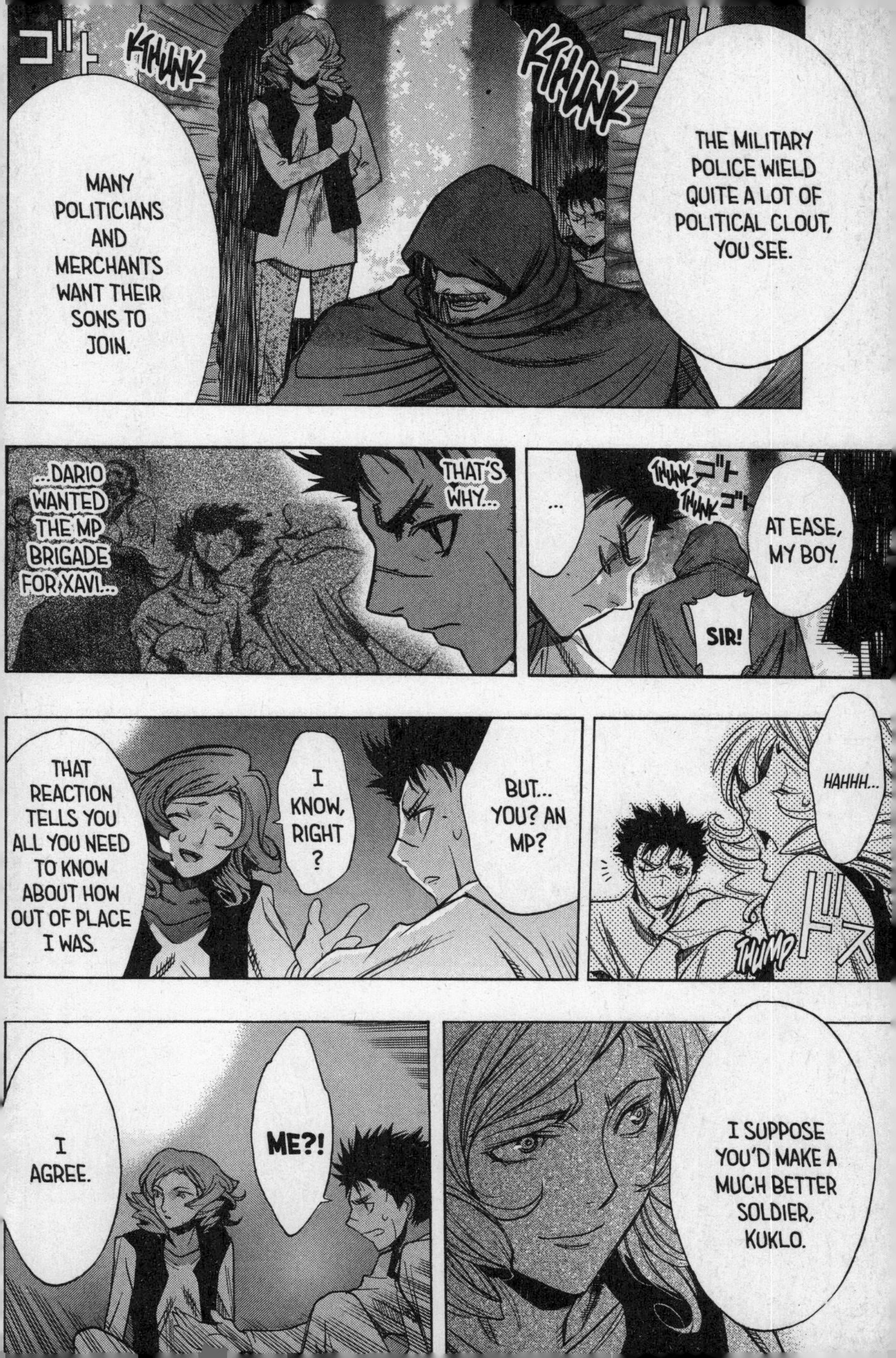
THE MILITARY POLICE WIELD QUITE A LOT OF POLITICAL CLOUT, YOU SEE.
ゴッ
KTHUNK
KTHUNK
ゴト
MANY POLITICIANS AND MERCHANTS WANT THEIR SONS TO JOIN.
THUNK ゴト
THUNK ゴト
AT EASE, MY BOY.
SIR!
...
THAT'S WHY...
...DARIO WANTED THE MP BRIGADE FOR XAVI...
HAHHH...
ドス
THUMP
BUT... YOU? AN MP?
I KNOW, RIGHT?
THAT REACTION TELLS YOU ALL YOU NEED TO KNOW ABOUT HOW OUT OF PLACE I WAS.
I SUPPOSE YOU'D MAKE A MUCH BETTER SOLDIER, KUKLO.
ME?!
I AGREE.

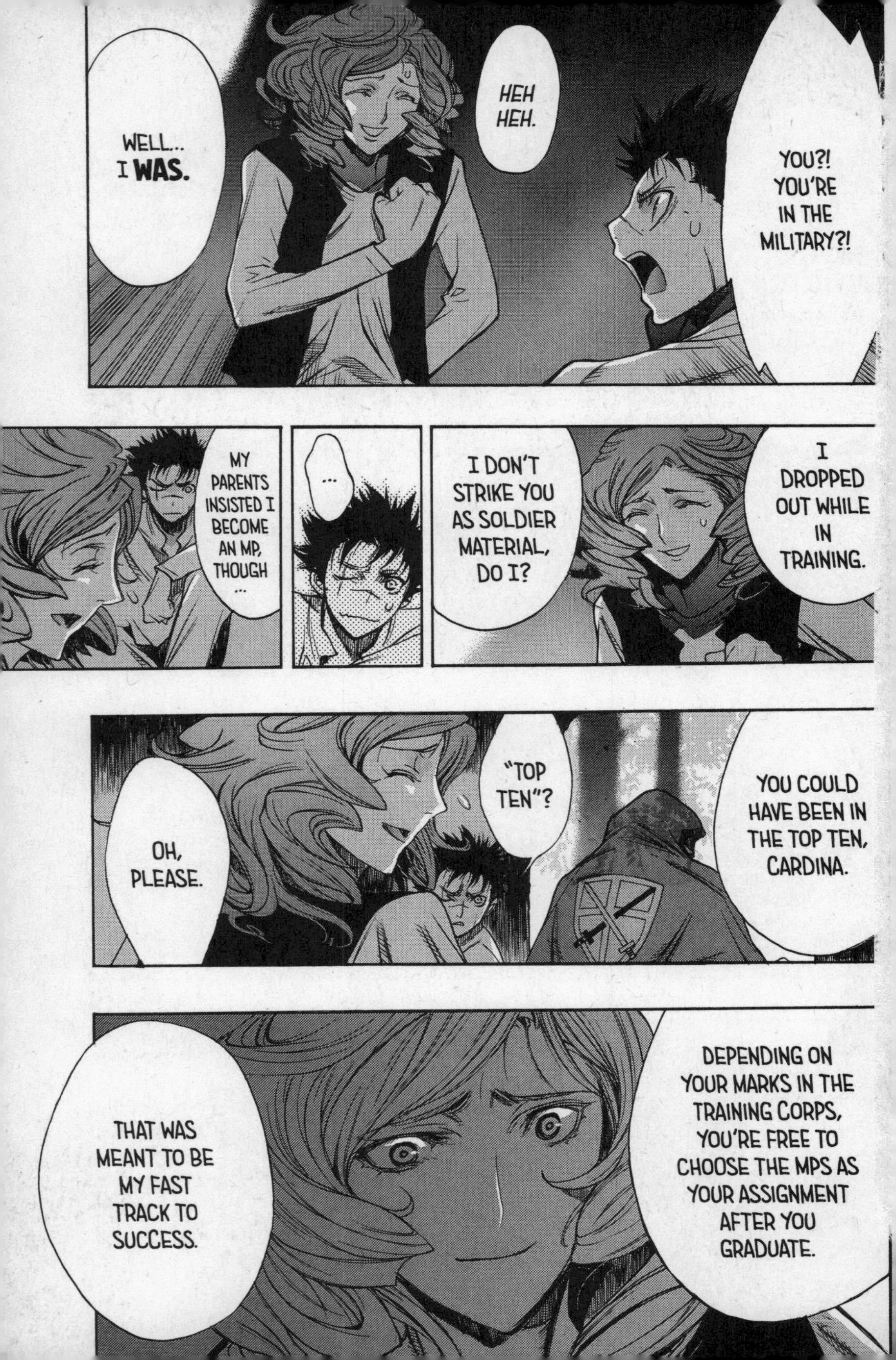
YOU?! YOU'RE IN THE MILITARY?!
HEH HEH.
WELL... I WAS.
I DROPPED OUT WHILE IN TRAINING.
I DON'T STRIKE YOU AS SOLDIER MATERIAL, DO I?
...
MY PARENTS INSISTED I BECOME AN MP, THOUGH...
YOU COULD HAVE BEEN IN THE TOP TEN, CARDINA.
"TOP TEN"?
OH, PLEASE.
DEPENDING ON YOUR MARKS IN THE TRAINING CORPS, YOU'RE FREE TO CHOOSE THE MPS AS YOUR ASSIGNMENT AFTER YOU GRADUATE.
THAT WAS MEANT TO BE MY FAST TRACK TO SUCCESS.

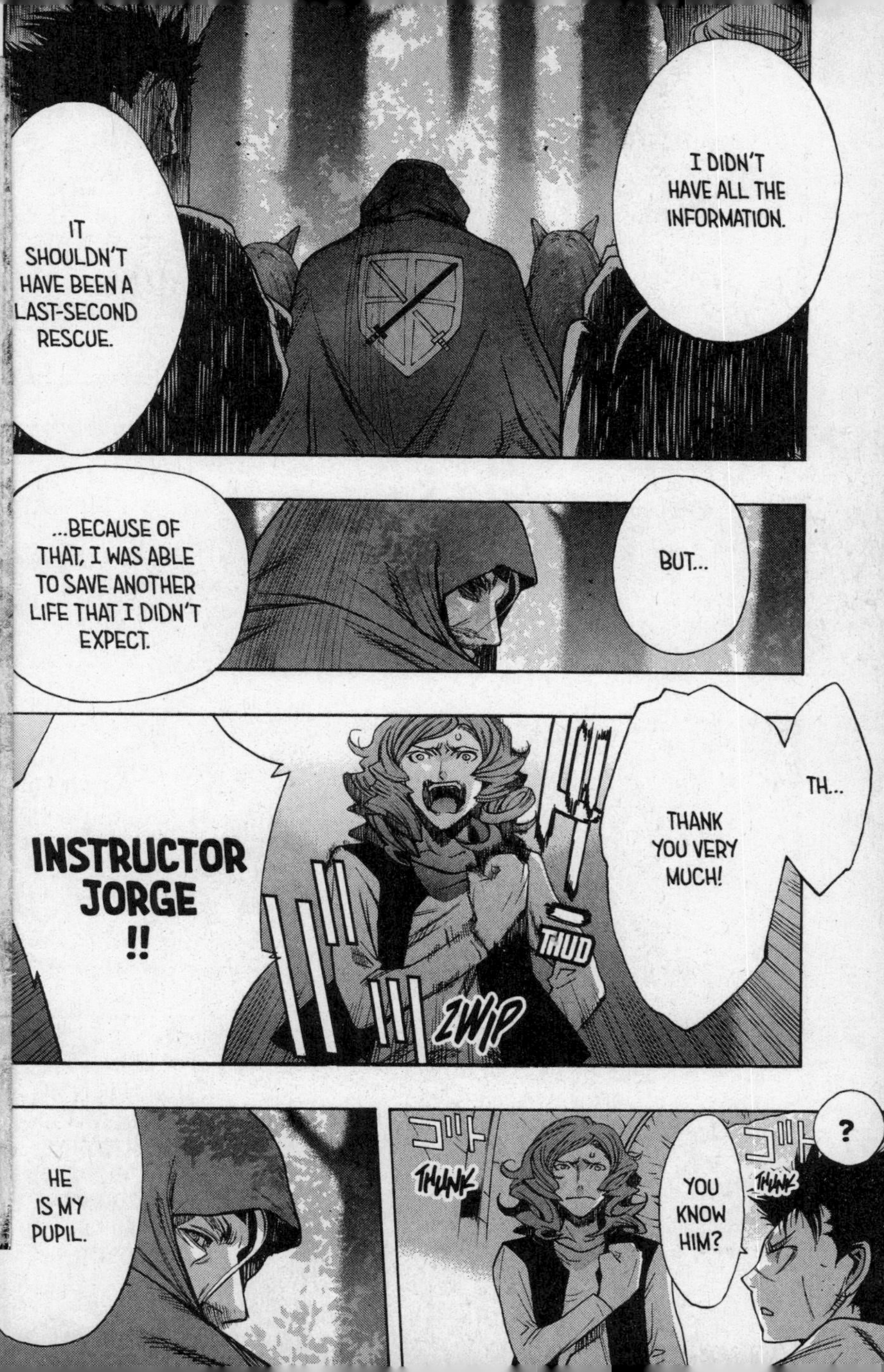
I DIDN'T HAVE ALL THE INFORMATION.
IT SHOULDN'T HAVE BEEN A LAST-SECOND RESCUE.
BUT...
...BECAUSE OF THAT, I WAS ABLE TO SAVE ANOTHER LIFE THAT I DIDN'T EXPECT.
TH...
THANK YOU VERY MUCH!
THUD
ZWIP
INSTRUCTOR JORGE !!
?
ゴッ
THUNK
YOU KNOW HIM?
ゴッ
THUNK
HE IS MY PUPIL.

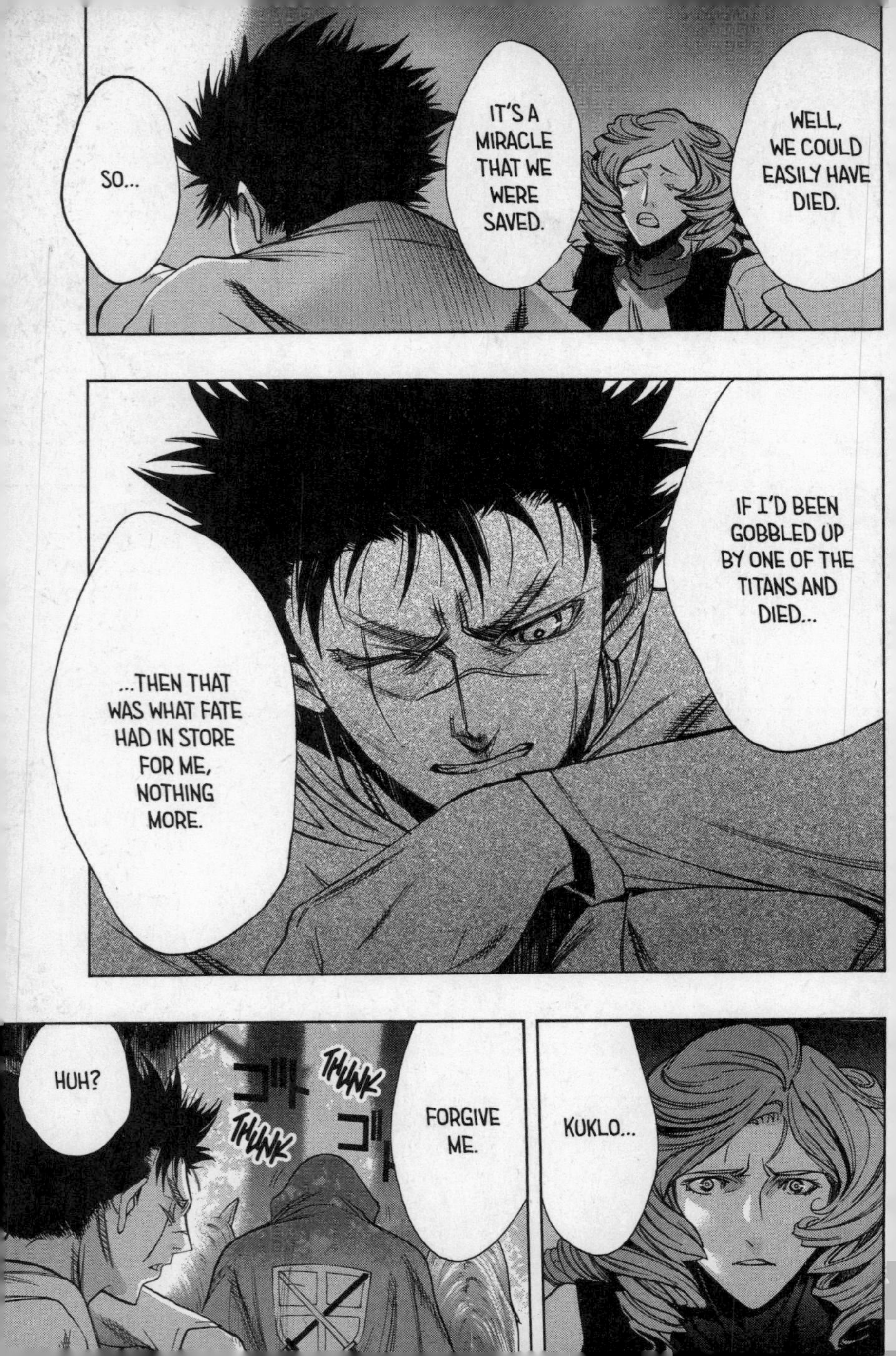
WELL, WE COULD EASILY HAVE DIED.
IT'S A MIRACLE THAT WE WERE SAVED.
SO...
IF I'D BEEN GOBBLED UP BY ONE OF THE TITANS AND DIED...
...THEN THAT WAS WHAT FATE HAD IN STORE FOR ME, NOTHING MORE.
KUKLO...
FORGIVE ME.
THUNK
THUNK
HUH?

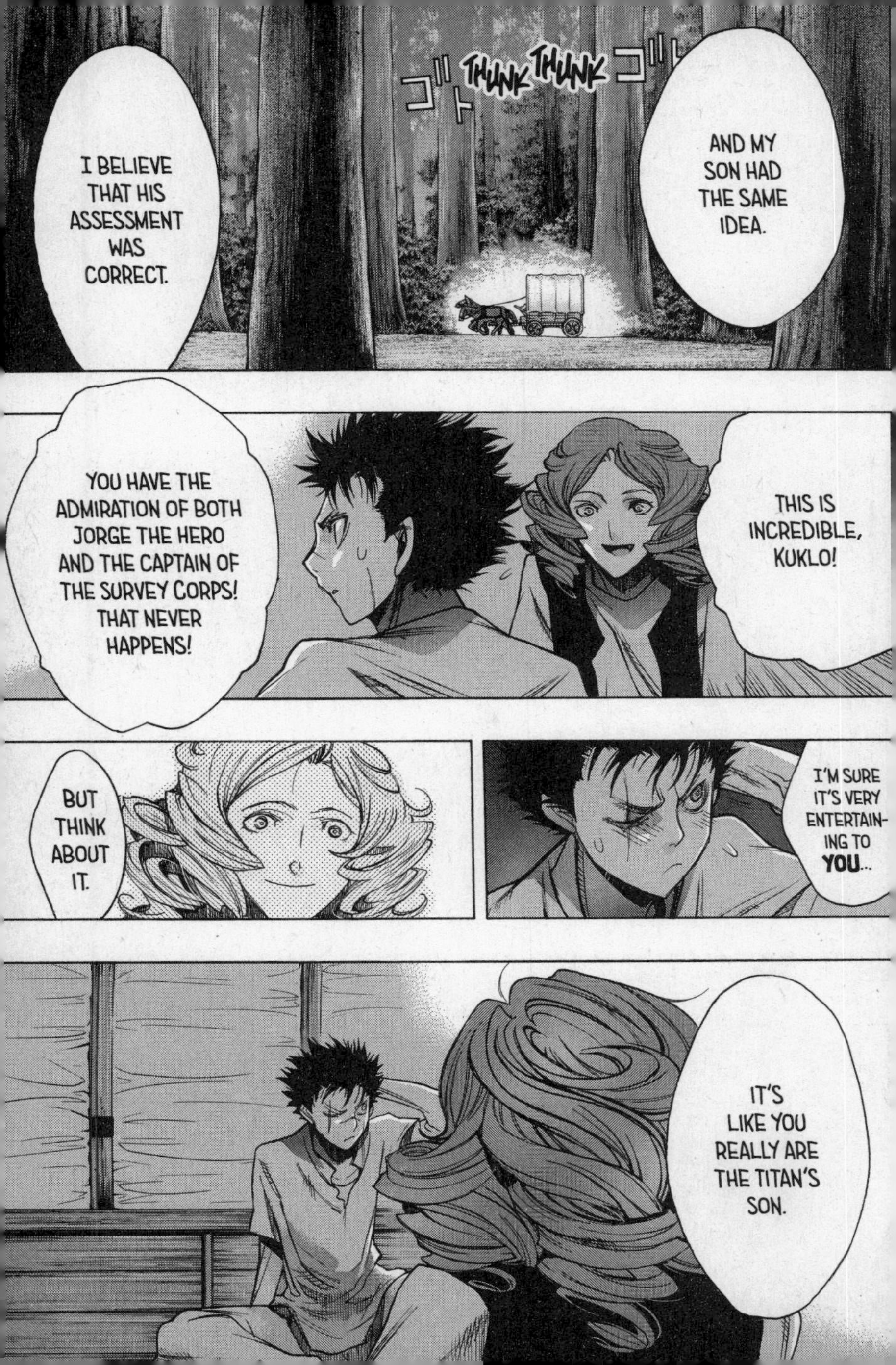
AND MY SON HAD THE SAME IDEA.
ゴト THUNK THUNK ゴト
I BELIEVE THAT HIS ASSESSMENT WAS CORRECT.
THIS IS INCREDIBLE, KUKLO!
YOU HAVE THE ADMIRATION OF BOTH JORGE THE HERO AND THE CAPTAIN OF THE SURVEY CORPS! THAT NEVER HAPPENS!
I'M SURE IT'S VERY ENTERTAINING TO **YOU**...
BUT THINK ABOUT IT.
IT'S LIKE YOU REALLY ARE THE TITAN'S SON.

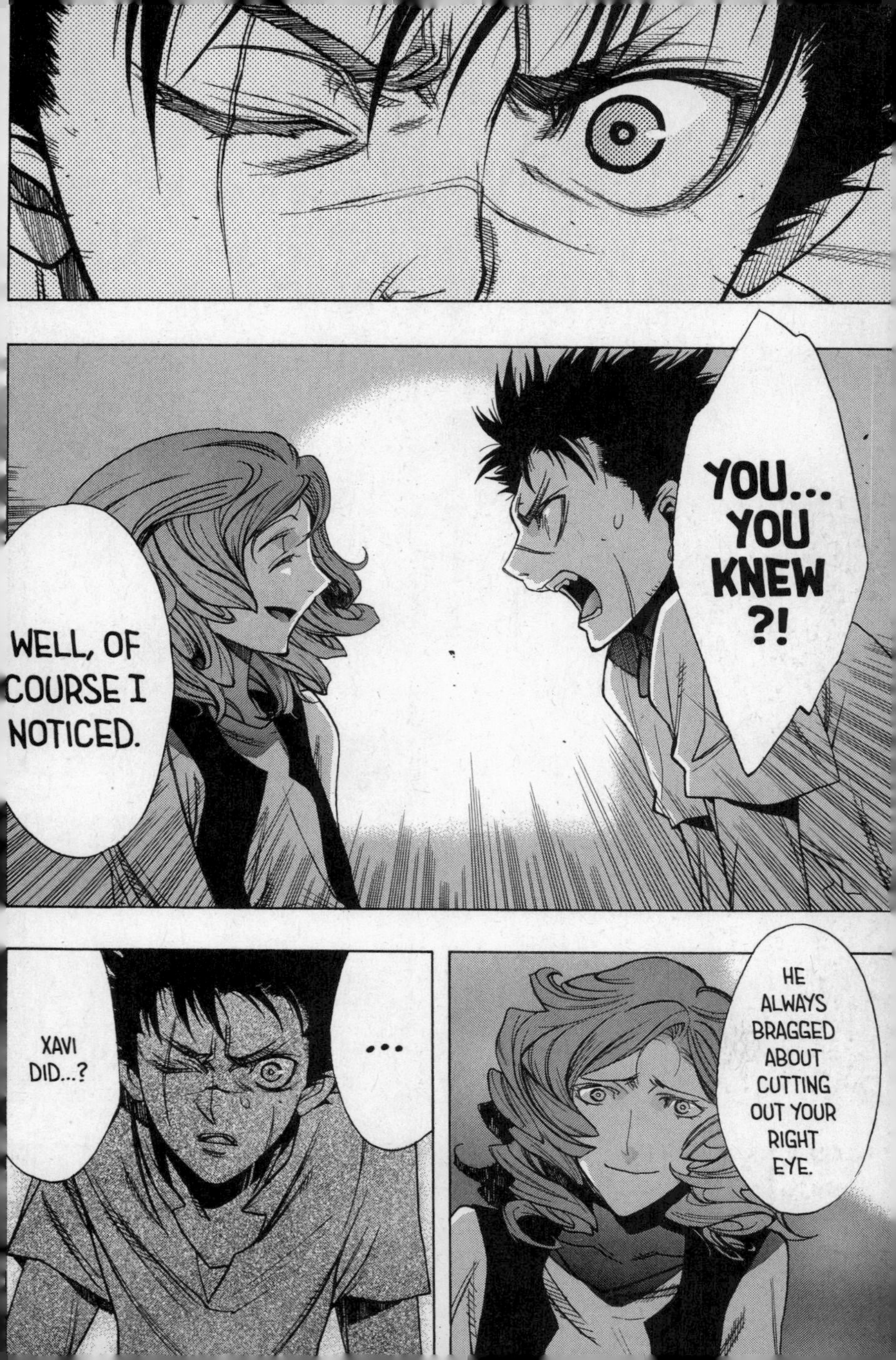
YOU... YOU KNEW?!
WELL, OF COURSE I NOTICED.
HE ALWAYS BRAGGED ABOUT CUTTING OUT YOUR RIGHT EYE.
...
XAVI DID...?

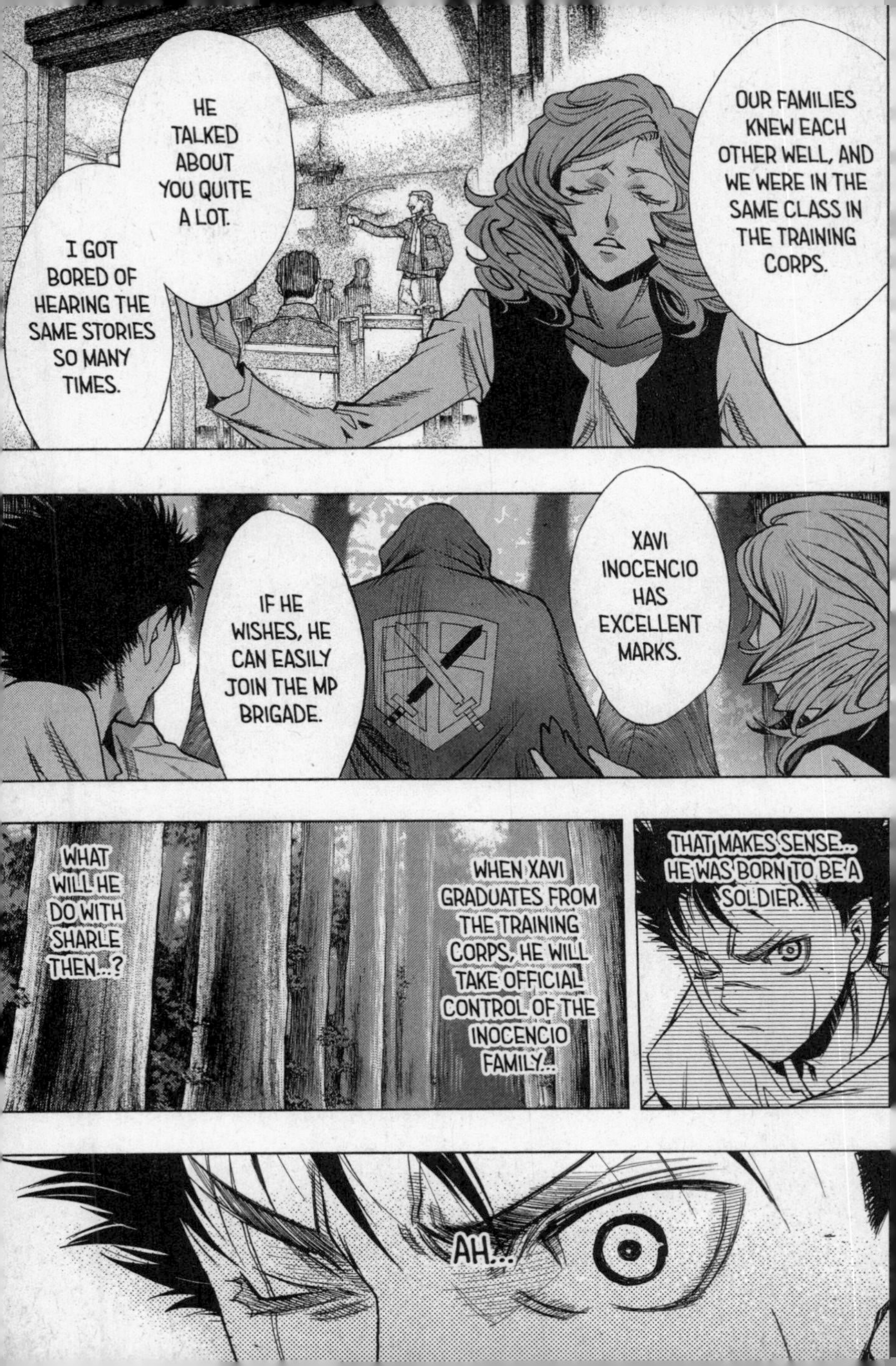
OUR FAMILIES KNEW EACH OTHER WELL, AND WE WERE IN THE SAME CLASS IN THE TRAINING CORPS.
HE TALKED ABOUT YOU QUITE A LOT.
I GOT BORED OF HEARING THE SAME STORIES SO MANY TIMES.
XAVI INOCENCIO HAS EXCELLENT MARKS.
IF HE WISHES, HE CAN EASILY JOIN THE MP BRIGADE.
THAT MAKES SENSE... HE WAS BORN TO BE A SOLDIER.
WHEN XAVI GRADUATES FROM THE TRAINING CORPS, HE WILL TAKE OFFICIAL CONTROL OF THE INOCENCIO FAMILY...
WHAT WILL HE DO WITH SHARLE THEN...?
AH...

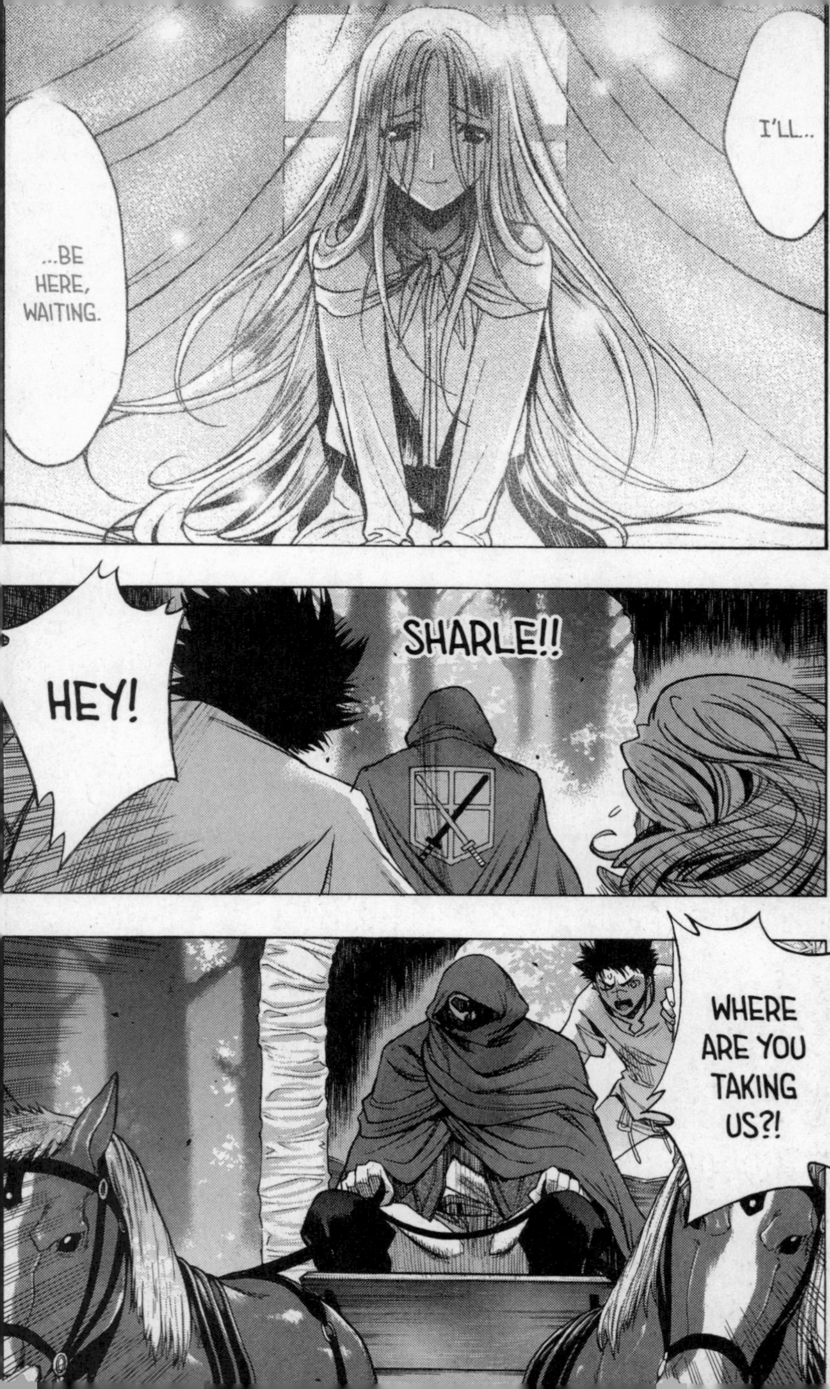
I'LL...
...BE HERE, WAITING.
SHARLE!!
HEY!
WHERE ARE YOU TAKING US?!

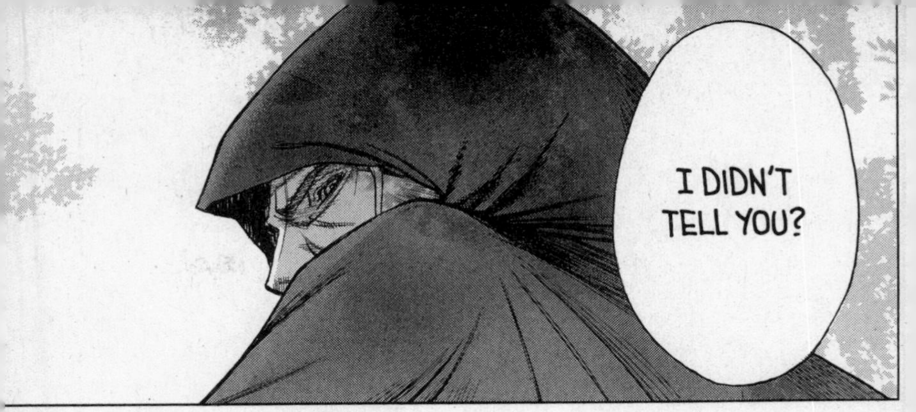
I DIDN'T TELL YOU?
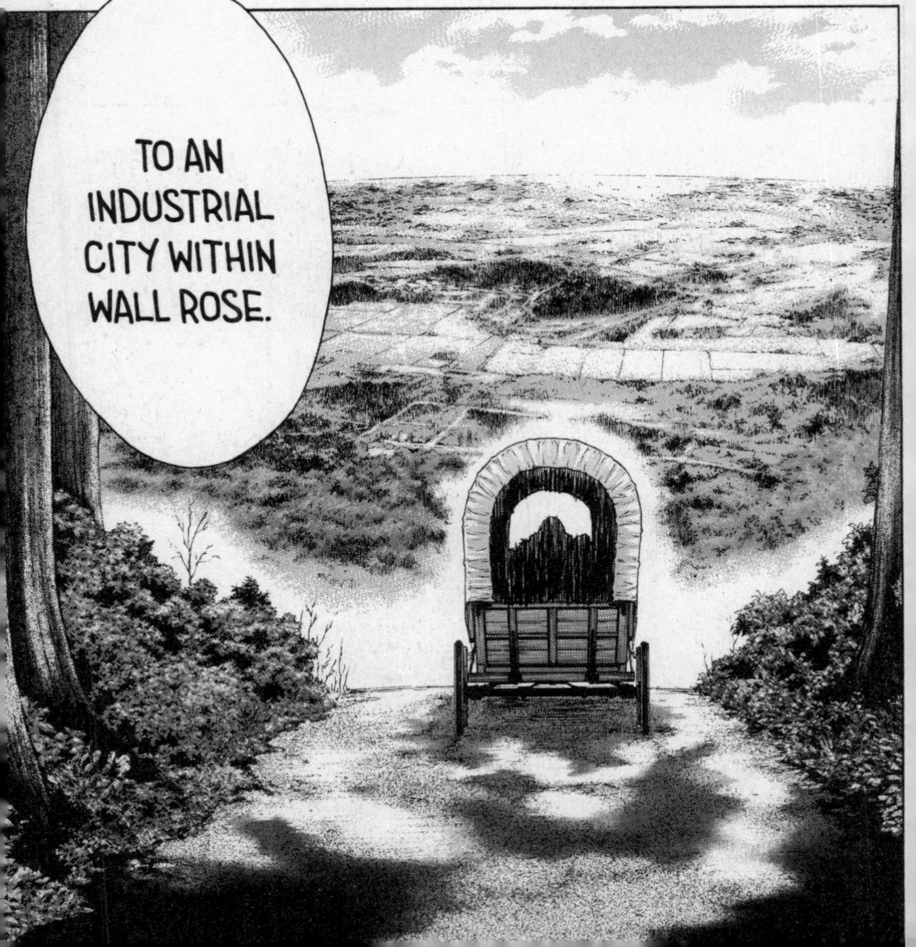
TO AN INDUSTRIAL CITY WITHIN WALL ROSE.

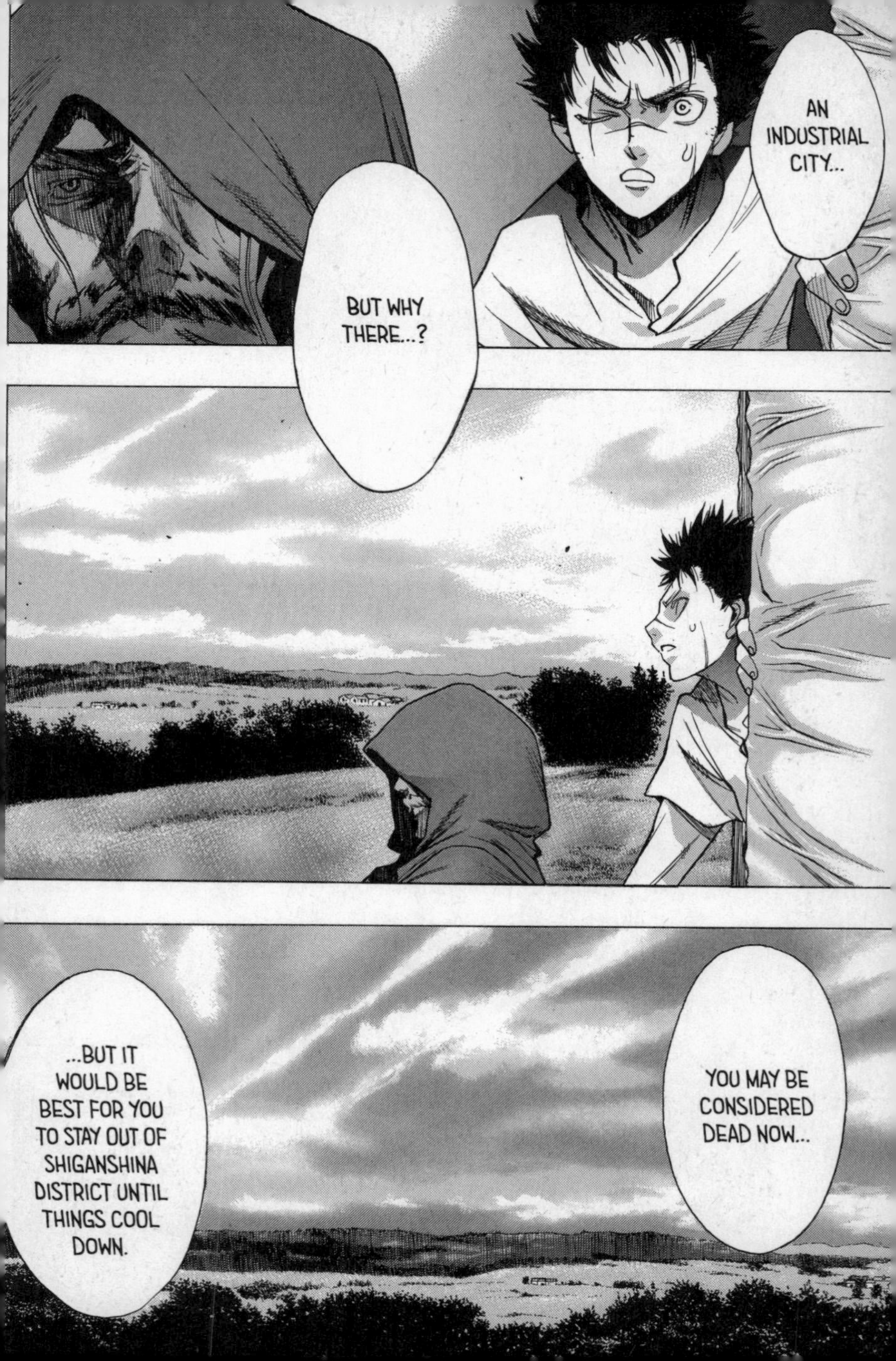
AN INDUSTRIAL CITY...
BUT WHY THERE...?
YOU MAY BE CONSIDERED DEAD NOW...
...BUT IT WOULD BE BEST FOR YOU TO STAY OUT OF SHIGANSHINA DISTRICT UNTIL THINGS COOL DOWN.

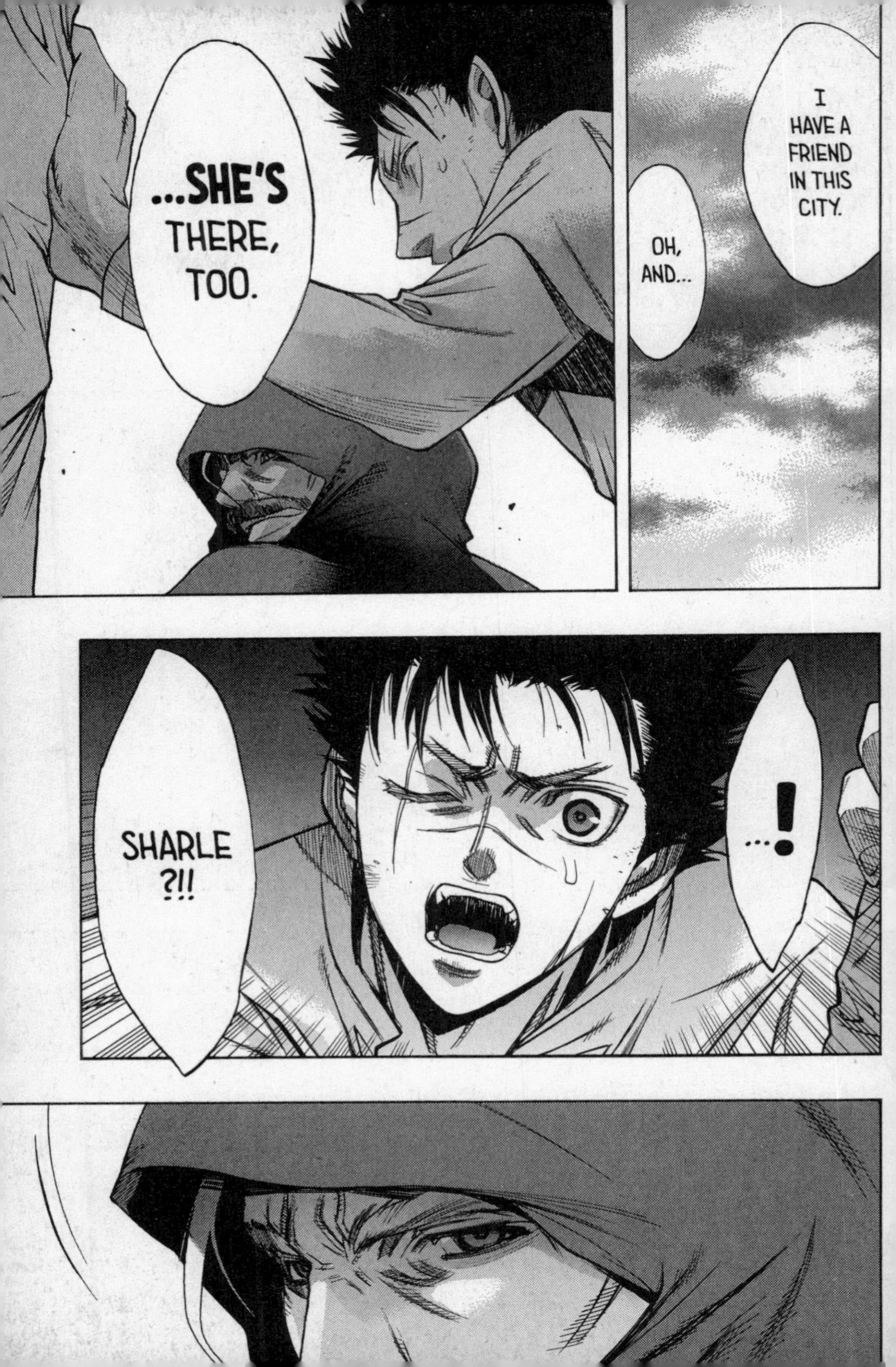
I HAVE A FRIEND IN THIS CITY.
OH, AND...
...SHE'S THERE, TOO.
...!
SHARLE ?!!

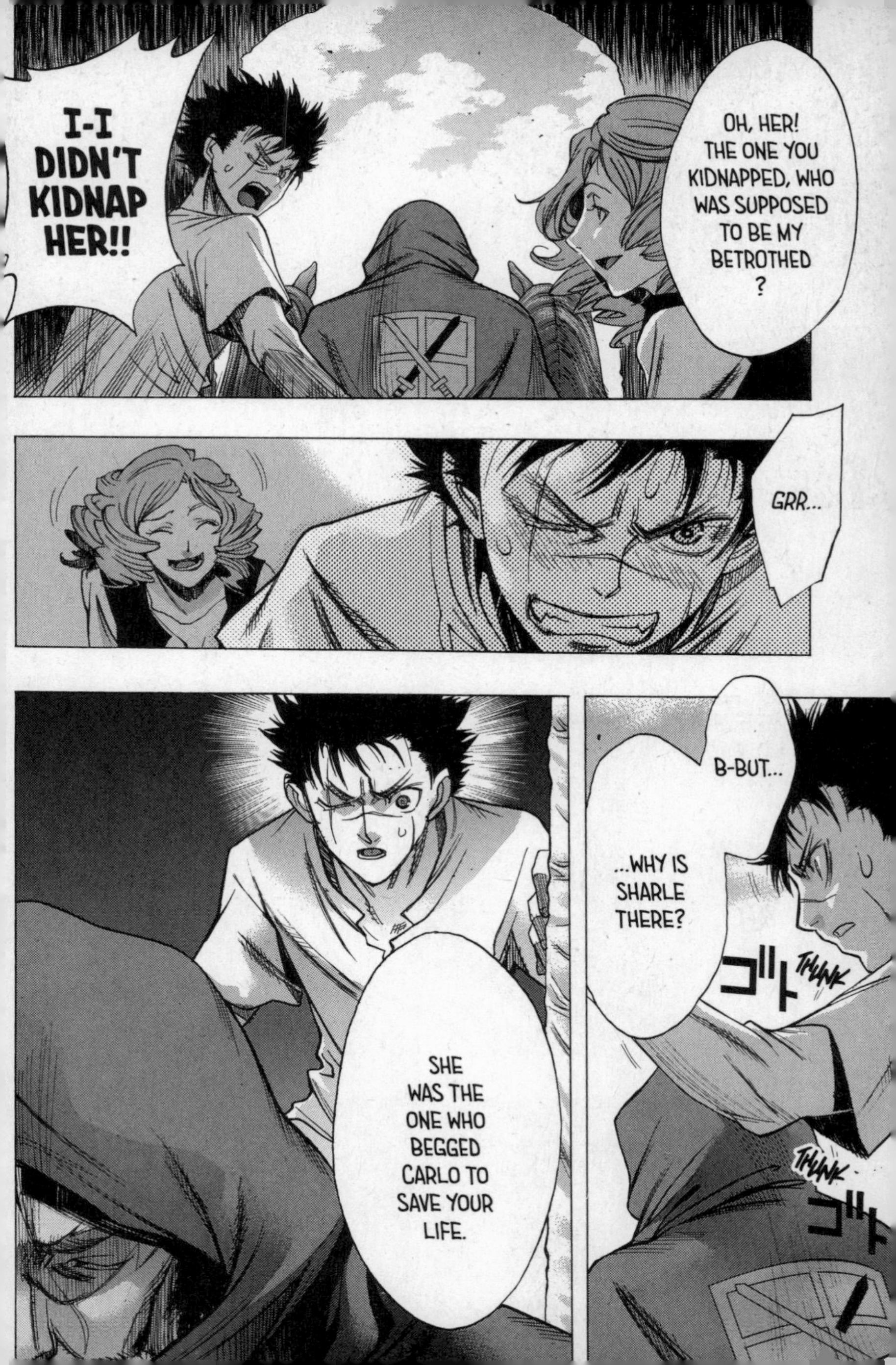
OH, HER! THE ONE YOU KIDNAPPED, WHO WAS SUPPOSED TO BE MY BETROTHED ?
I-I DIDN'T KIDNAP HER!!
GRR...
B-BUT...
...WHY IS SHARLE THERE?
ゴト
THUNK
THUNK
ゴト
SHE WAS THE ONE WHO BEGGED CARLO TO SAVE YOUR LIFE.

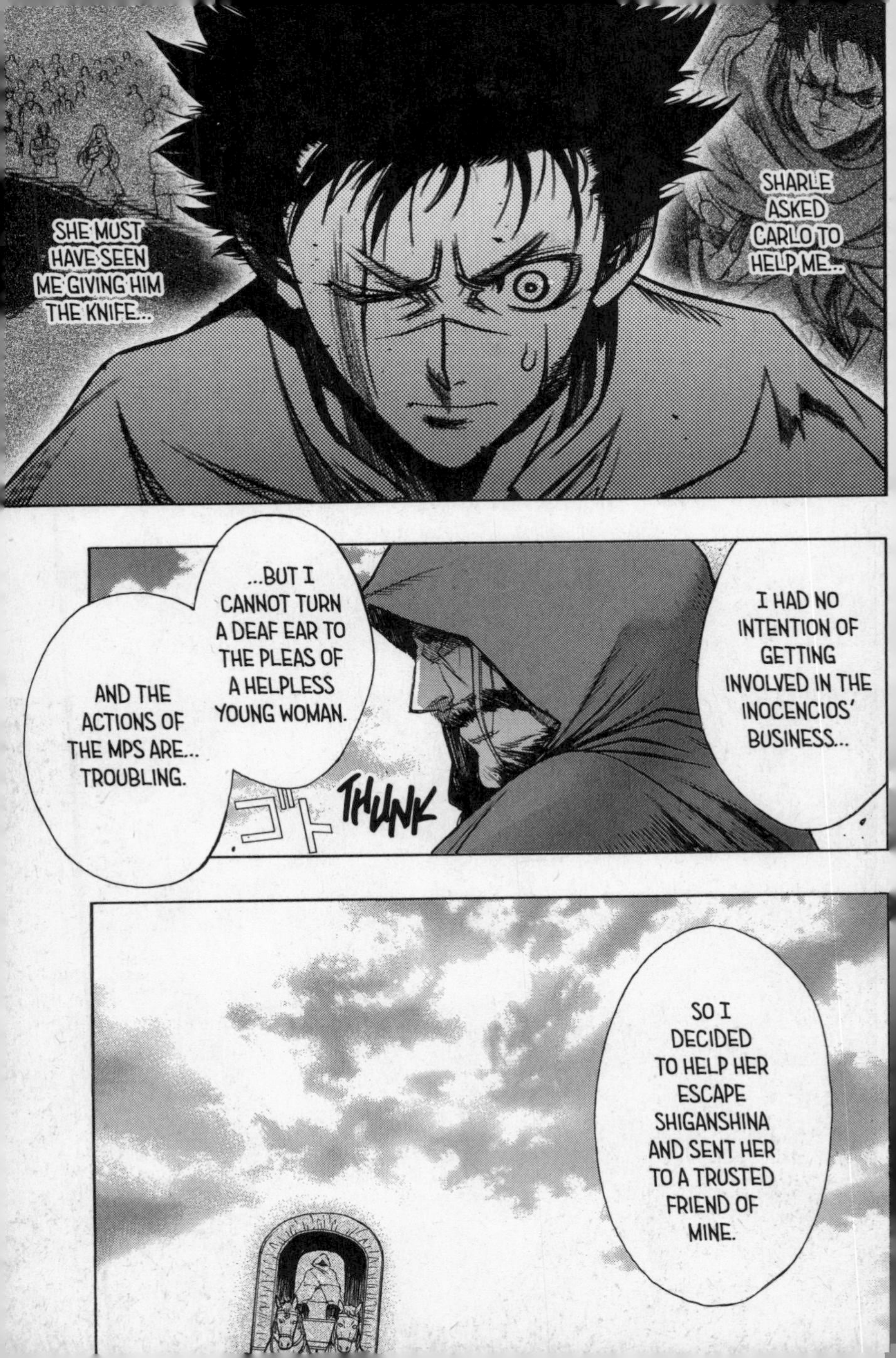
SHARLE ASKED CARLO TO HELP ME...
SHE MUST HAVE SEEN ME GIVING HIM THE KNIFE...
I HAD NO INTENTION OF GETTING INVOLVED IN THE INOCENCIOS' BUSINESS...
...BUT I CANNOT TURN A DEAF EAR TO THE PLEAS OF A HELPLESS YOUNG WOMAN.
AND THE ACTIONS OF THE MPS ARE... TROUBLING.
ゴト
THUNK
SO I DECIDED TO HELP HER ESCAPE SHIGANSHINA AND SENT HER TO A TRUSTED FRIEND OF MINE.

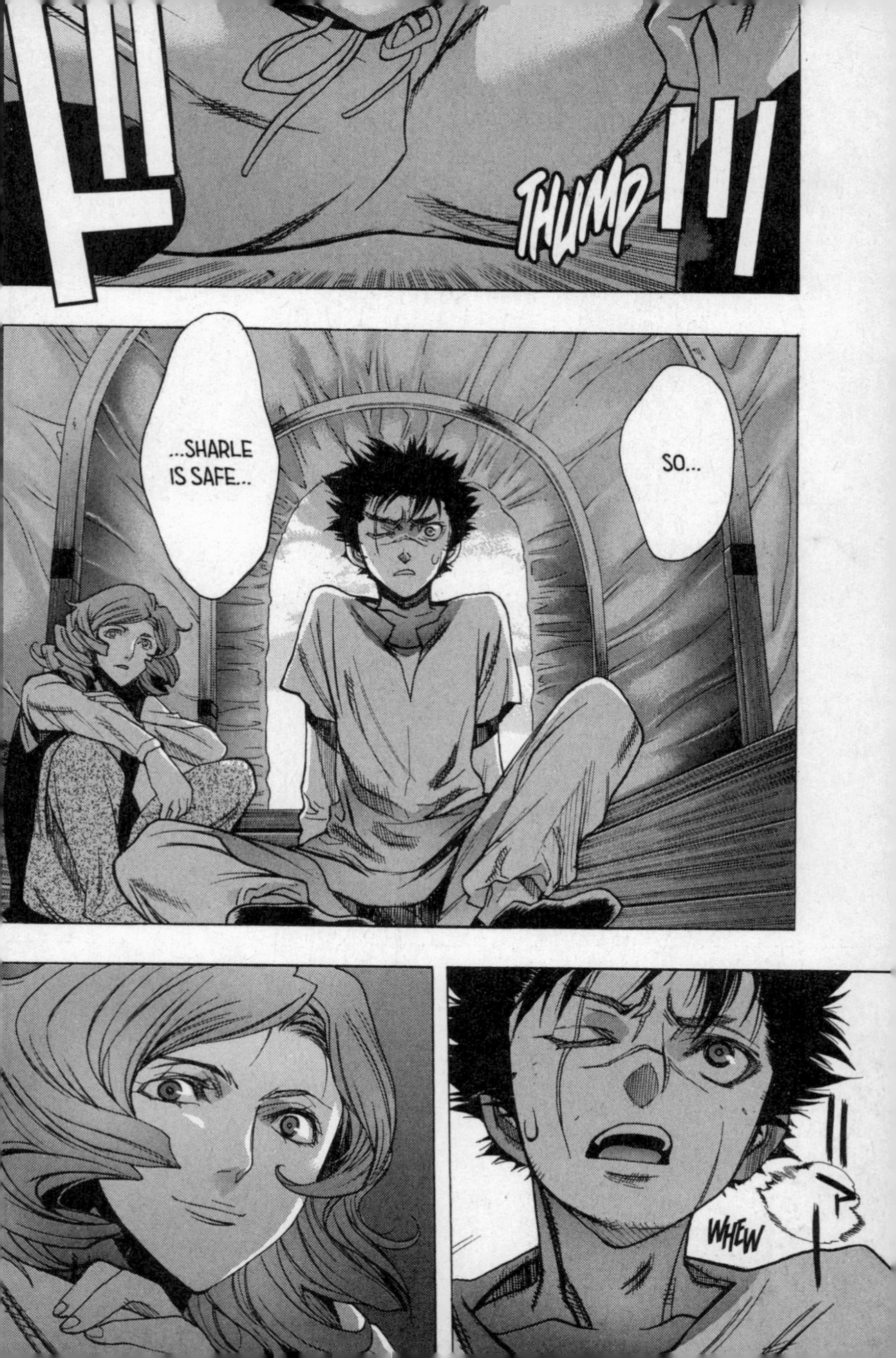
THUMP
SO...
...SHARLE IS SAFE...
WHEW

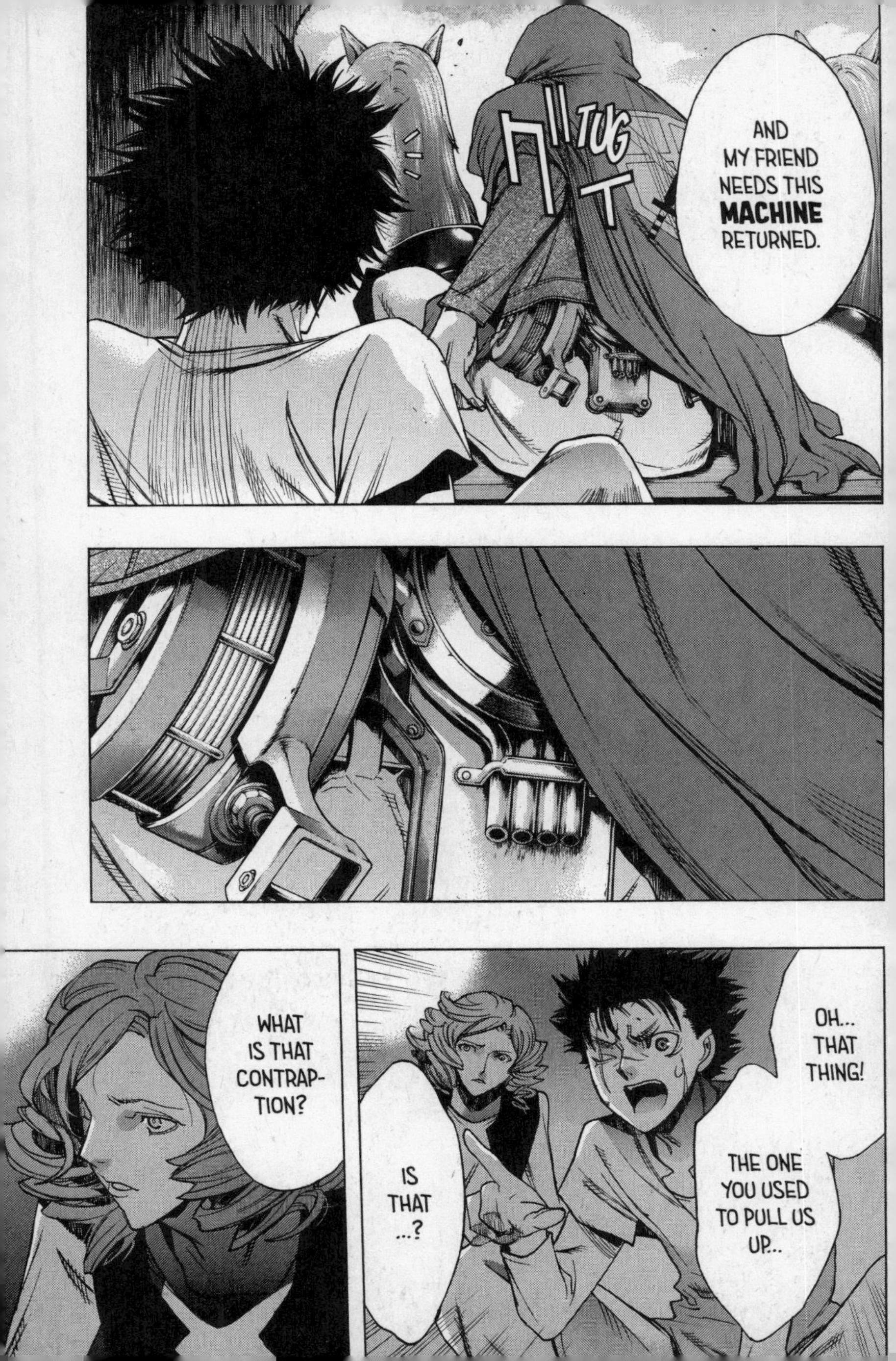
AND MY FRIEND NEEDS THIS **MACHINE** RETURNED.
TUG
OH... THAT THING!
THE ONE YOU USED TO PULL US UP...
IS THAT ...?
WHAT IS THAT CONTRAPTION?

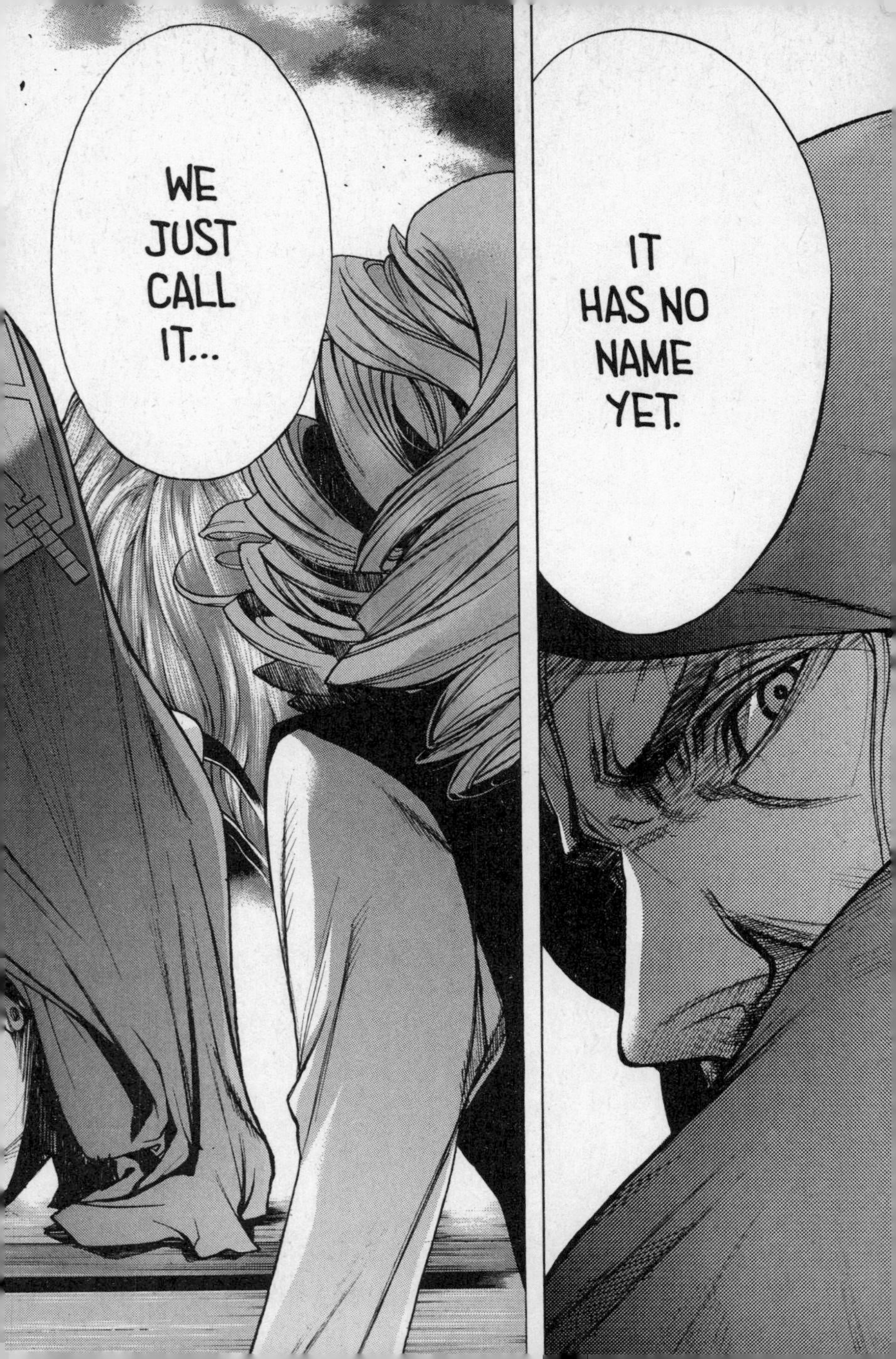
IT HAS NO NAME YET.
WE JUST CALL IT...

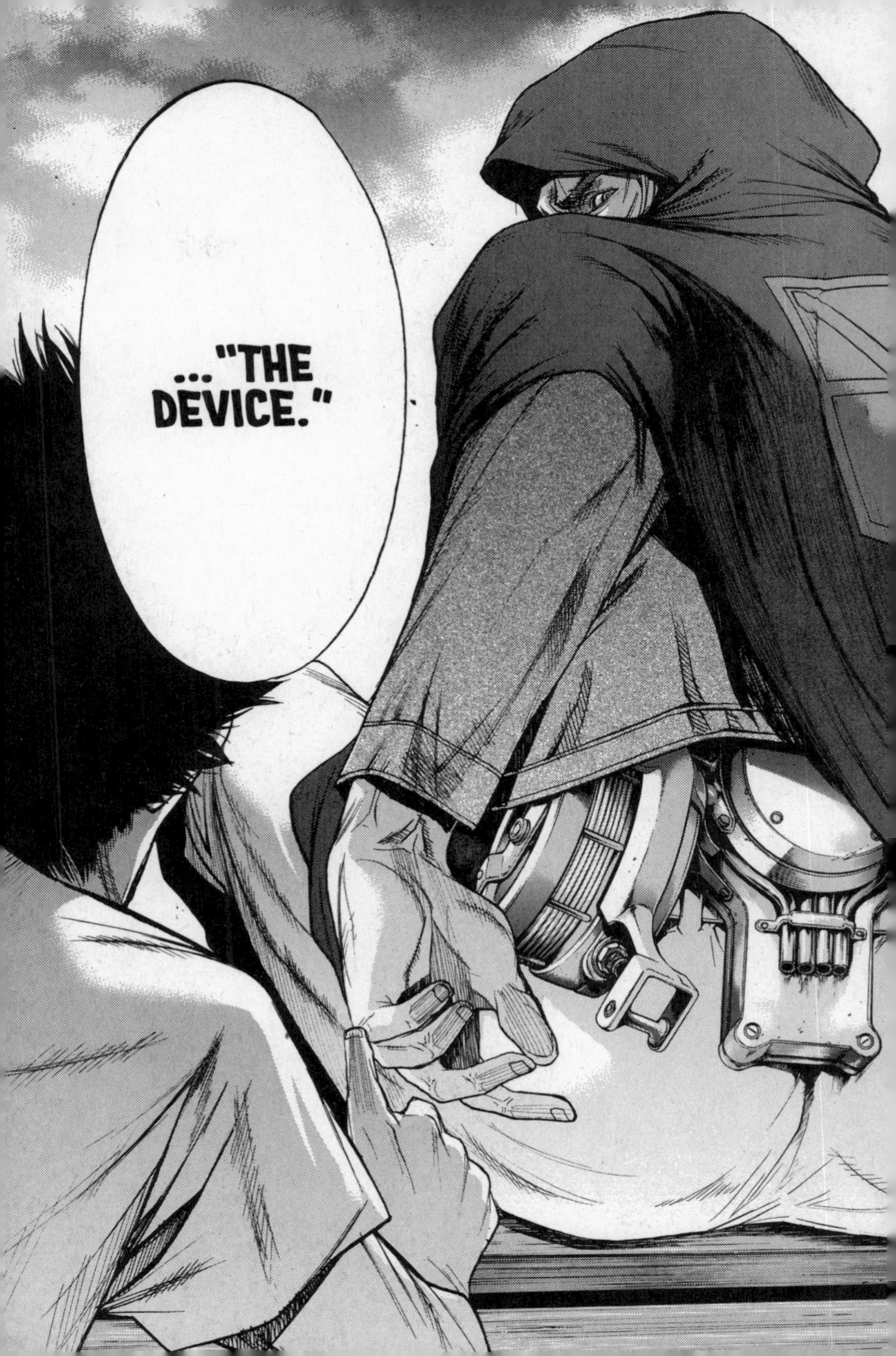
..."THE DEVICE."

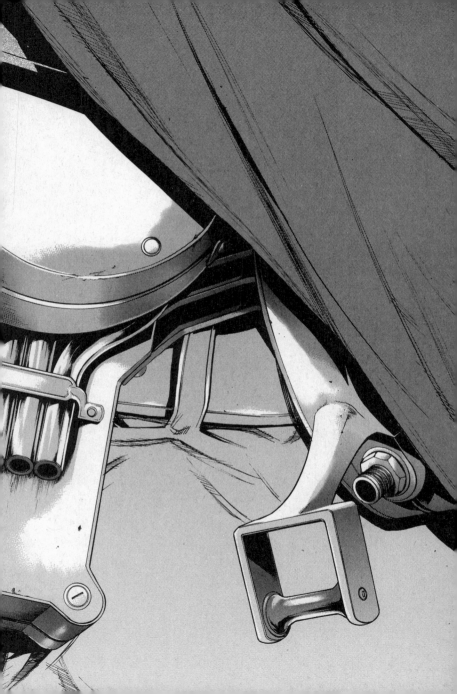

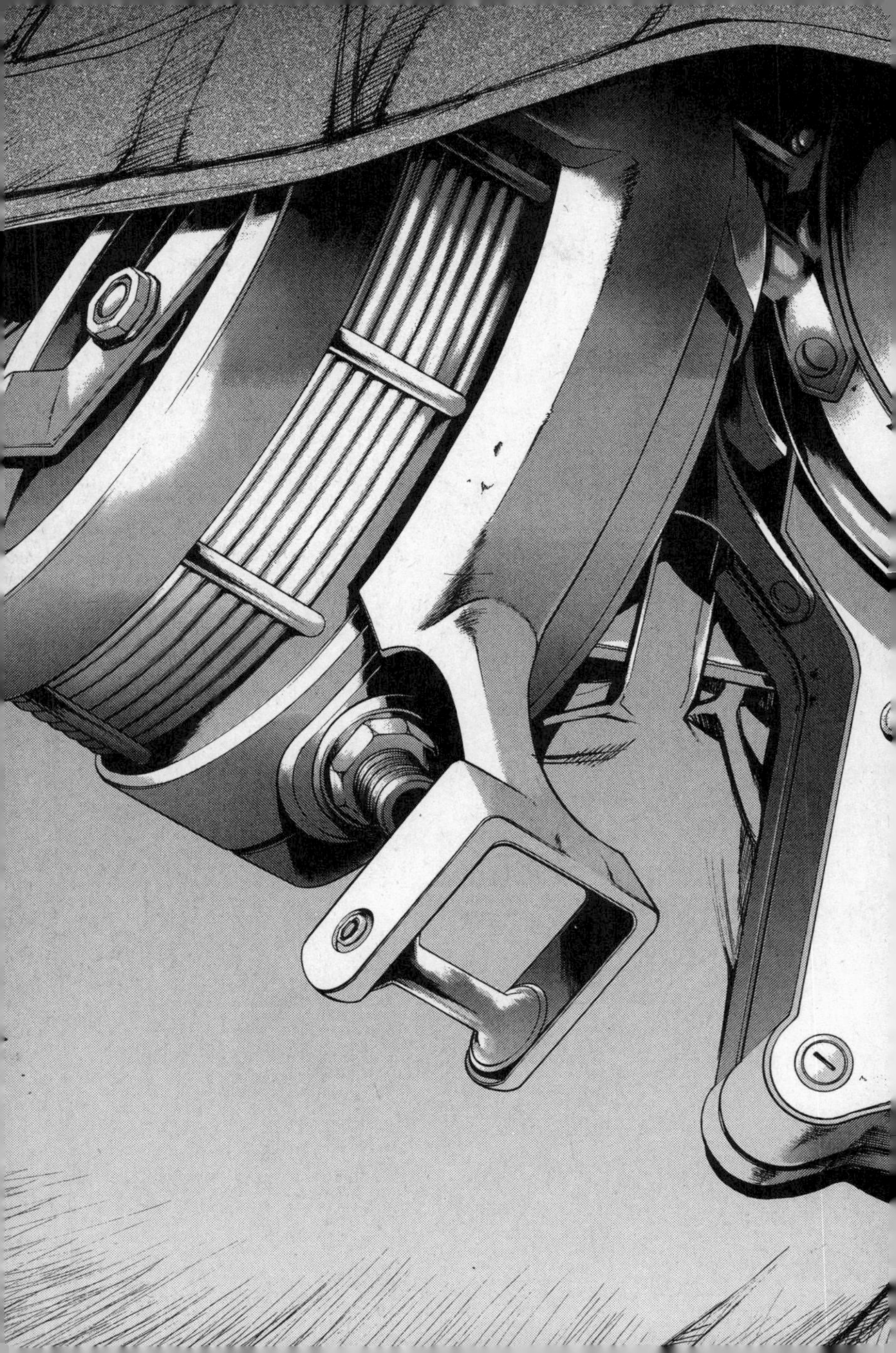

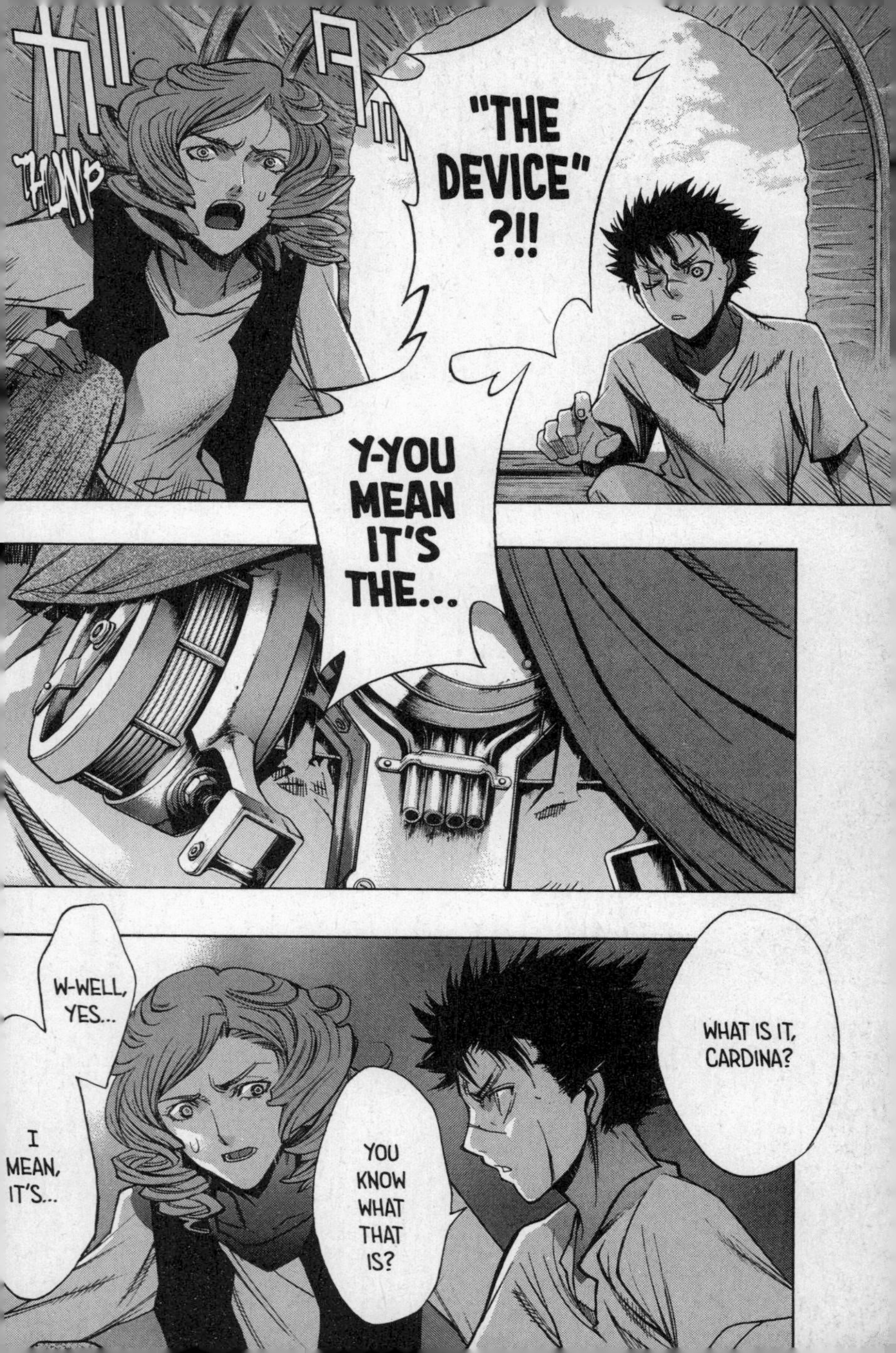

"THE DEVICE"?!!
THUMP
Y-YOU MEAN IT'S THE...
WHAT IS IT, CARDINA?
YOU KNOW WHAT THAT IS?
W-WELL, YES...
I MEAN, IT'S...

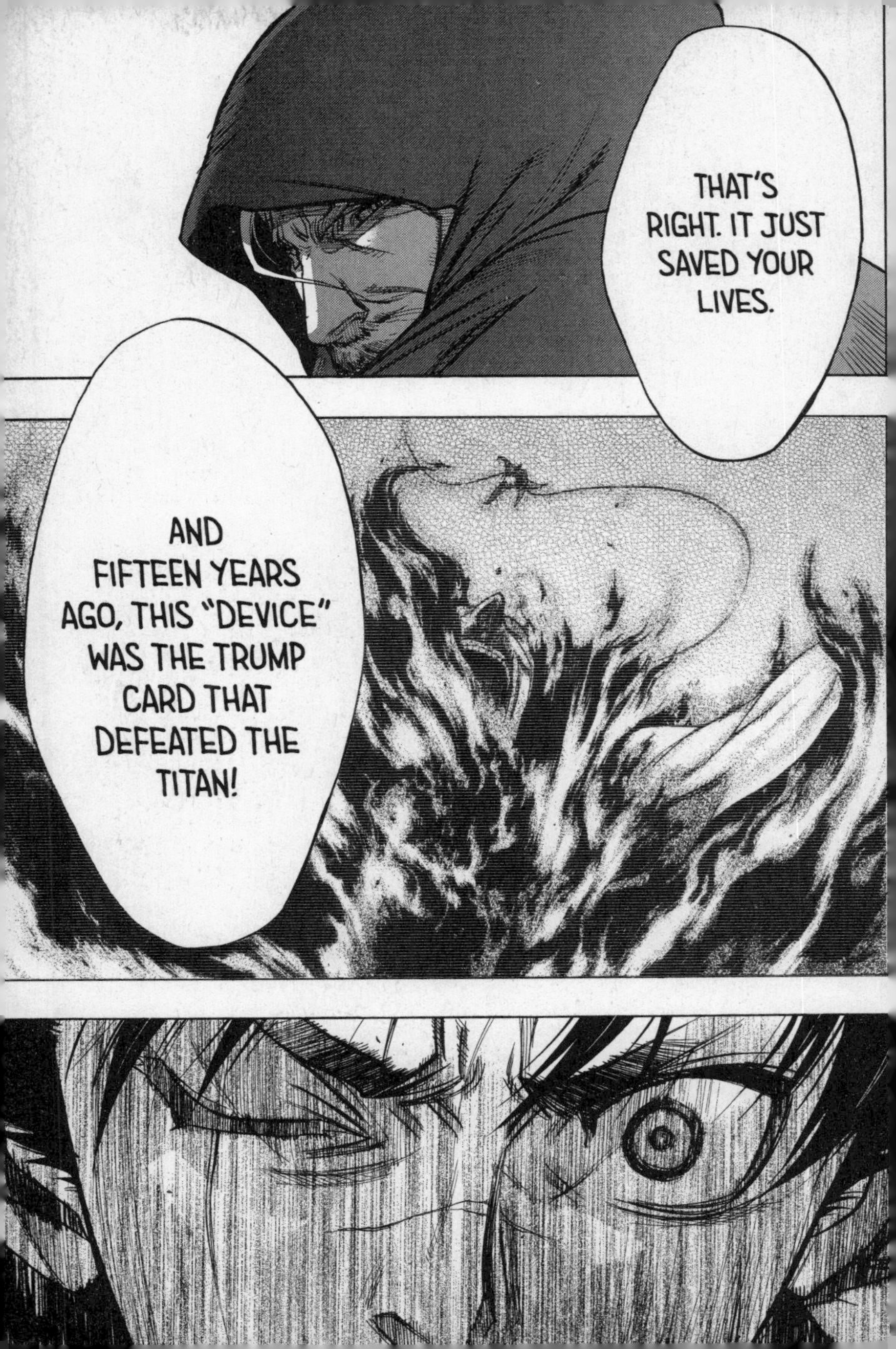
THAT'S RIGHT. IT JUST SAVED YOUR LIVES.
AND FIFTEEN YEARS AGO, THIS "DEVICE" WAS THE TRUMP CARD THAT DEFEATED THE TITAN!

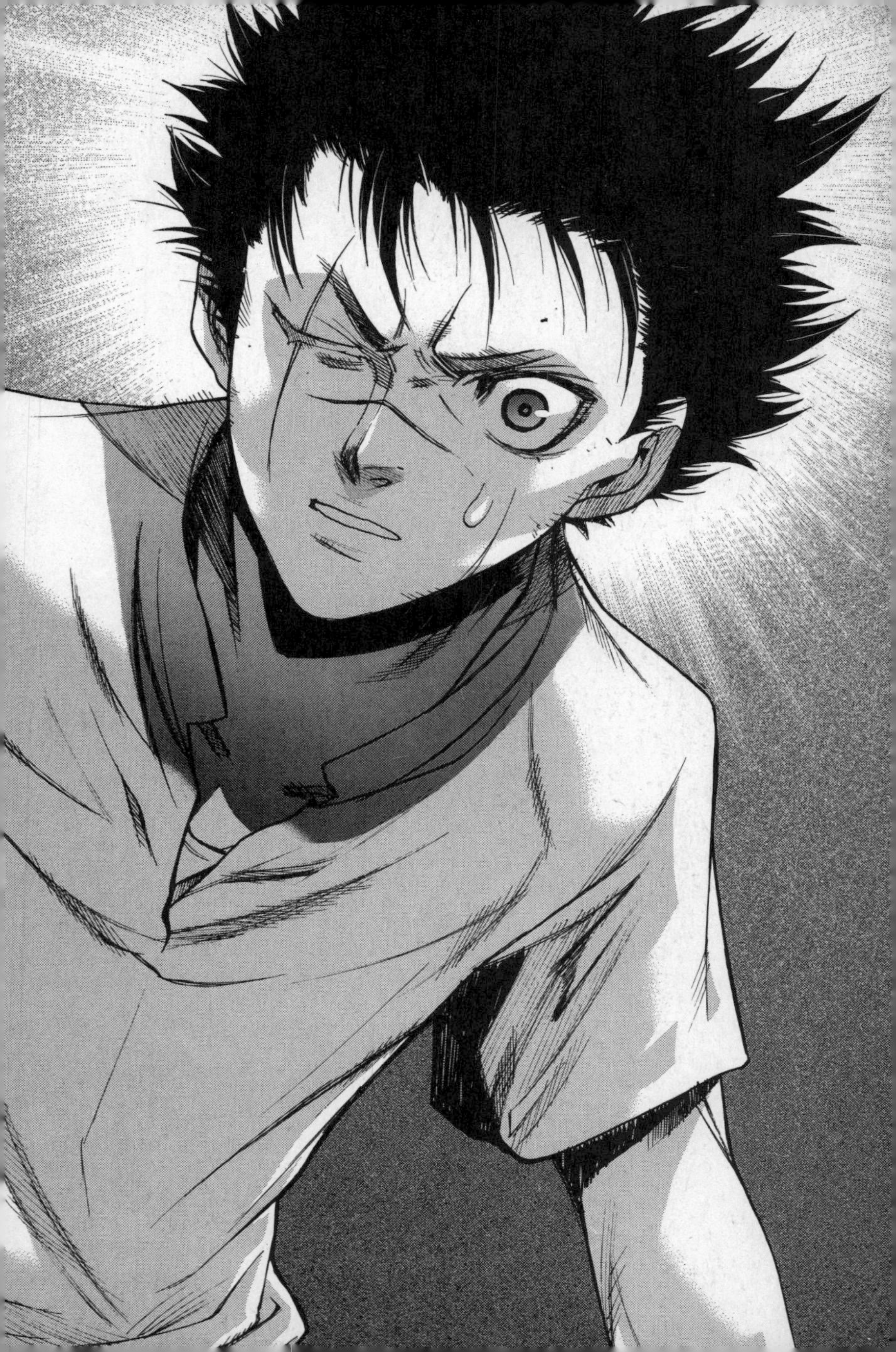

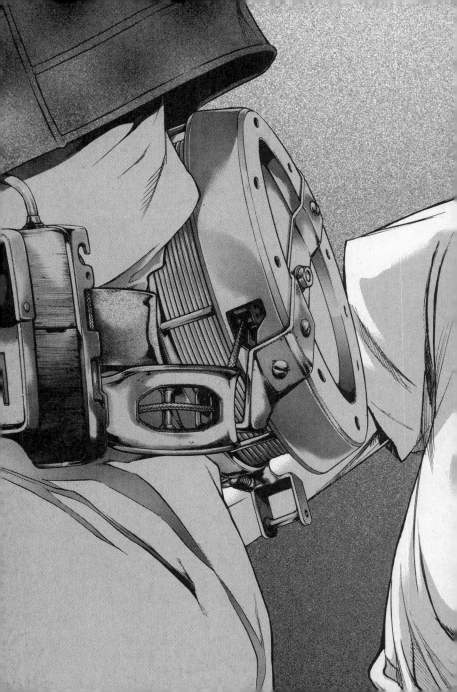

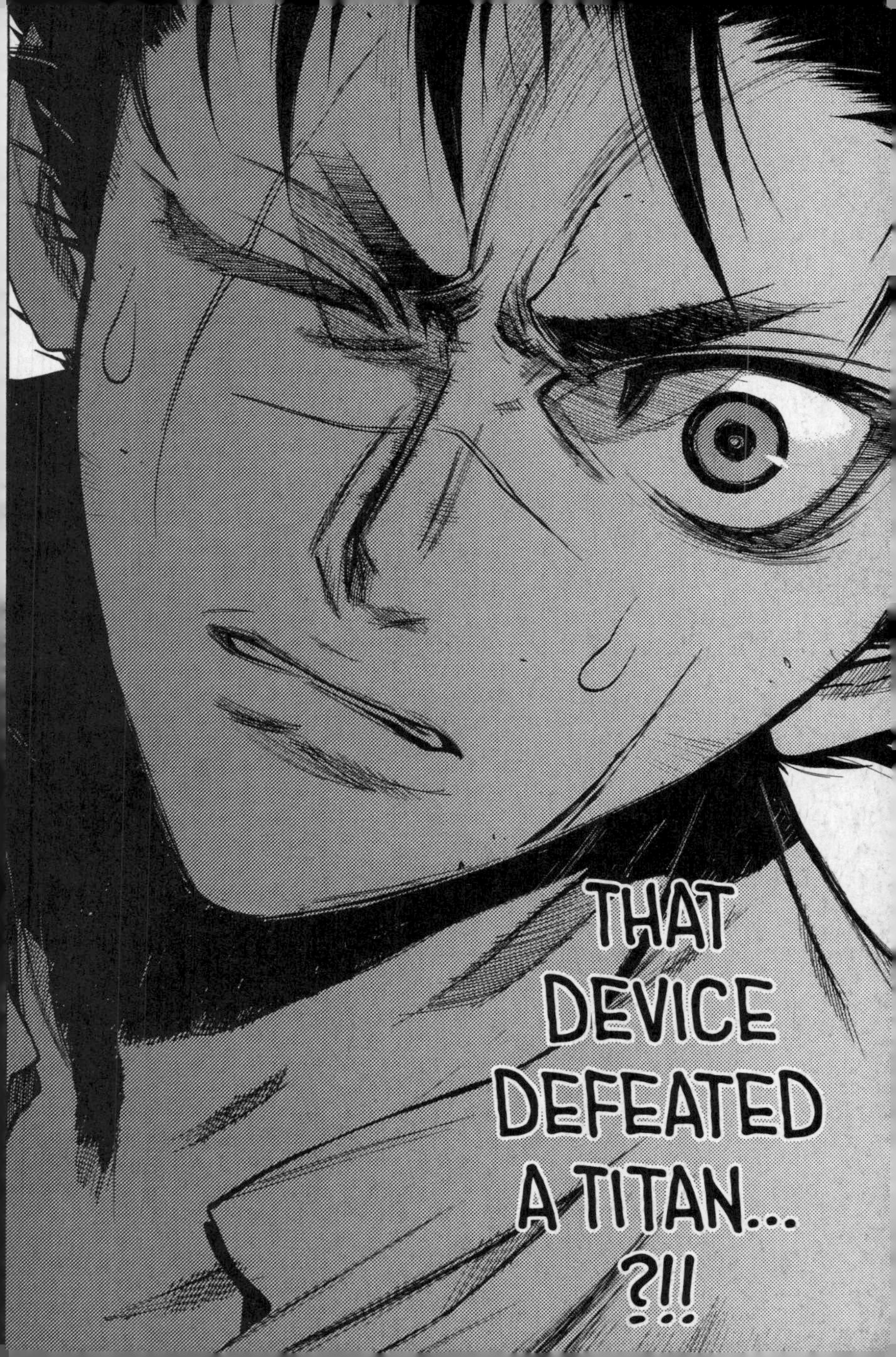
THAT DEVICE DEFEATED A TITAN...?!!

ATTACK on TITAN
BEFORE THE FALL

TO BE CONTINUED

Attack on Titan: Before the Fall
Sharle's Shiganshina Diary

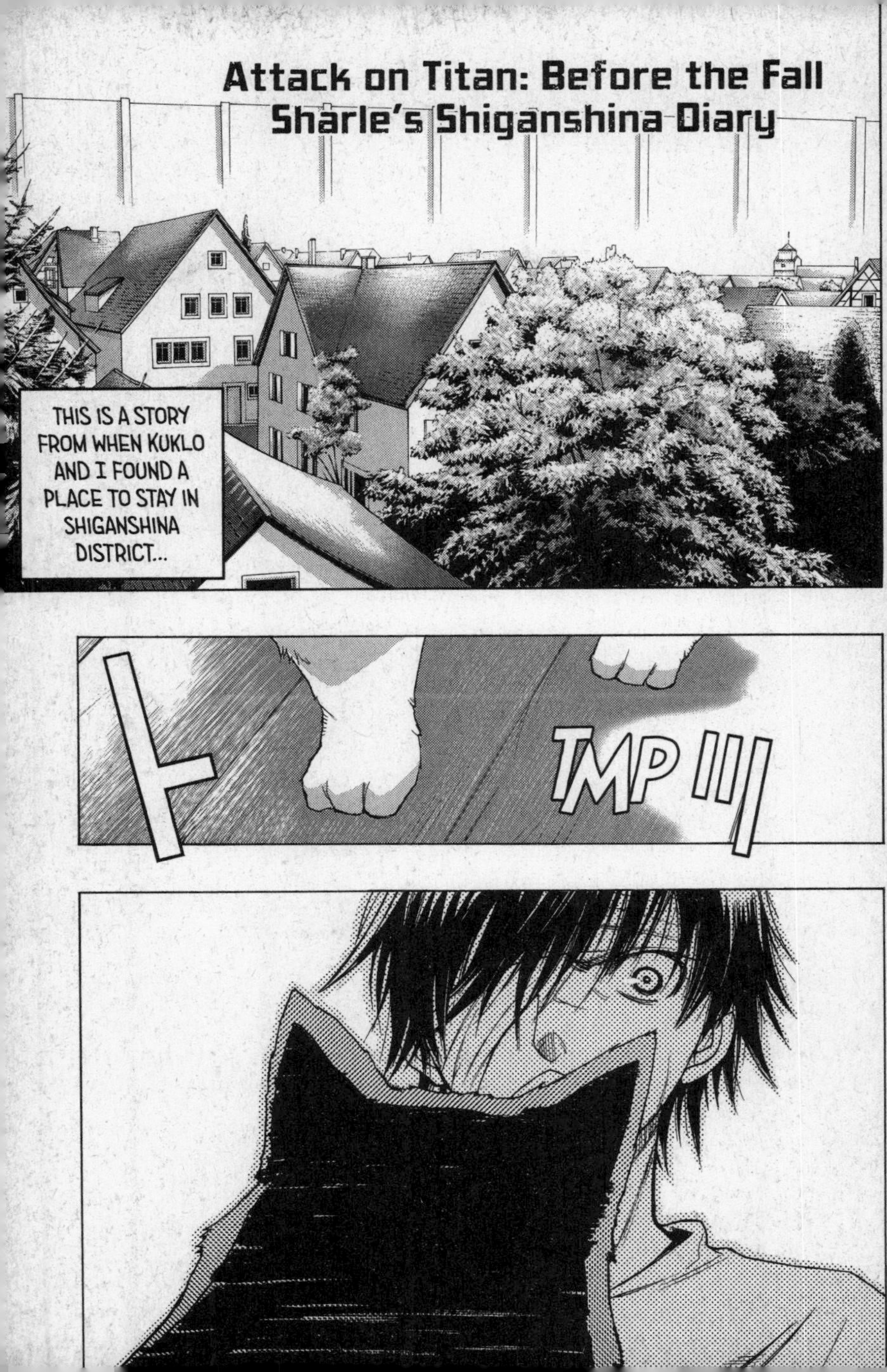
THIS IS A STORY FROM WHEN KUKLO AND I FOUND A PLACE TO STAY IN SHIGANSHINA DISTRICT...
TMP

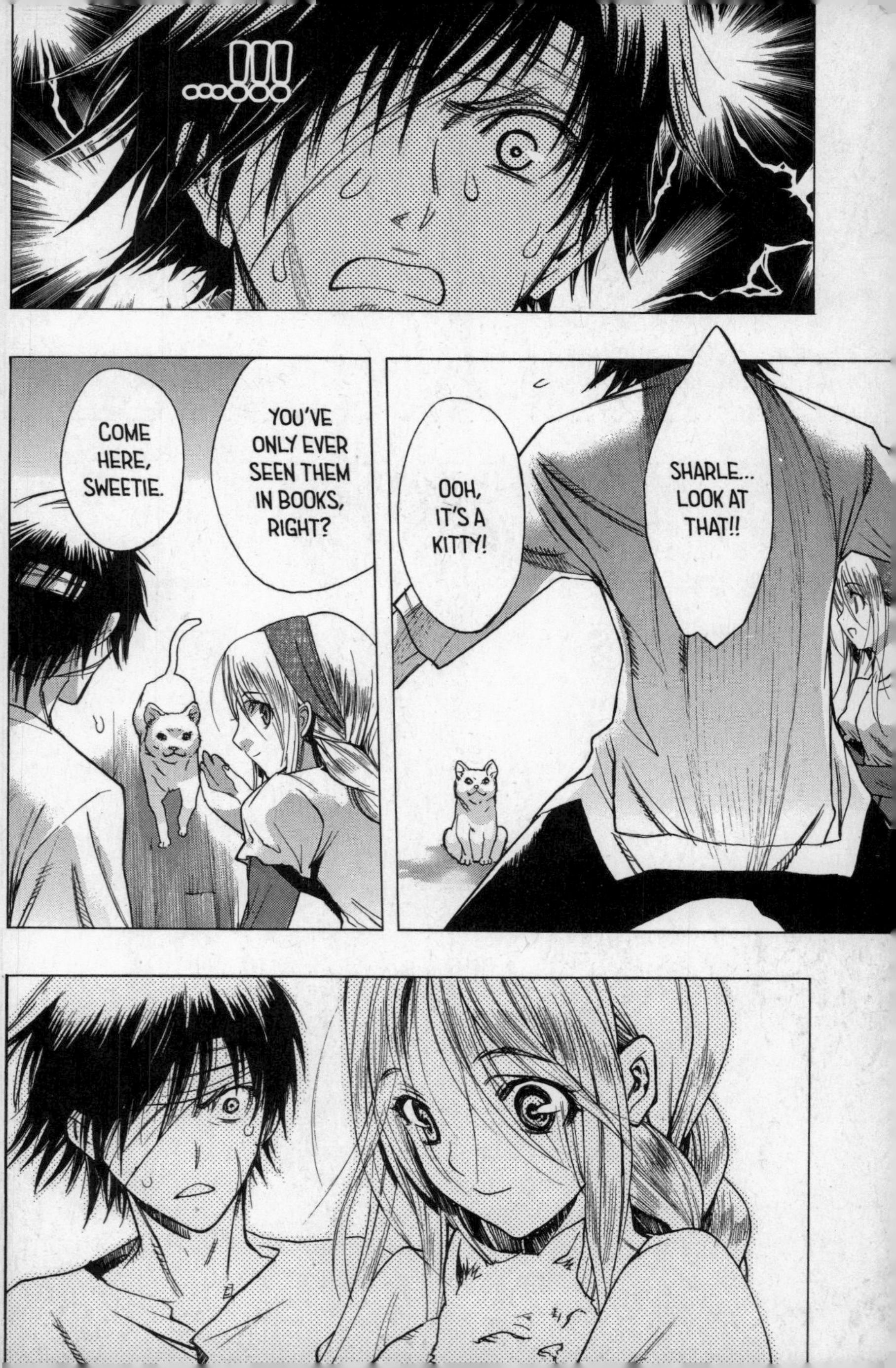
...!!!
SHARLE... LOOK AT THAT!!
OOH, IT'S A KITTY!
YOU'VE ONLY EVER SEEN THEM IN BOOKS, RIGHT?
COME HERE, SWEETIE.

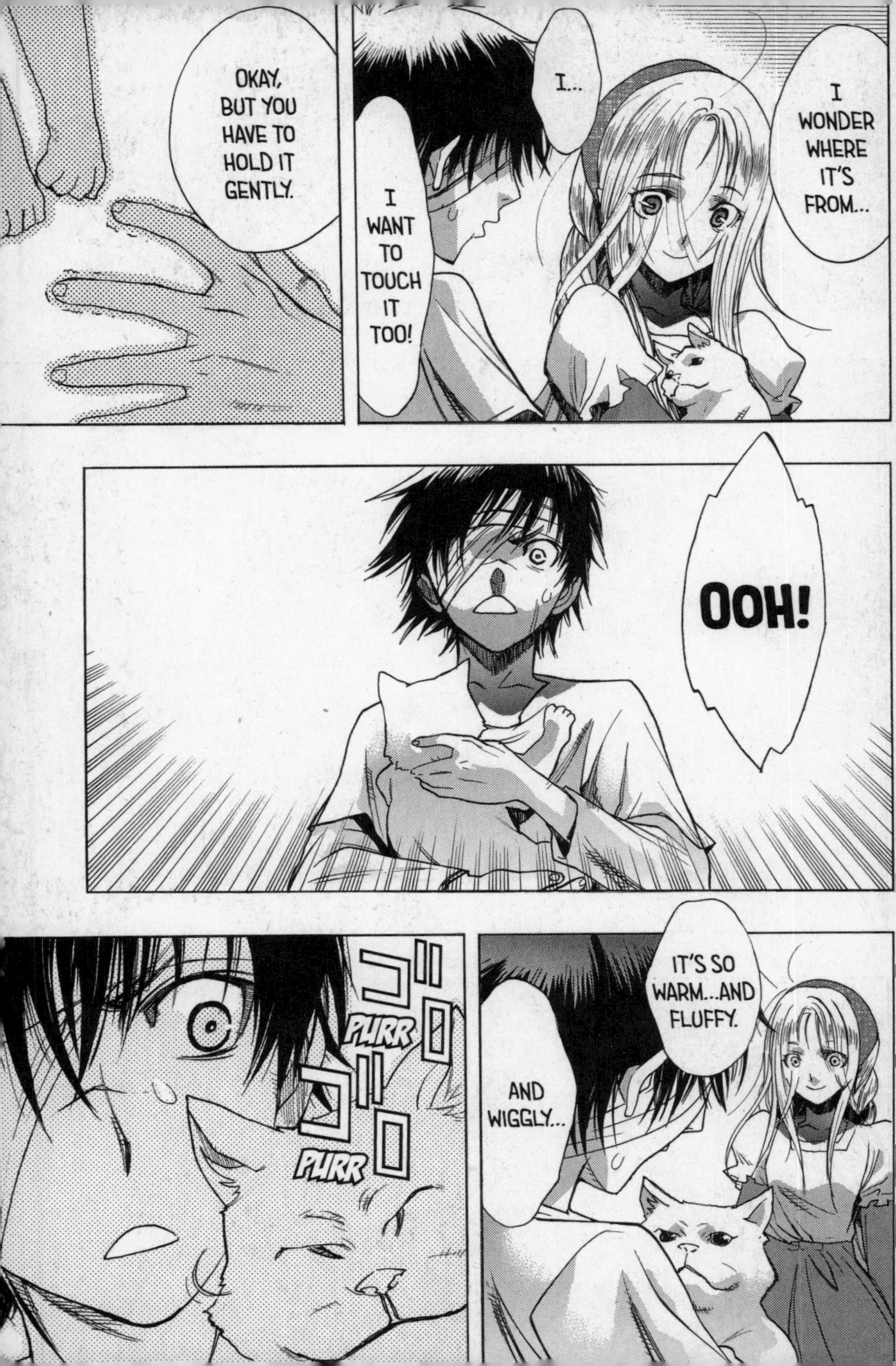
I WONDER WHERE IT'S FROM...
I...
I WANT TO TOUCH IT TOO!
OKAY, BUT YOU HAVE TO HOLD IT GENTLY.
OOH!
IT'S SO WARM...AND FLUFFY.
AND WIGGLY...
ゴロ
PURR
ゴロ
PURR

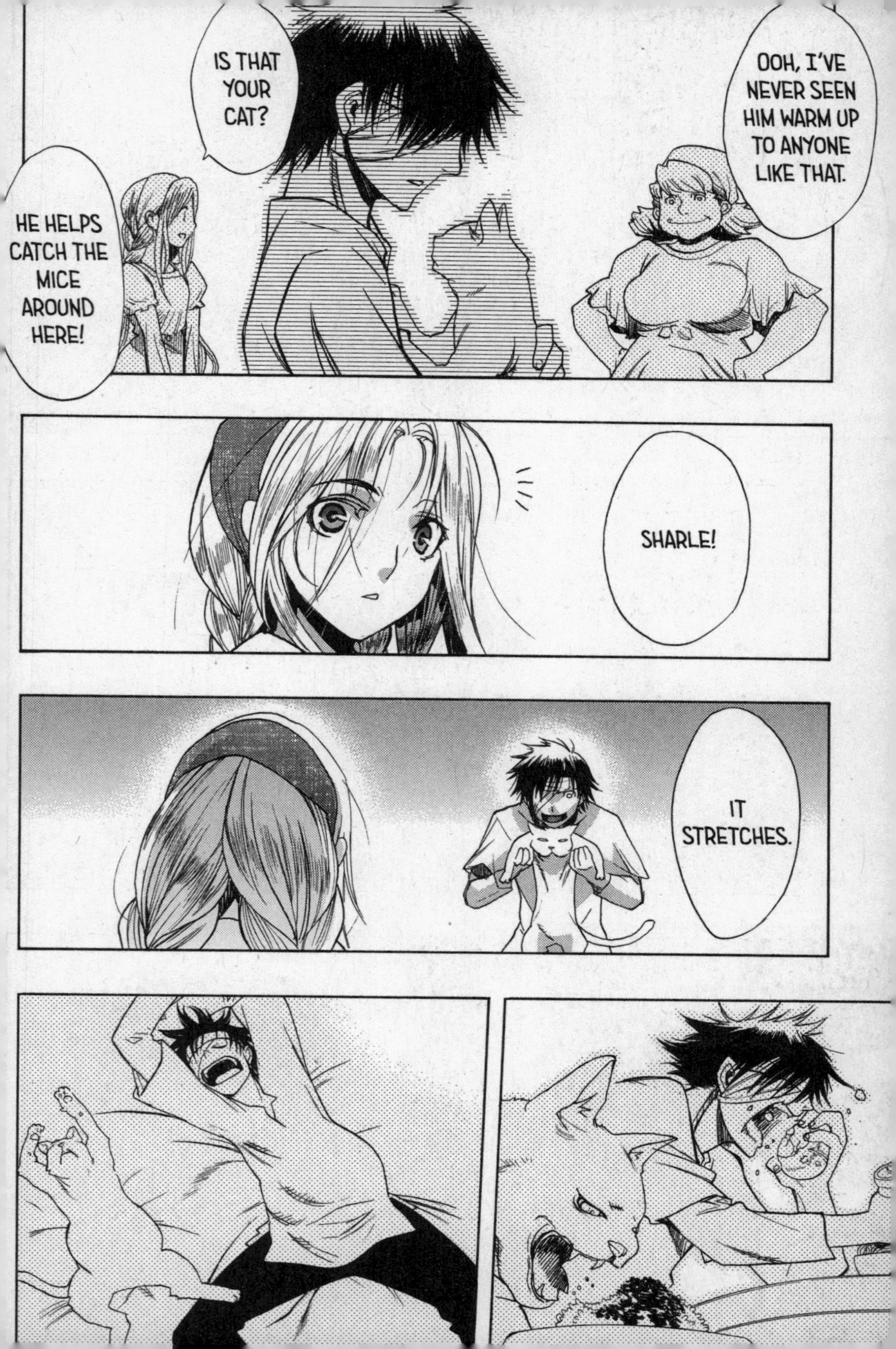
OOH, I'VE NEVER SEEN HIM WARM UP TO ANYONE LIKE THAT.
IS THAT YOUR CAT?
HE HELPS CATCH THE MICE AROUND HERE!
SHARLE!
IT STRETCHES.

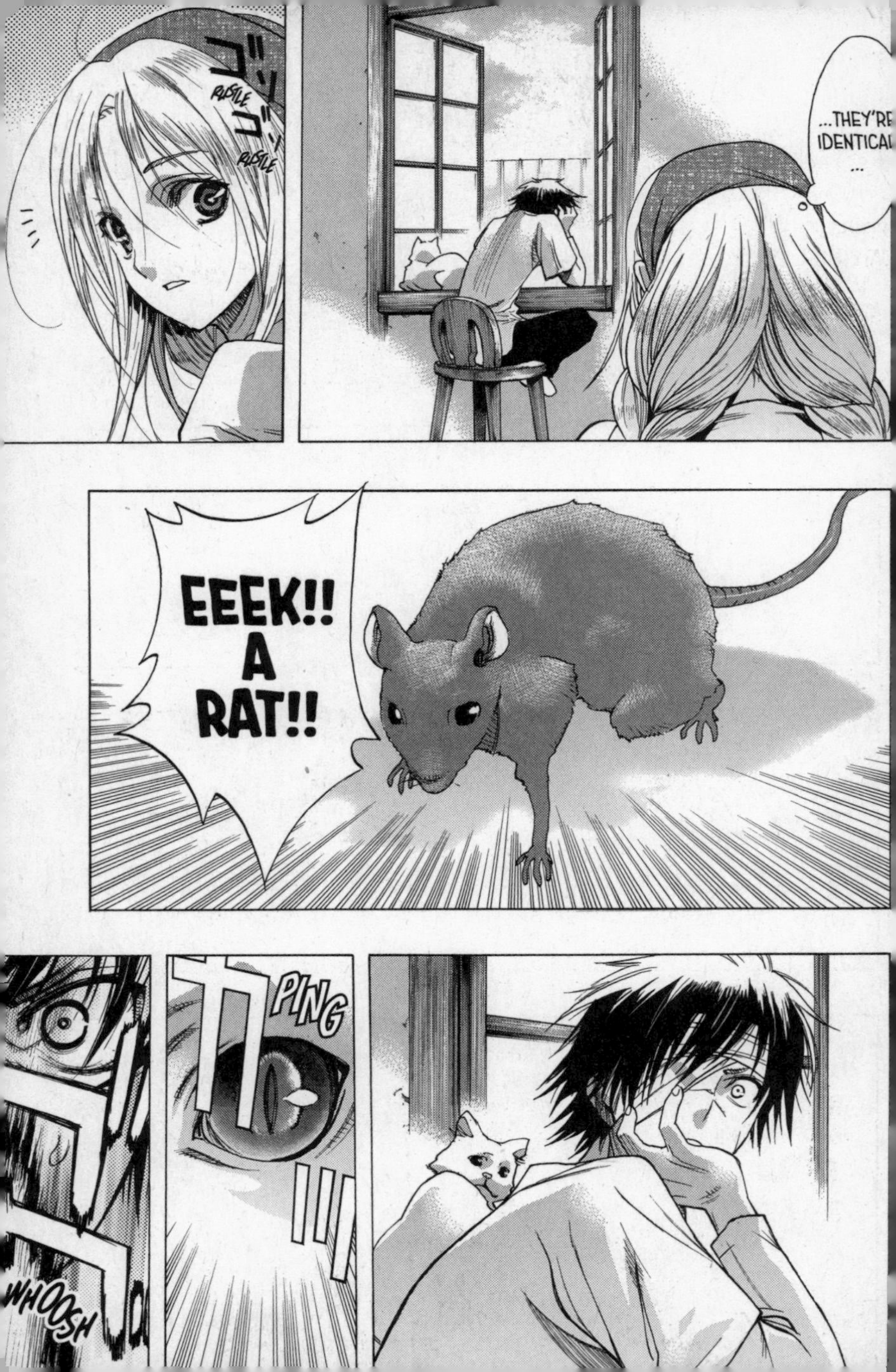
...THEY'R IDENTICA ...
RUSTLE
RUSTLE
EEEK!! A RAT!!
PING
WHOOSH

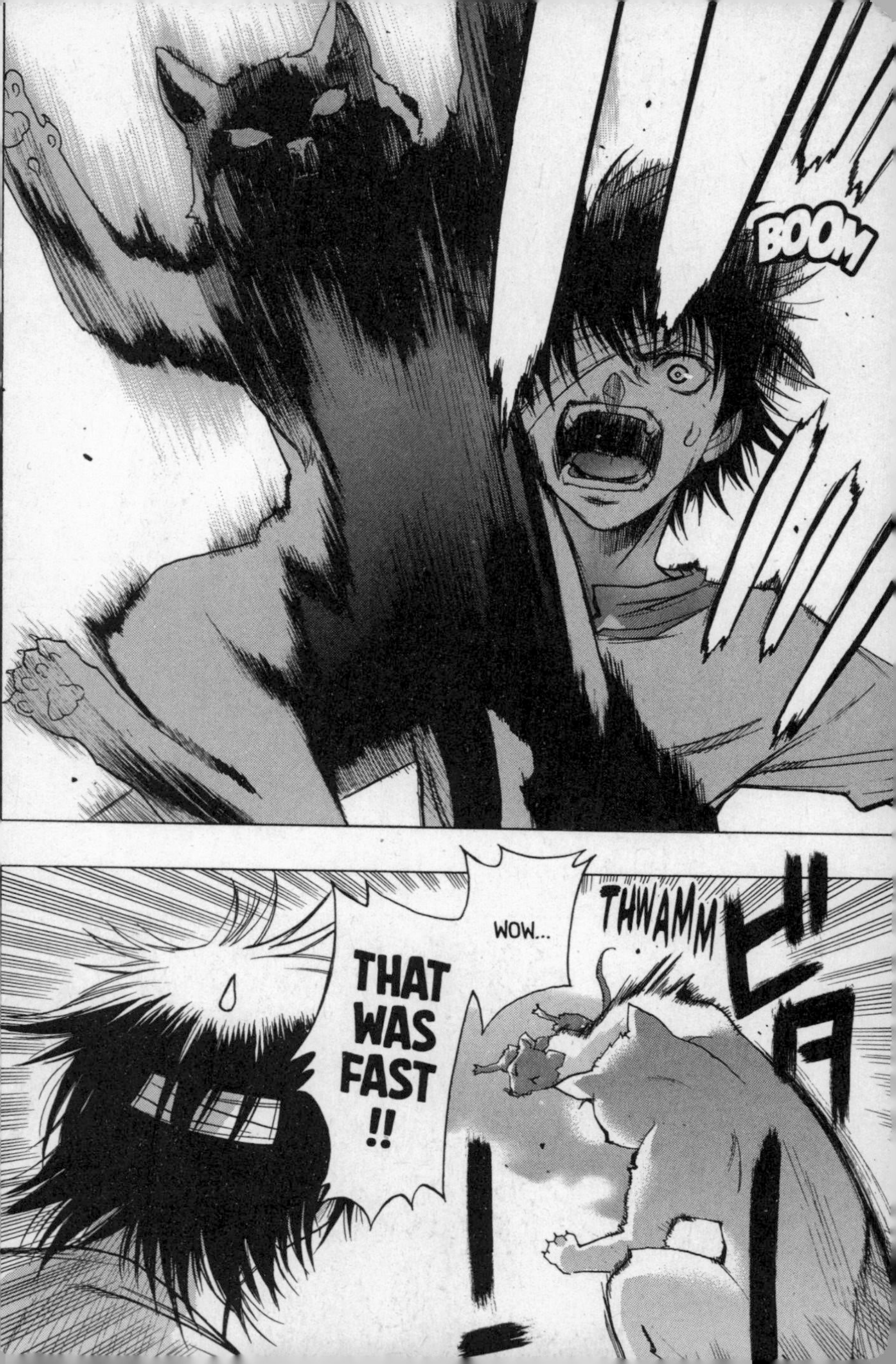
BOOM
THWAMM
WOW...
THAT WAS FAST !!

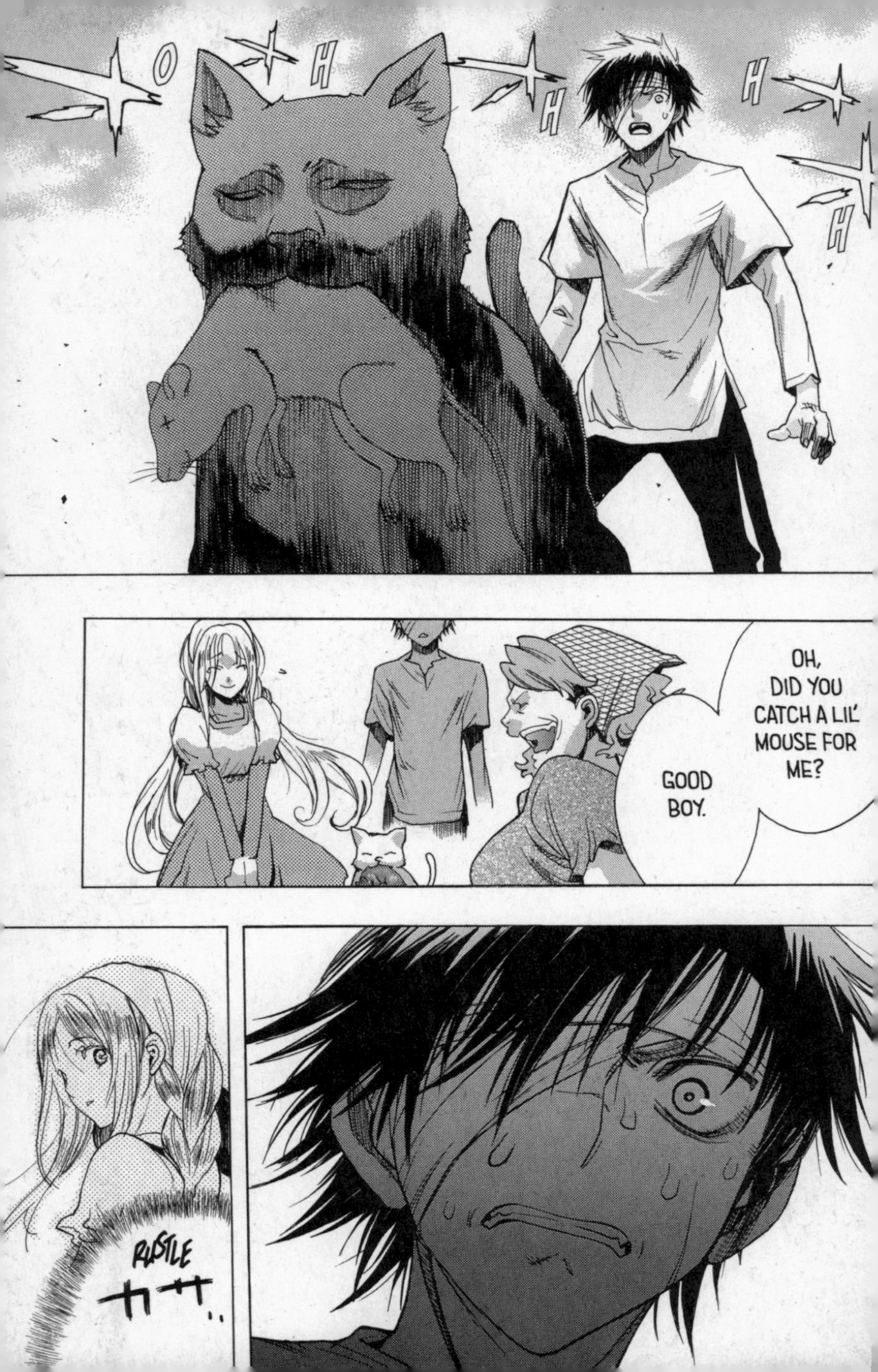
OHHHH
OH, DID YOU CATCH A LIL' MOUSE FOR ME?
GOOD BOY.
RUSTLE
カサ..

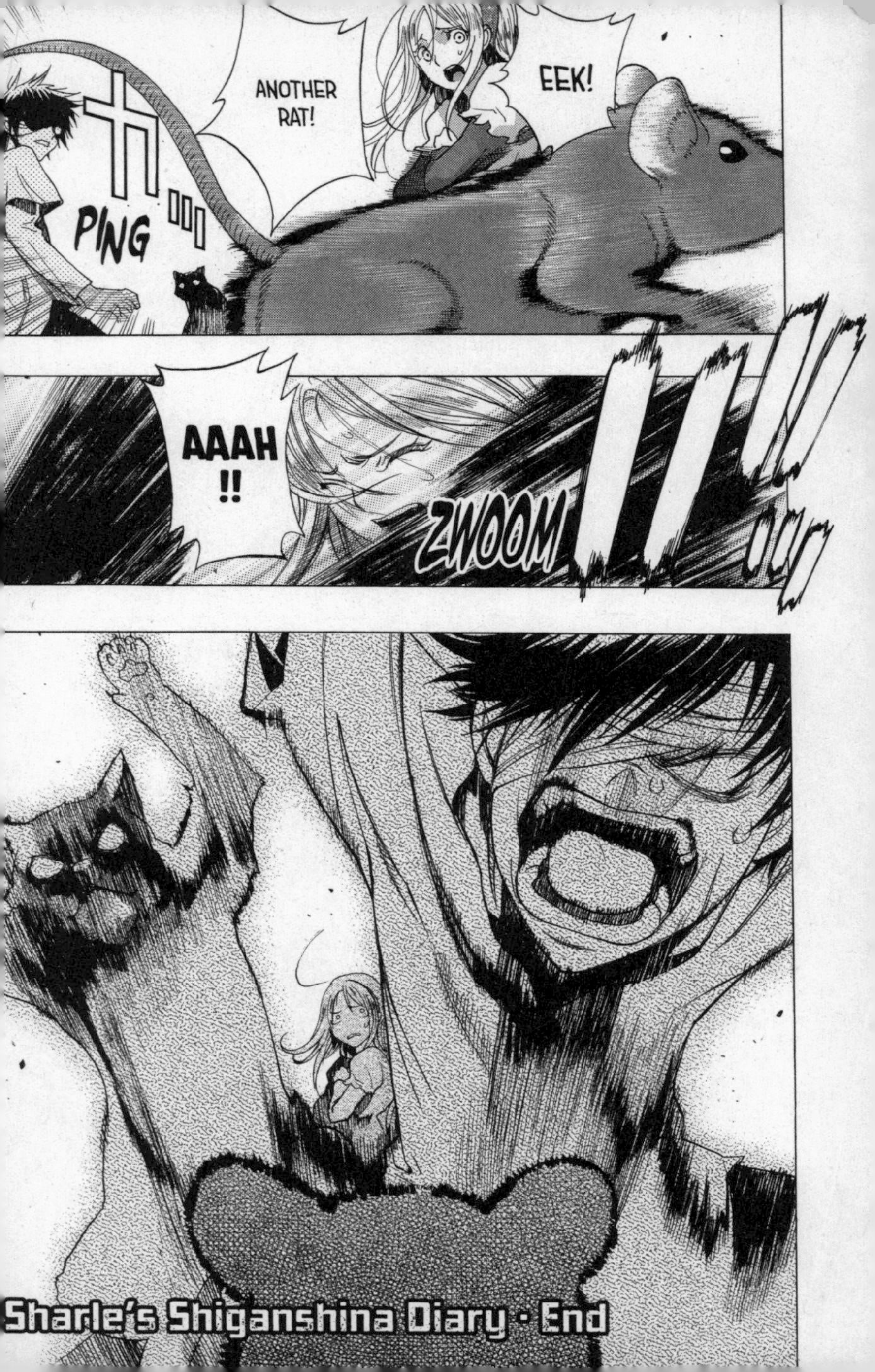

EEK!
ANOTHER RAT!
PING
ZWOOM
AAAH !!
Sharle's Shiganshina Diary · End

Translation Note

Naraka, page 34

The name for a type of realm in the Buddhist afterlife. A Naraka is something like purgatory in which the dead must live out a set period of time, undergoing hellish torment, until their karma is consumed and they can be reborn into a higher plane of life. Also known as "naraku" in Japanese.

A Kodansha Comics Trade Paperback Original
Attack on Titan: Before the Fall volume 4 copyright © 2014 Hajime Isayama/
Ryo Suzukaze/Satoshi Shiki
English translation copyright © 2015 Hajime Isayama/Ryo Suzukaze/Satoshi Shiki

Published in the United States by Kodansha Comics, an imprint of
Kodansha USA Publishing, LLC, New York.

Publication rights for this English edition arranged through
Kodansha Ltd, Tokyo.

First published in Japan in 2014 by Kodansha Ltd., Tokyo
as *Shingeki no kyojin Before the fall*, volume 4.

ISBN 978-1-61262-981-0

Character designs by Thores Shibamoto
Original cover design by Takashi Shimoyama (Red Rooster)

Printed in the United States of America.

www.kodanshacomics.com

9 8 7 6 5 4 3 2 1
Translation: Stephen Paul
Lettering: Steve Wands
Editing: Ben Applegate
Kodansha Comics edition cover design by Phil Balsman